YIDDISH LIVES ON

יִידיש לעבט
YIDDISH LIVES ON

Strategies of Language Transmission

REBECCA MARGOLIS

McGill-Queen's University Press
Montreal & Kingston • London • Chicago

ISBN 978-0-2280-1443-0 (cloth)
ISBN 978-0-2280-1444-7 (paper)
ISBN 978-0-2280-1550-5 (ePDF)
ISBN 978-0-2280-1551-2 (ePUB)

Legal deposit second quarter 2023
Bibliothèque nationale du Québec

Printed in Canada on acid-free paper that is 100% ancient forest free (100% post-consumer recycled), processed chlorine free

This book has been published with the help of a grant from the Canadian Federation for the Humanities and Social Sciences, through the Awards to Scholarly Publications Program, using funds provided by the Social Sciences and Humanities Research Council of Canada.

This publication is made possible by the generous support from the Vered Jewish Canadian Studies Program at the University of Ottawa.

We acknowledge the support of the Canada Council for the Arts.

Nous remercions le Conseil des arts du Canada de son soutien.

Library and Archives Canada Cataloguing in Publication

Title: Yiddish lives on : strategies of language transmission / Rebecca Margolis.
Names: Margolis, Rebecca, author.
Description: Includes bibliographical references and index.
Identifiers: Canadiana (print) 20220394695 | Canadiana (ebook) 20220395136
  | ISBN 9780228014430 (hardcover) | ISBN 9780228014447 (softcover) | ISBN
  9780228015505 (PDF) | ISBN 9780228015512 (EPUB)
Subjects: LCSH: Yiddish language. | LCSH: Yiddish language—Social aspects.
  | LCSH: Jews—Languages. | LCSH: Language and culture.
Classification: LCC PJ5113 .M37 2022 | DDC 439/.1—dc23

This book was typeset by True to Type in 10.5/13 Sabon

Contents

Tables and Figures

Preface and Acknowledgments

אַ פּאָר ווערטער אײדער איך הײב אָן

A por verter eyder ikh heyb on.

A few words before I begin.

This book is about the transmission of a lesser-spoken language across successive generations. It examines Yiddish in Canada since 1950, focusing mainly not on Haredi (ultra-Orthodox) speakers who use it every day but rather on those who have chosen to engage with the language in the secular world even as its numbers of native speakers have plummeted. In the process, it tells the stories of families, community activists, writers, young radicals, singers, actors, theatre directors, and filmmakers who have committed to speak, publish, sing, perform, and create dialogue on screen in Yiddish within multilingual contexts over the last seventy years. This diverse group has generated innovative strategies to connect with Yiddish as, variously, a link to a thousand-year-old Eastern European Jewish heritage, an integral part of an immigrant legacy, an alternative to mainstream Jewish community life, a way to access a rich cultural tradition, the voice of a literary or artistic muse, or a personal calling. Connectedness with secular Yiddish has evolved across multiple planes from native fluency to basic communication; as an ability to recite poetry, sing lyrics, or perform in a play, film, or video; or as a capacity to read and translate text; familiarity with a few terms or phrases; and as emotional connection.

Yiddish today sits amidst the ruins of a civilization decimated by the cataclysmic events and migrations of the twentieth century. One of multiple Jewish languages that evolved over two thousand years of diaspora experience – including Ladino (also known as Judezmo or Judeo-Spanish), Judeo-Arabic and others – Yiddish belonged to a historically persecuted minority with limited social mobility. Mass immigration from Eastern Europe around the turn of the twentieth century was accompanied by widespread linguistic acculturation as newcomers adopted the majority languages of their host countries (the United States, Canada, Britain, Australia, and others). Forces of modernization, industrialization, and cultural integration in Europe encouraged the adoption of languages such as Russian or Polish, with marked impacts by the interwar period. Spoken by a majority of the world's Jewish population on the eve of the Second World War, Yiddish faced linguicide as a thousand years of its history was obliterated by the Nazis in the Holocaust, the systematic, state-sponsored murder of six million Jews, an estimated 85 per cent of whom were Yiddish speakers. In the postwar period, the language faced repression in the Soviet Union, which had formerly endorsed secular Yiddish culture as part of the post-Revolution Communist state. As part of its nation-building process, the newly established State of Israel promoted the cultural hegemony of Hebrew (Ivrit) in the country as well as in Jewish communities abroad. Within immigrant centres such as Canada, Yiddish increasingly moved to the margins both as a vernacular and as a potent language of politics and culture.[1] The estimated number of native speakers in 2020 was about one million, a majority living in Haredi enclaves in the United States and Israel.[2] In contrast, secular Yiddish, which has almost no native speakers, has continually evolved in association with heritage, the arts, and identity politics.

The losses to Yiddish over the last century have been immeasurable. The developments that form the subject of this book can never bring back what once was. They do, however, point to the continued resilience of a diaspora language that emerged without a homeland, amongst a geographically diffuse population that faced persecution over centuries. The ongoing initiatives to preserve and promote the language that appear in this study take place despite – or sometimes because of – the devastation Yiddish has faced. This book explores how in each decade since the Holocaust, Yiddish has moved into new domains of creativity, activism, and inspiration. These developments have taken place among worldwide trends towards globalization and multilingualism, with language increasingly tied to identity formation rather than state apparatus. Secular Yiddish has become less and less utilitarian for its speakers, with its use evoking associations with any of the following: nostalgia, mourning, identification with countercultural politics, embracing alterity (otherness), rebellion and survival, the splendour of artistic creation, youth culture, and more. Scholars have characterized post-Holocaust Yiddish activity as "postvernacular," which is to say that the language has assumed deliberate, symbolic functions, sometimes superseding its communicative ones.[3]

This book investigates the ways in which a minority or heritage language can be meaningfully transmitted across multiple modes. It does so over a period of seventy years, beginning in 1950 when a sizable community of native speakers engaged in a wide variety of activities, through 2020, when few of the European-born generation remained and secular Yiddish was primarily being transmitted by new speakers as a second or third language. 2020 also significantly altered the Yiddish cultural landscape with the onset of the restrictions associated with the coronavirus pandemic, notably in a shift from in-person to virtual activity. The book focusses on Canada as a country with a particularly rich history of Yiddish engagement within a multicultural context. This is not a book about Jewish languages bur rather the story of one of them. That story is closely entwined with other languages, notably Hebrew. However, unlike Hebrew, which is tied to the State of Israel, Yiddish does not have a homeland where the language is spoken as part of travel or cultural exchange; nor does it function as a sacred or liturgical language within Judaism. My aim here is to tease out the ways in which Yiddish has not only survived but thrived in innovative ways four generations after the migration of its last group of traditional European-born speakers.

This study shares my personal journey as a new speaker, researcher, and teacher of Yiddish. However, the stories it tells were largely unknown to me before I began my scholarly research. As an English speaker who attended Montreal's Bialik High School, a secular Jewish day school where Yiddish has always been taught, I did not appreciate how remarkable it was to be learning the language as a young, non-Haredi person in the 1980s. Nor did I appreciate the cultural significance of the Dora Wasserman Yiddish Theatre, whose plays I attended with my high school classes and throughout my undergraduate degree in Yiddish Studies at McGill University. Even as a doctoral student in Columbia University's Yiddish Studies program in New York, I did not recognize how unusual it was that most of my courses were taught in Yiddish, that I could converse with my professors and fellow students in Yiddish, and that there was a community of native and new speakers ideologically committed to the language. At that time, I did not consider the history of the organization called Yugntruf (Youth for Yiddish), whose immersive Yiddish-language events and summer retreat I happily attended. The impetus for this book arose later, from a desire to translate my associative belonging into a scholarly examination of how Yiddish has been transmitted outside of the Haredi context.

As one example, the chapter on singing unpacks a dynamic that I had simply accepted as a norm within secular Yiddish learning. As a novice instructor of Yiddish at Columbia University in the mid-1990s, I was only dimly aware of the pedagogy I had absorbed during my own education and was passing on to my students by requiring everyone to sing a variety of Yiddish songs, sometimes analyzing them as works of folklore or literature but often just for fun. Singing was a component of my academic training that I subsequently integrated into my own teaching in university language courses as well as in adult education classes in Canada, the United States, and Israel.

This book is about strategies surrounding Yiddish language transmission in what I term "created language spaces": sites that are deliberately created to support the continuity of a language that is not commonly a mother tongue or widely spoken. I use the term "created" to underline the intentionality behind the organization and presentation of ventures to promote Yiddish continuity, and the resources and cultural capital that are deployed to do so. Created language spaces may encompass any or all of the following, and more: homes committed to raising native language speakers; children's community theatres that produce performances in the language; meetings of youth-run groups whose members function in the language; published texts, and events where writers share them; cultural festivals or community choirs where musicians perform in the language; subtitled on-screen experiences; and virtual gatherings. Fluid and flexible, adaptable, and constantly evolving, created language spaces form an indispensable means of secular Yiddish continuity by shifting the locus of transmission from biological families to cohorts who choose to engage with the language. The title – ייִדיש לעבט Yiddish lebt, meaning "Yiddish lives on" or "Yiddish is alive" – is deliberately provocative, suggesting that the viability of lesser-spoken and lesser-taught languages can be enacted in both innovative and deeply meaningful ways.

Each area of discussion focuses on a particular moment when ventures promoting Yiddish connection and continuity emerged in Canada. These include: transmission within families (1950s to today); participation in community youth theatre groups (1960s to 1970s); publishing, anthologizing, and translation (1970s to 1980s); singing in immersive and community spaces (1990s to 2000s); and new media such as digitization and social media, as well as subtitled cinema (2000 to present). Each is rooted in a specifically Canadian context with tendrils in the transnational Yiddish milieu that spans the United States, Latin America, Australia, Europe, and Israel. With each chapter devoted to a different era and model for continuity, I conceptualize the book as a series of expanding rings of engagement with the language and culture. These circles move from native speakers in the middlemost ring to those who engage with Yiddish through new media in the outermost ring (see figure 0.1). Although each is discrete, readers will note the interconnectedness of the circles and the recurring names of people, organizations, and ventures across the chapters of the book.

The objective of the book is to spotlight diverse strategies of minority language transmission. It does not suggest that secular Yiddish will once again become a widely-spoken native language. Rather, it investigates mechanisms to create spaces where the language can be used far more fully than individual words and phrases. My hope for this study is twofold: (1) that it elucidates how created language spaces have evolved within a transnational secular Yiddish world, with Canada as a case study; and (2) that it offers a model for the way other minority languages may support new modes of transmission, in particular among young people.

As a study of a recent and ongoing cultural phenomenon, this book has involved a great number of people who have lent their time, effort, and support. My heartfelt appreciation goes to them all. I want to take this opportunity to spotlight just a few.

To the many innovators of Canadian Yiddish cultural activity who so generously agreed to participate in interviews and the five hundred people who took part in my 2017 online survey on Yiddish use in Canada: I could not have told the stories in the book without your input. I wish to thank the experts who facilitated my access to primary source material, especially Eiran Harris and Eddie Stone at the Jewish Public Library; Janice Rosen at the Alex Dworkin Canadian Jewish Archives (formerly known as the Canadian Jewish Congress Charities Committee National Archives); and Christa Whitney and her team at the Wexler Oral History Project (Yiddish Book Center). I am also grateful to my research assistants at the University of Ottawa:

William Felepchuk, Rebecca Good, Michael Kent, Simon-Pierre Lacasse, Elizabeth Moorehouse-Stein, Jesse Toufexis, and Sacha Victor. I wish to acknowledge the financial support of the Social Sciences and Humanities Research Council of Canada as well as the Vered Jewish Canadian Studies Program and the School of Philosophical, Historical & International Studies at Monash University.

The external reviewers of the manuscript, Mark Abley, and the editors at McGill-Queen's University Press offered important feedback. Thank you to my colleagues at the University of Ottawa, the Association for Canadian Jewish Studies, Monash University, and further afield, who provided a collegial space for me to conduct and share my research and inspired me with new perspectives. A special thank you goes to Seymour Mayne, my long-time colleague and friend in the Vered Jewish Canadian Studies Program. Many thanks to the Yiddishists who been my teachers, project collaborators, and community over the last twenty-five years, as well as the students I have had the privilege of teaching at Columbia University, YIVO's Uriel Weinreich Program in Yiddish Language, Literature, and Culture, the University of Ottawa, the Steiner Summer Yiddish Program at the Yiddish Book Center, and the Naomi Prawer Kadar International Yiddish Summer Program. I am deeply grateful to my family: my parents for immersing me in Yiddish culture from a young age and my grandmothers and aunts for enthusiastically encouraging my interests.

My biggest debt of gratitude goes to Bena Margolis in her unicorn wings, who was an inspiration throughout, and my beloved Lindsay, who supported this project in every way possible. I dedicate this book to you.

NOTE

Unless otherwise indicated, the Yiddish in this book is transliterated according to the standards of the YIVO system. Names of people and institutions are spelled according to common usage. Unless specified, all translations from the Yiddish are my own.

YIDDISH LIVES ON

Introduction

A linguistic carrier of a thousand years of European diasporic Jewish civilization, Yiddish was spoken by a widely dispersed population across Eastern Europe and its immigrant centres into the twentieth century. Whereas its Sephardi branch, which settled in locations across the Mediterranean, developed other Jewish languages including Ladino, Yiddish developed within its Ashkenazi branch as its speakers moved through Germany and subsequently across Eastern Europe. Linguistically, Yiddish integrated the Middle High German of Ashkenazi Jewish settlement with elements of Hebrew/Aramaic and Romance languages and, once it became an extraterritorial language, components of Slavic and other languages. Yiddish evolved within a vast transnational network that developed over centuries and rode on waves of persecution and uprooting to travel with its speakers to new homes, including Canada. Over the last hundred years, it has been significantly weakened by linguistic acculturation, its European ancestral home decimated. In Canada, census statistics show a sharp drop in Yiddish use from a high of almost 100 per cent of Jews declaring it to be their mother tongue in 1931 to about 50 per cent twenty years later and some 3 per cent in 2020. Despite these diminishing numbers of native speakers, Yiddish has evolved across new domains as a robust locus of heritage, identity, and creativity. As a recent study of its new speakers asserts, "Yiddish stands out as a severely endangered language which, apparently, refuses to die."[1]

Historically, Yiddish was connected to no nation-state or army, with the notable exception of Soviet state support in the two decades following the 1917 Russian Revolution.[2] The trend towards "glottophagy" – the adoption of major languages over minor ones – was underway for Yiddish even before the Holocaust, as many upwardly mobile Jews were adopting languages such as Polish.[3] At the same time, Yiddish served as both a lingua franca for millions and a vehicle for wide-ranging cultural activity, with 75 per cent of the world's Jews, or an estimated eleven to thirteen million people, speaking it in 1939.[4] These speakers, who lived in Eastern Europe as well as in new immigrant centres, spanned the spectrum of socioeconomic, political, and religious orientation. By 1945, one out of every two Yiddish speakers were no more, and its historic European heartland lay in ruins.

As the survivors settled in immigrant communities or in the nascent State of Israel, acculturation to the dominant language and culture was the norm. Today, just a few thousand fluent speakers of secular Yiddish remain worldwide, comprising diminishing numbers of elderly native speakers and increasing numbers of new learners. Yiddish has remained a language without official state support with the notable exception of Sweden, where it receives funding as an official minority language.[5] In the State of Israel and pre-State Palestine, tensions between Yiddish and Hebrew within a complex multilingual context along with shifting public opinion, politics, and financial considerations have long shaped activity around the language. Whereas Yiddish was for decades supressed as a negative symbol of Jewish exile in the diaspora, its speakers created significant cultural outputs in the language, notably in literature; moreover, Yiddish has more recently experienced a resurgence, especially among younger generations.[6] As a stateless language without an academy, Yiddish lacks universally agreed-upon arbiters, and questions around orthography and new vocabulary remain contested. Statistics suggest that Yiddish barely exists as mother tongue or daily language outside of Haredi (ultra-Orthodox) circles today. In *Like Everyone Else ... but Different: The Paradoxical Success of Canadian Jews* (2001, revised 2018), Morton Weinfeld addresses the cultural capital associated with Yiddish within the Jewish mainstream: "Yiddish has become very important in the symbolic sense, used not only for communication but also to mark specific rituals or occasions, as songs, prayers, names of food items, and curses," although, he notes, its actual symbolic significance and role in strengthening Jewish identity is difficult to measure.[7] He suggests, "At some point, any ethnic culture in North America is inevitably diluted as fluency in the mother tongue is lost. For now, the symbolic uses of Yiddish and Yinglish count for much, indeed more than most other immigrant languages."[8]

This book shifts the focus from Yiddish as symbol to broader questions around language continuity. It examines the ways in which Yiddish has increasingly become a meaningful chosen space for expressing Jewish and other identities as well as diverse forms of new creativity. Since the immigration of the last generation of traditional European-born speakers after the Holocaust, multiple models have evolved for Yiddish transmission outside the home, and without state support. In tandem with other sites of Yiddish globally, Canada has been the site of enduring ventures to preserve, promote, and propagate connection with the language in the areas of theatre, youth activism, publishing, music, cinema, and new media. Some of the models offer means of direct language transmission; others offer gateways into acquiring or improving knowledge of the language, whether written or spoken. Over the last seventy years, Eastern European Jewish immigrants and their descendants as well as new speakers of the language have forged ways to connect with Yiddish as part of a multilingual matrix encompassing any or all of the following: Canada's official languages, English and French; pre-modern Hebrew as the language of Jewish sacred text and prayer; modern Hebrew (Ivrit) as a contemporary spoken language; and other languages such as Polish, Russian, or German.

Yiddish exists within two distinct communities: Haredi and secular. In the aftermath of the Holocaust, each group formed its own relationships to the language. Haredim (plural of Haredi, literally "fearers of God") refers to traditionalist (ultra-Orthodox) Jews who maintain a strict adherence to Jewish religious law (Halakha) and observance, and eschew the values and practices of the modern, secular mainstream. Haredim live in urban or semi-urban communities characterized by segregated educational, religious, and communal institutions, and they maintain distinctive language and dress.[9] Among the Haredim, Hasidim constitute today's largest group of Yiddish speakers. Originally followers of a mystical revival movement founded in eighteenth century Poland, Hasidim are organized into sects with charismatic leaders called *rebbes*, each of which maintains its own institutions and customs. In the recuperative efforts to rebuild their communities in aftermath of the Holocaust, these have come to form an interconnected network of enclaves spanning the United States, Canada, Israel, Europe, and Australia, both within major urban centres (e.g., Borough Park, New York; Outremont, Montreal; Mea Shearim, Jerusalem) and in separately established communities (e.g.,

the villages of Kiryas Tosh, near Montreal, or Kiryas Joel, New York).
Today, four generations after the Holocaust, Yiddish has come to function as a primary means of communication across multiple Hasidic
dynasties, such as Satmar, Belz, Bobov, Vizhnitz, Klausenburg, Skver,
Tosh, and Ger, where it is the first language learned and the vernacular of family, work, and community, with pre-modern Hebrew and
Aramaic reserved for study and prayer. The Hasidic world exists as a
stronghold for Yiddish as a linguistic connection with the traditional
Jewish community past and present as well as a means of asserting
separation from the rest of society. High birth rates and low attrition
have resulted in growing numbers. In his 2019 study, Dovid Katz estimates a rapidly growing population of between 500,000 and 1 million Haredi Yiddish speakers worldwide.[10] A 2022 study predicts that
nearly one in four Jews will be Haredi by 2040.[11]

The word "secular," in this study, denotes the language of immigrants from Eastern Europe who participated in a cultural life encompassing modern literature, theatre, politics, and education that has
since extended beyond their communities. In the milieu of secular
Yiddish, the numbers of native speakers have dwindled worldwide,
while opportunities to connect with the culture have expanded.
According to Dovid Katz, this group includes between 100,000 and
550,000 very elderly speakers raised in pre-Holocaust Europe, their
descendants, and smaller numbers of new learners of the language.[12]
As the native speakers pass away and the language is not being widely transmitted among their descendants, secular Yiddish has increasingly become the purview of new speakers.

This study focuses on the secular Yiddish group, for whom continued engagement with the language has taken place despite mainstream linguistic acculturation. Prominent within this group are Yiddishists, an international and diffuse network of individuals and
their organizations that have spearheaded activity in the areas of education, performance, activism, and publishing. A 2020 ethnographic
study defines "Yiddishist" as "a particular activist identity within a
larger, global network of Yiddish language devotees – often referred
to as 'the Yiddish world.'" In my own work, people who describe
themselves as Yiddishists consider Yiddish culture work to be a significant, if not a defining, part of their identity. They are, generally
speaking, culture-makers and culture-brokers: academics, musicians,
writers, organizers, and students who facilitate opportunities for
engagement within the Yiddish world."[13] Yiddishists include both

native speakers and increasingly, over time, new speakers. They comprise Jews and non-Jews who have come to embrace the concept of a Yiddishland as a virtual community grounded in the language and its culture.

Canada has been at the forefront of many innovative and enduring developments in post-Holocaust Yiddish life: a productive and enduring literary milieu; a robust community theatre and youth movement; community-based activism; music festivals, choirs, and other sites for communal singing; digital projects; and twenty-first-century cinema. This study spotlights Canadian innovations to the transmission of Yiddish. These endeavours evolved out of the dynamics of each place and the background and interests of the people who settled there. For example, Yiddish youth theatre features prominently because Montreal became home to Dora Wasserman (1919–2003), an actress trained on the Soviet stage who initiated activities for youth that blossomed into an enduring community theatre. The study is anchored in Montreal, Toronto, and Vancouver due to the critical mass of individuals and institutions in each city who promoted the continuity of Yiddish.

Elements of the Canadian story will be familiar to other places within an increasingly transnational Yiddish world. For many descendants of Eastern European Jewish immigrants, Yiddish has come to function as a heritage language, defined as "the vehicle whereby the cultural memory of entire peoples is transmitted over time from place to place, from community to community, and from generation to generation."[14] At the same time, Yiddish has also come to play a meaningful role for increasing numbers of people without a heritage connection. Built into the language is a longing for a better world rooted in the traditional Jewish hope for messianic redemption and also expressed in modern leftist revolutionary ideologies.[15] Over the last decades, this utopian impulse has become a source for new activist identities and inclusive subcultures.[16] As I discuss in this book, in the 1960s, a radical youth movement called Yugntruf published an activist manifesto in its journal after debating its tenets at a conference; in the 2020s, activists within a Queer Yiddishkeit subculture are congregating around groups such as the leftist Rad Yiddish.[17]

The Canadian Yiddish story is, in many ways, a familiar one. An immigrant group arrives fleeing persecution and in search of new opportunities and the native language is widely spoken within families and the wider community for the first generation; the children grow up bilingually or multilingually and then adopt the dominant language(s) of the new country – in this case the official languages of English or French – and raise their own children with varying degrees of exposure to the immigrant language. Continued connection with the immigrant language hinges on a number of factors, including the dedication of parents to its continued use inside and outside of the home; community networks of schools and other institutions to facilitate opportunities for language use; connections with a homeland where the language continues to be used; and a popular culture that generates the desire to engage with what has become an ethnic or heritage language. But, like elsewhere in the decades following the Holocaust, Canada has presented multiple barriers to transmitting Yiddish as a communicative language spoken with fluency in the long term. English appealed as the language of the mainstream and, by extension, of upward mobility and the notion emerged that speaking an immigrant language with children might limit their opportunities. This was compounded by two other factors: the rise of modern Hebrew (Ivrit) as the official language of the State of Israel and its dissemination as global Jewish language and culture, and a socioeconomic shift away from a working class, immigrant past and with it, the decline of leftist movements as ideological homes for Yiddish.

From 1901 to 1931, Canada's Jewish community increased from some 16,000 to over 155,000 as a result of mass immigration from Eastern Europe, with virtually the entire population declaring Yiddish as their mother tongue on the national census. These immigrants spoke multiple languages: Yiddish as an everyday language; Hebrew as the sacred language of study and prayer; and the Russian, Polish, Ukrainian, or Hungarian of their native countries. A final wave of Holocaust survivors and their families arrived in Canada after the Second World War, many of them Yiddish speakers. The children of these immigrants predominantly attended English-language schools and acculturated linguistically into that milieu. European-raised Yiddish-speaking immigration slowed to a trickle after the late-1950s, and that population aged and was little replenished. By 2001, after decades of immigration by Jewish people of non-Yiddish speaking origins (notably a sizable Sephardi immigration from north Africa and the Arab world, as well as newcomers from Israel and elsewhere), Yiddish was the mother tongue of only 6 per cent of Canada's 330,000 Jews.[18] The 2006 half-census findings showed that, for the first time, Hebrew had eclipsed Yiddish as

Table 0.1
Yiddish as mother tongue and in the home, compared to the total
Canadian Jewish population, 1931–2011

	1931	1951	1971	1991	2011*
Total Jews	155,700	204,800	276,000	318,000	391,700
Yiddish mother tongue	149,500	103,600	49,900	26,500	15,200
Percentage	96	51	18	8	2.5
Yiddish language of the home	n/a	n/a	26,300	6,600	6,860
Percentage	n/a	n/a	9.5	2	1.75

*Voluntary.
Source: Canadian census, rounded to the nearest hundred.

the mother tongue among Canadian Jews.[19] As table 0.1 shows, most Canadian Jews in the 1930s understood and could speak at least some Yiddish but by 2011, most could not. Few of the Yiddish-speaking immigrants who settled in Canada between 1880 and 1960 transmitted linguistic fluency to their grandchildren, regardless of their own attachment to the language.

In the immediate aftermath of the Holocaust, the survivors who carried the Yiddish language and culture to new locations faced two simultaneous draws: an ongoing, deliberate engagement with Yiddish, and acculturation to their new environments. In many cases, the trauma of the Holocaust meant the latter overtook the former, as survivors focused on adapting to life in their new homelands; sometimes, the former held sway as survivors of the Holocaust devoted themselves to Yiddish cultural work. One prominent example of this dual response can be found in poet and novelist Chava Rosenfarb and her husband, Dr Henry Morgentaler, who survived the Holocaust and arrived in Canada as a married couple, raised a family, and ultimately went their separate ways. Rosenfarb became a luminary in the Yiddish literary world, authoring novels and short stories that chronicled the Holocaust and its aftermath, particularly in her home city of Łódź. Morgentaler, in contrast, became Canada's most prominent advocate of women's rights to abortion. Rosenfarb and her husband abruptly ceased speaking Yiddish with their young son and enrolled him in an English school after an incident at a playground where a little boy inquired, "Doesn't he speak language?"[20] Despite this, their daughter, literature professor Goldie Morgentaler, became the foremost translator and scholar of her mother's work.

The Roskies family offers a further example of diverging approaches to the continuity of secular Yiddish. Having resided in the Jewish
cultural centres of Vilna/Vilnius (part of Poland until 1939, today
in Lithuania) and Czernowitz (Ukraine) in the early 1930s before
their flight to Canada in 1940, Mazsa and Leib Roskies established
their residence in Montreal as a centre for modern Yiddish culture.
They promoted the work of local as well as international writers and
artists and hosted lively gatherings in their home. For Mazsa, who
spoke an elevated and elegant Yiddish, the language offered a means
of prolonging the Jewish Vilna of her youth rather than an ideology.[21]
In his memoir, their youngest son, David, writes:

> And so, our home in Montreal, as was their home in Czernowitz,
> was a salon for Yiddish writers, artists, actors, scholars. Montreal
> was an extremely congenial place for my parents to arrive in
> 1940, because there was an infrastructure of Jewish secular insti-
> tutions, and they could enter into that immediately and become
> active on all fronts. The central Jewish organization in Montreal
> to this day is a unique organization called the Jewish Public
> Library ... And that was the cultural hub of the entire communi-
> ty. Writers came and read their work and were fêted, so that all of
> Yiddish culture made its way to Canada. And after having an offi-
> cial evening at the Jewish Public Library, it could also happen
> that my mother would invite them for a private soiree in our
> own home ... I grew up sitting underneath the piano at these lit-
> erary gatherings, at the feet, literally at the feet, of some of the
> greatest Jewish writers of all time. Avrom Sutzkever, Chaim
> Grade, Yankev Glatstein [Glatshteyn], not to speak of a whole
> group of important writers who were Montreal-based. Melech
> Ravitch, Yehuda Elberg, Chava Rosenfarb. And now we get to the
> crucial piece of it. The other key institution of Montreal was the
> network of Yiddish day schools ... So, we, all of us, all four of us
> [Roskies siblings], actually graduated from the same school, the
> Jewish People's School or Folkshule. And our teachers were also
> the personal friends of our parents. So, I would say that I grew
> up in a space that was called the *yidishe gas*, the Jewish Street,
> which is a concept in Yiddish. *Yidishe gas* means the home, the
> school, literally the street that speaks Yiddish, a Yiddish daily
> newspaper, Yiddish amateur theatre, Yiddish political parties.[22]

Three of the Roskies children went on to experience and promote secular Yiddish in diverging ways. Ruth R. Wisse (born Czernowitz, 1936) became a founding figure of the academic field of modern Yiddish literature at McGill University and subsequently at Harvard University. Beginning in the 1960s, she would introduce Yiddish literature to English readerships as a scholar, translator, and anthologizer.[23] In her graduate course at McGill University in the late 1970s, Aaron Lansky seeded the idea of a book exchange to access hard-to-find Yiddish texts, which grew into one of America's foremost Jewish institutions: the Yiddish Book Center. While she was a linchpin in the continuity of secular Yiddish, Wisse has staunchly renounced the notion of a secular Yiddish revival and disavowed any association with Yiddishism in her writing as a cultural critic and public intellectual.[24] Eva Raby (born Montreal, 1942) trained as a librarian and, after a period of departure from Yiddish, created a new model of Yiddish-language children's programming at Montreal's Jewish Public Library that yielded an album of Yiddish children's music titled *Kinder Klangen: Holiday and Play Songs for Children ... of All Ages*. In the 1960s, David G. Roskies (born Montreal, 1948) co-founded a radical countercultural youth movement called Yugntruf (Youth for Yiddish), and subsequently become a professor of Yiddish and Hebrew literature at the Jewish Theological Seminary, where he taught his advanced courses in Yiddish literature in Yiddish. Among his scholarly writings were studies that frame the secular Yiddish culture in Montreal as a "utopian experiment" and as part of a Jewish "usable past."[25] As promoters of diverse areas of, and approaches to, secular Yiddish culture, Wisse, Roskies, and Raby are discussed further at various points in this study.

The ongoing appeal of secular Yiddish is linked to its historic connection to multiple ideological and cultural nodes. These include (in no particular order): family or heritage relationships; leftist-oriented movements informed by anarchism, socialism, communism and broader values of social justice; as a vernacular in a symbiotic relationships with a sacred tongue (Hebrew/Aramaic); nostalgic associations with an imagined *shtetl* (pre-Holocaust Eastern European market town with a sizable Jewish population)[26] or immigrant quarter such as New York's Lower East Side; responses to destruction and memorialization, notably in the aftermath of the Holocaust; as a basis for cross-cultural relations; as a language aligned with countercultural identities; as a non-hegemonic language in women's or feminist culture or within queer culture; high literary production, with a rich modernist poetic and prose tradition; popular culture, notably comedic; and music, including klezmer, theatre music, and folk music. Each of these nodes can be reinvented and renegotiated, alone or in tandem, by groups or individuals. On the one hand, Yiddish transmission since 1950 must be understood in the wake of the Holocaust because it cannot be understood separately from that profound rupture. On the other hand, secular Yiddish continuity has been a deeply forward-looking, vital enterprise.

As a language that has over the last century marked a fecund site of leftist activism and wide-ranging cultural production, Yiddish has evolved as an inclusive space for those who are rediscovering their heritage as well as newcomers who are drawn to the language as a means of exploring their chosen identity. The new speakers of Yiddish form part of a wider trend of people who are drawn to lesser-spoken languages such as Breton or Catalan for discovery of heritage or ideological motivations. According to sociolinguistic studies of European minority languages, these new speakers can play a significant role in language revitalization while also raising issues of authenticity, authority, and legitimacy.[27]

While this study spotlights Canada, it is important to note that Yiddish has historically been – and continues to be – inherently transnational in character, spanning multiple Jewish homelands, real and imagined. For centuries, the language encompassed daily communication as well as creative expression, political activism, and identity building across a vast geographic territory that constituted its "Yiddishland." A Jewish diaspora vernacular that evolved first in German territories and subsequently in Slavic lands, by the late nineteenth century Yiddish flourished within a vast territory comprising millions of speakers. By 1939, the world's largest populations of Yiddish speakers lived in New York and Warsaw. The emergence of modern Yiddish literature, theatre, and film traversed multiple geographic locations as both the producers and their products – newspapers, literary journals, books, plays, or films – travelled internationally. Ideological organizations ranging from Orthodox to secular leftist maintained active chapters in Europe as well as in immigrant centres. After the Holocaust, the Yiddish map was reconfigured to foreground Canadian cities such as Montreal, Toronto, and Vancouver as well as New York, Buenos Aires, Melbourne, Tel Aviv, Antwerp, London, and other urban centres. As a result, Yiddish cultural initiatives after 1950 have tended to extend over multiple locations. In order to illustrate this point, I offer here a small selection of organizations dedicated to the promotion of secular Yiddish continuity in 2020. They do not include specific educational programs or research institutions, nor the many organizations dedicated to music and the arts. Kadimah Jewish Cultural Centre and National Library (Melbourne, Australia, founded 1911) hosts classes, reading groups, lectures, and performances;[28] the League for Yiddish (New York, USA, founded 1979) publishes Yiddish books and a journal;[29] Maison de la culture Yiddish Bibliothèque Medem (Paris, France, founded 1929, merged into its present incarnation in 2002), has a Yiddish library and cultural centre that offers courses;[30] the Peretz Centre for Secular Jewish Culture (Vancouver, Canada, founded 1945) offers courses for adults and youth as well as a community library and choir; the Yiddish Book Center (Amherst, USA, founded 1980) offers Yiddish courses as well as housing a large digitized collections of Yiddish materials;[31] YUNG YiDiSH (Tel Aviv, Israel, founded 1993) is a Yiddish library and a cultural centre/performance space.[32] In 2020, the transnational character of secular Yiddish was particularly evident in the music scene, as enhanced by a global circuit of festivals, as well as in cinema and new technology such as video sharing and social media.

ABOUT THIS BOOK

ייִדיש לעבט / *Yiddish Lives On: Strategies of Language Transmission* examines how voluntary engagement with Yiddish has evolved in the last seventy years in Canada. It covers the widely diverse group of people who have chosen to engage with the language far from its pre-Holocaust European heartland, in the face of widespread linguistic attrition and decreasing numbers of native speakers. They include graduates of the secular Yiddish schools and students in university classes, actors in Yiddish theatre and cinema, translators, academics in the field of Yiddish studies, musicians, and the many others. Their wide-ranging activities undermine the assumption that the survival of a migrant language requires a continuous influx of native speakers from abroad or transmission within families or ethnic groups. They suggest that a language continuity can occur in settings beyond learning it in the home or in school, and that these ways are constantly evolving.

Rather than framing Yiddish as a heritage activity, this book considers ventures that in some way break with the past: new modes of transmission between the generations or within publishing or activism, new avenues for performance, or new integration of technologies. Scholars have traced the history and cultural production of Yiddish in Canada, and especially in Montreal, during the opening decades of the twentieth century.[33] I focus instead on the lesser-known stories of those who have chosen to continue speaking, writing, or reading Yiddish after 1950, and those new speakers who have opted to learn it and create in it. I do not deal with all aspects of post-Holocaust Yiddish culture in Canada, and I considers some important aspects only briefly. Absent from the study are the many community groups that grew up organically among European-born Yiddish speakers to celebrate the language through events, clubs, reading groups, and conversation circles. I also do not discuss the development of Yiddish education at the post-secondary level. Instead, the book zeroes in on community-based models for engagement that have emerged to expand the reach of Yiddish for new generations and new learners.

This book explores initiatives that have fostered connection with the language across three generations since the arrival of last European-born speakers to Canada. These are: intergenerational transmission; book projects in the immigrant generation and translation in the second; youth theatre and activism in the second generation; music spanning the second and third generations; and application of new online, screen, and digital technology in the third. I trace the evolution and legacies of each model through the present day. As points of comparison, the book addresses the trajectory of Yiddish within the Hasidic world as well as twenty-first century examples of language revitalization for other lesser-spoken or less-commonly-taught languages, notably Scottish Gaelic and Canada's Indigenous languages. As such, the study forms part of an expanding scholarly literature on the revitalization of endangered languages.[34]

CREATED LANGUAGE SPACES
AND CONCENTRIC CIRCLES OF YIDDISH

As a lens through which to understand language transmission, I propose the term "created language spaces." These are deliberately constructed sites for people to engage with non-dominant languages: the home of a family raising children to be native speakers; a group whose members opt to speak or create or perform in the language; a gathering such as a festival or retreat; or opportunities for learning, creativity, or socializing, whether in person or facilitated by digital technologies. Created language spaces form the heart of the dispersed and mobile culture that has grown up around secular Yiddish, and are more about creating moments than about physical location. Rather than addressing the "why" of Yiddish after the Holocaust, the concept of created language spaces provides answers to the "how."

Created language spaces function like the "third places" proposed by urban sociologist Ray Oldenburg in his book *The Great Good Place*: those that exist between home (the first space) and work (the second space) where individuals can informally congregate to explore, negotiate, and build a sense of self or connection to others, for example cafes, libraries, or public parks. In the Hasidic world, the recuperative post-Holocaust establishment of dense urban enclaves has resulted in third places where Yiddish is widely spoken, such as shops or the playground. For secular Yiddish, the loss of the *yidishe gas* – neighbourhoods where the language was used on a daily basis – has reconfigured the locus of linguistic continuity to created language spaces. Whereas third places offer sites for ongoing language use, created language spaces carve out structured yet voluntary opportunities to encourage language continuity in collective settings such as groups or festivals. The notion of created language spaces also draws on scholarship that utilizes postcolonial theorist Homi K. Bhabha's concept of "third space" – transformational, in-between, hybrid spaces where identities interact and are negotiated – in order to frame projects that promote the continuity or revitalization of minority languages within formalized settings.[35]

For heritage, minority, lesser-spoken, or less commonly taught languages, created language spaces encompass a wide array of strategies for continuity that are often enjoyable but sometimes challenging, especially for new speakers. They can be inclusive in providing accessible points of entry into the language, or exclusive in requiring a certain level of language knowledge or cultural literacy. The strategies that support such spaces form the subject of this book, which posits that secular Yiddish remains a viable language in Canada, though in ways that are very different from the past.

I think of secular Yiddish language transmission in terms of concentric circles. I have organized this book around this image with traditional speakers – pre-Holocaust-born Eastern European immigrants – and their descendants in the centre, moving outwards in expanding rings to encompass a broader population. Each is associated with a strategy of transmission. In the inner circle is transmission of the language within families, predominantly from parents to children (chapter 2). The second circle involves transmission through community activism, largely piloted by those born into Yiddish-speaking families: formal education and support for Yiddish teaching, informal youth education such as theatre groups, and programming such as lectures geared toward a broader Jewish community with a shared heritage but not necessarily language fluency (chapter 3). The third circle is transmission within a community through literature, which assumes a high degree of fluency but in which books can also represent a component of culture with meaning beyond reading (chapter 4). Fourth is transmission through singing, which can encompass those without a Yiddish heritage and with varying degrees of language competency; through workshops and festivals, singing can function as a gateway to language transmission (chapter 5). The fifth – outermost – ring is governed by new technology and includes film in which the creators produce dialogue via translation into Yiddish and audiences take it out of Yiddish via subtitles. It also includes digital and online technologies, which position Yiddish within a globalized cyberspace, making it accessible to the widest possible group, connected virtually and interactively to a potentially infinite corpus of language and culture (chapter 6). Each circle has forged its own strategies of Yiddish transmission in created language spaces. (See figure 0.1).

The book also tracks overlap or drift among the circles and the extent to which involvement in multiple circles strengthens language transmission. The repeated appearance of names across multiple chapters demonstrates this feature. The book is also replete with newcomers to Yiddish who have engaged in processes of language acquisition and the expression of their own brand of future-oriented Yiddish engagement. In contrast to other models of concentric circles of language,[36] here the relationship of the inner to outer circles is determined not by geography but by other factors such as connection to the heritage of the Yiddish European heartland, chosen levels of engagement, ideological orientation, and creative inspiration. Those in the inner circle, the original carriers of the language and culture, rallied for Yiddish continuity and the promotion of the language and culture in the creation of new initiatives within the outer circles. For example, European-born activists deliberately spoke Yiddish at home and created school systems and other educational opportunities to transmit the language to their own children and subsequent generations. They founded cultural organizations and committees to create theatres, music festivals and retreats, university courses, and other ini-

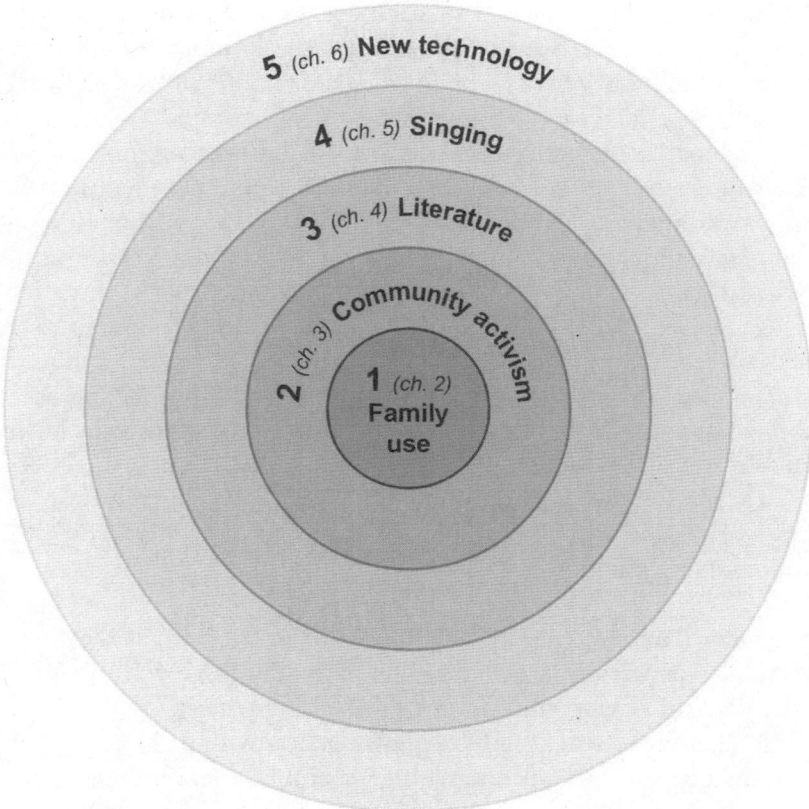

Figure 0.1 Concentric circles of Yiddish

tiatives. These, in turn, have offered a path of return or rediscovery for heritage speakers as well as way in for newcomers to the language who are drawn to it for ideological or creative reasons. Each generation adds new circles while also accessing the previous ones.

What becomes evident in any study of Yiddish is that there can be no full return to a pre-Holocaust language and culture. Collective experiences of dislocation and relocation, rupture and rebuilding have impeded the complete transmission of the civilization to future generations. The same can be said for any cultural group that has undergone upheaval due to mass emigration, war, or genocide. The focus here is not the losses to Yiddish but the degree to which subsequent generations have configured new domains for the language. Rather than relinquishing its hold as a language associated with a destroyed past, Yiddish has been actively reimagined in meaningful ways by new generations. What is lost in this process are the multilayered specificities of the experiences of millions of Jews who fully lived their lives in Yiddish within a multilingual context informed by what Benjamin Harshav's *The Meaning of Yiddish* terms "the semiotics of Jewish communication": their fluent everyday speech in its acrolectal (more prestigious or formal) and basilectal (less prestigious) varieties, their accents, idioms, and slang, with a cultural literacy particular to their times and places.[37] What is gained is active and innovative engagement with a rich language repository that shows no sign of abating in the present or future. Yiddish remains teachable, learnable, and malleable.

This book argues against a binary understanding of Yiddish as either alive or dead, with its vitality measured exclusively by its numbers of native or daily speakers. This measure in no way reflects the richness of the language and culture in Canada over the last seventy years. Rather, this study looks at shades of Yiddish using the following rubric:

1 Products or outcomes *in* Yiddish (not *about* Yiddish), be they Yiddish conversation, published texts, singing, stage performance, cinema, or other forms;
2 Collectively enacted spaces for engagement in Yiddish: not individuals learning or translating Yiddish but people coming together as speakers, activists, writers and readers, actors and singers, and learners.

All non-majority languages produce incentives and strategies to ensure their continued use among both native/heritage speakers and newcomers. Secular Yiddish offers a case study of a language that by and large no longer serves as a lingua franca or daily vernacular. It demonstrates how language spaces can be created in such a situation, with Canada as a site of particular innovation.

The story of Yiddish in Canada after 1950 is one of expansion and dynamism. It offers enterprising models of transmission in created language spaces, all of which have been successful in various ways, all still in progress. None have endeavoured to revive the prewar world; rather, they have enabled Yiddish to live beyond occasional words or phrases embedded in majority languages. The book presents Yiddish not simply as what was but as what is and what can be, a story that continues to unfold into the twenty-first century.

1

Yiddish Canada, Yiddish Ideologies

As the focus of this book, Canada offers a case study of a country that has developed its own strategies for Yiddish transmission within a global context. This chapter presents an overview of Yiddish in Canada and its changing representation in the media, followed by a brief section on Scottish Gaelic as a point of comparison. It then turns to the ideologies of Yiddish more broadly and the discourse around its "revival," "revitalization," or "renaissance," including the dynamics of secular and Haredi Yiddish and scholarly theories about the language and its continuity.

YIDDISH CANADA

Much of the infrastructure for Canadian Jewish life was laid by Yiddish speakers in the first decades of the twentieth century. Until the mid-nineteenth century, the country's Jewish population had largely arrived via Great Britain seeking new economic opportunities. They numbered in the hundreds and formed a socially and linguistically integrated English-speaking group. In 1851, after almost a century of Jewish settlement in British North America, more than half of the country's 354 Jews lived in Montreal and aligned themselves with the dominant English power in the British colony of Lower Canada, which would form part of Canada in 1867. Emancipated since 1832, Jews in Lower Canada held prominent positions in political life. Unlike the neighbouring United States, Canada did not experience a German-speaking Jewish immigrant wave; the first mass immigration – a striking contrast to the existing Anglo-Jewish establishment – would come from Eastern Europe. In 1881, the census showed 2,443 Jews in all of Canada, twice as many as ten years earlier: Eastern European immigration had begun.[1] By 1901, immigration increased the total Canadian Jewish population to over 16,000. In the peak year of 1913–14, over 18,000 Jews arrived in Canada, with immigration resuming after the First World War with less intensity. By 1931, the Jewish population of 156,726 formed the country's eighth-largest ethnic group, with some 96 per cent declaring Yiddish as their mother tongue.[2]

Canadian Yiddish cultural activity emerged in tandem with other Jewish centres worldwide, notably its nearby epicentre of New York. The point of entry for the majority of the over two million Eastern European Jewish immigrants who entered the United States from 1880 to 1920, New York evolved a vast network of Yiddish fraternal organizations, theatres, newspapers, schools, and other organizations to promote the language and culture. The geographic proximity between Montreal, Toronto, and New York facilitated exchange and collaboration.[3] The newcomers ranged in ideological orientation from traditional to radical, with streams of secular Yiddish mirroring a spectrum of political engagement.

The mass Jewish exodus from Eastern Europe coincided with proactive late nineteenth- century government policies to bring new immigrants to Canada. Between 1896 and the outbreak of the First World War, over three million immigrants settled in the country, increasing the total population by 43 per cent by 1931.[4] An open-door policy facilitated immigration of Eastern European Jews. Although federal policies aimed to encourage rural settlement and provide labour for farming, mining, and forestry, Jews formed the country's most urbanized population at close to 97 per cent in 1931, compared with 34 per cent for Canadians as a whole. By 1931, a large majority resided in Montreal (58,000), Toronto (47,000), and Winnipeg (18,000), with close to three quarters found in each city's Jewish immigrant neighbourhood.[5] They were drawn into semi-skilled industrial labour, in particular the nascent garment industry, and, despite government efforts, only a very small proportion settled on the farming settlements that the Jewish Colonization Association established before the First World War.[6] In sum, Canada's Jews formed an urban minority in a country whose makeshift immigration policy sought out a "stalwart peasant in a sheepskin coat, born on the soil, whose forefathers have been farmers for ten generations, with a stout wife, and a half-dozen children."[7] They joined a society in which antisemitism was embedded.[8] However, anti-Jewish sentiment in Canada was never systemic and, unlike in Europe, no state-sanctioned violence ever took place.

After decades of mass immigration, exclusionary policies restricted Jewish settlement in Canada as a 1931 Order in Council (PC 695) closed the door to immigrants.[9] Only a very few individual Jews were allowed into the country under special Orders in Council, and it became virtually impossible for Jewish refugees to enter Canada, even on a short-term basis.[10] Irving Abella and Harold Troper's bestselling *None Is Too Many* borrows as its title a Canadian official's interpretation of the federal government's immigration policy. Abella and Troper argue that Canada's record for the admission of Jews between 1933 and 1948 was among the worst in the Western world and that only limited success resulted from the efforts of the organized Jewish community – notably under its umbrella body, the Canadian Jewish Congress – to pressure Mackenzie King's government to permit entry to Jews fleeing Nazi Europe.[11] In the face of the antisemitism that grew more overt in the 1930s, Jews found themselves largely excluded from Canada's mainstream.[12] As Franklyn Bialystok observes, "The Jewish community was urban, proletarian, static in its growth, and outside the mainstream of economic power, social prestige, or political influence."[13] Canadian Jews formed a highly visible group living in dense urban neighbourhoods; they were working class; many were outwardly religious, founding houses of prayer and observing the Jewish food laws (Kashrut); others were leftist, prominent in the labour movement; and Yiddish formed the dominant common language.[14]

Montreal, the largest Jewish centre, was also the city with the least integration. It was by 1901 home to 45,000 of the country's 126,000 Jews, and it absorbed a third of Canada's Jewish immigrants in the first decades of the twentieth century. Jews represented the largest non-French and non-Anglo-Celtic ethnic group in the city, with Yiddish the third most spoken language, after French and English, by World War One. From 1900 through the 1940s, most settled in the Jewish neighbourhood of Mile End along "the Main" (Boulevard Saint Laurent), which bisected Montreal geographically and culturally into the numerically dominant working-class Franco-Catholic majority in the east and the economically dominant Anglo-Protestant elite in the west.[15] The British North American Act of 1867 had enshrined the binary character of the province of Quebec along reli-

gious and linguistic lines: a majority Franco-Catholic rural population dating back to the original French colony and an Anglo-Protestant
urban minority that dominated political and economic life in Montreal.[16] Each group maintained organizational infrastructures,
including educational systems, libraries, social services, and hospitals.
As their numbers grew, the Jews came to form what poet Irving Layton termed a "third solitude," sandwiched between, and yet separate
from, the two dominant groups.[17] Facing social exclusion from both
groups, the city's Jews established their own schools, libraries, and
social services, with Yiddish functioning as the community vernacular for the first half of the twentieth century. As Ira Robinson and
Mervin Butovsky suggest, "In cultural terms, the relative linguistic
and religious isolation of the Jews in Montreal ironically proved to be
a positive condition in encouraging the establishment of a well-knit
autonomous community life."[18] When many thousands of Jews left
Montreal after the 1976 election of the separatist Parti Québécois government, Toronto emerged as the country's Jewish population centre.
However, Montreal would remain home to a majority of Canada's
Yiddish writers, a permanent Yiddish theatre, and day schools teaching the language. In Quebec, where nationalist ideologies have come
to align identity with language, the competing pressures of French
and English, paradoxically, permitted more space for ethnic or minority languages such as Yiddish.

The very small number of Jewish refugees from Nazi Europe who
settled in Canada from 1933 to 1945 included prominent figures
who made major contributions to Yiddish literature, scholarship,
education, and theatre. A larger group of leading Yiddish artists and
luminaries settled in Canada after 1945. Members of the Jewish community rallied to integrate the newcomers and encouraged their
creative work. The displaced persons camps, which housed some
250,000 Jews across Europe at the end of the Second World War,
became temporary sites for a revivification of Yiddish cultural activity.[19] Many displaced persons settled in areas that had previously been
minor centres of Yiddish culture, notably Canada, which absorbed
the world's third-largest population of Holocaust survivors after
Israel and the United States. An estimated 35,000 survivors settled in
Canada from 1947 to 1956, about 15,000 of them in Montreal, where
they experienced the challenges of building new lives.[20] Overall,
between 1945 and 1960, Canada's Jewish population increased by 35
per cent, at least half of whom were survivors.[21]

The Holocaust survivors encountered a chasm separating them from the existing Canadian Jewish community. As Franklin Bialystok points out, the newcomers spoke Yiddish, Polish, or other European languages, whereas established Canadian Jewry was largely English-speaking. Many recent arrivals had experienced a prewar Europe far more sophisticated than the one the earlier immigrants had left decades earlier. In addition, the survivors' Holocaust experiences were often met with indifference, incomprehension, suspicion, or even hostility from Canadian Jews (What must you have done to survive? What must these experiences have done to you?).[22] This strengthened many survivors' connection to Yiddish, as they became involved with organizations relating to that culture. They joined existing groups while also creating their own formal and informal networks, many of which functioned in Yiddish for practical as well as ideological reasons.[23]

By 1961, Canadian Jewry – and Yiddish cultural life – was largely concentrated in Montreal (with a Jewish population of roughly 103,000), Toronto (89,000), and Winnipeg (19,000), with a growing community in Vancouver (7,000).[24] The major Jewish centres each had a Yiddish newspaper that continued to appear in the decades after the Holocaust: the *Keneder adler/Canadian Jewish Eagle* in Montreal (1907–88, a daily until 1963), *Dos yidishe vort/The Israelite Press* in Winnipeg (1915–81), and *Der yidisher zhurnal/The Daily Hebrew Journal* in Toronto (1912–62). Popular, community, and art theatre performances were staged across the country. A Canada-wide network of secular Jewish schools, including both supplementary and all-day schools as well as summer camps, offered curricula in Yiddish language and culture. A core population of Yiddish speakers still resided in the old Jewish neighbourhoods, bucking the trend to relocate to suburban areas. Newcomers who wished to connect with the existing Yiddish community were soon integrated into existing institutions as writers for the newspapers, teachers, actors, and leaders in local political organizations. They banded together with the pre-Holocaust arrivals to pioneer new ventures in and for Yiddish.

Montreal became home to a sizable and expanding Hasidic population. In the pre-Holocaust period, members of Montreal's small Hasidic communities spoke Yiddish, just as a majority of the new immigrants did.[25] For example, Hasidic rabbi Yudel Rosenberg (1860–1935) – author of the 1909 bestselling account of the supernatural *golem*[26] – was a regular contributor to the mainstream Yiddish daily *Keneder adler* and published works in a genre that scholar Ira Robinson has termed "disguised fiction."[27] Hasidic refugees from Nazi Europe, who struggled to transplant their decimated communities, published news of their burgeoning local population as well as nonfiction writing in the *Keneder adler*.[28] During and after the Holocaust, leaders of Hasidic sects settled predominantly in, and adjacent to, the Jewish quarter of Mile End, where they established networks of institutions. As Yiddish declined as a spoken language in the Jewish mainstream, it conversely increased in prominence as a vernacular in the Hasidic world. As suggested by the title of William Shaffir's study, "Safeguarding a Distinctive Identity: Hasidic Jews in Montreal," the voluntary Hasidic separation from the mainstream was supported by distinct educational institutions and infrastructure, even in dense urban neighbourhoods shared with other groups.[29] As part of this effort, one of the city's Hasidic groups, the Yiddish-speaking community of Tash, relocated from urban Montreal to a remote settlement in the rural Francophone region of Sainte-Thérèse in 1962.[30]

While the arrival of refugees and survivors of the Holocaust bolstered the language through new initiatives, the use of Yiddish within the wider Jewish community faced a steady decline. Census statistics suggest that the language required a continuous influx of native speakers from abroad because the dominant pattern in Ashkenazi immigration had been for new immigrants and their Canadian-born and -raised children to adopt English. With the last wave of immigration after the Holocaust, the relocation of Yiddish to the margins of Jewish life was compounded by the immigration of Jews with no historic connection to Yiddish and the increasing prevalence of Israeli Hebrew/Ivrit as the language of youth education. The widespread adoption of English as the language of the Jewish community was further hastened by the postwar exodus out of the old immigrant neighbourhoods, where a high density of Yiddish speakers had facilitated the use of the language in the home and on the street.[31]

By the mid-1950s, Canada housed a diverse population of some 200,000 Jews composed of four subgroups: a small but well established, English-speaking old guard; rapidly acculturating Europeans from the period of mass immigration and their children; recent Eastern European refugees and survivors of Nazi Europe; and a small but growing group of largely French-speaking, Sephardi Jews from North Africa and the Middle East.[32] In this new mix, English and French became the daily languages and Israeli Hebrew the shared Jewish language. As Yiddish declined as the Jewish lingua franca, neither were the Sephardi languages of Ladino (Judezmo) and its various dialects (e.g., Haketia) widely spoken in Canada.[33] In 1951, some 51 per cent of Canada's Jewish population declared itself Yiddish-speaking in the national census, down from the 1931 high of 96 per cent.[34] The three cities that housed a majority of the country's Jews all evinced declining numbers of Yiddish speakers by 1951: 67 per cent in Winnipeg, 62 per cent in Toronto, and 55 per cent in Montreal.[35] Meanwhile, the percentage of Jews who declared English as their mother tongue (the first language learned and still understood) was steadily on the rise, due in large part to the Anglicization of the Canadian-born children of Yiddish-speaking immigrants. Thus, in 1951, Yiddish was the mother tongue of some 85 per cent of Jews born outside the country, compared with 44 per cent of those born in Canada.[36] These changes caused demographer Leo Rosenberg to remark, "In 1951 and in subsequent years an increasing percentage of Canadian-born Jews are of the second and third generation, born in Canada, and are the children and grandchildren of Jews who had rarely or never heard Yiddish spoken in their parents' homes."[37] As sociologist Leo Davids later noted: "In 1951, the majority of Canadian Jews still reported Yiddish as their mother tongue, and younger Jews had a passive mastery of Yiddish – although they didn't speak it very often, they understood it fully and had no problem receiving communication from older Jews who would speak to their children and grandchildren in Yiddish … However, during the 1950s and later, it is apparent that the home use of Yiddish was increasingly mixed with English, and therefore the mother tongue of Jews whose childhood occurred in the period shortly after the Second World War would have combined English and Yiddish in most cases. This has been going on everywhere that Yiddish was spoken."[38]

The statistical changes in the mother tongue among Canadian Jews on the census from 1931 (Yiddish: 96 per cent, English: 2 per cent) to 1961 (Yiddish: 30 per cent, English: 58 per cent) indicate the rapid rate of linguistic acculturation.[39] By the 1970s, Yiddish in Canada could be perceived as endangered, a perspective most clearly articulated at that time by Jack Thiessen, emeritus professor of German at the University of Winnipeg: "When eastern Europe was destroyed, Yiddish lost its geographical base, and though enclaves may continue to exist in Mea Shearim, Williamsburg, Mont-real and Rio, the end is in sight. Sure, we have Yiddish courses in our universities. These are attended by students whose parents left them culturally rootless, and who are searching for their Zaida (grandfa-ther) and the shtetl (ghetto). For them it is therapy ... For those with a long view, Yiddish is an episode like Alexandria, or Spain, and is destined for the limbo of Aramaic and Ladino."[40] Thiessen observed a drop in Yiddish use as a marker of ethnicity among the younger generation of Canadian Jews, a fall that he predicted would end in its inevitable demise.

Cultural activists, known in Yiddish as "*kultur-tuer,*" rallied to create new avenues for continuity in Canada. A cadre of European-born sur-vivors of the Holocaust who immigrated to Canada dedicated them-selves to maintaining and expanding Yiddish culture. One prominent linchpin was Sara Mlotek Rosenfeld (1920-2004). Born into a family of leftist Jewish activists (Bundists), she was raised in Warsaw until she fled to the Soviet Union in 1939 after the German invasion. After spending the war years in Soviet Kazakhstan, she and her husband made their way to Canada and settled in Montreal in 1949. There she began to dedicate herself to Yiddish cultural activity, beginning with organizing the Workmen's Circle Chorus. In her longstanding capac-ity as executive director of the Canadian Jewish Congress National Committee on Yiddish, she promoted the language and culture via publishing projects, education for youth, music, and in activism local-ly as well as internationally. For example, the founder of the Yiddish Book Center in Amherst, Massachusetts, Aaron Lansky, worked close-ly with her in his campaign to rescue abandoned Yiddish books across Canada. According to Lansky, as one of the Center's first board mem-bers in the 1980s, "Sara mobilized a country," enlisting collectors nationwide and allocating temporary storage for the books in the basement of the Canadian Jewish Congress headquarters in Montre-al.[41] Lansky recalled that when Rosenfeld organized an international gathering of thousands of delegates to the Veltrat (the World Council on Yiddish and Yiddish Culture), "the speakers, as usual, pounded the podium and bellowed, '*Vu iz undzer yugnt?*' [where is our youth?], we, the elusive *yugnt*, were in the basement with Sara, on our hands and knees, sorting her latest haul of Yiddish books." Her 2002 appoint-ment to the Order of Canada made her "the closest thing to a Yiddish knight the world has ever seen."[42] Rosenfeld's efforts as an impresario would include directing Montreal's annual outdoor Yiddish Music

Festival and cofounding KlezKanada, an annual music retreat active from the mid-1990s to the present day. Her family played a significant role in the transmission of Yiddish: her brother, Joseph Mlotek, relocated from Canada to New York and become educational director of the Workmen's Circle; he and his wife, musicologist Eleanor Chana Mlotek, became world-renowned collectors of Yiddish songs. Her son, Moishe Rosenfeld, is a leading Yiddish actor and theatre producer in New York. Active across different concentric circles of secular Yiddish, their names recur in various parts of this book.

For Rosenfeld and her generation, dedicating themselves to Yiddish activism marked continuity with their prewar experiences. They came together to memorialize what had been lost but also to build anew. One approach to continuity has been an insider model that speaks to the traditional speakers of Yiddish: the European-born generation and their descendants. An articulation of this model is the hundreds of Yiddish clubs dotting Canada and the United States, which have over the last fifty years been prominent sites for engagement with, and celebration of, the language and culture. Such clubs are spaces to engage informally with the language, with participants arriving with varying levels of knowledge derived largely from home and family.[43] An example of an enduring Canadian club is the Toronto-based Friends of Yiddish (FOY).

FOY was founded in 1984 by a small group of insiders to European Yiddish culture "who shared the vision of ensuring the continuity and growth of the Yiddish language and the Ashkenazi culture … who continue to attract new members for whom *mameloshen* is their extra gene!"[44] In 2020, the welcome page of its website offered the following statement: "We are the last generation immersed from childhood in the Yiddish culture, and we want to cultivate an appreciation of the culture for the future. We talk about the golden chain and the links that intertwine, creating a beautiful expression of our Jewish identity. Yiddish is a piece of that cultural link that is the chain of Jewish life."[45] The website's "About" page indicates that the group comprises members with common goals and a shared background as children or grandchildren of European-born Yiddish speakers: "Who are we? We're the same as you. We're first, second and third generation Canadians who want a chance to hear a *Yidish vort* and a *freylikh lid* [Yiddish word and a happy song]. Sometimes, we almost *tsebrekh di tseyn* [break our teeth] as we try speaking Yiddish and we can't always find the right word. But then, it gets easier and easier and those of us who are more fluent are always willing to help. We laugh a lot too ... sometimes so hard, we can't speak any language!"[46] Until restrictions on gatherings due to the coronavirus pandemic in late 2019, FOY was hosting programming year-round in and about Yiddish, including lectures, literary readings, screenings of Yiddish films, sing-along sessions, and holiday parties. A newspaper article about the group quoted one of its members, Helen Smolkin, a native speaker with a history of involvement in Yiddish organizational life: "People say Yiddish is a dying language, it is not. At our events, you are surrounded by people with a passion and love for Yiddishkeit." [47]

With the passing of the European-born generation, Yiddish activism irrevocably changed from a European to a Canadian model of engagement. This transition had begun earlier as European-born activists sought ways to engage with their Canadian-raised children and grandchildren. By 2020, the transition to new speakers as carriers of Yiddish is evident even within the insider model of FOY, which offered scholarships for students seeking to study the language as new speakers rather than heritage speakers. Canadian-raised activists and artists would create their own sites for Yiddish continuity adapted to their experiences and interests. The fluidity and flexibility of Yiddish have helped to sustain it in its transition from an immigrant to an ethnic language and culture, and beyond.

In 2020, Canada maintains multiple outlets for an enduring and multipronged engagement with secular Yiddish with histories dating back several decades. To mention just a few: Montreal and Toronto house secular Jewish day schools that include Yiddish as part of the curriculum; they are the only cities in North America where this is the case. University programs at McGill University, University of Manitoba, University of Ottawa, University of Toronto, York University, and elsewhere have, at various points, offered full-year and intensive Yiddish language and culture classes. Montreal houses a permanent Yiddish theatre with annual productions, including a youth wing. In Vancouver, a Jewish cultural centre offers Yiddish education to children, houses a Yiddish folk choir, and runs a circulating library of Yiddish books. Yiddish music is sung, played, and danced to at public performances festivals and retreats in locations across the country.

In 2017, I conducted a national online survey on Yiddish use in Canada. The results are instructive, questioning assumptions about the present and future of Yiddish in Canada and indicating that people engage with the language in ways and in contexts not reflected in the census statistics. The survey asked ten questions about the respondent's use of Yiddish, most with multiple possible responses. I disseminated it via email and social media through people active in the Yiddish world across Canada as well as targeted reading groups, theatre groups, event lists, and newsletters. The respondents answered the questions anonymously but were asked to provide data about their age and the locations of their origin and current residence. The roughly five hundred respondents represent a self-selected group of people involved enough with Yiddish to learn of the survey. Almost all identified as Jewish, most of them as secular Jews. The respondents did not include any Hasidim, likely due to limitations on internet use in those communities combined with the secular and cultural character of the modes of dissemination (as discussed in the next chapter, members of Hasidic communities were interviewed face-to-face instead, using the same ten questions).

The respondents offered extensive data about their familial, professional, scholarly, and personal experiences with Yiddish. Respondents were asked about their areas of present involvement with Yiddish (speaking; reading; translating; listening to, watching, or performing Yiddish music or theatre; studying or teaching; attending Yiddish events), to list the Yiddish speakers in their families, where their Yiddish comes from (home/family, neighbourhood, school, university, self-study, music, reading), the duration of their involvement with Yiddish, what activities they engage with on a regular basis today (speaking with family, friends, community members, or colleagues; reading; singing; watching plays or movies), why they speak or are involved with Yiddish, whether they expect their grandchildren to be Yiddish speakers (yes, no, maybe), and how they identify in religious terms (from Haredi to no religion). The results indicate multifaceted engagement with Yiddish, with the respondents overwhelmingly identifying multiple areas of involvement and sources of knowledge. A majority indicated that while their Yiddish was not fluent or spoken on a regular basis, the language formed an important component of their lives and identities, and they sought out diverse ways of connecting with it. Most of the respondents offered lengthy responses to the open-ended question about why they are involved with Yiddish, mentioning family heritage, the richness of the language and culture, a love for music or theatre, and so on. The survey pointed to models other than family transmission, as many respondents indicated that

they learned Yiddish in school or by self-study; almost no one
expressed an expectation that their grandchildren would be Yiddish
speakers. These modes of transmission – from teachers to students,
among singers, within structured conversation or reading groups,
through reading texts or viewing subtitled films – represent ways that
new speakers are connecting with Yiddish as a living language across
multiple, intersecting spaces. In the next chapter, I will analyze this
data further, considering how it points to connections between language, culture, and identity.

MEDIA ANALYSIS OF YIDDISH IN CANADA

A significant shift has taken place with respect to the narrative around
Yiddish in Canada in the last thirty years, from "dead" and "dying," to
"reviving," "revitalizing," and undergoing a "renaissance." A brief analysis of media discourse surrounding secular Yiddish in mainstream
Canadian periodicals – English language, French language, and Jewish community newspapers – offers one lens through which to assess
these changes. The analysis reveals a shift towards associating Yiddish
with innovative projects to promote discovery of the language and
culture, notably among youth, rather than viewing it simply as an
expression of an immigrant or ethnic heritage.

In the 1970s, the term "Yiddish" appeared in mainstream newspapers in a wide variety of ways that signal its ongoing daily use as
well as its shift to a lesser-used heritage language. Articles and ads
show that Yiddish retained its hold among the Canadian Jewish
population alongside other languages spoken following immigration. For example, an article in the *Globe and Mail* announced that
York Cablevision, a recently created television company in Toronto, planned to offer programming in Portuguese, Italian, Greek,
East Indian [sic], and Yiddish,[48] while advertisements by car dealer-
ships offered service in Yiddish and several other languages.[49] Here
Yiddish use indicates continuity among native speakers in the
European-raised generation. The same continuity is found in articles about Yiddish theatre productions by an aging cadre of classic
stars; for example, "Ida Kaminska: Frail, Flexible and Dazzling."[50]
Yiddish received hundreds of casual mentions, for example in job
postings with preference given to those with Yiddish as a second
language or as hints in crossword puzzles. At the same time, as I discuss in chapter 3, articles in the Canadian press expressed concern

about the future of Yiddish and a desire to preserve it for future generations. Yiddish was also moving beyond its traditional speakers, but in popularized form. Two best-selling American books that presented the language to a mainstream readership – Leo Rosten's *The Joys of Yiddish* (1968) and Maurice Samuel's *In Praise of Yiddish* (1971) – appeared repeatedly in book reviews and feature articles.

The 1980s and 1990s, and the broader implementation of Canadian policies to promote multiculturalism, led to perceptible changes in how Yiddish was regarded. Articles employ reports about Yiddish events as opportunities to discuss wider issues relating to the survival of the language and culture. These explain what Yiddish is, what is at stake in the Yiddish initiatives taking place, and offer the perspectives of participants about the importance of maintaining the language. The articles are characterized by an increasing emphasis on Yiddish ventures that do not hinge on fluency: musical or theatrical performances, or educational opportunities for new speakers to be exposed to the language, such as university courses, adult education, or special programming for young children. For example, a 1988 article headlined "Yiddish, Anyone?" presents activities in Toronto: courses for adults at a community centre, weekly children's Yiddish classes, and performance of Yiddish theatre and music.[51] A 1997 article headlined "Yiddish Gets a New Lease on Life" discusses a North American revival of popular interest in the language.[52] Numerous articles review the role of the Dora Wasserman Yiddish Theatre in the preservation of Yiddish: for example, a 1999 article headlined "Director Refuses to Let the Curtain Fall on Yiddish: Dora Wasserman Uses the Theatre to Help Save a Language" cites sociologist Morton Weinfeld suggesting that the "unnatural death" of Yiddish as a language of daily life has lent preservation attempts a sacred value.[53]

A vast majority of articles published in the 2000s and 2010s focus on the future of secular Yiddish and how – not whether – it will be transmitted. Articles that report on the Canadian census evoke dismal news; for example, sociologist Leo Davids states, "The [2011] census data clearly show a viable Yiddish-speaking population only in the Montreal area. There are still a few thousand Yiddish-speaking children there. Elsewhere, there is no 'life' for the Yiddish tongue in Canada."[54] However, as soon as writers step away from the census statistics, they express optimism about the language's present and future. A

2012 article headlined "Colourful Language Still Has a Voice" states:
"The arguments about whether Yiddish is alive or dead have died
down. Its future is somewhat dependent on universities and community associations, but people like Professor Weiser [a professor of Yiddish at Toronto's York University] are committed to its future. It's a
way of passing on an inheritance. Yiddish remains a living language,
much reduced but in no danger of disappearing."[55]

Yiddish is often characterized as more than a vernacular. For example, a 2012 article by a journalist who studied Yiddish in the 1980s at
Bialik, a secular Jewish high school in Montreal, considers the
impacts of her education: "About Jewishness, I feel I understand in a
way that those who didn't learn Yiddish might not. Because there is
intellectual knowing, and emotional knowing, and bodily knowing,
and in language you get all of that."[56] Only in a small minority of
articles does Yiddish appear as a mere vestige of an immigrant past.[57]
Multiple articles spotlight new educational initiatives that are participatory, inclusive, and fun. A 2007 article about a program for tod-
dlers at the Toronto Jewish Library describes how children and their
parents and grandparents learn Yiddish songs and poems, and discusses "a surge of renewed interest in Yiddish and the rich culture
associated with it."[58] A 2016 article on an annual "Lyrics and Latkes
Sing-Along" presented by Montreal's Dora Wasserman Yiddish Theatre cites two members discussing the importance of the younger
generation learning to speak Yiddish.[59] An article in *Maclean's* magazine discusses how Yiddish courses are being successfully implemented in Canadian universities.[60] And journalist Joel Yanofsky's
2017 essay "What's the Yiddish Word for Comeback?" suggests that
Yiddish "could be going mainstream."[61] While a majority of this
newspaper and magazine coverage deals with Montreal or Toronto,
several articles note similar activity in the city of Winnipeg, once a
hub of Yiddish and now a site of new initiatives.[62]

These articles reveal optimism among groups interested the richness that the language has to offer the younger generation. The author
of "Inside the Burgeoning Yiddish Renaissance" (2018) suggests jetti-
soning the rhetoric around language "revival" in favour of a model for
engagement with Yiddish that exists outside of personal heritage:
"Despite what you may think, Morris [a non-Jewish student and
scholar of Yiddish] is actually a good representation of the future of
Yiddish: secular, urban, global, bookish, hipster. This is not the Yiddish of payot and textbooks, but of podcasts and online journals."[63]

Commentators also draw comparisons with other groups invested in language transmission. A 2019 podcast called "Yidd-ish?" asks the question, "Can a culture exist without the language that is central to it?" One participant notes, "This is an interesting discussion that is going on in Indigenous communities across Canada right now. Whether they continue the culture without the language. And most of them have concluded that they can't. And I would say the same for Yiddish."[64]

The evolving media discourse around Yiddish in Canada has parallels beyond its geographic borders, notably in the United States.[65] Interest in Yiddish increased dramatically in the 1990s and 2000s along with new ventures in the areas of education and performance. While sometimes articles conflated activity about Yiddish with its revival, they consistently pointed to renewal in language learning and creativity, especially among younger cohorts.

SCOTTISH GAELIC: A COMPARISON

While this book focuses on Secular Yiddish language transmission in Canada, I offer a brief discussion of Scottish Gaelic as another lesser-spoken language that is undergoing revitalization in Canada and abroad. The comparison raises important questions about the potential impacts of state recognition and government support of lesser-spoken languages, and the role of new speakers in maintaining their continuity. The example of Scottish Gaelic will be used at various points in this book to tease out some the themes relating to such languages, notably with regard to music and broadcasting.[66]

Some fifty thousand speakers of Scottish Gaelic reached Canadian shores escaping upheaval and persecution during the height of British colonial expansion in the late eighteenth century. Settling primarily in Nova Scotia, they made up the largest ethnic group in the province by the early twentieth century, when their numbers began declining. Due to cultural repression, assimilation, and the relocation of its speakers to urban centres, the transmission of Scottish Gaelic within families declined precipitously in both its native Scotland and in Canada.[67] In the 1970s, however, the language experienced an upsurge in Canada due to grassroots revitalization efforts.

Educational and cultural programming within community organizations has been instrumental to Scottish Gaelic continuity. The most prominent of these organizations is the Colaisde na Gàidhlig/

The Gaelic College (founded 1938), located in St Ann's, Cape Breton Island, a historic bastion of Scottish Gaelic in Nova Scotia. Built with funds raised in the community, the college offers classes in the language, song, history, instrumental traditions, and traditional arts (sewing, spinning, weaving, cooking) in weekly as well as intensive themed weekends or weeklong sessions. As the only institution of its kind in North America, the college brings together an international cohort of students of varying ages – youth aged ten to seventeen as well as adults – who have diverse backgrounds and skill levels.[68] In late 2019, the college's director of education, Kenneth MacKenzie, observed that while a majority of students stem from heritage families, with previous exposure to the language ranging from extensive to minimal, roughly a quarter come from other backgrounds; some perceive Scottish Gaelic as offering an alternative to mainstream culture.[69]

The continuity of Scottish Gaelic has benefitted from state support in both its native Scotland and in Canada. Under the language planning body created in 2005 under the Gaelic Language Act (Bòrd na Gàidhlig), the Scottish government, parliament, and local councils instituted plans that included public signage as well as public service provision. Gaelic language education developed at the primary and secondary school levels, including a number of immersive Gaelic schools.[70] During the same period, Scottish Gaelic in Canada received state recognition and funding. With a third of the province's population tracing its roots back to Scotland, the Nova Scotia government formed the Office of Gaelic Affairs (Oifis Iomairtean na Gàidhlig) in 2006, dedicated to "Renewing Gaelic language and culture in Nova Scotia." In addition to generating new speakers through second language learning, the Office of Gaelic Affairs promotes the recognition of Scottish Gaelic speakers as "an integral part of the identity of the province" and "a founding language and cultural group." Its mandate includes support for community language courses, mentorships that pair up new and fluent speakers, extra-curricular immersion programs, and opportunities for study in Scotland.[71] With this government support, the teaching of Scots Gaelic courses in Nova Scotia has grown from just a single school with fifteen students to a total of seven schools with over three hundred students by 2015. In 2017, the province published a resource guide for educators titled *Gaelic Nova Scotia* to celebrate the contributions of Gaelic speakers and encourage pride and connections with Gaelic language, culture, and identity within local communities.[72] Scottish Gaelic spaces are being integrated into the mainstream; for example, the province's "Gaelic Month" offers events to raise awareness and celebrate language, culture, heritage, and identity, with the 2021 marking the twenty-fifth anniversary of the event with the theme, *Air Adhart Le Chéile*/Forward Together.[73] With new ties established with Scotland in the renewal of the language and culture, and Canada hosting programs such as student exchanges, Nova Scotia forms a stronghold of Scottish Gaelic in the world.

Unlike Scottish Gaelic, contemporary Yiddish is not tied to any state apparatus that supports its integration into the mainstream. There are no government-coordinated annual campaigns, themes, or published educational guides that reflect a specific point of view about what the language is or should be. Rather, secular Yiddish continuity continues to depend on voluntary engagement and the work of non-profit organizations within a loosely connected cluster of ventures. However, the languages bear much in common in terms of their grassroots activities and in the changing profile of their speakers to new learners.

With population of native speakers of Scottish Gaelic dwindling, scholars have posited that the future of the language is increasingly shifting to youth and new speakers.[74] By 2019, there were only about two thousand Canadian speakers, with only a few hundred native speakers; the rest were second language learners who acquired the language from family members, or, increasingly, through educational programs.[75] New learners include both those with and without Scottish Gaelic heritage, with a tendency among new speakers to internalize elements of ethnic identity as part of the language acquisition process.[76] In recent years, the goal of expanding new Gaelic speaker networks through second language education and programming have become increasingly significant to language advocates and policymakers, who recognise the difficulties of reinstating the transmission of a language in the home once it is interrupted. New speakers have become a "crucial demographic" for the sustainability of Scottish Gaelic in both Scotland and in Canada.[77] A recent study found that rather than a global objective of "native speaker" fluency, speakers were more oriented towards a "new-speaker model" and "considered a native-speaker target as inauthentic." While they participated in Gaelic cultural networks with older, "traditional" speakers, some also constructed their own identities as new speakers.[78]

Canadian learners form a distinct cohort. For example, recent fieldwork by Stuart Dunmore has found that new language learners in Nova Scotia were far more enthusiastic than their counterparts in Scotland to adopt the ethnonym "Gael" as an ethnolinguistic identity marker.[79] Dunmore found that in new speakers in Nova Scotia were also motivated to attain higher levels of oral fluency.[80] In 2020, he observed an optimism associated with the Canadian Gaelic community, which "now exists almost entirely as a network of speakers rather than a geographically concentrated ethno-culture," in contrast to the evident decline of its native speakers in Scotland. The passing of the last of the traditional native speakers has rendered the "the perceived authenticity of heritage-motivated new Gaelic speakers" less contested in Nova Scotia than in Scotland."[81] The future of Gaelic in Nova Scotia on an upward trajectory, with a growing population of enthusiastic new speakers.

In both the Scottish Gaelic and secular Yiddish contexts, the traditional speakers had largely passed away by 2020, leaving new speakers to determine the future of the language. Both languages rely increasingly on new learners, who bring their own ideological motivations to the study of the language. Another crucial difference lies in a decades-old ideological debate around the future of Yiddish as a language of multiple, often opposing ideologies, within a diverse and sometimes contested space. One factor is the existence of two distinct post-Holocaust Yiddish communities to which I will now turn: the secular and the Haredi.

SECULAR AND HAREDI YIDDISH

Since the 1950s, Yiddish has increasingly split into two branches in Canada as well as globally: Haredi Yiddish, a daily language of family and community life and a linguistic boundary against the mainstream, and secular Yiddish, most often associated with identity and cultural production. The limited contact between the two groups has resulted in two distinct sites of Yiddish, with different worldviews and different grammatical and spelling systems for the language.

The secular Yiddish world is geographically dispersed, and increasingly comprised of new learners of the language as well as artists, activists, and enthusiasts from diverse backgrounds. It grew out of the nineteenth-century ideological battles of European Jewish modernity. This period of Haskalah (Jewish Enlightenment) produced a corpus of modern literature in both Yiddish and Hebrew by Mendele Moykher Sforim (Mendele the Book Peddler, pen name of Sholem Yankev Abramovitch, 1836–1917), Sholem Aleichem (Sholem Rabinovitch, 1859–1916) and I.L. Peretz (1852–1915), to be followed by hundreds of writers of diverse backgrounds and ideological and literary orientations worldwide.[82] Leftist political movements employed Yiddish to reach the Jewish masses both in Eastern Europe and in new immigrant centres. These evolved organizations that promoted Yiddish continuity with an enduring and global reach. The Jewish Labour Bund (Algemeyner Yidisher Arbeter Bund in Lite, Poyln un Rusland/General Jewish Workers' Union in Lithuania, Poland, and Russia, popularly known as "the Bund") was formed as a secular Jewish socialist party in Russia in 1897. It established affiliated groups in Jewish immigrant centres worldwide during and after the Second World War to promote a secular, leftist, Jewish diaspora culture and the Yiddish language. The Bund's influential core principle of "*doikayt/doykeyt*" (hereness) locates the continuity of the Jewish people in the strengthening of their diverse local diaspora communities, rather than in a single Jewish homeland.[83] The Poale Zion/Farband (Workers of Zion), founded as a workers' movement in a split with the Bund in 1901, espoused a Labour Zionist ideology. The Workmen's Circle/Arbeter Ring (recently renamed The Workers Circle), was founded as a fraternal organization in New York 1897 and then formed chapters across North America to promote secular Jewish culture. Jewish Communists were active in an array of activities. The interwar period marked the highpoint of secular Yiddish with a cultural life that included a periodical press, literature, theatre, music, and education, oftentimes in association with a spectrum of Jewish leftist political movements.

An ideology known as "Yiddishism" gained traction as a movement against linguistic assimilationism as well as the anti-Yiddish sentiment of the late nineteenth century.[84] It crystalized in the wake of the 1908 Czernowitz Conference, the first international gathering in support of the language, which promoted a model of legitimating Yiddish through activities such as language planning and standardization; the event also signalled the beginning of an ideological orientation that espoused the language and culture as a core element of Jewishness.[85]

1925 marked the founding of the YIVO Institute for Jewish Research (Yidisher Visnshaftlekher Institut/Jewish Scientific Institute), which would form a centre of scholarship, including history, linguistics, demographics, education, literature, and folklore, first in Vilna/Vilnius and subsequently in New York.[86] As part of its activities, in the 1930s the YIVO devised and promoted a system of standardized grammar and spelling known as "*klal-sphrakh*" (Standard Yiddish) that has been widely adopted in the secular milieu.[87] This supraregional Standard Yiddish – as opposed to its regional variants (dialects) – is widely used by Yiddishists and new speakers more broadly.[88]

A concurrent concept of Yiddishkeit/Yidishkayt (Jewishness) emerged among immigrant communities in North America to denote the essential qualities associated with Yiddish. The term – which traditionally refers to observing a Jewish way of life and continues to do so among the religiously observant – was recast in a distinctly secular guise to denote an alternative understanding. Irving Howe's popular 1976 history of Eastern European Jewish immigration to the United States, *World of Our Fathers*, noted: "That phase of Jewish history during the last two centuries is marked by the prevalence of Yiddish as the language of the east European Jews and by the growth among them of a culture resting mainly upon that language. The culture of Yiddishkeit is no longer that of traditional Orthodoxy, yet it retains strong ties to the religious past. It takes on an increasingly secular character yet is by no means confined to the secularist elements among Yiddish-speaking Jews. It refers to a way of life, a shared experience, which goes beyond opinion or ideology."[89]

Haredi Yiddish has evolved along a very different trajectory with numerous sects of Hasidim, interconnected through transnational networks, representing a stronghold for the language. Hasidim are largely descendants of refugees from, or survivors of, the Holocaust. They form part of interconnected enclaves whose members relocate for study or marriage. Within Satmar, the most insular of the Hasidic sects, the Romanian-born leader Joel Teitelbaum (1887–1979) espoused the use of Yiddish as an expression of strict separation from the mainstream, even as Hungarian served as the shared language of many of his Hasidim after the Holocaust in their adopted homes worldwide. As the largest Hasidic group, Satmar has had a profound influence on other Hasidic groups. Under the Teitelbaum rabbinic dynasty, the Satmar sect has actively supported and promoted the use of Yiddish in daily life, including the publication of newspapers.[90]

The smaller Vizhnitz sect has also, like the Satmar, expressed a clear commitment to the language: for example, the Vizhnitzer Rebbe held a gathering late in 2016 where he urged that Yiddish use in Hasidic households in America and Israel "needs to be strengthened" and implored his followers to speak to their family members and other members of the group exclusively in Yiddish.[91]

Multigenerational family transmission is augmented by public institutions in Hasidic communities. Schools not only teach Yiddish as a subject but also employ it as a means of teaching other subjects on the curriculum; synagogues and halls for advanced communal study (*beys-medresh* or *kollel*) employ the language as a shared vernacular. In addition, Yiddish use is normalized in Hasidic urban enclaves by being widely spoken in neighbourhood shops, parks, and on the street. For those Hasidim who do not speak Yiddish on a regular basis and employ other, non-linguistic conventions such as clothing to maintain their distinctiveness, Yiddish can still occupy a role. For example, the deliberate adoption of Yiddish cadence or accent or the insertion of Yiddish terms into an English sociolect, which scholars term "Yeshivish" or "frumspeak," can be a valuable identity-marker, in particular for those who are learning to become religiously observant.[92] Further, the language can be employed in specific situations: for example, the largely non-Yiddish speaking Chabad Hasidim will listen to the *sichos* (speeches) of the last Lubavitcher Rebbe in Yiddish.

A body of scholarly literature on the Hasidim and their use of Yiddish worldwide points to a deliberate use of the language as a means of maintaining a distinctive and separate identity. Jeffrey Shandler writes that contemporary Hasidic Yiddish varies from that of their pre-Holocaust ancestors in substance as well as orientation, and it is "used today as a barrier, rather than a bridge, between Hasidim and other Jews."[93] Miriam Isaacs posits Hasidic Yiddish use as a "one-way barrier" to the secular world, as well as a manifestation of positive values – *haymish* and *frim* (familiar and pious) – and a link with a collective past.[94] Tatjana Soldat-Jaffe identifies Haredim as a form of Jewish ethnicity and Yiddish as a marker of that ethnicity: "As a status symbol, Yiddish indicates the cultural values of the community, and, as such, Yiddish can still function in the construction of ethnic boundaries."[95] Ayala Fader's ethnographic study examines intergenerational transmission from mothers to children among Brooklyn Hasidim. She points to the gendered nature of Yiddish use, with men speaking "Hasidic Yiddish" and women speaking "Hasidic English," or Yiddish-inflected English.[96]

Without the emphasis on language planning and standardization that have been central to Yiddishist ideology, Hasidic Yiddish has developed very differently from secular Yiddish in both its spoken and written forms.[97] Chaya Nove has compellingly argued for scholarly recognition of the distinctiveness and significance of Hasidic dialects, in which the language is undergoing change as a native vernacular.[98] One area of difference from the Standard Yiddish predominantly used by secular Yiddish speakers is pronunciation, with dialects of Hasidic Yiddish largely derived from Central Yiddish, which was historically spoken in Poland, Galicia, and part of Hungary. In terms of grammar, scholars of American Hasidic Yiddish have noted a loss of distinctions of gender and case as a result of contact with English, which lacks these linguistic features[99]; this is tendency is also found in other minority languages.[100] A further outcome of contact with English has been the incorporation of local (i.e. English) terms into Yiddish. Rather than create Yiddish terms for new concepts as per the Yiddishist model, Hasidic Yiddish will integrate a word such as "cell phone" (versus the terms coined by speakers of Standard Yiddish speakers: *tselke* or *mobilke*). Miriam Isaacs suggests that this flexibility is at the root of the successful transmission of Haredi Yiddish: "While linguistic laxity by Haredim may be criticized by purists, there is reason to conjecture that it is this very quality about the language that is key to its survival against unlikely odds ... The experience of the Haredim demonstrates that adherence to formal accuracy in language is not as important for continuity as a willingness to allow variation, language mixing, and borrowing."[101] As a culture that prioritizes traditional textual knowledge, today's Haredim do not identify themselves as producers and consumers of modern Yiddish culture. However, as discussed elsewhere in this volume, Hasidic communities do produce a wide array of media with Yiddish content: newspapers and journals, memoirs, novels, musical recordings, and children's literature and board games. All of these comply with the norms of Hasidic communities around gender, modesty, and values.

FRAMING THE DISCOURSE AROUND YIDDISH

Whether Yiddish is dying or being preserved, revived, or revitalized has been debated in both popular and academic discourse over the last decades. Its decline as a spoken language has been well documented; a recent study, *Language Diversity Endangered,* refers to Yiddish as "perhaps the most famously 'dying' language."[102] The Endangered Languages Project website lists Yiddish as "at risk," despite attributing to it over 1.2 million speakers, with a geographic justification: Yiddish is no longer widely spoken in its European territory of origin, with most speakers located in America and Israel.[103]

At the root of this paradox is the widening gap between the secular Yiddish world and Haredi speakers discussed above. In the secular realm, spoken Yiddish qualifies as endangered according to measures of mother tongue and daily use. Only a few thousand people outside of Haredi enclaves worldwide are native speakers or use Yiddish on a regular basis, whereas a much larger number are connected to the language on an occasional basis as learners, singers, actors, or members of conversation and reading groups. In contrast, within the rapidly growing Hasidic world, where Yiddish use forms part of a collective imperative to maintain a pre-Holocaust Eastern European Jewish civilization, the language is far from threatened. In her 2006 article, "Imagining Yiddish: A Future for the Soul of Ashkenaz," Janet Hadda observes the widening split between the inward-oriented Yiddish culture of Haredim and what she terms the "neo-Ashkenaz," a "wildly inclusive," highly accessible culture that transcends ethnic boundaries.[104] Secular Yiddish in "neo-Ashkenaz" centres on music, theatre, and other forms of performance, as well as the translation of Yiddish literature, rather than being spoken every day. While in many ways it is the torchbearer of Yiddish as a living language, the Hasidic world is largely disconnected from much of the cultural production that, since the late nineteenth century, has formed the heart of secular Yiddish culture. By the same token, the cultural production of the Hasidic world remains largely unknown or inaccessible to secular devotees of Yiddish. However, the barriers between these worlds are being breeched by growing interest among secular activists, cultural workers, and scholars in Haredi Yiddish, and by the presence of former Haredim among those who are bringing Yiddish to secular Jews and non-Jews as teachers, scholars, and artists.

Some recent scholarly studies situate contemporary Yiddish firmly within the Hasidic world. Linguist Dalit Assouline writes, "Yiddish, a language spoken by millions of traditional and secular Jews prior to the Second World War, is preserved today almost exclusively in several ultra-Orthodox communities, where it functions as a powerful sym-

bol of a distinct ethnic and religious identity."[105] Alexander Beider
likewise characterizes the present-day status of Yiddish as primarily
the purview of Haredi Jews.[106] Dovid Katz interrogates the gap
between "two groups of 'Yiddish involved Jews' who barely speak to
each other": the Hasidim and "the modern Yiddishist camp."[107] He
locates the site of Yiddish revitalization squarely within the Haredi
world and cites estimates there will be eight to ten million Hasidic
Yiddish speakers by 2075.

Any discourse around a language as dead, dying, or revived is complex. This is evidenced by recent scholarship around Hebrew, which
served for over two millennia not only as the language of daily prayer
and sacred textual study but as a vehicle for transnational diasporic
literary creation and written communication. A recent study argues
that Hebrew has been imbued with tremendous symbolic power and
creativity, despite not functioning as an everyday vernacular for
much of its history.[108] Linguist Ghil'ad Zuckermann observes that
the study of Hebrew "offers unique insights into the dynamics
between language and culture in general and in particular into the
role of language as a source of collective self-perception."[109] Jeffrey
Shandler analyzes what he calls the "trope of Yiddish as moribund,"
which dates back two centuries to the Haskalah. He writes, "The
trope of Yiddish as a dying or dead language has ... proved something other than a sociolinguistic assessment both before and after
the Holocaust. It has served, instead, as a discursive frame for
addressing the shifting stature and significance of Yiddish in modern Jewish life."[110] A recent blog post by the editors of a Yiddish
Studies journal headlined "Yiddish Lives! *Loshn* of the Living Dead,"
parodies rhetoric of the language as "dying" by including images of
Yiddish writers and other cultural figures altered to look like zom-
bies. They write: "Certainly over the past two centuries there have
been many attempts to provide Yiddish with a final resting place.
We are all familiar with these stereotypes of the language: Yiddish as
a dead language of the past that must be laughed at or mourned for,
a source of laughter or tears, but never an essential living part of
contemporary life, Jewish or otherwise. And yet, Yiddish continues
to inspire: Yiddish as the model for radical utopian futures, the language of a new borderless world; or Yiddish as the language of growing Hasidic communities."[111]

Elegiac associations with Yiddish are deeply embedded in the discourse around the language. Yiddish poetry and prose have long been

embedded in Holocaust commemorations, and the language invoked to signify rupture and loss. Writing in 1990, literary scholar Anita Norich interrogates this association and its implications for the language:

> [Yiddish] is the language of the majority of Holocaust victims and has increasingly become a metonymy for them, as if it constituted the very shrouds they were denied. As a language of mourning and commemoration, it is a sign of absence, carrying the authority of the dead with whom one cannot argue and who therefore always have the last word. This situation is further complicated because the words are becoming unrecognizable and indecipherable. Also prevalent in the popular imagination is a perception of Yiddish as the earthy language of the folk, an expression of the wit and irony born of adversity well met. To use Yiddish phrases is to dramatize one's knowledge of and connection to the roots of Jewish culture. Yiddish is seen as embodying Jewish fortitude and as encapsulating modern Jewish history. And, with its recent revival, it seems to promise that even this terrible history may be redeemed. There is a Yiddish expression that says 'English redt men; Yidish redt zikh' [English is spoken; Yiddish speaks]. It is indeed as if, in a troubling sense, Yiddish speaks but is not spoken Yiddish is no longer understood as a language composed of signifiers but as itself a sign of rupture and loss. To view it in this way is to see it – perhaps to distance and dismiss it – as completely separate and framed, an entity that can be regarded with awe or amusement.[112]

The twenty-first century discourse around secular Yiddish as "dying" has further hinged on the passing of its last pre-Holocaust, European-born and -raised generation. Jews in both Europe and immigrant centres had long been engaging voluntarily with Yiddish as a marker of identity and gravitated to its performative outputs, such as theatre, even as they spoke or adopted other languages; perhaps the most famous example is Franz Kafka.[113] But after the Holocaust, Yiddish was no longer as widely spoken and transmitted as it had been, for example, among the 375,000 Jews of Warsaw, who made up almost third of the city's population before the Nazi occupation in 1939. Those speakers who came of linguistic maturity in prewar Eastern Europe were the last to experience Yiddish as a language with infinite potential in all of domains and registers – in the home, the street, the political arena, high literature, and popular culture – across a broad religious, socioeconomic, and ideological spectrum as part of a global population of fellow speakers. In his 2004 book, *Words on Fire: The Unfinished Story of Yiddish*, Dovid Katz writes:

> For anyone to whom modern Yiddish, and its literature and culture are dear, the most bitterly painful time is the present. The secondary Holocaust blow is hitting hard and is coming to its devastating climax. The last secular Yiddish *masters* – writers, teachers, cultural organizers, scholars, journalists, performers, artists and so on, who came to intellectual or cultural maturity in pre-Holocaust Eastern Europe, are disappearing daily. In mid-2003, Montreal, for example, was still on the conceptual map of high-end secular Yiddish culture because of the presence of great prose writer Yehuda Elberg (born in Poland in 1912); the untiring, inspirational organizer of Yiddish cultural institutions and events, Sara Rosenfeld (born in Poland in 1920); and the fabled founder of Canada's Yiddish theatre, Dora Wasserman (born in Ukraine in 1919). By mid-2004, they were all gone. It is rather unfair to complain to God (or to doctors) when people in their eighties and nineties who have lived through a lot come to the end of life in peace surrounded by loved ones. By late 2004, Montreal, with no disrespect to its many enduring Yiddish resources (far outstripping many cities with much larger Jewish populations), had fallen off the map as a centre boasting major living masters.[114]

That same year, in "Ways of Escape: Yiddish," included in his volume *Spoken Here: Travels Among Threatened Languages*, Mark Abley likewise describes the dwindling and aging audiences for Montreal's Yiddish theatre and as readers of secular Yiddish literature; its Hasidic speakers, he suggests, offer the language's last stronghold.[115] 2020, a generation later, marks a further transition for secular Yiddish as the last cohort who learned the language in pre-Holocaust Europe are passing away. As a recent study of Yiddish in Australia points out, these speakers not only form the last generation to have raised their children in an immersive Yiddish environment that encompassed family and community institutions, they were also the builders and supporters of Yiddish organizations such as schools, theatres, libraries, and festivals.[116]

Though native carriers of European Yiddish were not being replenished, the 1980s and 1990s marked a sea change in the global activity around secular Yiddish. This diverged from what had come before by appealing to a new generation that might not have been previously exposed to Yiddish, whether Jewish or not. Language and culture courses at universities, including intensive summer programs in Canada, the United States, Europe, and Israel, expanded. This period also marked significant new developments in the Yiddish world: the popularization of the new genre of klezmer music – Eastern European Jewish instrumental traditions paired with lyrics sung in Yiddish – and accompanying festivals; the fusion of Yiddish and radical queer sensibilities in activism and performance that become known as Queer Yiddishkeit (Queer Yiddishkayt); the restoration and screening of prewar Yiddish films at festivals internationally; and a worldwide ingathering of books under the aegis of the Yiddish Book Center (Amherst, USA). These initiatives attracted popular interest and scholarly attention, both among the descendants of Eastern European Yiddish speakers and among newcomers. However, at the height of this new activity in the 1990s, questions remained as to its implications for Yiddish. From her position as Chair of Yiddish Studies at Harvard University, Ruth R. Wisse published a magazine article that staunchly argued against the idea of a Yiddish renaissance in America: "For all the talk of revival, Yiddish actually has only a handful of trained scholars who are capable of translating, editing, teaching and interpreting its vast and varied accumulated heritage; it can claim even fewer creative artists sufficiently at home in the language to renew its performance repertoire."[117]

Over the last twenty-five years, secular Yiddish has become a flashpoint in the discourse around contemporary Jewish identity. Even as prominent American academics – many of them children of the European-born survivor generation – participated in the debate around its place in American life, others integrated the language into their academic work. For example, Joshua A. Fishman pioneered sociolinguistic theories of language revitalization born out of his efforts to promote secular Yiddish.[118] His 1991 *Yiddish: Turning to Life*, is a bilingual anthology that traces the twentieth-century growth of the language in both secular and Orthodox contexts.[119] Jonathan Boyarin's 1996 *Thinking in Jewish* is a work of critical theory that employs the language as a lens through which to interrogate Jewish

identity politics from the vantage point of "the intermediary generation, child immigrants or children of immigrants from Jewish Eastern Europe."[120] Scholars of Yiddish and contemporary Jewish culture
who were newcomers to the language joined in, offering alternative
models for positioning language and culture within scholarship, as
well as in cultural life more broadly. For a generation of new speakers, Yiddish resonated in new ways within American Jewish life. For
example, David Shneer and Karen Aviv's 2005 *New Jews* identified
Yiddish as one of multiple "viable routes for constructing Jewish
identity" and predicted that immersive trips to study Yiddish and discover the rich Jewish heritage of Eastern Europe would become
more common.[121] Increasingly, academics have played a prominent
role not only as researchers of post-Holocaust Yiddish but as participants in its continuation.

The turn of the millennium brought a surge of academic interest
in Yiddish. The most influential twenty-first century theory, that of
"postvernacular" Yiddish – in contrast to vernacular or full-language
Yiddish – was first proposed by Cecile Kuznitz in a 2002 article,
"Yiddish Studies.["][122] Jeffrey Shandler expanded on the theory, suggesting in his 2006 book, *Adventures in Yiddishland: Postvernacular
Language and Culture*: "The language's secondary, symbolic level of
meaning is always privileged over its primary level. In other words,
the fact that something is said (or written or sung) in Yiddish is at
least as meaningful as the meaning or the words being uttered – if
not more so."[123] For Shandler, the concept of postvernacular Yiddish forms part of a fundamental post-Holocaust reorientation of
the map of Yiddishland, historically rooted in Europe, to newer
immigrant centres, in particular in America.[124] Cultural politics
around Yiddish have been defined by the divide between before
and after the Holocaust, aligned with communicative usage versus
symbolic levels of meaning.[125] Shandler suggests that the language
has become inherently performative: "Increasingly, Yiddish speech
must be willed into existence, constructed and monitored with
unprecedented deliberateness ... Because fluency in Yiddish is
increasingly less common, those who stage festivals and other
events celebrating Yiddish culture cannot assume that participants' devotion to the language's secondary, symbolic level of
meaning is matched by their competence in Yiddish at its primary, vernacular level."[126] Most significant to this study is Shandler's
conceptualization of the patterns of language transmission asso-

ciated with modern Yiddish culture: "Although Yiddish culture is often vaunted as a 'golden chain' forged by an unbroken succession of biological generations, it might be better understood in the modern era as proceeding through cohort generations, manifest in youth movements, political parties, trade unions, literary circles, educational institutions, various immigrant, refugee, and survivor associations, and so on."[127] As Shandler points out, some of the language's most ardent proponents have been new learners, notably renowned linguist Max Weinreich (1894–1964). Many of those invested in Yiddish today are likewise choosing to engage with the language outside of organic family transmission. I discuss this last point more fully in the section on Queer Yiddishkeit (chapter 5).

The postvernacular Yiddish theory has elicited multiple responses. Netta Avineri's essay, "Yiddish Endangerment as Phenomenological Reality and Discursive Strategy," posits that secular Yiddish is indeed endangered according to accepted measures and argues that proponents of secular Yiddish form a "metalinguistic community" for whom the language is key to group identity despite not necessarily being spoken or learned. One feature of this group is "nostalgia socialization," in which Yiddish is linked to a lost past.[128] Avineri suggests that it is this group that engages in public discourse about Yiddish today, and that its members experience Yiddish as endangered due to a lack of contact with the rapidly growing group of Hasidic speakers.[129] Amelia Glaser's recent article, "The Idea of Yiddish; Re-globalising North American Jewish Culture," investigates the place of Yiddish within the identities of American Jews and suggests that in the mainstream, the language has shifted from a mode of communication, or *signifier*, to a subject, or *signified*.[130] Glaser identifies three areas where fluency in, or awareness of, Yiddish is significant for American Jews today: Yiddish as a diaspora language and a borderless and inclusive expression of Jewishness; access and connection to a collective memory and heritage; and a collaborative and progressive minority subculture of the present. She observes, "Yiddish, as an element of Jewishness that is separate from religion, the State of Israel, and genetics, can accommodate shifting paradigms in the definition of Jewish identity."[131] Precisely because it has been historically marginalized, Yiddish offers an alternate channel for asserting Jewish identity. With the continued renewal of interest among diverse groups, sites for Yiddish language are expanding. As she suggests, Yiddish can function as a *"lieu de mémoire"* (a space of memory), something to be evoked within collective consciousness.[132] With the destruction of the pre-Holocaust European locus, the language can serve as a carrier of political or religious identity, history, and culture.

Ethnomusicologist Abigail Wood 's *And We're All Brothers: Singing in Yiddish in Contemporary North America* proposes an inclusive approach to Yiddish continuity. Rather than dwelling on the language's decline, she suggests "imagining a vital Yiddish present – post vernacular or otherwise."[133] She interrogates the multifaceted apparatus that underpins the vibrant secular Yiddish culture that has emerged globally: "For those with eyes to see, Yiddishland is a real, tangible place, here and now. A thriving contemporary, North America-centred subculture coalesces around a network of institutions involved in the teaching and promotion of Yiddish culture. If not definable by language or spatial borders, today's Yiddishland is created by interpersonal networks based around shared cultural reference points."[134] Within this framework, Yiddish exists within its own particular modes of time and space: "If today's Yiddish culture is little spatialised within conventional frameworks and borders, it is nonetheless strongly felt as a kind of 'counter-space', a Yiddishland that is in part defined by its transformation of mundane, everyday spaces."[135] Wood invokes Michel Foucault's concept of "heterotopia" – multilayered, discursive "other" spaces where the ordinarily incompatible imagined and real can co-exist – to characterize the spaces created by activities such as singing as "heterotopic instantiations of Yiddishland."[136] Lacking a geographic centre or ancestral homeland as a point of orientation, Yiddishland is invoked and enacted through engagement with language and culture outside of regular time and in chosen settings, whether gatherings in private homes, classroom workshops, or singing in parks.

Shandler's 2020 *Yiddish: Biography of a Language* identifies four ways in which secular Yiddish transmission has become characterized by discontinuity since the Holocaust: from a mass to a niche language; from being rooted in Eastern Europe to dispersion in multiple centres; from a native language to one voluntarily acquired in adulthood, including by non-heritage speakers and non-Jews; and as a language of alterity and opposition to religious, cultural, or political hegemonies or heteronormativity.[137] For its Hasidic speakers, the language forms a "linguistic gatekeeper" that expresses their connections to tradition while also articulating boundaries between themselves and wider mainstreams.[138] Meanwhile, younger creators of secular culture are engaging with new themes and formats as "contemporary Yiddish culture increasingly involves people who are not native speakers of the language and whose connection to it does not conform to a conventional model of a heritage language."[139] Given the multilingualism of most Yiddish speakers within a diasporic context, Shandler suggests applying the model of "translanguaging" – which emphasizes the linguistic repertoire of speakers over the boundaries between languages – to study the hybridity of language use today.[140]

The "postvernacular" character of Yiddish is shared by other Jewish diaspora languages, notably Ladino (Judezmo/Judeo-Spanish). The two languages had very different trajectories, Ladino arising among a smaller Sephardi population in the Iberian Peninsula where historical factors discouraged the development of a mass popular culture.[141] Among immigrants, Ladino was transmitted primarily as a spoken language, with few remaining native speakers but growing interest from new speakers. Devin Naar's 2019 study, "On Words Reclaimed and the Fate of Ladino," describes his own rediscovery of the language he heard from his grandparents growing up and to which he was now exposing his son via literature, phrases, expressions, and songs, without the expectation of fluency: "Perhaps, then, Ladino has moved toward attrition once again, but now as it wanders toward a new digital afterlife, the possibility emerges of a new future, a new 'explosion' of *Sefaradizmo*, of Sephardicness, in a new direction – not as a daily vernacular nor merely a dead language to be studied in university, but rather as a 'post-vernacular' to be learned and used by choice among individuals and communities in order to connect with, reinvigorate, and transform their culture, their identity, and their community."[142] Like Yiddish, Ladino is undergoing a resurgence of interest among young learners with, as well as those without, a heritage connection.[143]

Against debates around the present and future of secular Yiddish, one thing is certain: those who are engaging with the language are doing so deliberately and they are leaving their own imprint upon it. Whether we use the labels "Yiddishism," "Yiddishkeit," or "secular Yiddish," or terms such as "revival" or "revitalization," or Ghil'ad Zuckermann's "reinvigoration of Yiddish as a secular language,"[144] to characterize the extensive networks that have evolved to promote its continuity, the language exists on a continuum. Over the last decades, Yiddish in the non-Haredi milieu has been transmitted through a variety of strategies. Those strategies are the subject of this book. The next chapter turns to secular Yiddish as a spoken language that is transmitted within families. It compares secular and Haredi modes of intergenerational transmission in Canada to interrogate strategies for continuity in two very different contexts.

2

Yiddish Spoken in Families
The 1950s to the Present

When the thousand-year-old European Yiddish heartland experienced a mass exodus between 1880 and 1920 and near annihilation in the Holocaust, Canada represented one of many adopted homes. Since 1950, Yiddish has existed in Canada as a transplanted orphan from a place that exists only in collective memory. While the language and its heritage continue to occupy an important place in Jewish cultural life, most people who are involved with Yiddish in today's non-Hasidic mainstream do not speak it fluently or on a regular basis.

This chapter examines the transmission of Yiddish within families in Canada. I focus on its use as a functional vernacular spoken in full sentences to express a multitude of ideas and in varying settings, rather than the use of discrete words or phrases embedded in another language or format, for example as proverbs. This communicative use of Yiddish is open-ended and implies fluency across different spheres. This chapter examines the mechanisms that facilitated – and continue to facilitate – the intergenerational transmission of Yiddish by juxtaposing the Haredi and non-Haredi worlds. I suggest that both Haredi and secular Yiddish transmission among the generations constitute created language spaces. The Haredi space is writ large: under community leadership, members collectively raise their children as native speakers and evolve strategies to employ the language for wide-ranging functions as an insider language within a non-Yiddish-speaking majority culture. Outside of the Haredi world, individual families who opt to raise their children in Yiddish determine the strategies that work best for them.

Here we find the crux of the polarization that has increasingly characterized Yiddish in Canada – and globally – since the Holocaust.

Within the Haredi world, members of Hasidic sects engage with Yiddish by speaking it on a daily basis as a deliberate way of maintaining boundaries from the modern, secular mainstream. In contrast, the non-Haredi group largely connects with Yiddish outside of sustained, everyday usage. This may include study and structured conversation, translation, singing, listening to music or watching plays or films, as the basis for a cultural or countercultural identity. Focusing mainly on the non-Haredi group, this chapter asks questions about language transmission through speaking it to one's children, arguably the most natural and effortless way of passing on a language: Why is there continued interest and engagement within families in a language that so few people speak? What strategies facilitate the acquisition of the spoken language in remove from a wider community of speakers?

The chapter begins in the bull's eye of the concentric circles of secular Yiddish (see figure o.1). It investigates the relatively infrequent use of the language among the non-Haredi group in four ways: (1) discussing Yiddish within wider dynamics of language transmission in Canada; (2) presenting the counterpoint of the Hasidic world; (3) offering a case study of non-Haredi Canadian families in which Yiddish has been transmitted to a third generation as an everyday language; and (4) exploring the results of an online survey on Yiddish use in Canada that suggests trends in the intergenerational transmission of the language. In addition to statistical analysis of census and population surveys and scholarship on language transmission, this chapter draws on three primary sources, which have been subjected to qualitative analysis: the results of the above-mentioned survey; a series of interviews conducted with members of Montreal's Hasidic communities; and interviews conducted with non-Haredi parents raised in Canada who have transmitted Yiddish to their own children.

DYNAMICS OF LANGUAGE TRANSMISSION
IN CANADA

Among the ideologies carried by the mass immigration of Eastern European Jews to Canada in the first half of the twentieth century – notably Orthodoxy, Zionism, the Left – was an imperative to promote Yiddish transmission to future generations. By the 1910s, newcomers to Canada were developing a wide-ranging system of schools and summer camps that offered instruction in Yiddish as well as the study of song, literature, and folklore. Communities across the country founded libraries, theatres, newspapers, and other sites of Yiddish. Many of these ventures outlasted the first generation and supported the transition of an immigrant language into an ethnic language of the second generation. At the same time, wider trends – linguistic and cultural integration, increasingly non-Yiddish Jewish migrations to Canada, the prominence of Israeli Hebrew within educational and communal life, the decline of the Jewish Left – have undermined the intergenerational transmission of spoken Yiddish. It has become remarkable to find non-Haredi families where it has been transmitted to grandchildren or even children as a fluently spoken language. In countries of mass immigration like Canada, where adopting the official languages formed an integral part of the process of acculturation, speaking Yiddish beyond the second generation has been rare.

Yiddish in Canada exists at the intersection of several tendencies that have encouraged language loss. Transmitting any immigrant language across consecutive generations presents multiple challenges. When newcomers are transplanted to a country with a majority language other than their own, they tend to adopt the dominant language even if they continue to speak their native tongue to their spouses and children or within their communities. When their children attend local schools, they learn to speak the language of the adopted country fluently; those who continue to speak the immigrant language do so as bilinguals. Without sustained community support and a sizable population of speakers, the language of their parents becomes relegated to the home. Parents may lack ways of encouraging continued engagement with the language, and children may lack opportunities for practice or else choose not to speak the language. Their own children are even less likely to speak it, especially if their spouses do not share the same linguistic background. In the absence of wider reinforcement within the linguistic community, a primary factor behind ethnic language transmission is whether parents deliberately choose to speak a minority language to their children and whether they find ways to do so successfully. Yiddish fits in this pattern of intergenerational language transmission in Canada.

Historically, the Yiddish language has been far more likely to be transmitted when its speakers have lacked access to dominant languages, which is far from the case in Canada. In late-nineteenth-century Tsarist Russia – which encompassed most of the Eastern European Jewry and where Jews were legally excluded from significant areas of public life – 97 per cent of the Jewish population declared themselves speakers of "the Jewish language" (i.e., Yiddish) on the 1897 census.[1] As legal limitations were lifted after the Russian Revolution of 1917, increasing numbers became speakers of Russian, Polish, and other languages, with census statistics indicating a growing gap between larger numbers of mother-tongue speakers and declining numbers of everyday speakers of Yiddish.[2] The mass emigration of Eastern European Jews in the late nineteenth and early twentieth centuries further weakened the hold of Yiddish as the Jewish lingua franca. In Canada, the newcomers rapidly adopted English, and in more recent decades, many have become proficient in French as well.

The trajectory of Yiddish as a vernacular in Canada is complicated by the multilingualism of its speakers. While virtually all of Canada's Jews in the peak year of 1931 declared Yiddish as their mother tongue, it was common for the new arrivals to additionally speak one or several Slavic or other European languages, as well as having knowledge of Hebrew. Their linguistic acculturation was complex: many used Yiddish as a home language and spoke it to their children, while others opted for Polish, Russian, or another non-dominant language, or spoke various languages in combination. Demographic study of changes within the Canadian Jewish community between 1931 to 1961 indicates that while their numbers were relatively small, mother tongues during the period of mass immigration included languages like Polish, Hungarian, German, Russian, and French.[3] Language choices were motivated by ideological, familial, emotional, or other factors, in particular in the aftermath of the cataclysmic events of the Holocaust. For example, some parents opted to speak English with their Canadian-raised children and Yiddish with each other when they did not want the children to understand; others deliberately spoke Yiddish with their children as an expression of continuity, sometimes speaking Polish with each other when they did not want the children to understand, and so on.

Since the 1950s, Hebrew has largely subsumed the role of the Jewish ethnic language in Canada, in particular as part of children's education. Within traditional Eastern European Jewish civilization, Hebrew and Yiddish functioned in tandem within a system of diglossia (internal bilingualism), in which pre-modern Hebrew/Aramaic served as the primary language of prayer and sacred text and Yiddish as vernacular. Hebrew maintained its function as the global Jewish language while Yiddish was linked to the Ashkenazi experience. As postwar waves of Sephardi immigrants arrived from countries such as Morocco and Algeria, Yiddish further ceded its role as the lingua franca of Canadian Jewry. With the founding of the State of Israel in 1948, Jews living in the diaspora expressed their moral and financial support and promoted Israeli forms of culture: music, dance, food, and language. Pre-modern Hebrew maintains its role as a language of prayer and sacred text, while Israeli Hebrew has assumed the role of the vernacular of the State of Israel and the basis of an Israeli culture that in some settings – notably summer camps and festivals – has become synonymous with Jewish culture. Canadian census statistics indicate that Hebrew use has increased steadily in the mainstream Jewish community. The 2006 census indicated that Hebrew had entirely superseded Yiddish as the Jewish "ethnic" language.[4] On the 2016 Canadian census, some 75,000 people declared themselves to have a knowledge of Hebrew, including some 20,000 who declared it to be their mother tongue (mostly Israelis and their families living in Canada). In comparison, 21,000 people declared knowledge of Yiddish, some 13,000 for whom it was their mother tongue (most of them elderly).[5] It should be underlined, however, that knowledge of Hebrew and Yiddish are by no means mutually exclusive within the Canadian Jewish community.

While the status of Hebrew as a heritage language appears secure within its dual spheres – sacred and cultural – the motivations for an attachment to Yiddish as a heritage language in the secular sphere appear less evident. Hebrew is taught in day schools, and travel opportunities to the State of Israel facilitate immersive linguistic experiences across all ages. The language is transmitted intergenerationally among Israelis in Canada via a network of cultural organizations, by engaging with their homeland through return trips, or by accessing mass media. Because it is not tied to a state apparatus, Yiddish lacks these ties and offers no economic or political advantages to its speakers. Unlike many other heritage, ethnic, or second languages, there is no geographic state to travel to, welcome immigrants from, or benefit from culturally. Even the once-existing sense of a transnational Jewish collective with Yiddish as its shared denominator has faded. Outside of the Haredi milieu, the language has almost no native speakers and the few who are raised from birth in Yiddish are often the children of new learners. Secular Yiddish transmission among kin has become increasingly voluntary, determined within individual families.

STATISTICS AND SCHOLARSHIP ON YIDDISH
IN CANADA

Clear patterns are borne out by census statistics. Yiddish was a mass immigrant language in the first decades of the twentieth century, when waves of newcomers settled across Canada. But even during that period, Yiddish was transmitted incompletely to the second generation and rarely into the third. Canadian statistics reveal a shift away from Yiddish as a spoken language as early as the 1930s. From the 1931 high of 96 per cent (slightly higher in the provinces of Quebec and Manitoba), by 1981, only 11 per cent of Canadian Jews declared Yiddish as their mother tongue and 9.5 per cent as the language of the home. In 2006, the number had dropped to 3 per cent out of some 373,000 Canadian Jews. As early as 1931, a mere 3 per cent of Canadian Jews had declared themselves not able to speak English on the census, underlining the dominance of that language even among the immigrant generation. While the percentage of Jews born outside Canada who declared Yiddish as their mother tongue dropped from 99.4 per cent in 1931 to 83.5 per cent in 1951, among Canadian-born Jews the numbers fell from 95.8 per cent in 1931 to 37.8 per cent in 1951.[6] While children of European-born Yiddish speakers did maintain a connection to the language, far fewer did so as a regularly spoken vernacular.

The inverse case exists for the country's Hasidim, who have increasingly transmitted Yiddish over the last decades. The designation of Yiddish as a means of maintaining a distinctive Hasidic identity by Satmar and other sects has resulted in the language being spoken with greater fluency among younger speakers than their elders. Patterns within this group explain a noteworthy statistic on the Canadian census: after years of steady decline, the numbers in the category of "Yiddish language of the home" increased from 3,100 to 6,700 between 2006 and 2011. What is perhaps most notable about the 2006 Canadian census statistics is the information tabulated with the period of immigration: 56 per cent of Canadians who declared Yiddish as their mother tongue were non-immigrants.[7] These Canadian-born speakers are members of Hasidic communities, and, if current trends of large families and high retention continue, the population is slated to grow over the next decades.[8] For Hasidim located primarily in and around Montreal, Yiddish is a language of daily use, which suggests long-term continuity and vitality. For many, it is the mother tongue of children born into the community and the dominant spoken language of family and community life. As a first language learned by children of these communities, Yiddish carries with it the status of *heymish*, or "insider" language.[9] Given this upturn and the passing of the last generation of European-born speakers, the number of Hasidic speakers will continue to overtake that of secular speakers. Hasidim represent a growing population with hubs in New York, Jerusalem, London, Antwerp, Melbourne, and other centres that form a transnational community.

The 2018 *Survey of Jews in Canada* suggests connections between attitudes towards Jewishness and Yiddish in the country today. As the first population survey to specifically explore "the perspectives of Jews in Canada, addressing themes of identity, practice and experience," it offers close analysis of a representative sample of 2,335 out of a total Canadian Jewish population of some 392,000.[10] The findings identify that population as 80 per cent Ashkenazi (of Eastern or Western European origin), 10 per cent of Sephardi or Mizrahi origin (from Southern Europe or the Middle East), and the rest unidentified or "other." Canadians identify as Jewish in multiple ways: religion, culture, descent, or a combination of all three. Only a minority (some 20 per cent) define their Jewishness through practices such as the observance of Jewish law, synagogue attendance, or participation in cultural activities.[11] A subsequent article by two of the survey's authors suggests that younger Jews are gravitating towards models of Jewish identity outside of religious observance or involvement in established organizations.[12] The survey identifies a correlation between respondents placing a high importance on being Jewish and an identification with religious Orthodoxy (89 per cent), Yiddish as mother tongue (86 per cent), and belonging to a Jewish organization (82 per cent).[13] The survey links Yiddish as a language learned in childhood with heightened connection to Jewish identity. Those who identify with religious Orthodoxy, are over the age of 75, and whose mother tongue is Yiddish are far more likely to seek out Jewish themes in books, films, or plays.[14] The educational programs that generated the greatest interest included Hebrew or Yiddish courses.[15] The authors additionally suggest that the decline of humour as "an essential element of Jewishness" may be attributed to the depletion among young adults of "Jewish humour's richest reservoir – the Yiddish language."[16]

A close reading of the results suggests a number of findings relating to Yiddish transmission. In terms of mother tongue, English represents 71 per cent of the total sample, Yiddish and Russian 7 per cent apiece, Hebrew 5 per cent, French 4 per cent, and 7 per cent

Table 2.1
Yiddish mother tongue by age cohort

Age cohort	Yiddish mother tongue
18–49	55 (31.8 per cent)
50–69	48 (27.7 per cent)
70+	70 (40.5 per cent)
Total	173 (100 per cent)

Table 2.2
Yiddish mother tongue by denominational category

Denominational category	Yiddish mother tongue
Traditional	70 (43.8 per cent)
Conservative	44 (27.5 per cent)
Liberal	11 (6.9 per cent)
Nondenominational	35 (21.9 per cent)
Total	160 (100 per cent)

Note: Percentages don't total exactly 100 because of rounding.

other, placing Yiddish equal or higher in prominence to all mother tongues other than English. This is particularly notable given that while the last immigrant generation of Yiddish speakers were Holocaust survivors, the other languages have been replenished by more recent and ongoing immigration from the former Soviet Union, Israel, North Africa, and France. A survey co-author, Robert J. Brym, provided the data I have used to construct table 2.1, which reveals that the language is being transmitted across multiple generations, in particular among more religiously observant Jews.[17]

Table 2.1 indicates that of the 143 respondents who indicated Yiddish mother tongue on the survey, about 40 per cent are seventy years of age or over. The others are divided approximately equally between eighteen- to forty-nine-year-olds and fifty- to sixty-nine-year-olds, at around 30 per cent each. These findings suggest that among the respondents, Yiddish is being transmitted beyond the survivor generation and their children.

Table 2.2 indicates that some 44 per cent of respondents claiming Yiddish as their mother tongue adhere to traditional religious observance: Orthodox, Modern Orthodox, or Haredi. Some 28 per cent are Conservative, 7 per cent are Liberal (identifying with the Reform,

Table 2.3
Age cohort by denominational category for respondents with Yiddish
mother tongue (percent in parentheses)

Denominational category	Age cohort		
	18–49	50+	Total
Traditional	40 (83.3)	29 (25.4)	69 (42.6)
Conservative	1 (2.1)	49 (43)	50 (30.9)
Liberal	0 (0)	10 (8.8)	10 (6.2)
Nondenominational	7 (14.6)	26 (22.8)	33 (20.4)
Total	48 (100)	114 (100)	162 (100)

Note: Not all percentages total exactly 100 because of rounding.

Reconstructionist, or Humanist/Secular Jewish denominations), and some 22 per cent identify as "non-denominational." Brym suggests that this last category comprises people from families with leftist roots in a historical affiliation with Socialist or Communist movements.[18]

Table 2.3 shows that the overwhelming majority (83 per cent) of the younger (eighteen- to forty-nine-year-old) respondents claiming Yiddish as a mother tongue identify with traditional denominations.

As Brym points out, these tables do not address the question of whether a revival of Yiddish is taking place among younger Canadian Jews because they deal with mother tongue rather than language use today.[19] However, this data does indicate that the Yiddish language has been transmitted intergenerationally beyond the second generation of immigration, notably among more observant Jews, whether or not this entails continued use beyond childhood. Yiddish appears here as a marker of religious observance among its youngest speakers.

These statistics and analysis of Canadian Yiddish language use are situated within a wider body of scholarship that has emerged since the 1960s about the role that language retention plays in maintaining ethnic identity. Joshua Fishman's pioneering 1966 study, *Language Loyalty in the United States*, argued that a powerful feeling of heritage continues to exist despite the loss of an ethnic language in the shift to English. Charles Hobart offered a Canadian perspective that same year, finding that the grandchildren of Ukrainian immigrants often expressed renewed interest in their ethnicity even after their own parents became alienated from it.[20] In Canada, study of the relationships between language retention and ethnic identification gained traction as part of the new discourse around multiculturalism of the 1970s and 1980s. Works from this era point to the complexities of the connections between language and ethnic identity for Canadian Jewry. For example, Morton Weinfeld argued in 1981 that attachment to ethnic identity can occur in meaningful ways without language or other markers of cultural distinctiveness. His statistics revealed ethnic language use to be significantly lower for native-born members of ethnic groups. In the case of Canada's Jews, where the scores for ethnic language use appear far higher than the national average, Weinfeld points out that these statistics encompass both Hebrew and Yiddish: "The required use of the latter in religious services even as Yiddish is lost raises the average for the Jewish group."[21] Fishman's influential theories of language revitalization in the 1990s argued that the continued use of a minority language in the home and outside of the classroom was essential to reversing language shift for threatened languages.[22] Other scholars at that time suggested that whereas the home might previously have been considered the last bastion of language use, this is not always the case for longer established community languages.[23] Recent scholarship on the transmission of minority or ethnic languages across diverse groups and countries shows that a key factor in transmission of a language is whether caregivers speak it to their children.[24]

A study by Statistics Canada analyst René Houle examines the period from 1981 to 2006 and analyzes data from multiple ethnic groups across three generations to determine the factors at play in language transmission. Foremost are exposure in the family, with mothers bearing the primary responsibility of passing on immigrant languages, and the "marriage market," with marrying out of the ethnic group drastically reducing the transmission of immigrant languages. Canadian-born children are more likely to marry outside of the ethnic group and hence less likely to transmit the languages of their immigrant parents. Higher educational levels render it more likely that a parent will transmit one of Canada's official languages rather than an ethnic language. By the third generation, all ethnic language transmission drops sharply, with just 10 per cent of grandchildren sharing their grandmothers' tongue, as compared to 55 per cent in the second generation. The highest rates of transmission are found among groups where couples marry within the ethnicity and where ongoing immigration is continually bringing in new speakers.[25] Although the Canadian Multiculturalism Act supports programs to promote diversity in Canada, these activities are not a primary factor in the ongoing transmission of immigrant languages.

Houle concludes, "As first-generation immigrants age, their descendants are experiencing rapidly decreasing immigrant-language transmission, which is at risk in certain groups with a pool of aging speakers and no longer able to renew itself (the German, Portuguese, Hungarian and Polish groups), notably through new migratory flows."[26]

Houle's findings intersect on multiple levels with questions around Yiddish transmission. Given the time of mass immigration between 1900 and 1925, with a smaller post-Holocaust wave, Yiddish forms part of a wider category of European languages (including Italian, Polish, Hungarian, and German) that are not, as a rule, being transmitted intergenerationally. Yiddish has become a "heritage" language – that is, a non-dominant language familiar to a particular ethnic group – in a Jewish population with Eastern European roots that has overwhelmingly adopted English as its mother tongue. For those new immigrants who do arrive speaking a Jewish language, that language tends to be Israeli Hebrew, which is also the heritage language spoken and taught most widely in the mainstream Jewish community. Although Jewish out-marriage levels have remained relatively low (23 per cent in Canada compared to 50 per cent in the United States),[27] marrying within the group does not represent a factor in the transmission of Yiddish outside of the Haredi milieu today, since very few non-Haredi Jews speak the language at all. This situation is due to the timing of the Eastern European immigration combined with wider attitudes towards language transmission, with new arrivals strongly encouraged to adopt English.

Since the 1980s, Canadian multiculturalism policies have encouraged a variety of ethnic cultural activities, but they have provided relatively little support for ethnic language maintenance. Jack Jedwab argues that non-official languages are not essential to the country's model of multiculturalism. While Canada formally enshrined English and French as its two official languages in 1971, the country's policies and programs did not support the promotion of non-official languages.[28] Further, while the 1982 Canadian Charter of Rights and Freedoms expressed a commitment to preserve and enhance the multicultural heritage of Canadians, it did not specify how this was to be accomplished. When legislation established a department of multiculturalism in 1991, a concurrent law called for the creation of a heritage languages institute to develop standards for the training of teachers and for curriculum design; this institute was deferred a year later and never materialized. Jedwab concludes, "In the Canadian multicultural paradigm, knowledge of non-official languages hasn't been deemed essential to ethnic belonging. In effect, a strong sense of belonging to one's ethnic origins does not require knowledge of the associated language."[29] He offers a quotation from Canada's minister of multiculturalism, Jason Kenney, in 2009: "I think it's really neat that a fifth-generation Ukrainian Canadian can speak Ukrainian – but pay for it yourself."[30] As I argue elsewhere, multicultural policy has had a mixed impact on Yiddish by supporting areas such as Yiddish publishing and education while, at the same time, encouraging the linguistic integration of its speakers into the Canadian mainstream.[31]

Given all of the above, why would we expect anything but the tiniest minority of speakers more than six decades after the last major wave of Yiddish-speaking immigrants? For the purposes of this book, a more instructive question becomes: how do those who do go against the dominant trends of immigrant language loss transmit Yiddish as a spoken language within families into the third generation and beyond? There are two models: (1) a group model, as evidenced by the Hasidim; and (2) an individual model, as evidenced by those who choose to transmit the language to their children within a predominantly non-Yiddish speaking environment.

HASIDIC YIDDISH AS A GROUP MODEL OF LANGUAGE TRANSMISSION

Hasidic Jews represent continuity with the dominant historical pattern of Yiddish use in family and community settings. Within traditional modes of internal Jewish bilingualism, Hasidim employ Yiddish for intersecting reasons: expressing continuity with a Jewish past; heightening their distinctiveness and separating themselves from the mainstream; maintaining and reinforcing group solidarity; and facilitating communication among Hasidim worldwide so that, for example, a Hasidic person in Antwerp can speak with another in New York.

Canadian census statistics point to a steady expansion of Yiddish among Hasidic populations in the Montreal area. In 2006, the city was home to a majority of the country's Yiddish speakers despite the fact that the total Jewish population of Montreal (71,380) was half that of Canada's largest Jewish community in Toronto (141,685). That year, Montreal had 13,515 self-declared Yiddish speakers of all ages, compared to 10,345 in Toronto. The statistics can be attributed to Montreal's historical primacy in Eastern European immigration as well as the infrastructure that was created in the opening decades of the twentieth century to promote the Yiddish language and its culture. They also point to more recent developments in the expansion of Canadian Hasidic communities, a majority of whom reside in the Montreal area. In 2006, of Canada's 9,305 Yiddish speakers over the age of seventy-five, 4,390 lived in Toronto and 3,345 in Montreal; however, out of 1,345 Canadian Yiddish speakers under the age of five, 1,180 were residents of Montreal, while 140 lived in Toronto.[32] The maintenance of spoken Yiddish in Montreal and the relative youth of the city's Yiddish speakers can be attributed to the rapid expansion of its Hasidic communities due to large families and high retention. Yiddish has shifted from being an immigrant language to a vehicle for perpetuating tradition and group identity. In a 1993 study, Leo Davids declared of the Hasidim, "Yiddish is safe among them!"[33]

A series of in-person interviews conducted with members of Montreal's Hasidic communities for this study suggest a common understanding of the place of Yiddish in contemporary Canadian Haredi life. While representing a small sample, the responses are consistent across different sects and three generations: the respondents uniformly expressed the centrality of Yiddish within their lives and the lives of their communities. Under the authority of Hasidic leadership, Yiddish is endorsed and promoted as the language of instruction in schools and as a dominant language of the home, community, and public life. With the language part of the daily experience within family and communal settings as well as Hasidic media, its speakers are relatively unselfconscious about their linguistic particularity. They do not express a struggle for linguistic survival of Yiddish or fear of its imminent decline; rather, Hasidic speakers of Yiddish understand their language to be flexible and open-ended. In addition to questions about who in the family speaks Yiddish today (the response from all participants being "everyone"), respondents were asked to choose the answer(s) that best applied to the questions below. The responses to the survey questions represent those provided most often by the interviewees, regardless of age, place of origin, or gender:

1 I learned Yiddish: at home from my family; in school as a child.
2 Today, I speak in Yiddish with other people every day.
3 I speak Yiddish with: my family; my friends; members of my community; work colleagues.
4 I speak Yiddish because: some variant of "It is my first language."

5 True: I expect that my grandchildren will be Yiddish speakers and speak to their children in Yiddish.

The interviews were based on the ten-question survey on Yiddish I conducted in 2017 (see the previous chapter and below) and were undertaken in 2017 and 2018 by Steven Lapidus, a Yiddish-speaking scholar of Canadian Jewish Hasidism.[34] The respondents comprised five men and three women ranging in age from twenty-one to sixty. All of them resided in the Montreal area and were members of Hasidic sects that promote the use of Yiddish among their members: Satmar, Vizhnitz, and Belz. Their voluntary participation in the study indicated a degree of interest in or commitment to the subject. As part of a research project conducted by an outsider to their communities, most of the interviewees opted to speak in English, a language that they acquired in adulthood. Subjected to qualitative thematic analysis, these Canadian interviews further substantiate the development of a Hasidic Yiddish distinct from secular Yiddish.[35]

A married couple interviewed from the first generation – respondents with grandchildren – stated that all members of their families spoke Yiddish every day. Born in Brooklyn in 1961 and raised in Williamsburg and Borough Park, New York, Mrs R.A. learned Yiddish at home and in school, where classes were held in Yiddish and where she was also formally taught to read and write the language. When asked why she speaks Yiddish, she responded very simply, in English, "It's my mother tongue." When asked if she had anything to add, she said, "I always spoke Yiddish. I don't know. I mean, that was my first [language] in our house when we were little kids. When I got older, we started speaking more English. [Yiddish] is my natural language." Her husband, Mr E.A., born in Montreal's Mile End in 1958 and raised there, learned Yiddish at home as well as in school. He offered the following reasons for speaking Yiddish: "This is my language. My father spoke Yiddish, my grandfather, my great-great grandfather going back. I'm Jewish, I speak Yiddish." All of their children and grandchildren attended or currently attend Hasidic schools in Yiddish that also offer variable degrees of English and French instruction. Both Mrs R.A. and Mr E.A. unhesitatingly expected their grandchildren to speak the language with their own children.

In the second generation – people with children but no grandchildren – all of the respondents indicated that they had learned Yiddish at home and spoke it every day with their families and friends, and within the community. One interviewee, Mr E., had attended a *kheyder* (Hasidic school) in Buenos Aires held in Spanish because of the many Sephardi children in attendance who were not Yiddish speakers. All of the respondents expected their grandchildren to speak the language with their own children. Their reasons for speaking Yiddish were straightforward and the question was almost inevitably accompanied by a surprised laugh. Mr Y.P., born in 1973 and raised in the private community of Sea Gate, Brooklyn, speaks Yiddish because "It's my mother tongue, that's the easiest language that comes to mind." Mr S.K., born in Williamsburg, New York in 1973 and raised there, speaks Yiddish because "That is the best language that I know and another equally main reason is because people to whom I speak, by who I am surrounded or hanging out with, it is primarily their language. It wouldn't make sense if I started to speak to them in English." Mrs E., born in Outremont, Montreal in 1979 and raised there, responded in Yiddish to the question as to why she speaks Yiddish (presented in transliteration to convey the particularities of her Hasidic dialect): "*Azoy bin ikh ousgevaksn; ikh bin a yid*" (This is how I was raised. I am a Jew.). Her husband, Mr E., born in Argentina in 1978 and raised there, indicated that he speaks the language because "It's my language." Mr G., born in Manchester, England in 1977 and raised there, who speaks Yiddish "every minute of every day," responded: "It's a funny question ... It's my language. It's the way I identify myself as a Yiddish-speaking *Hasidishe* person."

In the third generation – people in their early 20s – Mr H.G., born in Williamsburg in 1996 and raised there, seemed taken aback by the question: "Because ... because my father and mother speak Yiddish. This is the first language I grew up with." He shared that everyone in his family speaks Yiddish all the time. Asked whether he formally studied any Yiddish growing up, he again seemed bemused by the question: "It's a part of you," he said.

The participants characterized their Hasidic Yiddish as a language in flux within their Canadian context. Mrs R.A. remarked upon the incorporation of English into Yiddish, and wider shifts to the language more broadly: "The Yiddish like what you read in [secular] books, from back then, have very, very complicated words. Is that supposed to be real Yiddish? That Yiddish, even I don't have half the words. The language is always changing." Her husband, Mr E.A., observed that in pre-Holocaust Poland, even non-observant Jews spoke Yiddish. He drew a parallel between the inclusion of words of

Polish origin in pre-immigration Europe and the insertion of English
words today. Both agreed that Montreal Yiddish has fewer English
words than the Yiddish spoken in the United States, with Mr E.A. suggesting that English is far more widely spoken in the US and therefore has a greater linguistic influence, whereas in Montreal, one is
more likely to hear French or ethnic languages. Mr Y.P. observed that
many words have "evaporated" from Yiddish so that speakers are
entirely unaware that they are using an English term; for example, the
word "steps" has become completely incorporated into Yiddish in
place of the terms his father used: *shtign* or *trep*. Mr Y.P.'s familiarity
with the secular Yiddish press (e.g., the New York *Forverts/The Jewish
Daily Forward*) and Yiddish authors like Sholem Aleichem and Isaac
Bashevis Singer allowed him to observe differences between secular
Yiddish produced by its European-born speakers, who came of maturity before the Holocaust, and Hasidic ("Hasidish") Yiddish. He characterized the way it was spoken in Poland in the past as "pure Yiddish,"
which would not be widely understood today, even among Hasidic
speakers. In addressing the question of Yiddish spelling, Mr G. offered
that as a writer for the contemporary Hasidic Yiddish press, printed
with various spelling systems, he occasionally consulted with his children, who read extensively in Yiddish, on questions of orthography.
Together, these observations suggest increasing confidence among the
younger generations about Yiddish usage in all of its forms.

The interviewees identified shifts between the generations, with the
younger speakers integrating more English into their Yiddish and
women tending to speak more English than men.[36] Mr S.K. stated that
his sisters would speak to their friends in English when they were
growing up in the 1990s, despite the protestations of their father, and
that they continue to speak English amongst themselves today. However, young men in his community would only speak Yiddish with
each other and it would be odd if, for example, he were to speak English in synagogue. Mrs E. agreed that women tend to incorporate more
English into their Yiddish, especially high school girls, who often
speak to each other in English. She also stated that she used French in
addition to English on a regular basis. Her husband, Mr E., who, as
mentioned, attended a Spanish-language Hasidic school in Buenos
Aires, spoke more Spanish as a child than his own children speak English today. He noted that among Satmar Hasidim, the boys tend to
speak mostly in Yiddish, while usage among the girls will vary within
families: parents who want to preserve the tradition and do not want

"Yiddish to be a second language" insist that their daughters speak only Yiddish at home, while in other families, women speak English for much of the day. Mr E. recalled the disparity in Yiddish use among Satmar women in pre-Holocaust Hungary: one of his grandmothers grew up in a small village and spoke Hungarian at public school but only Yiddish at home, while his other grandmother, who came from the city of Satmar, spoke only Yiddish. Mr H.G., the youngest of the respondents, pointed out differences between Yiddish spoken in Williamsburg and Montreal, with the former having a more "*hasidishe, frum* language," and the latter being more "classy," with a richer vocabulary and fewer English loan words. He shared that he occasionally speaks English with his Montreal-born wife – not his children, siblings, or parents – because she is comfortable in the language.

Mrs R.A., Mr E.A., Mr S.K., Mr E., Mr H.G., and Mr G. spoke in English during the interviews, with the men having studied English as adults on their own initiative. These respondents employed all of the linguistic markers of Yiddish speakers: Yiddish intonation in the "rise-fall contour" (a distinctive upwards-downwards inflection);[37] clearly discernible Yiddish accents (for example, the distinctive pronunciation of "ng" with a hard "g" sound: "goinG"); Yiddish syntax (for example, "I went yesterday to the store" or "I want that you should go"); and the insertion of Yiddish words such as "*bikhlal*" (totally). Mrs E. gave her interview in Hasidic Yiddish, with influences from English; for example, "*Frauen indz mixed men a sakh english mit di yidish*" (presented in English transliteration to convey the linguistic features of her Hasidic Yiddish: "We women mix a lot of English into our Yiddish").

For all the Haredi respondents, Yiddish functions as a core Jewish identity marker. Mrs R.A. and Mr E.A. stated that they would never speak to their own children in English, and Mr S.K. concurred. Mrs E. stated that she spoke primarily in Yiddish with her husband, Mr E., and used English when she did not want her children to understand what they were saying. This inversion of the very common assertion by children of Yiddish speakers outside of the Hasidic world – their parents used Yiddish when they did not want their children to understand – signifies a full circle back to Yiddish as a dominant vernacular. Although my informants offered their own perspectives on these questions rather than purporting to be representative of the Hasidic world as a whole, their responses underline the extent to which Hasidic Yiddish is removed from being a symbolic language of an immigrant past or ethnic identity; it is a full language of everyday use.

This is signalled by the tendency of the older respondents to provide far more involved responses to why they speak Yiddish than the younger ones, who seemed taken aback by the very question and provided short responses stating the obvious (e.g., because it is my language) after a moment of surprised silence. The pattern is in sharp contrast to Netta Avineri's observation of "nostalgia socialization" among secular speakers, in which a loss of fluency over the generations has been accompanied by increasing talk *about* Yiddish rather than *in* Yiddish. Within their families and communities, Hasidic speakers of Yiddish talk *in* Yiddish rather than *about* it.

THE INDIVIDUAL MODEL
OF YIDDISH TRANSMISSION

Intergenerational transmission of Yiddish weakened almost immediately after Eastern European mass immigration in the 1920s, both quantitatively and qualitatively. My study *Jewish Roots, Canadian Soil: Yiddish Culture in Montreal, 1905–1945*, points to the speed of linguistic acculturation within the community even during this earlier period. One measure was Yiddish-language writers beyond the first immigrant generation. The norm was for the children of Yiddish-speaking immigrants to turn to English while integrating some Yiddish terms, phrases, or grammatical forms into their writing. Poet and novelist A.M. Klein (1909–1972), novelist Mordecai Richler (1931–2001, grandson of Yiddish-Hebrew writer Yudel Rosenberg), poet Irving Layton (1912–2006), poet and short story writer Miriam Waddington (1917–2004), poet and novelist Leonard Cohen (1934–2016) are among the most famous Canadian examples. Klein, who was embedded in both cultural milieus, was a leading translator of both Yiddish and Hebrew into English; he also promoted Yiddish writing and art in *The Canadian Jewish Chronicle*, where he was editor.[38] Miriam Waddington, who established a close friendship with Yiddish writer Ida Maza, published translations from the Yiddish.[39]

The turn to English was not due to a lack of institutional support; Jewish schools prioritized Yiddish literature and composition and exposed the students to literary works and opportunities to create and publish. Rather, two factors were at play: the second generation was linguistically more at home in English and, most importantly, they were able to reach a wider audience in that language. The one notable exception was the Shtern-Krishtalka family, which included three generations of published Yiddish writers by 1960.[40] The difficulty lay in transmitting the level of Yiddish required to produce literature in Canada, even with a system of secular Jewish day schools, camps, clubs, and youth journals to support it. Since 1950, the transmission of Yiddish – not just as a literary tongue but as a spoken, everyday language – has become increasingly exceptional in the Canadian mainstream. This section examines two cases of individual family Yiddish transmission in the same light as the Shtern-Krishtalka family of fifty years earlier: examples of a rare phenomenon, both in Canada and globally. By way of introduction, it discusses the dynamics of non-Hasidic intergenerational Yiddish transmission in Canada. The goal is to discern what contributes to continuity of fluently spoken Yiddish across three generations.

As a non-official language in Canada, Yiddish is increasingly imparted within families through what linguists term "private language planning": the deliberate creation of an enriched home milieu by parents speaking a non-dominant language with their children. Such planning has occurred despite the decline of educational institutions, which encompassed leftist-oriented secular Jewish schools that functioned in Yiddish and in which the language formed a core part of the curriculum, in tandem with youth groups and summer camps. The decline of Yiddish as a dominant community language, combined with the attrition of educational opportunities for its instruction, means that the burden of language transmission has fallen upon those who choose to raise Yiddish-speaking children as a component of ethnic continuity. Compared to the private language planning that happens within individual families who opt to speak Yiddish with their children, Canada's Hasidic communities can be understood as engaging in a form of "public language planning" under the leadership of their community authorities.

In contrast to public language planning undertaken by the state or a governing body, private language planning takes place informally among parents. Private language planning can include multiple scenarios: (1) one parent speaking a non-dominant language to a child; (2) parents switching between or mixing multiple languages; or (3) consecutive language introduction, in which the dominant language is not introduced for the first years of a child's life.[41] As discussed below, scenarios 2 and 3 have historically yielded the transmission of Yiddish within the home into the second generation. It is the first scenario that has yielded success in the rare instances in which the children of immigrants have transmitted the language to their own

children in the third generation. Language learning methods for
rearing children in a non-dominant language within a multilingual
household include One-parent-one-language (OPOL), which is predi-
cated on the premise that language is transmitted most effectively
within a household by each parent consistently speaking his or her
native tongue with the children.[42] This dynamic of having one parent transmitting Yiddish to his or her children alongside a second
non-dominant language is borne out in the case of the two families
I discuss below: the Botwinik family and the Berman family.

Yiddish bilingualism in Canada (and worldwide) among non-
Haredi children since 1950 has increasingly become the purview of
parents committed to the transmission of the language. Ingrid Piller,
who has published extensively on the topic of intergenerational language transmission, examines childhood bilingualism as the purview
of "elite bilinguals": "middle-class international couples, expatriates,
academics who raise their children in a non-native language."[43] This
applies to Yiddish if one includes under the category of "elite" those
most ardently committed to the continuity of Yiddish as a living, spoken language. Indeed, choosing to raise children in Yiddish requires
intense dedication and resourcefulness: How does one locate Yiddish-
speaking playmates or babysitters for the children? What games, toys,
apps, and audiovisual materials are available in Yiddish, in particular
those that can compete with mainstream offerings? As one non-
Canadian example, a secular family in Melbourne, Australia, that
opted to raise their children entirely in Yiddish created an internet
group called "Mames un Tates" (Moms and Dads, established 2009)
to offer a virtual immersive experience for their children in the
absence of playmates.[44] As discussed in the next chapter, a rare case
of community-building for parents raising children in secular Yiddish is found in New York, where a play group called Pripetshik was
formed in the 1980s by members of Yugntruf.

While parents relate to their children's bilingualism in very positive
terms, they may lack effective strategies to promote transmission and
engagement in the home.[45] Even parents who successfully transmit a
language may experience tensions when, for example, their children
display linguistic rebellion and either question or refuse to speak the
language.[46] Sabine Little offers a useful model for home language as
heritage language that she terms "Great Aunt Edna's Vase": a treasured
heirloom may evoke feelings of love, pride, ambivalence, guilt, or conflict; it may be cherished or discarded. While that vase represents a

complicated inheritance, how much more so is the case for an inherited language.[47] A study titled "It's My Language, My Culture, and It's Personal!" suggests that a parent's choice to transmit a heritage language to children within an interethnic family can be motivated by a desire to affirm or construct a relational sense of cultural identity and distinct in-group membership.[48] For Yiddish speakers, the sense of transmitting a distinct identity and set of values is closely bound up with the language. Given the very deliberate – and statistically unusual – choice to transmit Yiddish outside of the Hasidic world today, the language enjoys a marked advantage: its young speakers are made acutely aware of their linguistic distinctiveness in ways that can support the process of transmission.

The findings in this next section indicate that those Canadian-raised parents who have chosen to transmit Yiddish within their households have been tremendously resourceful. They have shaped created language spaces for their children through enjoyable activities such as conversation, stories, and songs. Their children tend to evince positive attitudes towards the language and culture along with an appreciation of the legacies they have inherited. However, they represent a tiny minority within a minority of today's Yiddish speakers.

THE BOTWINIK FAMILY

Di tsukunft fun yidish iz in fornt fun undz. (The future of Yiddish is in front of us.)
Leybl Botwinik, Ottawa, 30 October 2016

The Botwinik family, with its successive generations of Yiddish speakers spanning pre-Holocaust Europe into the present day, represents a rarity. In this family, childhood bilingualism in Yiddish in the second and third generations took place because of parents with an exceptionally strong ideological framework. The Botwinik family comprises three generations of Yiddish speakers: Polish-born David (1920–2022), in the first generation; four children raised in Montreal in the second: Rivl (b. 1955), Leybl (b. 1959), Sender (b. 1964), and Yankl (b. 1965); and over a dozen grandchildren ranging in age from six to thirty-six in late 2016. Both David and his Italian-born wife, Silvana, were postwar immigrants to Canada who had survived the Holocaust. In a one-parent-one-language scenario, each parent spoke their native language to the children: David spoke Yiddish, his wife Italian. The four children became multilingual speakers in a house-

hold that included Yiddish, Italian, English, and French, as well as
Hebrew learned at school.

David Botwinik, a composer, musician, and music teacher, was sin-
gularly devoted to the continuity of Yiddish upon settling in Montreal. He describes the rich Yiddish cultural life he had experienced in his
native Poland, growing up in Vilna (Vilnius) and subsequently resid-
ing in Łódź in the immediate postwar years. Yiddish served as the language of his daily life and advanced musical studies in Vilna; he viewed
operas translated into and performed in Yiddish and dreamed of composing his own. In postwar Łódź, he found receptive audiences for his
Yiddish songs. Botwinik settled in Rome, where he attended the Santa
Cecilia Conservatory. He recalled his impressions of arriving in Montreal in 1956: "I found a rich cultural environment. There was a daily
Yiddish newspaper, the *Keneder adler* (*Canadian Eagle*), the large Jewish
Public Library where Yiddish was spoken and where there were many
Yiddish cultural events, as well as Yiddish-speaking societies and institutions. I found work as a music teacher in the Jewish Peretz School,
where Yiddish was central."[49] In addition to serving as a music teacher
and choir director at the Peretz School and United Talmud Torah
schools for thirty-five years, Botwinik's extensive involvement in the
Yiddish milieu included working on musical projects with theatre
director Dora Wasserman and local poets Ida Maza and M.M. Shaffir.

Botwinik was a Yiddish maximalist who was uncompromising in his
devotion to the continuity of the language.[50] He later recalled, "I saw
that the Yiddish atmosphere in Montreal was not the same as it had
been in Vilna, Warsaw, and other towns in Eastern Europe. I embarked
on various projects to encourage maintaining Yiddish as a living language." These efforts included penning letters to newspapers to encourage more extensive Yiddish use within the local Jewish community and
publishing Yiddish-language magazines by and for young people.[51]
Botwinik maintained an unwavering commitment to the importance
of spoken Yiddish. In an oral history conducted in 2011 (in Yiddish), he
offered the following thoughts on the future of the language:

A lot of work needs to be done. We need people who are interested in Yiddish as a spoken language. Because reading – everyone
can read, there are people doing that everywhere. But speaking –
Folks say, Oh, you want to speak Yiddish? What's wrong with English? English doesn't need to be worried about. English is everywhere. You can't stop English. But Yiddish must be spoken. One

can speak English as well. But for Yiddish – we need culture-evenings, culture-mornings, times set aside for the culture. And Yiddish should be spoken in the home. If people are used to speaking Yiddish, they'll speak it consistently. And of course, they'll know English and will be able to speak it in the broader society that doesn't know any Yiddish. So English is spoken as needed. Do you understand? But Yiddish is more important.[52]

Botwinik cited the danger as represented by his own experience as an instructor in the United Talmud Torah schools, which discontinued its teaching of Yiddish in the late 1950s: "We dropped the reins. We let the horse go its own way. They began to speak, speak and speak [English] and Yiddish was discarded." He emphasized the need for steadfastness to ensure linguistic continuity: "First of all, we must be stubborn. And if something is to be done, it needs to begin with the youth. This will determine if Yiddish will continue to exist. If, heaven forbid, something happens and it is thrown away, then we are abandoning an inheritance. I transmitted it to my children that way so that they would be able to transmit it to their children."[53]

Botwinik actively involved his own children in his efforts by using Yiddish as his primary language of communication with them and instilling in them an activist commitment to the language. His youngest son, Yankl, recalls in his memoir, *Chicken Soup with Chopsticks*, the deep-rooted devotion to Yiddish his father ingrained in him. He describes how growing up, most of his peers had been raised "with Yiddish spoken around them but not *to* them"; they could understand the language but could speak it only with difficulty. As a result, they came to view Yiddish as a "secret language" spoken when they were not intended to understand their elders, or they harboured negative, disdainful attitudes to it as a language of the past. In contrast, his father fought for Yiddish, criticizing the community for its neglect of the language, and recruited his four children as young adults to fight alongside him. Yankl recalls: "Over a number of years, particularly during high school and college, I felt that we were more than a family: we were an ideological movement. My father tried to impress upon me the belief that Yiddish was an important means of stemming the rapid slide to assimilation that was occurring the world over ... Yiddish was the natural antidote: an immediate link to the idealized pre-Holocaust world of Eastern Europe where Jewish culture flourished and healthy ideals and values guided human behaviour ... Religion wasn't sufficient. Language, because we use it and think in it all the time, is a very effective means of identifying with a people and its experiences."[54] What the children heard at home was that while many were promoting Hebrew, no one was promoting Yiddish, and so they became language activists. According to Yankl, "The Botwiniks were the mavericks, standing out in the secular Montreal Jewish community, ridiculed by some, admired by others, and not afraid to speak out for a noble and righteous cause."[55]

In addition to being raised as fluent Yiddish speakers and language activists, the Botwinik siblings spearheaded and directed new youth-oriented publishing projects that were exceptional for their time. Even in Montreal, where the Jewish People's and Peretz Schools (JPPS) and Bialik High School taught Yiddish alongside Hebrew and encouraged their students to publish in Yiddish in school magazines and offered awards for literary creativity, one finds just a handful of Canadian-born authors who published poetry or prose in the language outside of school-sponsored publications.[56] When the Botwinik children were young adults, the family produced four issues of a magazine titled *Der nayer dor* (The New Generation, 1978–82). These were colourful and filled with content of interest to young people: essays promoting the use of Yiddish alongside articles about popular science, short lessons on Yiddish grammar next to cartoons and puzzles. The editor of the magazine and its main contributor, Leybl Botwinik, was one of a very small group of Yiddish authors worldwide who were the children of the last European-born generation. As a recent Bialik graduate, he published a science fiction novel called *Di geheyme shlikhes* (The Secret Mission) in 1980, one of a very few literary works published by an author from the generation born after the Holocaust (the novel is discussed more fully in the next chapter). Botwinik characterizes writing science fiction in Yiddish as an ideological matter: within a culture oriented towards the future, authors should produce creative work that is compelling to them and their readership, not simply repeat what has already been done. Similarly, he asked why were there no comics or cartoons in Yiddish when perhaps their creation could inspire others to seek out creativity in the language? As a result, Leybl included comics in *Der nayer dor*.[57]

All four Botwinik children speak Yiddish with their children today. The eldest daughter, Rivl, moved to Israel to live in a Haredi enclave of Jerusalem where the language functions as a daily vernacular. Her younger brother, Leybl, resides in secular Israel and raised his four

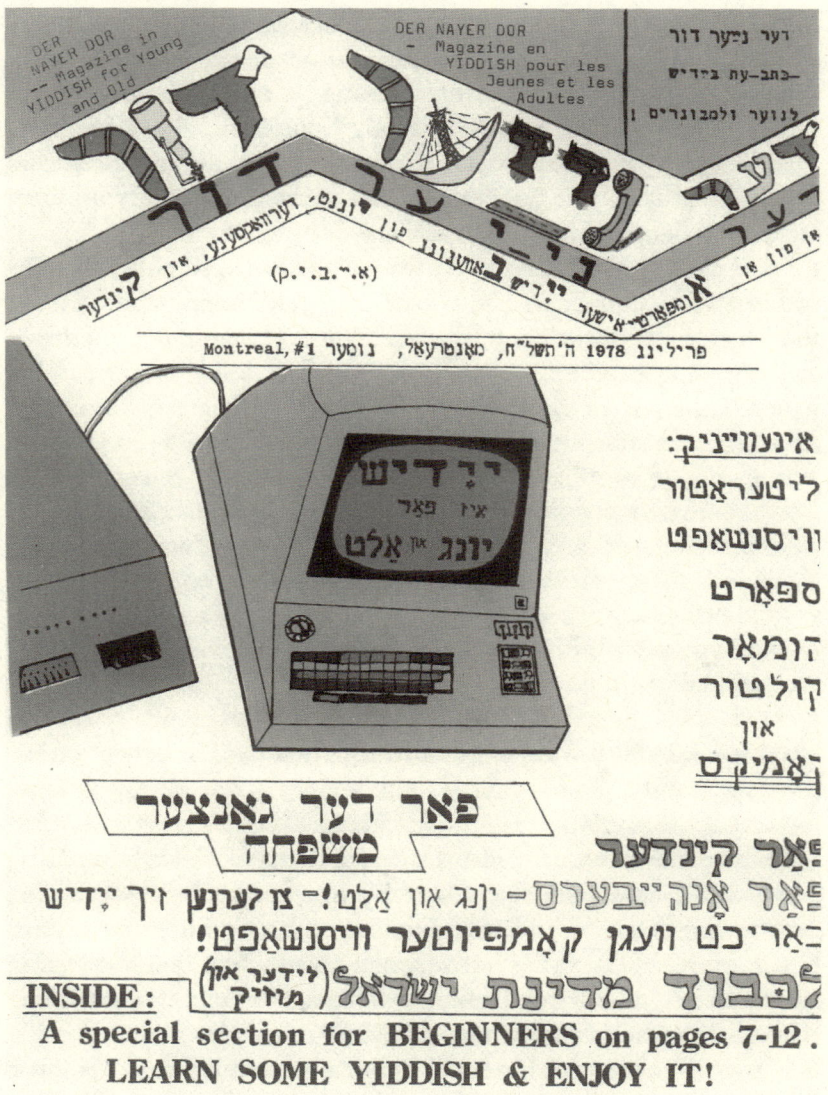

Figure 2.1 Cover of *Der nayer dor* #1, 1978

children to speak Yiddish with him while his Israeli-born wife, Malka, who is of Libyan origin, speaks to the children in Hebrew and has also learned to understand some Yiddish. Sender, who resides in Philadelphia, married the American-born Naomi, who learned Yiddish in university. She shared his commitment to speaking the language with their two children. A musician, Sender compiled and published the

collection of fifty-six of his father's original solo and choral compositions in *From Holocaust to Life: New Yiddish Songs* (2010), and recently
released an album of fifteen of the songs.[58] The youngest sibling,
Yankl, resides in Ottawa with his Hong Kong-born wife, Bina Ester,
and they have raised their large family in a multilingual home, in
which he speaks to them in Yiddish and she in Cantonese, with English as the shared family language.

I participated in a goodbye meal Yankl and Bina Ester hosted at the
end of a visit from Leybl and two of his adult children from Israel,
and I had the opportunity to interview them.[59] Before the interview,
they responded to the same questions as the Hasidic respondents discussed earlier. Their responses to the first two questions were the
same as my Hasidic interviewees.

  1 I learned Yiddish: At home from my family; In school as a
     child.
  2 Today, I speak in Yiddish with other people: Every day.

The third question indicated a narrower domain of Yiddish usage,
here limited to close contacts:

  3 I speak Yiddish with: My family; My friends; Members of my
     community.

The main difference lay in the question "I speak Yiddish because,"
to which their responses included: "We have a responsibility to pro-
tect the language and culture and to pass on the treasures to the next
generation" (Leybl), and "I know it. I'm able to transmit and enrich
my children's worldview, I like the language" (Yankl). Leybl's son,
Nathaniel (born in Israel in 1992, raised there), indicated that in addition to speaking it with his father on a daily basis, he speaks Yiddish
a few times a year with family and others who are aware that he
speaks the language because "I can and it is unique." The responses
were not self-evident to them as they had been to the Hasidic respondents discussed above. In a secular context, the answers required more
explanation than, "because it is my language."

According to Leybl, his father taught his children to love Yiddish
through music and shared with them stories about his youth in Vilna,
where it was the language of all aspects of daily life. This became the
model for their use of the language at home: the children used Yid-

dish to talk about films and current affairs, to play games, and to speak with each other so that its use would remain natural. The method that both Leybl and Yankl employed with their own children was to be more fun as a parent in that language: their Yiddish-speaking selves had better stories and activities so their children wanted to speak Yiddish with them. Rather than a formal pedagogical approach, each used songs, stories – especially bedtime stories "so that they would enter their dreams" (Leybl) – games, and humour. During the interview, both Leybl's adult children interjected in Yiddish with the names of favourite tales, which they still remembered. Yankl recalled playing a game in which he would pretend not to understand an English phrase like "I am tired," and repeat it using a similar-sounding Yiddish word, like *"du bist tayer"* (you are dear [to me]), in order to teach new vocabulary. They played Go Fish and Rummy-Q in Yiddish to teach numbers and colours. Leybl, who raised his children in Israel, where negative attitudes towards Yiddish as a language associated with exile prevailed at the time, never insisted that his children speak the language with each other; however, his assertion, "but if they wanted something, they had to ask for it in Yiddish," was met with knowing laughter. A computer scientist by profession, he shared that when he helped his daughter with her computer homework, he did so in Yiddish. While neither Leybl nor Yankl expected their children to speak as fluently as them, their children indicated a strong interest in maintaining the language.

Leybl and Yankl expressed a forward-looking and optimistic view of Yiddish that identified the language as a bond between the past and the future. Although their parents were survivors, the Holocaust was not a primary motivation behind the continued use of Yiddish in their home. Leybl observed, "You cannot rebuild what is gone. Jews always build new things but do not forget what was." As a self-identified futurist, Leybl stated that his transmission of Yiddish was motivated by building for tomorrow. The clearest expression of this optimism was watching Yankl and Bina Ester's young children speaking Yiddish effortlessly with each other and with their older Israeli cousins during the interview; their teenaged son told me in fluent Yiddish that they all opt to speak the language with each other whenever they visit.

Another example of intergenerational Yiddish transmission is offered by the Berman family. For Ana Kuper Berman, a long-time teacher of Yiddish in Canada's secular Jewish schools and the grandmother of Yiddish-speaking children, the interconnected strands of language continuity are rooted in, and supported by, formal education. Born in Russia in 1940, Berman was raised as a native Yiddish speaker by Bundist parents who settled in Montreal in 1950. She attended the secular leftist Avrom Reisen School of the Workmen's Circle and acted in Dora Wasserman's Yiddish youth theatre. She trained as teacher in Montreal's United Jewish Teachers' Seminary and became a kinder-garten teacher at the Peretz School, an all-day secular Jewish school where Yiddish formed a core part of the curriculum.[60] Berman's entry into teaching occurred when a teacher was going on maternity leave and another educator, Yena Fishman, requested that Berman be per-mitted to assume the role while completing her studies. The two worked together and Fishman, who had been a teacher in Poland before the war and "was a treasure trove of Yiddish material for chil-dren," mentored Berman for five years.[61] Berman subsequently taught Yiddish at Montreal's Bialik High School and, after relocating to Toronto, at the Bialik Hebrew Day School, where she was active from 1981 to 2007. At the time of my interview in 2018, in addition to lead-ing a conversation group for adults in Toronto and being involved with Yiddish reading groups, Berman was proudly speaking the lan-guage with her grandchildren.

Berman and her Canadian-born husband, a graduate of the Calgary Peretz School, decided that they wanted their children to speak Yiddish as they were growing up so that they could communicate with Berman's parents "in the language that they loved and felt most com-fortable [in.]" Berman and her husband practiced speaking to each other in Yiddish before their two sons were born and spoke only Yid-dish at home so that it was accepted as natural. Berman's training as a teacher involved acquiring a repertoire of interactive songs and stories for every occasion, which facilitated raising her own children in an immersive environment. At the time of my interview, both of Berman's sons were speaking Yiddish to their own children. Berman saw her grandchildren several times a week and they spoke Yiddish together; she noted that "If I speak to my sons in English, my grandchildren remind me to speak Yiddish." The language formed part of a multilin-gual household: the sons spoke to their children in Yiddish on a daily basis, in addition to English and French; two of her grandchildren also spoke Mandarin, which they learned from their mother.[62]

Two points emerge from the examples of the Botwinik and Berman families: one can successfully transmit Yiddish within a multilingual home and the key to engendering a willingness to speak Yiddish among children is to render the experience both meaningful and enjoyable. Challenges include the lack of a community of other children who speak Yiddish; preschools and other early childhood education opportunities; and the availability of resources such as contemporary children's books, games, television shows, and films. Both Yankl and Leybl Botwinik drew on their own knowledge and interests to create stories and games; Ana Kuper Berman integrated a rich repertoire of Yiddish children's songs. Each of them drew on their own immersive exposure to Yiddish from a European-born carrier of its culture to shape created language spaces for their children. For new learners of Yiddish who opt to speak Yiddish with their own children – not an unheard-of phenomenon in the secular Yiddish world – forming sustainable created language spaces that are both enjoyable and encourage language use is particularly challenging. Recordings of Yiddish children's music or online resources aimed at children can render this challenge less difficult (see chapter 6). Far more common than the transmission of spoken Yiddish to the third generation is the partial continuity of elements of Yiddish culture – songs, stories, and games – while raising children within a dominant language such as English, a topic that lies beyond the scope of this chapter.

ONLINE SURVEY

As I discuss in the previous chapter, to gather data about Yiddish use in Canada today, I conducted a short online survey that revealed a diversity of modes of language connection.[63] It ran Canada-wide from September through December of 2017. I targeted email invitations to contacts including language instructors in university programs and community settings, performers, and cultural organizations.[64] The survey was also posted on social media sites (Facebook and Twitter) and forwarded via email by the respondents to their own networks. Deliberately brief, the online questionnaire contained eight multiple-choice questions and two open-ended questions that took an average of five minutes to complete. The mainstream outreach, combined with the inclusive and open-ended format of the survey (which did not assume fluency in Yiddish) cast a wide net. The survey received 485 responses from a variety of respondents, a significant sample size. Ranging in age from under twenty to over ninety, they comprised established figures in the worlds of education, translation, and music as well as newcomers to the language. They spanned different origins and backgrounds and included many people who self-identified as Jewish, ranging from secular to traditional, as well as a small number of non-Jews.

The respondents across all age groups indicated that they connect with Yiddish across multiple domains. Of the 485 respondents, 308 indicated that they spoke Yiddish, representing a majority across all age categories except for those born between 1963 and 1982, where the total was just slightly less than half. Most of the respondents who spoke Yiddish stated that they acquired it from their families or schools as children, but also worked independently to improve it; many had attended university or other language classes, engaged in independent study and read Yiddish texts, or were involved in some form of Yiddish performance. All indicated that they engaged in at least two of the following on a regular basis: reading or writing in Yiddish; research; translation out of or into the language; listening to or singing Yiddish music; performing in Yiddish theatre; participation in conversation or study groups; teaching; and attendance at events such as Yiddish-language lectures, plays, or concerts. Music represented the largest area of engagement, with roughly half of respondents reporting singing in Yiddish on a regular basis. This result points to the ongoing legacy of music as a site of continuity and innovation, with multiple respondents citing it as their initial access point into Yiddish. The results indicate a broad swath of created language spaces to support Yiddish continuity, sometimes in addition to and sometimes in place of its transmission within families.

A vast majority lived in cities with a strong Yiddish presence – Montreal, Toronto, and Vancouver – where a variety of organizations continued to offer programming in the language. The survey respondents, especially among those who identified with secular Jewishness (Yiddishkeit/Yiddishkayt), often aligned Yiddish with social justice. The open-ended responses to the survey – "I speak Yiddish / I am involved with Yiddish because" – revealed a shared discourse. One element was the connection to family and the past: honouring, remembering, and identifying with family ancestry, with the terms "heart" and "soul" recurring, as well as concepts of comfort and home. Another was the preservation of a Jewish collective past leading to a responsibility to uphold Yiddish, both the language and its surrounding culture. A third area was a love for the language, which was extolled for its expressiveness.

For the purposes of analysis, respondents were grouped into five cohorts with a common denominator of shared experiences and cul-

Table 2.4

Percentage of Yiddish speakers by respondent's age cohort (number of respondents in parentheses)

	Born 1981–98 (42)	Born 1965–80 (50)	Born 1946–64 (204)	Born pre-1946 (100)
No one in family	17	22	7.4	9
Self	42	30	56.4	66
Spouse/significant other	2.4	6	19.6	43
Parents	31.9	58	71	45
Grandparents	53.7	60	43.1	33.1
Siblings	12.2	8	26.5	29
Children	2.4	4	9.8	12
Grandchildren	0	0	0.98	6
Other	4.9	8	4.4	5

tural norms or values: born before 1946 ("the Silent Generation"), born 1946 to 1964 ("Baby Boomers"), born 1965 to 1980 ("Generation X"), and born 1981 to 1998 ("Millennials"). The largest number of responses originated from the Baby Boomer group (204 responses), which can be explained by several factors: as the children of the last generation of European-born Yiddish speakers, they would have been exposed to the language in a potentially immersive way (a combination of family, schooling, cultural activities, social events); with their parents' generation dwindling in size, they might be more likely to seek out Yiddish activities; and as recent retirees, they might have more time to devote to pursuing an interest such as Yiddish. The responses also suggest multigenerational networks. Among the cohort born before 1964 for whom Yiddish was commonly cited as a mother tongue or a language learned early in life, respondents who spoke Yiddish indicated that they did so with multiple family members across generations: parents, spouses, siblings, and children.

However, the patterns revealed in the responses are not necessarily what one might expect for family language transmission. Table 2.4 is a summary of the responses to the following multiple-choice survey question: "The Yiddish speakers in my family are (please choose all that apply): No one; Me; My spouse or significant other; My parents; My grandparents; My siblings; My children; My grandchildren." The table is based on a total of 396 responses (89 did not provide dates of birth). While the results are speculative, they suggest some interesting trends.

The percentage of respondents who declared themselves Yiddish speakers was highest among the oldest born pre-1946 cohort (two thirds) and then decreased to just over half among the Baby Boomers and again to under a third for the Generation X group. This trend is not surprising, given the shift in the status of Yiddish from an immigrant to an ethnic/heritage language and the decline of widespread institutional support for its transmission (e.g., day schools or camps). The decline among the oldest two cohorts in the percentages of Yiddish speakers among spouses/significant others and siblings is likewise to be expected. (The lower numbers for grandparents and parents may be due to the present-tense construction of the question, "The Yiddish speakers in my family *are*," as most of the parents and grandparents of the people in these age categories had passed away.)

The survey indicates a shift from the family home and childhood classroom to other sites for Yiddish transmission. One notable finding is an increased proportion of self-declared Yiddish speakers among the youngest group of Millennials to 42 per cent, compared to 30 per cent in the Generation X cohort. This youngest cohort also reported a higher statistic for siblings who speak Yiddish than the Generation X cohort (12 per cent versus 8 per cent). However, when one further compares the Millennials to Generation X, one finds less family exposure overall to the language: while over half of Millennials reported that their own grandparents speak Yiddish, a statistic that is quite close to the 60 per cent reported by Generation X, fewer than a third (31.9 per cent) indicated that they have Yiddish-speaking parents. This figure is significantly lower than the number of self-declared speakers in the cohort (42 per cent) and represents close to half of the total reported by the Generation X cohort (58 per cent). Conversely, the responses among the two cohorts born before 1964 for numbers of grandchildren who speak Yiddish – 6 per cent and 1 per cent respectively – imply that these groups are not transmitting Yiddish as a spoken language to the third generation. Although these numbers may well increase with time, the survey question "I expect that my grandchildren will be Yiddish speakers: true; false; maybe," received an overwhelming response of "false" from all respondents. These findings suggest that the increase in Yiddish speakers among this youngest cohort cannot be explained simply through intergenerational transmission. Rather, younger speakers appear to be seeking out opportunities to engage with Yiddish outside their biological families in the multiple settings that exist for this purpose today. The survey supports what chapter 5 of this book discusses in depth: over the last thirty years, engagement with Yiddish is increasingly taking place in a Yiddishland that is enacted through events and activities and the building of interpersonal networks around the language.

Because the survey respondents are self-selecting and the responses are self-declared, the findings are particularly illuminating: the youngest cohort is proclaiming itself to be more Yiddish-speaking than its predecessors, despite having been less likely to hear the language spoken in their own homes growing up. Their higher rate of proficiency can be attributed to a renewed interest in the language and the acquisition of Yiddish through university courses or self-study. It may also be due to an over-reporting of proficiency in the language: someone from the younger generation may identify as a Yiddish speaker if, for instance, that person had taken one language course, while older respondents, exposed as they may have been to generations of fluent, native speakers, might not consider that same person to qualify. For Millennials, Yiddish does not appear to be shared within their own households: only a tiny minority declared that they had a spouse/significant other or children who spoke Yiddish: 2.4 per cent for both, a small number even if one factors in those not in a relationship or who might not have children yet. This implies that Yiddish represents a personal pastime or professional interest rather than a shared family pursuit. It suggests that Yiddish continuity will increasingly take place in created language spaces outside the home, and in adulthood.

FUTURES FOR YIDDISH TRANSMISSION

Outside the Haredi world, Yiddish no longer relies primarily on family transmission for its survival and growth. It is possible to engage with Yiddish as a heritage speaker or new speaker without exposure in the childhood home. Involvement with Yiddish can take place through participation in a combination of created language spaces: language classes, conversation groups, song workshops, theatre performances, and so on. Further, Yiddish is no longer the sole purview of Jewish immigrants from Eastern European and their descendants. As I discuss in chapter 5, theories of Queer Yiddishkeit offer alternative models for Yiddish continuity where the language is transmitted among cohorts rather than within biological families. As a historically non-territorial language without a single geographic or political centre, Yiddish, in many ways, predates recent trends towards globalization and multilingualism. Its use has for decades raised questions of legitimacy and authenticity, especially among newcomers. A recent study suggests that new speakers of Yiddish in the twenty-first century, both Jewish and non-Jewish, experience tensions around the legitimacy of their language use: for example, around what constitutes the correct accent or dialect. They may ask whether a standardized, classroom version of the language is acceptable or whether one must adopt a version of the language associated with a particular geographic location or group. [65] Another study of the category of "new speaker" interrogates the concept of linguistic legitimacy – the capacity to produce the correct linguistic forms in the appropriate situations – and suggests that it is destabilized by the death of its traditional speakers. The category of "new speakers" has potentially become a descriptive as well as prescriptive label that engenders hierarchical divisions between "old" and "new" language.[66] There is no single definition of what constitutes authentic Yiddish, and the language's evolution raises interesting questions about the value and even the meaning of authenticity. With new speakers increasingly at the fore of secular Yiddish, the language has moved into new domains and new models for continuity.

The next chapters of this book move from the middle outward in the concentric circles of secular Yiddish to explore the initiatives of successive generations as they engage with, and promote, the language. In adapting itself to wider trends, each approach and medium offers innovative models of Yiddish language engagement outside of family transmission, notably among the younger generation.

The strategies evolved by the generation of Yiddish speakers born before the Holocaust had lasting resonance for their children. They created youth-oriented spaces combining new systems of education in schools, camps, and theatre groups, sometimes in tandem with the deliberate maintenance of Yiddish as a language of the home. Formed and nurtured by these initiatives, the younger Canadian-raised generation, whose Yiddish world encompassed home, school, and extracurricular activities, gravitated towards domains that fit with the wider Canadian worldview of the 1960s and 1970s – notably performance and youth activism – to promote Yiddish into the future. This is the subject of the next chapter.

3

Yiddish in Youth Theatre and Activism
The 1960s and 1970s

The 1960s and 1970s marked a transitional time for Yiddish in North America in its concurrent decline as a Jewish vernacular and popularization within public culture. Leo Rosten's *The Joys of Yiddish* (1968) and Maurice Samuel's *In Praise of Yiddish* (1971) introduced the sounds and culture of Yiddish to broad audiences, as did the hit musical film, *Fiddler on the Roof* (1971). "Yinglish" – a term coined by Rosten for the borrowing of Yiddish words, phrases, and intonation into English[1]–increasingly entered the mainstream. Yiddish works appeared in translation and on university curricula while a youth-driven counterculture imagined and enacted fresh ways of being Jewish that included a new Yiddish movement.

In Canada, pervasive changes in the country's linguistic and cultural landscape mobilized a core of Yiddish activists. This period generated new initiatives by European-born Yiddish speakers – many of them Holocaust survivors – to transmit their language and culture. It also marked the advent of new projects to encourage Canadian-raised youth to use Yiddish as a living language. These ventures dedicated to enhancing continuity complemented earlier models of Yiddish transmission that had evolved in schools and camps in the first half of the twentieth century. Together, they fit the model of created language spaces as deliberate and participatory sites for Yiddish use, particularly oriented towards youth.

For certain members of the last generation of European-born speakers raising children of their own, transmitting the fullness of Yiddish civilization to their progeny became paramount. This coincided with a broader interest in ethnicity that took hold in the 1960s in North America. Yiddish activists known as *klal-tuer* worked to stave off the decline of the language and ensure cultural continuity through rich and varied community programming for all ages. In Canada, the enduring and resilient system of Jewish schools founded in the 1910s was bolstered by new teachers and students, and initiatives in lectures, plays, concerts, and book publishing flourished. Yiddish activism would become increasingly visible within the mainstream Jewish community as organizations banded together to support ventures across the country under the aegis of the national advocacy group, the Canadian Jewish Congress. However, despite the richness of the Yiddish offerings by, and for, the European-born generation, the place of the language in Canadian Jewish life increasingly became a point of discussion within the community, in public life, and in the press: With declining numbers of speakers of Yiddish, what would the future hold? Would Yiddish maintain a foothold in the cultural turbulence of the 1960s and 1970s?

For a Canadian-raised generation of Yiddish speakers, the language did not represent the same kind of cultural imperative as it did for their immigrant parents. A study in Melbourne characterizes the impetus shared by Yiddish-speaking Holocaust survivors worldwide as they rebuilt their lives in new settlements as an "imperative to nurture distinctiveness, sustain a sense of community, and promote cultural maintenance and generational transmission."[2] While their parents sought to nurture a community-based identity and promote the continuity of their civilization to future generations, for children raised in North America, English offered access to a mainstream culture far removed from the Europe of their parents. Even those whose mother tongue was Yiddish and who were reared in homes staunchly devoted to the language could not fully hope to sustain their parents' civilization.

And yet, Yiddish forms a vital element in the lives of a segment of Jewish youth raised in Canada in the 1960s and 1970s. These youth activists, like other members of their generation who would remain committed to Yiddish in the long term, tended to share a number of features. They were the children of Holocaust survivors whose parents had participated in Jewish youth movements in Europe and remained involved with ideological organizations that supported Yiddish, notably the Bund. They were raised in Yiddish-speaking homes where the language was highly valued, often in association with an enduring commitment to one or more ideological movements. They grew up in immigrant neighbourhoods where the language was widely spoken. Their parents exposed them to Yiddish culture via music, literature, theatre, and community programs, and they were educated in secular Jewish schools where Yiddish formed a core part of the curriculum (*shuln,* singular *shul* or *shule*) and their associated summer camps, and were involved in extracurricular youth activities where they employed Yiddish with their peers.

In the model of concentric circles of secular Yiddish, this activity sits in the second ring from the middle to encompass the activism of the European-born generation and their Canadian-raised children (see figure 0.1). Both engaged with Yiddish in a forward-looking manner by employing strategies oriented towards young people. Like a rope made up of multiple strands, their efforts encompassed various sites where Yiddish might be transmitted: the home and neighbourhood; youth and adult education; performance and the arts; activism. For the generation raised in the aftermath of the Holocaust outside of the European Yiddish heartland, the rope had to be deliberately refashioned. While formal education offered one means for ensuring continuity, Holocaust survivors and their children spearheaded new models for young people to connect with Yiddish in meaningful ways, notably via the performing arts and youth activism. Some of these ventures were supported by formally established committees on the national and regional levels, while others were initiated and carried out by Canadian youth. The more strands were interconnected and the more young people were actively engaged with them, the more productive and complete the transmission of Yiddish to the next generation would be. As Jewish institutions engaged in discussion and activism led by the prewar, European-born generation, young people participated in, and generated, their own responses. These youth formed a bridge between the Old World of pre-Holocaust Europe and the New World of postwar Canada and created a hybrid Yiddish culture.

Drawing on archival materials, print media, and interviews, this chapter presents three enduring modes of youth-oriented community activism: (1) by adults for youth in a community model: a drama workshop that became the Dora Wasserman Yiddish Theatre (DWYT); (2) by youth for youth in an international model: a group and journal formed by and for young people in Yugntruf-Youth for Yiddish; (3) by adults for youth in a national and regional model: the Yiddish Committees of the Canadian Jewish Congress. Each one targeted young people as the carriers for Yiddish at the transitional moment when the language was on the decline within the mainstream. It begins with a brief introduction that frames these activities within a broader historical context.

YIDDISH IN THE 1960S AND 1970S:
POLITICAL LIFE, EDUCATION,
AND PUBLIC DISCOURSE

The postwar generation came of age during a period of transition when Jewish institutions increasingly began to supplant the family in the transmission of Yiddish. Harold Troper's study, *The Defining Decade*, presents the 1960s as transformative to Canadian Jewry on multiple levels: increased legal and social inclusion in the mainstream brought new opportunities for engagement and ethnic pride; at the same time, the country's Jews faced renewed waves of antisemitism, and assimilation offered its own challenges. The decade ended with a newfound form of Jewish identity based in activism and multicultural ideals, as well as intensified bonds with the State of Israel. These shifts within the Jewish community occurred against wider change on the national level, with the 1960s marking the emergence of a distinct identity for Canada. Almost a hundred years after Confederation – a century of ongoing cultural identification with Great Britain – Canada would adopt its own anthem ("O Canada") and a new flag bearing a maple leaf.

The country was entering the early stages of discussion that would result in Canada's policies of official multilingualism. The Royal Commission on Bilingualism and Biculturalism, established in 1963 to examine the changing linguistic and cultural makeup of a country traditionally defined by English and French, came to encompass the country's other ethnic groups. A study by Richard Menkis finds that initially Canadian Jewry, as represented by the Canadian Jewish Congress, reacted with ambivalence to political debates around multiculturalism, preferring to be recognized as a religion rather than one ethnic group among many.[3] However, other Jewish groups were buoyed by developments related to the Royal Commission on Bilingualism and Biculturalism; for example, in 1965 the Canadian arm of the Jewish Labour Committee (JLC, founded 1936), a secular advocacy group, presented a brief to the commission that underlined "the traditional right of every ethnic group to maintain and cultivate its particular values and cultural heritage."[4] By 1971, a Canadian Jewish Congress plenary session called for Yiddish and Hebrew to be treated as a unit within discussions of multiculturalism and for the investigation of potential state funding in support of ethnic cultures.[5]

Meanwhile, the government of Quebec was driving its own sweeping political and social process to transform the province from a

Catholic state into a modern, secular one. This Quiet Revolution (révolution tranquille) would have direct impacts on Yiddish in Montreal. The Liberal government of Premier Jean Lesage (elected in 1960) introduced wide-ranging reforms including a new Ministry for Cultural Affairs, and the inclusion of a Jewish representative – longtime director of Montreal's Jewish Public Library, David Rome – on its Arts Council. Lesage's government established the Royal Commission of Inquiry on Education in the Province of Quebec (better known as the "Parent Commission") to reform the educational system and promote the universal accessibility of secular schooling; it also established a Ministry of Education to create a state-funded system through to the college level. Through the introduction of government grants to support teaching the state-mandated curriculum in the province's parochial schools, including its Jewish day schools, the Parent Commission led to renewed discussion of Jewish education.[6] In a recent study, Simon-Pierre Lacasse argues that, in contrast to the antisemitism associated with Quebec during the Second World War and the political upheavals of the 1970s and 1980s, the "New Quebec" of the 1950s and 1960s "invigorated Jews as a religious and cultural minority rather than marginalizing or alienating them. While Jewish activists remained critical of the expanding ambitions of the Quebec state and of the rise of nationalism in the province, they took the opportunity to advance Jewish claims and adopted a largely positive outlook on their communal future in Quebec."[7] Jewish activists and writers expressed optimism about the changes, with Canada's largest Anglo-Jewish newspaper, the *Canadian Jewish Chronicle*, publishing positive and nuanced articles about Quebec politics and culture.[8] Yiddish intellectuals outside of Canada commented positively on these developments; for example, renowned poet, critic, and journalist Jacob Glatstein (Yankev Glatshteyn) published an article in a New York Yiddish daily in 1962 characterizing the crystallization of national identity in Quebec as a "great drama" that is "of particular interest for Jews who are themselves fighting for their survival among the nations." It was proudly reprinted in English translation in the *Canadian Jewish Chronicle*.[9]

This period saw drastic changes to the linguistic make-up of the Canadian Jewish community. An analysis of the 1961 census that appeared in the *Canadian Jewish Chronicle* underlined the deep-rooted connections between Yiddish language, identity, and class during a time of rapid linguistic, social, and economic transition. Journalist Ben Taube suggested that Canadian Jews – both immigrants and Canadian-born – were deliberately underreporting their ethnic origins but not their religion, resulting in a rapidly increasing discrepancy between the two (255,000 Jews by religion but 81,000 fewer by ethnicity). According to Taube, "the real keystone is language": those who did not speak Yiddish also did not tend to identify as Jewish by ethnicity. The upward economic mobility of the population appeared to herald a decline in the place of Yiddish, with lower-income groups more likely to maintain a connection to Yiddish and, by extension, their Jewish ethnicity, than their higher-earning counterparts.[10] Further, the once-prominent Jewish Communist movement had undergone rapid attrition after the political upheavals of the 1950s, when increasing anti-Communist sentiment across Canada and the mass movement of the Jewish population out of the working class resulted in the loss of Yiddish as a vernacular of the Jewish left.[11] While Yiddish remained a vital component of an aging European-born Jewish community into the 1970s, its future among the Canadian-born and -raised generation lay in question. Further, as part of the rising prominence of the State of Israel in Canadian Jewish life after the Six Day War, Israeli culture – folksong, folkdance, and the use of Israeli Hebrew (Ivrit) – became increasingly embedded within mainstream Jewish education and community activity.

Despite increasing rhetoric about the inexorable transition away from Yiddish as Jewish vernacular, members of both the older and younger generations expressed attachment to the language. Two voices appearing in the *Canadian Jewish Chronicle* a few weeks apart in 1955 offer evidence of this. The first voice is that of Montreal-born Irwin Cotler (born 1940), future international human rights lawyer and federal Minister of Justice, then a fourteen-year-old student at Herzliah High School and winner of a community public-speaking contest about Jewish identity. In an address published under the headline "Yiddish Language and Literature Is Indispensable to Jewish Life," the young Cotler implicated his Canadian-raised generation in the continuity of Yiddish:

> Yes, my friends, the old order changes, yielding place to new, but can we get along without the old expressions and idioms that though the years have filtered in our homes, our schools and our lives and have become permanent fixtures associated with our customs, festivals and holidays? Can we divorce ourselves from the Yiddish newspapers and periodicals which ever since printing was

invented have kept us informed accurately and fully, not only on community matters, but on all aspects of Jewish life concerning our brothers and sisters in every corner of the globe? Can we shut our eyes to the works of the writers or our ears to the strains of "Das Pintele Yid" or "My yiddishe mame"? We cannot divest ourselves from Yiddish language and literature, any more than we can divest ourselves from any of our limbs. It has become a part of our being, a part of our moods, a part of our Jewishness. Yiddish language has become a part of ourselves, and as such is definitely indispensable to Jewish life.[12]

The second perspective is represented by A.A. Roback (1890–1965), a Polish-born psychologist, scholar of Yiddish, and advocate of the language and culture. A graduate of McGill University, he maintained a life-long connection with Montreal after he left for the United States. Under the title of "Yiddish: Foundation of Jewish Culture," Roback argued that Yiddish was essential for the survival of Jews as an ethnic group and advocated the need for a strengthening of the existing culture:

I cannot envisage a Jewish culture existing in the Diaspora without the medium of Yiddish, which has been nourished by the folk spirit and which, in turn, fosters the creative imagination of its intellectuals ... The promotion of Yiddish culture in this country has been handicapped not only by the inroads of assimilation but by a general misconception of its riches, the lack of funds among its devotees, and perhaps worst of all, the inefficiency and lack of drive of those charged with the responsibility of maintaining Yiddish cultural media ... There can be only one course for Jewish survival: Let us make for the intensification of Jewish life through the cultivation of Yiddish letters and art.[13]

With Canadian Jewry no longer primarily European-born and Yiddish speaking by the 1960s, what could the new place of Yiddish be? For Hasidic populations, the answer to this question was highly utilitarian: one of the defining characteristics of the sect of Tosher Hasidim that relocated from urban Montreal to form Kiryas Tosh (Tash) in a rural area of Quebec in the 1960s was a deliberate use of the Yiddish language as the enclave's lingua franca.[14] For the Jewish mainstream, for whom English and French were rapidly assuming the role of vernacular as well as the languages of literature, art, and wider religious and community life, the place of Yiddish within Jewish Canadian life would have to be renegotiated and re-envisioned.

The pride and joy of the secular Yiddish community were its children's schools, which embodied the hopes for transmission of the language and culture. Formed in the 1910s, the movement of secular Yiddish schools expanded rapidly in Canada in the 1920s and 1930s, from preschool through high school, in both full-day education and extension classes held on afternoons or weekends and in tandem with teacher-training programs and adult education.

In North America, the *shuln* movement encompassed nearly a thousand schools in some 160 communities between 1910 and 1960.[15] Within a largely working-class group of recent immigrants, the *shuln* formed part of a wider way of life shared by members of Jewish political groups. They encompassed an intersecting and transnational web of social relationships and institutions as well as offering a site for any of the following activities: attending meetings and participating in activism such as picket lines; singing in choirs; taking part in reading groups; playing in mandolin orchestras or in sports leagues; fundraising for the cause; and attending concerts, lectures, or literary events. Regardless of their ideological orientation, the *shuln* positioned Yiddish language as a repository of Jewish culture and taught literature, Jewish history and culture, Jewish holiday celebration, the arts, and current events in Yiddish. Singing formed a core part of the curriculum, with Yiddish songs specially composed by teachers for use in the classroom and by school choruses. During their heyday from the 1920s into the 1940s, the *shuln* made great efforts to modernize their pedagogy, publishing pedagogical texts as well as special magazines for and by children and holding conferences at the national and regional levels to provide teacher training. They were complemented by extracurricular activities for the students such as clubs, orchestras, sport leagues, and summer camps to create a year-long learning experience.[16]

To their founders, the *shuln* offered the means of transmitting Jewish values based on a particular worldview. In Canada, four distinct leftist-oriented movements were most active in this role: the Jewish Labour Bund, which espoused a secular Jewish socialist worldview; its offshoot, the Poale Zion/Farband, which espoused a Labour Zionist ideology; the Workmen's Circle/Arbeter Ring, which promoted secular Jewish culture; and the Socialist or Communist-affiliated United Jewish People's Order or UJPO (Fareynikter yidisher folks ordn), which grew out of a 1945 merger between two leftist fraternal orders: the Workmen's Circle and the Toronto Jewish Labour League.[17]

Montreal housed an especially ambitious system of Yiddish-oriented schools. Rather than non-sectarian public schooling, education in the province of Quebec was divided on a confessional basis into French-Catholic and English-Protestant school systems. The designation of the Jews as Protestant within this denominational system promoted the establishment of a robust Jewish day school system. Within this network, the city evolved a system of *shuln* that mirrored the ideological divisions of its Jewish immigrants to position Yiddish as a carrier of Jewish history and culture: (1) the Poale Zion's National Radical/Farband schools, which evolved into two streams in the 1910s: the more leftist-oriented Peretz Shule (Peretz School), which promoted Yiddish over Hebrew, and the more centrist Yidishe Folkshule (Jewish People's School), which included both Yiddish and Hebrew; the schools would merge in 1971 as the Jewish People's and Peretz Schools (JPPS); (2) the Arbeter Ring/Workmen's Circle Avrom Reisen afternoon school; and (3) the UJPO's Morris Winchevsky Shule.[18] Montreal's United Jewish Teachers' Seminary (Yidisher Lerer Seminar, founded 1946)[19] would offer rigorous courses in Jewish studies as part of a two-year teaching diploma, including classes in Yiddish and Hebrew language and literature, Jewish history, the Bible, and pedagogy. Although the Hebraist United Talmud Torah would offer classes in Yiddish into the 1950s, the language did not form part of its core curriculum.

In the rest of Canada, the network of active *shuln* likewise evinced various ideological orientations and schisms. For example, Winnipeg's Peretz Shule, founded in 1913 by member of the Jewish Labour Bund and labour Zionists, became the first modern Jewish day school in North America in 1920; the school grew steadily until there were six hundred students in seven grades in 1949 and produced several offshoots due to ideological differences.[20] Smaller cities such as Calgary, Edmonton, Hamilton, Ottawa, and Saskatoon also offered diverse Yiddish day school education.

By the 1920s the *shuln* were complemented by corresponding networks of camps to create the possibility of full-year Jewish education, with their widest influence in the 1930s. Of the forty Yiddish secular overnight and day camps that operated in North America between the 1910s and the 1960s, eight of them were located in Canada, with the largest and most enduring of these found in proximity to Montreal or Toronto.[21] The secular Yiddish camps – like the *shuln* – were founded by idealists and closely bound up with the politics of their sponsoring movements; their ideological and political orientation and particular emphasis on Yiddish varied from camp to camp as well as over time. These residential camps allowed for intensive programming to reinforce the regular school curriculum. The staff were drawn from within the movement's own ranks and were committed to its ideals, including teachers from the regular *shuln* as well as *shul* graduates, who also served as counsellors and role models.[22] Camps created an immersive environment in which Yiddish could fulfill multiple functions as a language of formal education, communication ranging from conversation to announcements, and games or song. One study of the Canadian camps characterizes them as "a twenty-four-hour opportunity to teach socialist values in Yiddish in the context of a 'fresh air' country camping experience."[23]

Yiddish in the *shuln* and camps was directly impacted by shifts in Jewish language use and the increased marginalization of the Jewish left in Canadian life. After peaking in the 1920s, the movement began to decline: the overall numbers of students attending the *shuln* in North America went down from an estimated 23,000 in 1930 to 12,000 in 1961.[24] By the 1940s, a majority of the corresponding camps had closed as formal education of Yiddish diminished. The structural and ideological changes implemented by the *shuln* systems in response to local and international events – the Great Depression and the Second World War, the Holocaust, the decline of the Jewish left, the creation of a Jewish state in Israel – marked the introduction of new curricula that promoted culture over ideology and gave more prominence to Jewish traditions and to Hebrew.

The increasing prominence of Israeli Hebrew (Ivrit) posed a particular challenge to Yiddish in youth education. The dynamics of Hebrew and Yiddish in the secular Jewish schools had been complex from the outset, with some *shuln* teaching both languages while others initially opted for a Yiddish-only curriculum in the 1910s. The establishment of the State of Israel in 1948 spurred the increasing adoption of Hebrew as the Jewish lingua franca in the schools, as well as the distinctive pronunciation of Israeli Hebrew, which differed from the Ashkenazi pronunciation traditionally used by Yiddish speakers. In the 1950s, Jewish schools that had been teaching Yiddish because of the immigrant make-up of their student body began to offer only Hebrew; for example, Montreal's United Talmud Torah Schools (founded 1896) ceased to offer Yiddish as part of its curriculum. Within the curricula of the schools, Yiddish began to shift from a spoken vernacular to a heritage language associated with literature and song, while Hebrew increasingly took on the role of the Jewish communicative language. In those schools that remained committed to Yiddish after the 1950s, teachers devised new ways to keep it meaningful. By the 1950s, Montreal secular Jewish schools had become a model for Yiddish cultural continuity in North America.[25]

The arrival of Holocaust survivors and the last generation of European-born Yiddish speakers – including prominent writers, pedagogues, actors, and activists – bolstered Yiddish education. They joined the schools as instructors and pioneered new educational ventures; their Yiddish-speaking children joined the student ranks. Extensive connections evolved between the Yiddish literary milieu and the secular Jewish schools. For example, in Montreal, the *shuln* were under the leadership of prominent local literary figures: Shimshen Dunsky as vice-principal at the Yidishe Folkshule, Yaakov Zipper as principal at the Peretz Shule, and Sholem Shtern as principal of the Morris Winchevsky Shule. The *shuln* also provided stable employment to the city's Yiddish writers – J.I. Segal, M.M. Shaffir and others – who, in turn, integrated literature into their students' education.

School alumnae who remained actively involved with Yiddish recall how the *shuln* cultivated connections between their students and the literary world. Eva Raby (born Roskies, 1942) recalls how her teachers at Montreal's Yidishe Folkshule would proudly announce visits by Yiddish writers to the school as part of their sojourns in the city.[26] Yiddish teacher Sheva Zucker (born 1951) recalls a youth culture within Winnipeg's Peretz Shule in which she was able to tell a young friend that a certain Yiddish writer had visited her home and signed her autograph book, and that friend was impressed.[27] *Shuln* activists developed strategies to enable Canadian-raised children to engage with Yiddish literature. For example, the recitation of literary texts offered a way to connect with Yiddish belles-lettres at school and also at community events. In this vein, Montreal cultural activist Rivka Augenfeld (born 1946) recalls regularly performing Yiddish poems and other texts at community events from her early childhood in the 1950s; these recitations were enthusiastically received.[28]

Three Canadian exceptions to dominant North American trends of postwar decline point to the lasting resilience of Yiddish youth education. First, 1945 marked the founding of Vancouver's Peretz Shule, which was established as a leftist supplementary school to provide children with an apolitical, secular Jewish education. In 1961, the school moved to a larger building that continues to house the city's Peretz Centre for Secular Jewish Culture, which remains active in the promotion of Yiddish.[29] Second, in 1961, Toronto's Bialik Hebrew Day School was founded by Toronto's labour Zionist movement, with Yiddish taught as an integral part of the curriculum alongside Hebrew; the school grew steadily and continues to offer Yiddish instruction. Third, Montreal's all-day schools, including the Folkshule and Peretz Shule, underwent marked growth in the 1960s due to the introduction of state subsidies for nongovernment parochial schools.[30]

In the 1960s, as Yiddish transformed from an immigrant to an ethnic language, the *shuln* assumed an increasingly significant role in the transmission and maintenance of the language. For example, the authors of a 1976 study, *Non-Official Languages: A Study in Canadian Multiculturalism*, note the high rate of Yiddish class attendance among school-aged children in their discussion of education and language retention.[31] Comprehensive children's education offered one means of transmitting Jewish values based on culture and ideology, as well as transmitting the Yiddish language itself. These activities were augmented by new initiatives in informal education and activism.

A new overnight summer camp called Camp Hemshekh generated its own brand of Yiddish youth culture. It joined Camp Boiberik (founded 1923) as a place where, as a recent study suggests, "post-World War II educators shaped their programs in hopes of ensuring the future of Yiddish after the Holocaust, infusing the language into official camp life even as it ceased to be used for everyday communication between campers."[32] Founded in 1959 by Bundists and other secular, Yiddish-speaking Holocaust survivors, Camp Hemshekh – which means "continuity" – offered an immersive, participatory, and peer-led environment that attracted sizable contingents of campers and staff from Montreal and Toronto to its camp in New York State each summer. The camp expressed the activist spirit of the 1960s and 1970s for English-speaking youth for whom Yiddish evolved from being the language of their parents to a meaningful aspect of their identity. Its 1965 mission statement offered the following principles: "community cooperation and solidarity; a feeling for social justice; knowledge of the Yiddish language and a close tie in with modern Jewish culture and the basic elements of self-identification with our Jewish heritage."[33] While the dominant language among the campers was English, Camp Hemshekh promoted Yiddish by injecting it into every aspect of the camp schedule: formal announcements and signage; singing multiple times a day; a camp newspaper with Yiddish content; Yiddish language classes at various levels; and Yiddish literature seminars. Cultural events featuring well-known guests from the Yiddish world took place on Friday nights. Great efforts were made to teach Yiddish to those campers who arrived not speaking the language, especially through singing and dramatic performances.

In an oral history, Moishe Rosenfeld (born 1949), a Montreal-raised Yiddish and English-language actor, producer, and promoter of Jewish musical theatre, reveals the lasting influence of Camp Hemshekh. Rosenfeld was born into a transplanted family of prominent Polish Yiddish scholars and activists who settled in North America after the Holocaust; his mother was legendary Yiddish activist Sara Mlotek Rosenfeld. A student at Montreal's Yidishe Folkshule, Rosenfeld became a camper at Hemshekh starting in its first year. He recalls the central position of Yiddish language and culture in the camp from its beginning: "We had Yiddish classes, Yiddish sing-alongs, Yiddish creative things. We had College Day and Olympics and all of those things, those competitions, where best Yiddish song was one of the categories, best original Yiddish, best original English. So Yiddish was in the air, as they say, it was in the air, in our hearts, in our lives."[34] Rosenfeld identifies Yiddish as a meaningful and integrated element of the staff and camper culture. Fluid connections between the Montrealers and New Yorkers forged lasting friendships, romantic relationships, and marriages within a community whose hundreds of members have remained devoted to each other decades later. Rosenfeld remarks, "If they went to Camp Hemshekh, then Yiddish is special."[35]

Among the variegated roles that Yiddish occupied within camp life, the most important lay in the area of performance, in particular after the arrival of Zalmen Mlotek (born 1951) – who would go on to become a leading figure in Yiddish music and theatre – as Camp Hemshekh's musical director at the age of seventeen. The camp developed as an intergenerational meeting place and a site for the refashioning of Yiddish culture for the youth of the 1960s and 1970s. It offered a network to promote enduring language activism and was instrumental in the success of the Yugntruf Yiddish movement and its journal.

THE DORA WASSERMAN YIDDISH THEATRE

A vibrant and expanding site of Yiddish youth activity in the 1960s and 1970s – and beyond – is Montreal's Dora Wasserman Yiddish Theatre (DWYT), which remains Canada's only permanent Yiddish theatre company. The youth wing of the theatre, known as the Children's Programme, the Children and Youth Programme, and, most recently, YAYA (Young Actors for Young Audiences), has involved generations of young people in theatre training and performances since 1951.[36] While the DWYT evolved to include elaborate, award-winning productions with large, intergenerational casts, its roots lie in Yiddish drama training for children and youth, a legacy that continues into the present.

Dora Wasserman (1919–2003) was born in Ukraine, trained as a student of drama with the GOSET (Moscow State Yiddish Theatre) under the eminent director Solomon Mikhoels, and completed a four-year theatre program just before the outbreak of the Second World War. Having survived the war acting in a theatre in Kazakhstan, she performed in displaced persons camps before settling in Montreal in 1950. There she undertook a variety of Yiddish-language activities through local organizations: literary recitations in the *shuln*, song performances at cultural events, and drama workshops for children. Students would gravitate towards her drama sessions from local Jewish schools. Wasserman recalled, "Finding Yiddish-speaking children then was not a problem."[37]

A partner to the Wasserman's theatre programs was the Jewish Public Library (Yidishe Folksbiblyotek, JPL), founded in 1914 as a non-partisan lending library, which served as a cultural centre for the city's Jewish community and hosted an array of programming for youth and adults that expanded in the postwar years.[38] The first of her theatre sessions, which took place at the Library, involved Yiddish-speaking children from the Avrom Reisen School. The Library had previously provided support to a successful wartime theatre studio directed by actress Chayele Grober (1898–1978) under the name Yidishe Teater Grupe (Yiddish Theatre Group, YTEG, 1939–42);[39] it would play a pivotal role in supporting Wasserman's projects. After the first production of Wasserman's youth theatre in 1950, the director of the Library, David Rome, included a stage and auditorium in his architectural plans for the new building (opened in 1953) because of the high calibre of the performance.[40] The Library would host a performance by theatre students to mark its fiftieth anniversary in 1964.[41]

Wasserman's program offered participatory and embodied education in Yiddish literature, song, and culture to the younger generation. Rather than promoting passive language acquisition, Wasserman's theatre participants engaged with the language through movement, singing, and recitation while also being steeped in Yiddish culture. The children took part in weekly workshops of "imagination games" consisting of Yiddish-language improvisation and skits, and sang Yiddish songs; in the process, they were exposed to works of Yiddish literature.[42] Within a few years of the group's founding, Wasserman began to invite members, who were by now teenagers or young adults, to meet once a week at her home to sing songs, discuss cultural issues, and socialize in Yiddish in what became known as "The Friday Night Group." Wasserman's sessions, for which David Rome also acted as mentor, offered informal education in Yiddish as well as broader Jewish culture that included meeting a range of writers and artists and composers from Canada and abroad.[43] The group staged several ambitious productions and many of its original members would later join the adult casts of Wasserman's productions.

In 1958, under the aegis of the Yidishe Folkshule, Wasserman founded a drama group made up of graduates from the school, with which she remained active for the next decade. The group employed the Stanislavski method, integrating improvisation with staged performances. A newspaper review of a 1962 production of Sholem Asch's classic play, *Onkl Mozes* (Uncle Moses), praised the performance and Wasserman for "demonstrating admirably that it is possible to present stimulating Yiddish theatre in Montreal with a group of amateur thespians." The review noted the potential future role of this theatre troupe in Montreal.[44] The review appeared just weeks after an editorial about the downsizing of professional Yiddish theatre in the city that read: "Is there a revival of Jewish theatre in Montreal? By all indications, there is presently a determined effort on the part of individual groups to preserve the best in Jewish theatre for those who still appreciate it. The players are grouped in small companies, sometimes comprising only two or three people, with fine reputations in Europe. The days when large 'troupes' would come here from New York seem at an end and it is to the credit, therefore, of these small roving ambassadors of good Jewish theatre that they are prepared to give their best for what, unfortunately, must prove to be meagre financial gain."[45]

A report published by Chayele (Eileen) Thalenberg in the Yiddish-language *Yugntruf* (Youth for Yiddish) journal in 1965 details the

activities of Wasserman's theatre group from the perspective of one of
its teenaged participants. Thalenberg describes the transition of the
group from a Saturday morning session of Yiddish stories and song
for young children at the Jewish Public Library a decade earlier to its
present incarnation with the original members having grown into
teenagers. The group had split into two groups (ages eight to twelve
and thirteen to fifteen) to perform Yiddish plays as well as ambitious
adaptations from works of Yiddish and world literature, including
Avrom Goldfadn's operettas, the folktales of Hershel Ostropol, the
works of classic Yiddish writers I.L. Peretz and Sholem Aleichem, a
Yiddish-language adaptation of Oscar Wilde's children's story *The
Happy Prince*, and a production of *Andorra* (1965) by Swiss dramatist
Max Frisch. Thalenberg provides an insider's account of the "Friday
Night Group" that met with Wasserman at the Jewish Public Library:
during the rehearsals, the members read a play several times; Wasserman highlighted the characters' features, discussed the plot and its
points of conflict with the group, and distributed the parts; the members then met with David Rome to discuss the play's meaning and the
difficulties inherent in staging it. In addition to sessions devoted to
dramatical works, the group staged literary evenings with local or visiting Yiddish writers, tackled dance or theatre exercises (*études*), and
attended plays in English, French, or Yiddish. Thalenberg discusses in
depth the group's most challenging project: a Yiddish adaptation of
Frisch's *Andorra*, a post-Holocaust parable that had been staged only
once in North America. While the play posed significant challenges
in terms of staging, she observed, "for young people, nothing is hard,
especially when they buckle down."[46]

While professional Yiddish theatre featuring a cadre of international
prewar stars was fading, Wasserman's Canadian youth theatre was on
the rise. By 1967, it was the last local company to perform regularly in
Yiddish. As audiences grew, so did the number of performances per
year. After a decade housed at the Yidishe Folkshule, the group's
anniversary performance was staged at the city's grandiose Monument
National Theatre, selling out performances of *Tevye*, a play based on the
beloved stories of Sholem Aleichem. Wasserman's theatre then found a
permanent home at the recently built Saidye Bronfman Centre for the
Arts, which also provided a budget for its operations and professional
staff to assist with choreography, design, sets, and lighting.[47]

The new arrangement allowed Wasserman to apply her methods in
a more sustained manner. In the Soviet tradition, Wasserman's theatre

training favoured a collective approach: leading and secondary roles were distributed equally, and works were chosen to facilitate this system. Jean-Marc Larrue observes that "joining the group was a little like joining a religious order" in the commitment expected by all participants: each cast member attended every rehearsal, which entailed rigorous practice and repetition of all dialogue, music, movement, and dance.[48] In 1968, Romanian-born composer Eli Rubenstein joined the group, and he would collaborate with Wasserman to compose and arrange songs for the next quarter century. Until that point, music had comprised individual songs or background accompaniment; now, it assumed prominence in large-scale performances. The first of Rubenstein's performances, *A Shtetl Wedding* (1969), featured fourteen songs especially composed for the play – solos, duets, and choral pieces for a cast of over fifty – as well as carefully choreographed crowd scenes. After popular success and rave reviews from critics, Wasserman and Rubinstein created other ambitious musical comedies based on classic works of Yiddish literature: *The Sages of Chelm* (1970), *Benjamin III* (1971), and *The Little Shoemakers* (1976). These were staged to critical acclaim, repeatedly revived, toured internationally, and served to enhance the theatre's reputation. Wasserman adapted works by other Yiddish writers and also collaborated with living writers, including Montrealers Shimshen Dunsky, Mordecai Husid, and M.M. Shaffir. Her plays dealt with contemporary social issues such as immigration and family relationships. She established a special relationship with Nobel Prize laureate Isaac Bashevis Singer and produced singular dramatic adaptions of his works.[49] By the late 1970s, Wasserman was offering after-school programming in Children and Youth Drama groups held in Yiddish at the Saidye Bronfman Centre and was proposing the revival of a free-standing youth arm of the Theatre under the name Young Actors for Young Audience (YAYA).[50]

Although the existence of ethnic-language theatre was not unique among Canadian immigrants during this period, Wasserman's Yiddish theatre stands out because of the active and enduring involvement of the younger generation. Alexandra Pritz's 1977 study of Ukrainian theatre offers an instructive comparison. Ukrainian theatre professionals who arrived in Canada after the war translated their experience and energy into amateur theatre in that language. Several Ukrainian groups in Toronto, Winnipeg, and Edmonton in the 1950s shared actors and resources, and had repertoires that included plays written both in Ukraine and in Canada, alongside newer works of

world theatre translated into Ukrainian.[51] However, unlike Wasserman's theatre, the Ukrainian community theatre did not reach out to
youth raised in Canada, who lacked adequate knowledge of the language. The absence of an estranged generation of younger speakers
within a community-based theatre led to a decline in Ukrainian-
language theatre, along with a concurrent and increasing emphasis on
dance and song. Pritz concludes: "The loss of the Ukrainian language
was reflected more strongly in Ukrainian theatre than any other form
of cultural expression."[52] In contrast, the DWYT entered its heyday during a weakening of Yiddish-language continuity and performance,
both locally and abroad. By the 1960s, a formerly flourishing Yiddish
commercial theatre scene had virtually disappeared worldwide, yet
Wasserman's theatre developed alongside – and in connection with –
a nascent Québécois theatre. In the 1960s, Wasserman sought out the
technical support of Gratien Gélinas (1909–1999) – widely considered to be the founder of contemporary Québécois theatre – and he
became a lifelong colleague and friend. Among her commissioned
translations was a highly acclaimed production of Montreal playwright Michel Tremblay's *Les belles-sœurs* in 1992.[53]

Several factors placed Wasserman's theatre in a unique position to
attract young people raised in Canada during the 1960s to 1970s.
Muriel Gold's 1972 thesis, which compares three Montreal theatres,
outlines the philosophy and the primary objectives for the group: (a)
to preserve the Yiddish language in Montreal, (b) to build an audience
for Yiddish theatre, (c) to develop the imagination 'on a wide scale
through freeing the body' through a variety of exercises, (d) to develop the child's inner resources which will lead him [*sic*] to an understanding and love of theatre.[54] These goals integrated Wasserman's
youth-oriented vision with a commitment to developing the potential of all of her students on individual as well as collective levels in
several ways. First, Wasserman deliberately conducted her drama sessions in an inclusive and informal environment, with a focus on the
young actors themselves rather than the outcome. Second, Wasserman's energy and vision encouraged voluntary participation by a
cadre of self-selected youth who had been exposed to Yiddish at
home, as well as through the local cultural milieu. Third, the theatre
performed a broad repertoire that included works by living writers,
thereby exposing the participants to contemporary Yiddish culture in
a meaningful and interactive manner. Fourth, the theatre was supported by the broader community and its institutions, notably the

Jewish Public Library, Jewish schools, and the Saidye Bronfman Cultural Centre. Moreover, the theatre was embraced by local audiences, both Yiddish-speaking and non-Yiddish speaking.

The DWYT played a significant role in the perpetuation and promotion of Yiddish language and culture in Canada. In recognition, Wasserman was awarded the Jewish community's Performing Arts Award (1972) with the following words: "Dora Wasserman and her Yiddish Drama Group productions have possibly done more to revive interest in Yiddish and the Yiddish theatre than almost any other single individual or group in Montreal."[55] She would also go on to receive the Order of Canada, the Order of Quebec, and a Masques Award for Lifetime Achievement from the Académie québécoise du théâtre. In 2019, a memorial plaque to mark the centenary of her birth was erected in the Dora Wasserman Woods, situated in the park across from the theatre. It reads: "Dora Wasserman led the fight to preserve Yiddish culture in Montreal and built tolerance and understanding between communities, something we need more than ever."[56]

Most significantly for the purposes of this book, Wasserman's theatre helped to shape a generation of youth committed to Yiddish as a living language. Her innovative projects amounted to no less than a cultural imperative in their commitment to, and successful promotion of, the continuity of Yiddish among a younger, Canadian-born generation.[57] The theatre supported Yiddish usage and fluency, confidence among its members, and a strong and abiding sense of Yiddish as a vital, living language. There is significant overlap between the participants in Wasserman's theatre and the young people who mobilized to inaugurate a radically new model for transmission that came to be known as Yugntruf, which I discuss in depth below. A 1971 article by Chana (Anna) Fishman Gonshor in the *Yugntruf* (Youth for Yiddish) journal underlines the significance of the DWYT. Fishman Gonshor recalls the founding of the theatre group some fifteen years earlier and points to its current incarnation with over forty members, all "united by a passion for Yiddish and the Yiddish theatre." She ascribes the group's success to several factors: Dora Wasserman's utter dedication; the maturing of the original children's group into young professionals (lawyers, teachers, engineers, architects) who remained strongly dedicated to the theatre; and the support of Yiddish secular school activists. Fishman Gonshor identified Wasserman's remarkable gift for innovation in finding a suitable repertoire for the theatre, with the most recent performances playing to packed houses that included university students with an interest in Yiddish. The DWYT, according to Fishman Gonshor, "is not only an institution where young Jews can experience the Yiddish theatre. It has emerged from, and influences, the renaissance of Yiddish cultural consciousness in North America."[58] This and other articles in the *Yugntruf* journal dedicated to the topic of the DWYT or that mention the DWYT underline its significance in shaping a generation of youth committed to Yiddish that translated directly into youth-led activism.

YUGNTRUF AND YOUTH ACTIVISM

Founded by a group of teenagers and young adults in the summer of 1964, Yugntruf (Call of Youth/Youth for Yiddish) developed as a grassroots movement under the leadership of the North American-raised generation that came of age in the 1960s and 1970s. Its founders and members resisted dominant ideological trends that relegated Yiddish to the sidelines as relic of the immigrant generation. Yugntruf marked a sharp break with the past as those involved were largely not fluent, and had to make a conscious effort to speak Yiddish to their contemporaries. Although its primary sphere of influence would be New York – the world centre of secular Yiddish activity due to the size of its Jewish community – a number of its key leaders were born and raised in Canada.[59] Its activities would encompass gatherings, campaigns, and annual conferences, as well as an enduring Yiddish literary journal produced by and for youth. Yugntruf resembled movements for other endangered languages more broadly: it was spearheaded by intellectuals, it was uncompromising in its call to speak Yiddish, and its journal was highbrow and contained much discussion of the language question.

Yugntruf did not emerge ex nihilo. The movement built upon the activism of its European predecessors dating to the 1908 Czernowitz Conference. It was also inspired by an earlier incarnation of an American movement by the same name, which was active immediately after the Holocaust. The Yugntruf membership of the 1940s was raised in Yiddish and hoped to counteract the decline of the language.[60] Its journal of the same name was edited by the young Uriel Weinreich (1926–67), who would in his early twenties author a textbook geared towards American youth, *College Yiddish*, and go on to become a pioneering linguist and scholar of the language.[61] In contrast, the 1960s Yugntruf spoke to a generation whose connection to Yiddish as a spoken language was far more tenuous. It emerged as one of several Jewish countercultural movements in the 1960s such as the Havurah movement and Neo-Hasidism.[62]

At the helm of Yugntruf in the 1960s were leaders who drew on interconnected strands promoting Yiddish continuity: families where Yiddish was spoken and valued among multiple generations, often in tandem with an adherence to an ideological movement; attendance at secular schools and summer camps where Yiddish formed part of the curriculum; participatory activities involving Yiddish, such as theatre. The created language spaces they constituted represented a merger of the Eastern European revolutionary movements of their parents with the North American counterculture of the time. Prominent among the transplanted European movements was the Bund, whose activists worked to create transnational networks that promoted ideological and cultural continuity to the next generation; one example is Camp Hemshekh, which was attended by a majority of the founding members of Yugntruf. But Yugntruf also stood apart from such initiatives, founded for youth by their parents. In contrast, Yugntruf was spearheaded and directed by their North American-raised children, who would strive to revitalize Yiddish explicitly for their own generation. Within a Yiddish world that was religiously and politically fragmented, the non-partisan Yugntruf transcended ideological lines: secular, Conservative, and Orthodox; Zionist and leftist.

Yugntruf began as the brainchild of sixteen-year-old Montrealer David Roskies (born 1948), today a professor of Yiddish and Hebrew literature. Like so many in his youth activist cohort, Roskies grew up steeped in Yiddish. He recalls the strong interconnections between pre-Holocaust Europe and his parents' adopted home in Canada, which cemented the family's strong connection to the Yiddish language after they arrived in Montreal.[63] For Roskies, the Yidishe Folkshule and Yiddish theatre offered two essential sites for Yiddish continuity in addition to the home. Until grade seven, he received full-day education where the Jewish Studies curriculum was conducted in Yiddish; he then continued his education at the Yidishe Folkshule supplementary high school (*mitlshule*) three times a week. Roskies's education imbued him with a rich knowledge of Yiddish civilization that encompassed its history, literature, traditions of song and folklore, and language. In addition, from the age of thirteen until he left for university four years later, Roskies took part in a half a dozen productions with Dora Wasserman's drama group; he would attribute his ease as a public speaker in Yiddish within Yugntruf to that training. Three thick scrapbooks documenting his performances and achievements through his teen years – ranging from newspaper clippings to correspondence with community leaders – reveal a steadfast commitment to Yiddish performance and activism.[64]

Looking back, Roskies outlines the factors that led to the creation of Yugntruf:

> So, I'm now fifteen years old, and I'm beginning to see that there are other forces out there, much more dynamic, and that Yiddish culture really is in crisis, and it's obvious demographically. There are no new writers appearing. The average age of the people at these [Yiddish literary] gatherings is sixty plus. Whenever I would go to a Yiddish cultural event, me and my friend Khaskl would be the only young people in the audience. So, when I was sixteen, I started a Yiddish youth movement. I won't belabour the point, but it was a quixotic but very brave effort to revive Yiddish culture, and it was part of the youth revolution. We were beginning to understand that we had the possibility of changing the world.[65]

A pivotal experience in Holocaust commemoration served as an impetus for Roskies's activism. When he was fifteen, his parents took him to an event marking Holocaust Remembrance Day (19 April) which featured two speakers from New York: poet Yankev Glashteyn in Yiddish, and journalist Shmuel Margoshes in English. Roskies was incensed: Everyone else in the room had grey hair and he was the only young person, so why use English? Roskies wrote a typewritten letter of complaint, in English, to the head of the Canadian Jewish Congress cultural committee expressing his outrage at the decision to introduce English in order to attract young people. The experience seeded his vision: "Make Yiddish young again. Put Yiddish back where it belonged, into the mouths of people who could stand up and fight."[66] Within a year, this concept would become a reality at a special Yiddish-language commemoration of the Warsaw Ghetto Uprising that Yugntruf co-organized.

Roskies evinced a strong commitment to Yiddish as a teenager. A private letter he wrote at fifteen to Michael Astour, then professor of Yiddish and Russian at Brandeis University, in response to his article on Jewish territorialism appeared in the New York journal *Afn shvel* (On the Threshold). Here Roskies expressed his appreciation of the journal, which he had read cover to cover, and the clarity of its Yiddish. He conveyed a desire to create a meaningful Jewish life in the Diaspora, with Yiddish being very dear to his heart. Yiddish was his mother tongue, the language of his ancestors, a flexible language with a vast literature. Assimilation marked a constant concern, wrote Roskies, and he was distraught by the indifference of parents failing to provide their children with a Jewish education even as centuries of Yiddish language and culture were ebbing away.[67] Astour, in turn, praised Roskies's dedication to Yiddish linguist Mordkhe Schaechter (1927–2007), who mailed Roskies a volume of rules for the standardized Yiddish spelling devised by YIVO in the 1930s.[68] Roskies became an ardent promoter of modern Yiddish orthography, which he had not been taught in school.

Roskies recalls the beginnings of Yugntruf as an "aha moment." From his position as a professor at New York's Jewish Teachers' Seminary, Schaechter recommended that one of his students, Gabriel (Gavi) Trunk – a young Bundist and Camp Hemshekh camper – contact Roskies during an upcoming visit to Montreal. The two met and decided "on a lark" to speak Yiddish together: "So we started speaking Yiddish to each other, and it was the first time in my life that I'd ever spoken Yiddish horizontally, rather than vertically. I never spoke Yiddish to my siblings – only to my parents, only to older people, and only to my teachers." The transformative visit prompted a breakthrough: a vision of building a community of peers with whom he could speak exclusively in Yiddish, despite the challenges posed by a lack of vocabulary to talk about everyday life or subjects of interest such as sports. He recalls the effort associated with gaining the necessary facility in the language: "So the first hurdle was learning to speak Yiddish as my lingua franca among my peers."[69]

Yugntruf soon moved into action. Following the visit, Roskies penned a letter to Trunk – the first Yiddish letter he had ever written to someone his own age – which suggested that they establish a Yiddish magazine for young people. Trunk read the letter out loud to the students in his class at the Teachers' Seminary, and Schaechter encouraged the class to reach out to Yiddish-speaking young people worldwide. In continuity with the activism of a generation earlier, Schaechter also suggested that they adopt the name *Yugntruf*, the title of the magazine that Uriel Weinreich had published fifteen years earlier. Yugntruf's "call to action" drafted by Trunk's class was published "in every Yiddish newspaper in the free-world," and further disseminated through the networks of Camp Hemshekh. With Roskies at the helm in Montreal and Trunk in New York, Yugntruf's leadership comprised teenagers from Yiddish-speaking homes; with the exception of Roskies, a majority were Bundists with strong connections to Camp Hemshekh. Yugntruf chapters were organized in Montreal, New York, Philadelphia, and Toronto.

From its inception, Yugntruf presented a paradigm shift in Yiddish transmission: led by North American raised youth, non-partisan and international in scope, and forward-looking. Correspondence David Roskies penned to the older generation underlined the project as a youth initiative. In April of 1964, Roskies produced a letter in Yiddish appealing to individuals worldwide whom he knew to be "strongly interested in Jewish/Yiddish issues and problems" where he proposed the model of a journal produced by a core group of youth from Montreal and New York; rather than seeking support or guidance, his request was for the names and contact information for any potential contributors aged fourteen to nineteen.[70] The response was immediate and enthusiastic. In a letter penned to Avrom Sutzkever, editor of the prestigious Tel Aviv literary journal *Di goldene keyt* (The Golden Chain) in early June, Roskies reported the Yugntruf mobilization efforts had resulted in dozens of letters from young people worldwide; he had further secured contact information for youth in Venezuela, France, and Brazil.[71]

The group's leadership, working in tandem in Montreal and New York, soon undertook wide-ranging campaigns to implement their vision. In his announcement of the imminent formation of the Montreal chapter, Roskies underlined the youth orientation of the journal in a collective "we" voice. The essence of his message was that, given increasing talk about the downfall of the Yiddish language, we, the youth, cannot wait for our parents; we have a simple but important plan: Yugntruf, both a journal and a movement. Roskies noted that since Montreal occupied a prominent position in the contemporary Yiddish world, it behoved the city to show what was possible. In this spirit, an inaugural meeting of Yugntruf would take place on 21 June at the Yidishe Folkshule, with the only adult present to be the writer Melech Ravitch, who would serve as the group's mentor.[72] The New York Yugntruf chapter also held its first meeting on 21 June. The New York group met with Uriel Weinreich, who offered guidance based on his own experience editing the earlier incarnation of the *Yugntruf* journal, as well as Mordkhe Schaechter, who would become the group's mentor and advocate.

The New York group under Trunk's leadership also prepared a letter addressed to young people worldwide asking them to become partners of the journal and to publicize the project, and calling for submissions.[73] Meanwhile, the Montreal and New York chapters divided up the tasks surrounding outreach and promotion and filled executive positions. As part of this process, they debated ideological questions entirely in Yiddish, and some swore oaths to speak only in Yiddish amongst themselves.[74]

The Yugntruf leadership drafted and disseminated a "call to arms" to some fifty Yiddish newspapers and periodicals worldwide. The announcement, signed by a dozen young people from Montreal and New York, reads:

> The ideological groups of young people being raised in Yiddish across the wide world, which until now have had no fixed address, no connection, and no organization, will be able to assemble around this publication. We aspire for *Yugntruf* to become a gathering site for budding young literary talents and a tribune for young activists and fighters for Yiddish. *Yugntruf* will become the spiritual laboratory where the Yiddish writers of tomorrow will be moulded: the Yiddish editors, cultural activists and readers of tomorrow … We appeal to everyone, common people (*folksmentshn*) and intellectuals, religiously observant and secular, to lend a hand so that this humble beginning will grow into a mighty, international Yiddish youth movement.[75]

From the perspective of its leadership, Yugntruf marked a conscious return of Yiddish continuity to the younger generation. Just as the vanguard of modern Yiddish culture beginning at the end of the nineteenth century – its leading writers, artists, and activists – were people in their teens and twenties, Yugntruf marked a reorientation towards youth in response to a crisis facing Yiddish language and culture. In a dramatic shift, the invitation calls for transnational partnerships outside the ideological schisms that had long plagued the Yiddish world. This radical "call to arms," published whole or in part in dozens of Yiddish newspapers and periodicals worldwide, yielded immediate expressions of support from the European-born generation of writers and activists.

Yugntruf held its founding gathering on 30 August 1964 in the auditorium of the YIVO, New York's foremost scholarly institution for Yiddish. An invitation from the organizing committee had been disseminated two weeks prior and advertised admission at no cost.[76] Some ninety delegates attended, the majority in their teens and primarily from New York, Montreal, and Toronto. The events surrounding the conference expressed the youthful enthusiasm of the fledgling organization. Roskies recalls the Montreal delegation travelling by train, led in song by member Raizel Fishman (Candib); they arrived to find banners in the hall stating, "First commandment – To Speak Yiddish," and "Jews speak Yiddish and Yiddish is beautiful." The militant focus on youth as opposed to the establishment was underlined by rules dictating that only young people had voting or speaking rights at the event; older observers had to request permission to speak, even if they were offering praise and support.

Roskies's opening address, delivered in Yiddish, set the tone for the event: "Who are we? Are we a group of enthusiastic youth who want to publish a journal? Are we a Yiddish youth group that is gathering once a year in New York to have fun at a conference? Are we wild fanatics with impossible ideals? Are we self-aware young people who have taken on a project and are not afraid of the results? Are we really *ready* to roll up our sleeves and get to work? Do we know exactly *what* kind of work we have taken on? Do we feel the enormous burden that lies on our shoulders?" [emphasis in the original] Roskies continued that it was incumbent upon the youth to revitalize the Yiddish language, to fight assimilation, to maintain "our literature, our culture, our identity." He employed revolutionary language – "We have courage, we will fight, we will turn the world upside down! We are not afraid of anyone!" – and then pointedly asked, "But are we really ready?" The goals of creating a journal and an international youth movement must not fail, he said, because the very future of the Yiddish language lay in their hands: "Only we, the youth, can save it, our generation must become the *Yiddish* generation, because there will most certainly not be anyone to follow. We must prepare them but first we must prepare ourselves." Roskies urged the delegates to hold strong in the face of adversity. The small movement would grow, he predicted, with local chapters emerging worldwide with the support of the entire Yiddish-speaking world: "We must not disappoint them, we must not and we will not!" Finally, he called upon the group's members to engage with Yiddish in practical as well as idealistically-oriented tasks: raising funds, gathering subscriptions, advertising, editing, discussing, and thinking. He concluded that the event marked the beginning of "the Yugntruf Epoch, with us as the founders."[77]

The opening address was followed by reports from Yugntruf committees in New York and Montreal, greetings from delegations and well-wishers, and a series of reports about the journal in its planning stages. Further greetings from well-wishers and a presentation of a draft of the Yugntruf constitution were followed by discussion and voting. The day then ended with group singing. Roskies later recalled that eminent linguist Max Weinreich (father of Uriel Weinreich and founder of the YIVO), approached him and urged him to join the ranks of Yiddish scholarship, whereas Roskies's own career plan was to become an avant-garde Yiddish filmmaker.[78] Roskies did ultimately become a scholar of Yiddish and Hebrew literature, but his recollection of the exchange underlines that the objective of Yugntruf was to forge new avenues for a new generation rather than slip into existing models.

Yugntruf's constitution emphasizes the imperative for young people to make deliberate use of the language in speaking, reading, writing, and singing. In ten principles that were reprinted, after extensive discussion, in the second issue of the *Yugntruf* journal, Yiddish is presented as "more than a linguistic means of expression" for its multilingual members: "Yiddish is a symbol of ethnic (*folkish*) identification" that connects them to Jewish life globally. It is an expression of Jewish creativity connecting its speakers to a long history and distinct worldview across all classes. Yugntruf would fight on behalf of the Yiddish language, long maligned by its own speakers and in a time of crisis due to the massive losses of the Holocaust, Soviet persecution, and the indifference and self-hatred of millions of Jews. It is up to the youth to take up arms and inject new vitality into Yiddish. On a practical level, members would be held to extremely high standards in entrenching the language in their lives. Yiddish must form a language of daily speech and writing, not just be reserved for special occasions such as singing at holiday gatherings. As such, Yugntruf members must constantly improve their own Yiddish through study and reading as part of a lifelong commitment. They must practice what they preach by speaking Yiddish with everyone who knows the language and routinely reading Yiddish publications. They must take an active role in Yiddish life, including Yugntruf and other organizations, by giving their time, energy, and money for the common good, with the motto, "*di yidishe yugnt far dem yidishn folk*" (The Jewish Youth for the Jewish People).[79] For Roskies, this process included painstakingly altering his elocution , notably the Yiddish "r" sound, by practicing in front of a mirror after he was criticized for his English-sounding pronunciation.[80]

Three months after the organization's founding conference, the first
volume of the quarterly *Yugntruf: Alveltlekher yidisher yugnt-zhurnal*
(International Yiddish Youth Journal) was published by a committee
jointly located in Montreal, New York, and Philadelphia. The journal
is elegantly produced, with high-quality, typeset articles, using a Standard Yiddish that is clear, idiomatic, and spelled in a consistent fash-
ion. The contributions from across the Americas and Europe include
essays on the present and future of Yiddish, Yiddish film, Yiddish literature, and contemporary political life; letters to the editor; original art-
work; a crossword puzzle; and announcements of marriages between
members. A close examination of the inaugural issues reveals what
amounted to a revolution, in tandem with other militant youth-led
movements of the 1960s, both in content and rhetoric. *Yugntruf* began
with a strong opening statement by its editor, Leybl Zilbershtrom,
titled "*Mir zaynen do!*" (We are Here!). Zilbershtrom expresses in
strongly worded language that the group must put personal ambitions
aside and work toward the future to reverse what he terms a "persistent
wheel of pessimism": because people know less Yiddish, they speak it
less, they write it less, in a perpetual cycle of decline. What is required
is a commitment from youth not only to advocate on behalf of Yiddish
but to speak the language themselves.[81] Several of the young writers
take a critical stance towards the older generation: a voice from Brazil
challenges the idea that the younger generation is responsible for the
current state of Yiddish; on the contrary, the author argues, the ani-
mosity towards the language comes from their elders.[82] An article by
an American writer blames the older generation for young people's
lack of immersion in Yiddish; he castigates in particular newer immigrants who neglected to speak Yiddish with their children in order to
acculturate them more easily and, in the process, lost the opportunity
to build a linguistic bond between the generations.[83]

This inaugural issue of the journal indicates that the reach of Yugntruf was wide from the outset, both among the youth and the older
generation. The Canadians included active members of the Dora
Wasserman Yiddish Theatre as well as a Camp Hemshekh representative. Several Jewish organizations offered subsidies, office space, and
mailing lists; Camp Hemshekh offered technical support; over two
dozen Yiddish-language journals and newspapers in the United
States, Poland, Mexico, Tel Aviv, Argentina, and Montreal published
articles about or reprinted the text of Yugntruf's inaugural announcement.[84] Subsequent annual gatherings held in New York attracted

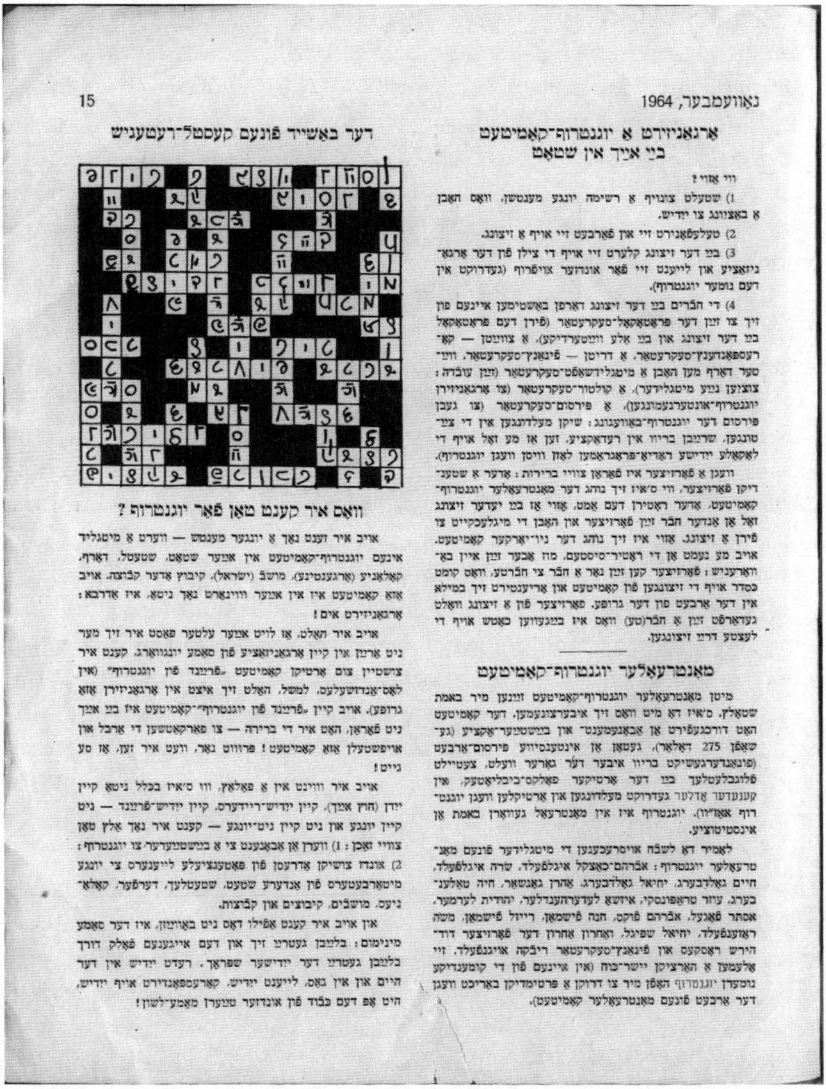

15　　　　　　　　　　　　　　　　נאָוועמבער, 1964

דער באַשײד פֿונעם קעסטל-רעטעניש　　　　אַרגאַניזירט אַ יוגנטרוף-קאַמיטעט בײַ אײַך אין שטאָט

וואָס איר קענט טאָן פֿאַר יוגנטרוף ?

מאָנטרעאַלער יוגנטרוף-קאַמיטעט

Figure 3.1　Page from the inaugural issue of the *Yugntruf* journal, November 1964. This page of the journal includes sections on how organize a local Yugntruf chapter, the activities of the Montreal committee, what readers can do for Yugntruf, and the answers to the previous crossword puzzle.

growing numbers of participants, who reported on the initiatives of their Yugntruf committees and debated the principles of the organization: for example, whether activities could take place in a language other than Yiddish (they voted no) and if the group required an age limit (they voted yes).[85] Activities organized under the auspices of Yugntruf included performance groups – theatre, choir, and dance – for young people, Yiddish forums to discuss issues in Jewish life, the creation of special programs for Yiddish clubs, a network of international pen pals, and a correspondence course for advanced study in Yiddish.[86] By its second year, Yugntruf chapters were active worldwide, as far afield as Sydney, Australia.[87]

Montreal occupies an important place in the history of Yugntruf as the site of its first active local committee. In the month leading up the appearance of the first *Yugntruf* journal in November of 1964, the treasurer of the local committee, Rivka Augenfeld, circulated a Yiddish letter to solicit financial support for the project in local circles. The letter opens: "Yiddish and Yiddish culture are in a troubled state. The only hope lies in our hands. We, the youth, are the Yiddish speakers of tomorrow, the Yiddish readers of tomorrow, the Yiddish cultural activists (*kultur-tuer*) of tomorrow. We have come together under the common goal to maintain and promote Yiddish and Yiddish culture across the world." The letter pointedly concludes, "Yugntruf was not founded for older folks but rather for the young because the youth represent our survival, our future."[88] A report from the committee in the inaugural issue of the journal expressed pride at the group's accomplishments: with over twenty active members, the group had raised substantial funds and undertaken ambitious local and international publicity campaigns.[89] The committee's report in the subsequent issue reported seven meetings held in the homes of members which combined planning and publicity campaigns with guest speakers from Montreal and elsewhere. Topics included Yiddish in Brazil, a lecture by McGill professor (and Roskies's sister) Ruth R. Wisse on Yiddish literature, and David Roskies's presentation on standardized Yiddish spelling. A symposium titled "What is Yidishkayt?" yielded a heated debate from three perspectives: religious, nationalist, and cultural/secular. The group also hosted a hootenanny with communal singing.[90] These activities indicate the varied domains – scholarly, activist, cultural – through which the young members actively connected with Yiddish in their lives. These created language spaces merged the legacies of Yiddish with their own current interests.

Finally, the Montreal chapter organized a special youth commemoration of the Warsaw Ghetto Uprising in partnership with the Montreal Jewish Youth Conference. The well-attended evening featured ten young people reciting a script of memoirs, resistance poetry, and modern lamentations under Roskies's direction. As several of the youth – Bryna Wasserman, Chana Fishman (Anna Fishman Gonshor), Roskies, and others – were members of the Dora Wasserman Yiddish theatre, the bulk of the material was in Yiddish.[91] The event brought Roskies's original impetus for youth-oriented Yiddish culture full circle.

The *Yugntruf* journal indicates close ties between the DWYT and youth activists in the 1960s and 1970s, and the significance the young people attributed to Dora Wasserman's model of fostering living Yiddish through performance. As discussed above, one of Yugntruf's most active members, Chayele Thalenberg, positioned the DWYT as a vibrant site for youth engagement with Yiddish.[92] In the special 1971 issue of *Yugntruf* dedicated to Yiddish theatre in America, the DWYT features prominently, including Chana Fishman's article that situates the theatre within a "renaissance of Yiddish cultural consciousness in North America."[93] Roskies's editorial, signed under the pseudonym "A. Montrealer" and titled "Der amerikaner yidisher teater: vos tut men?" (The American Yiddish Theatre: What Can Be Done?), discusses the decline of Yiddish theatre in other North American centres, even in its former hub of New York City, and calls for its renewal among youth, concluding: "The fate of the new Yiddish theatre now lies in our hands!"[94] These articles demonstrate the core of the movement: engagement with Yiddish as a site of vibrant creativity and empowerment. [95]

Responses to Yugntruf in the transnational Yiddish milieu spotlight a widening gap between the prewar and postwar generations of activists. Roskies would look back some fifty years later and observe: "On the one hand, we felt that we were the progeny and the future, and that we were undertaking the revitalization of the Yiddish language"; on the other hand, "we had witnessed the *khurbn-beys-yidish* (destruction of Yiddish), and it was clear that everything was going under. Not only because of the collapse of the Yiddish cultural milieu established by the European-born Eastern European immigrant generation but because the older generation did not believe that there would be posterity." Despite praise for Yugntruf, the European-born generation believed themselves to be the last before the end of modern Yiddish culture and did not believe in the capacity of the youth to intercede effectively before all was lost.[96]

While naysayers would continue to question the value of its American-born brand of youth-led Yiddishism in subsequent decades, Yugntruf became an enduring hub for newcomers to the

Yiddish language. Yugntruf formed part of expanding Yiddish activity in the late 1960s and early 1970s in the context of renewed debate about the place of Yiddish, this time with a focus on *why* versus *whether* Yiddish would retain its earlier centrality to Canadian Jewish life. As discussed below, Yugntruf was on the agenda of the National Conference on Yiddish in 1969, which meeting would result in the creation of a system of Yiddish committees under the aegis of the Canadian Jewish Congress, including participation by founding members of Yugntruf (David Roskies, Raizel Fishman, Chana Fishman, and Rivka Augenfeld).[97]

As an example of the prevailing discourse of the time, a 1972 article in the *Canadian Jewish Chronicle* featured two Toronto-based writers from different generations presenting opposing perspectives on the decline of Yiddish. The negative stance was offered by the journalist and scholar Jacob (Yankev) Beller, a member of the European-born prewar generation who blamed those who championed a Yiddish devoid of Jewish content. He asked, "Where can a Yiddishist today make use of Yiddish?" Using Yugntruf as his example, he argued: "It is the youth themselves upon whom the Yiddishists have laid such hopes who best expose the emptiness and hollowness of the secular-Yiddish camp, with their deep interest in and search for the fundamental principles of Jewishness."[98] A positive stance was offered by Victor Topper, co-founder of Toronto's Bialik Hebrew Day School, who discussed the rediscovery of Yiddish among Jewish youth, including in university courses, in what he termed a "survival and revival." Topper pointed to the growth of Bialik, where Yiddish was being taught as an integral part of the curriculum alongside Hebrew. He also highlighted the regional committees for Yiddish that had evolved under the aegis of the Canadian Jewish Congress in the 1970s, whose local events – lectures, concerts, and plays – were attended by people of all ages, including "teenagers and young married couples." He concluded, "The youth of Canada want Yiddish and need Yiddish so that they may drink from the cup of their almost forgotten heritage."[99] Topper represents the viewpoint of a generation raised in Canada that participated in Yiddish activity, and subsequently created opportunities for meaningful engagement for their own Canadian-born children. It is to the activities under the aegis of the Canadian Jewish Congress that this chapter now turns.

YIDDISH COMMUNITY ACTIVISM
OF THE 1960S AND 1970S:
THE CANADIAN JEWISH CONGRESS

The 1960s marked a crossroads for the continuity of Yiddish in the Canadian Jewish community. The Anglo-Jewish press expressed tensions between two perspectives: efforts to transmit Yiddish as a distinct culture to the Canadian-raised children of immigrants on the one hand, and the inevitability of its absorption into North American life on the other. An example can be found on a single page in the *Canadian Jewish Chronicle* in the fall of 1960. Here one article notes that Montreal's Jewish Peretz Shule opened its fundraising campaign with increasing registration and a wide-ranging cultural program for children that featured courses in Yiddish.[100] Next to it is a satirical commentary titled "Yiddish Culture Marches On," which finds evidence for Yiddish growth in the use of the word *chutzpah* by an American politician.[101]

Activists noted with alarm the widening gap between European-born, prewar Yiddish speakers and the younger generation raised in Canada. A Canadian report on the 1963 Symposium for Yiddish in Paris under the headline "Yiddish in Our Days" opened with a series of questions: "How many Jews still use Yiddish as their daily vernacular? How many read Yiddish literature? Is there a future for Yiddish?" The author noted the lack of young people at the gathering, suggesting that because Yiddish was not being taught in mainstream schools, few children were learning to speak it.[102] In a report on the symposium three years later, the author again noted the absence of youth representation: "Nevertheless, there is a revival of interest in Yiddish. The tragedy is in the wide gap between the revived interest and the actual level of knowledge and use ... Yiddish cannot be carried by sentimentality, nostalgia and the diligent study of experts. At the same time, would anybody suggest Yiddish schools in this day and age, while Hebrew is the most vital – some say the only – link between Israel and the Diaspora and the language of the Jewish faith?"[103] Canadian youth were increasingly identified as a potential force for Yiddish continuity and revival. For example, in an article published in 1970, Ben Lappin, a Canadian Jewish Congress official, observed the decline of secular Yiddish culture and called for a youth-led renaissance rather than a "piecemeal rehabilitation" led by older members of the Canadian Jewish community.[104] This discourse would feature prominently in the 1960s and 1970s.

Within a climate of uncertainty about the continuity of the language, a community of seasoned activists of the older generation began to band together to consolidate and coordinate their efforts through the Canadian Jewish Congress (CJC). Founded in the wake of World War One and reconvened in 1934 as Canada's national Jewish organization, the CJC aimed to represent all elements of the community. In the 1960s, the CJC offered a nation-wide platform to support both Yiddish and Hebrew as cornerstones of Jewish life. For example, the CJC expressed a commitment to supporting education in both languages by subsidizing teacher training in Montreal's United Jewish Teachers' Seminary.[105] However, as Yiddish usage in the mainstream declined and Hebrew solidified, everincreasing attention was given to Yiddish.

During this period, Ruth R. Wisse began to influence the direction and scope of the Yiddish-oriented activities of the CJC. A recent graduate of literary studies at McGill University, she had taken on the role of press officer of the CJC, which included publishing its *Bulletin* and putting together its communications and conferences. Her education in both the English and Yiddish milieus allowed her to move fluidly and serve as a bridge between them. She established friendships with major literary figures in both languages and brought them together; for example, during Avrom Sutzkever's inaugural North American visit in 1959, which took place in Montreal, she arranged for him to meet English-language modernist poets Louis Dudek (1918–2001) as well as A.M. Klein. Sutzkever encouraged Wisse to enrol in graduate studies in Yiddish literature at Columbia University in 1960. As a professor, she would go on to champion the inclusion of Yiddish literature at McGill University as well as its translation into English.[106]

The CJC Plenary Sessions passed multiple resolutions pertaining to Yiddish and implemented them via its officers. A 1962 resolution recognizing "the fundamental importance for Jewish Survival of strengthening and fostering the Jewish languages, Hebrew and Yiddish" contained five elements: the establishment of university chairs in Yiddish and Hebrew language and culture; the inclusion of both Hebrew and Yiddish in every public program held under the auspices of the CJC, the CJC official letterhead, and every issue of the *Congress Bulletin*; the CJC sponsorship of cultural programs in Hebrew and Yiddish; and the training of secretaries and stenographers in the Yiddish language. The final resolution read: "We further urge the National Executive of Congress to take whatever other measures may be necessary to ensure that the two Jewish languages, which are the repositories of the greatest values which our people has created, shall become better known and more widely utilized both within the framework of the CJC and within the Jewish Community as a whole."[107] At the 1968 plenary session of the CJC, a resolution on Hebrew and Yiddish included nine points, of which all but one pertained directly to Yiddish. These called for the inclusion of Yiddish in all CJC communications and publications; the creation of a Yiddish column in the CJC *Bulletin*; the publication of a Yiddish literary magazine; the organization of a National Yiddish Conference; and support for Yiddish theatre, choral, and dance groups. According to the plenary report, delegates from across the country – notably Montreal, Toronto, and Winnipeg – urged the creation of a "special department of Yiddish within the confines of the Congress structure. It was felt that strenuous efforts must be made to encourage younger people to become acquainted with the rich Yiddish heritage of literature and culture."[108] The CJC oriented its activities towards youth both in terms of support for programming and the inclusion of younger voices in its gatherings.

In May of 1969, a first event was held in Montreal to "study the problem of the Yiddish language in this country." The intergenerational event, which was the brainchild of Joseph Kage, national director of the Jewish Immigrant Aid Services (JIAS) and a scholar of Jewish immigration to Canada,[109] brought together eight hundred delegates from across Canada as well as representatives from fraternal organizations, Zionist organizations, women's groups, and schools. The wide-ranging programming featured a popular lecture in English by Maurice Samuel (author of the 1971 American bestseller *In Praise of Yiddish*) and a "literary oratorical" about the Yiddish language written by Montreal poet Melech Ravitch and performed under the direction of Dora Wasserman. The event featured workshops for youth groups, educators, religious leaders, and writers to discuss recommendations for advanced Yiddish education. The participants included a diverse group of young and seasoned writers: Anglo-Jewish writer Adele Wiseman and Yiddish writers Chava Rosenfarb and Rokhl Korn; teachers from Montreal's secular Jewish school system such as Yaakov Zipper, Shloime Wiseman, Leib Tencer, and Shimshen Dunsky; and McGill professor Ruth R. Wisse, as well as several community rabbis. Also present was Yugntruf founder, David Roskies.[110]

The event was positioned within broader cultural movements in the province of Quebec. While the province's Jewish community was his-

torically excluded from the French-Catholic milieu, secularization in
Quebec's Quiet Revolution of the 1960s repositioned language rather
than religion as a defining feature of Québécois identity. The conference keynote address was delivered in English by Quebec's minister of
culture, Jean-Noël Tremblay, a vocal nationalist, who expressed "affini-
ties between the fight of French Canadians and the Jewish people for
the preservation of their respective national cultures," and promised
that the "Quebec government will cooperate in future with the Jewish
authorities in all their cultural endeavours."[111] This discourse of rapprochement dates to the 1950s, when, after a history of estrangement
between the province's Jews and French Catholic majority, Québécois
and Jewish groups piloted new ventures to foster cultural exchange
and understanding, including organized dialogue.[112]

One concrete outcome of the event was the creation of the CJC
National Committee on Yiddish, whose dual objectives were to
serve as a hub for Yiddish activity in Canada and to support the
activities of its three regional committees – Western, Central, and
Eastern – in the strengthening of Yiddish culture.[113] The committee
would form a focal point for Yiddish into the 1970s under the leadership of its chair, Polish-born Arthur Lermer, while its chief advocate for the next three decades would be Montreal activist Sara
Mlotek Rosenfeld. At a second national conference held in Montreal in November of the same year, Kage shared a working paper in
which he made a number of proposals. These included a direct
appeal to youth, the publication of a regular Yiddish column in the
country's Jewish periodicals, the creation of educational materials,
the inclusion of Yiddish courses in public schools, the introduction
of "Yiddish themes" in television and radio programs, the inclusion
of Yiddish speakers at conferences, and convening an international
conference on Yiddish and Jewish culture.[114] Here one finds all the
characteristics of the activism of the 1960s: it increasingly took place
on an institutional level, it identified Yiddish as a core component
of Jewish identity, and it attempted to appeal to young people by
proposing courses, pedagogical materials, and other meaningful
programming for youth.

The CJC plenaries of the 1970s promoted Yiddish among younger
people in educational as well as performative contexts. The 1971 Plenary Assembly included resolutions pertaining to the production of
Yiddish textbooks and the inclusion of Yiddish language and culture
in the curricula of Jewish educational institutions.[115] The 1972 session

reported extensive Yiddish cultural activity already in place, as supported by the committee's national and regional offices: pedagogical materials; course development at both high school and university levels; preparation of literary anthologies and biographies of Yiddish writers; and events featuring local and international speakers, theatre productions, film screenings, and Yiddish song and dance.[116] Among the 1974 resolutions specifically geared to promoting Yiddish among the young was "to encourage Yiddish drama groups, choirs and other cultural projects."[117]

In a newspaper article marking five years of the National Committee on Yiddish, Lermer expressed the aspirations of the committee: "While we do not harbour any illusions about reviving Yiddish as a vernacular, the role of Yiddish as a basic component of the plural Jewish culture can hardly be exaggerated."[118] In addition to consolidating all Canadian organizations involved with Yiddish cultural activity, the committee's work included the publication of *Kanader yidisher zaml-bukh/Canadian Jewish Anthology/Anthologie Juive du Canada* (edited by Chaim Spilberg and Yaakov Zipper, 1982), which features poetry, prose, and essays on Canadian Yiddish culture in Yiddish, English, and French. It also sponsored festivals and public events in Toronto and Montreal which drew tens of thousands of spectators. However, the committee's focus, as Lermer indicated, centred on augmenting youth engagement across Canada. Initiatives included pedagogical materials for the schools; integrating Yiddish within summer camp programs through youth group tours; supporting the development of Yiddish theatre in Montreal, Toronto, and Winnipeg; the offer of new Yiddish courses at the University of Toronto as well as Jewish student organizations (e.g. Hillel) and local institutions (the Young Men's Hebrew Association [YMHA]); and ongoing efforts to integrate Yiddish into the curriculum of all Jewish schools. Lermer highlighted the legacy of children's education in the country: "It behoves Canada to be in the forefront, for it was in this country that pioneers laid the foundation for our Jewish school system, particularly in the Folks & Peretz sector. It was they who understood the importance of preserving Yiddish side by side with Hebrew."[119]

While the CJC's National Committee on Yiddish was primarily a project of the pre-Holocaust, European-born generation, its activities intersected in significant ways with the activities of Canadian-raised youth. In particular, initiatives were launched under the aegis of the CJC to support and augment existing projects on the regional level.

These included multiple collaborations between secular Yiddish schools and the Dora Wasserman Yiddish Theatre. For example, in 1974, Montreal's Yiddish Committee coordinated educational programs for children and youth in summer camps across the province. The project was run by Bryna Wasserman – the daughter of Dora Wasserman – and included members who were closely involved with Wasserman's Yiddish theatre.[120] It included twenty trips to sleepover and day camps for a total of forty-three performances, reaching some three thousand children and teenagers. A report considered this highly successful due to the involvement and enthusiasm of the camp counsellors and staff, who in some cases were taught the plays before the performances.[121] One such event presented a Yiddish play ("with English assistance") of a wedding scene with music, singing, and dance that did not require any knowledge of the language. Photos from Pripstein's Camp, a residential camp in rural Quebec whose curriculum included both Hebrew and Yiddish, depict enthusiastic participation by both the actors and campers. In addition to Wasserman's Yiddish Drama Group all donning shirts that said "Yiddish," handmade posters were put up on the walls, reading *Yidish is a tayere zakh* (Yiddish is a precious thing), as well as other slogans.[122]

LEGACIES OF YIDDISH YOUTH ENGAGEMENT

The models that grew out of 1960s and 1970s Canada have left a lasting imprint on the transmission of Yiddish. With the disbanding of the Canadian Jewish Congress in 2011, nationally coordinated cultural activity – including committees for Yiddish – has ceased in Canada; however, local groups continue their activities. Two initiatives to grow out of this period specifically to support Yiddish engagement for and by youth have left lasting legacies: the DWYT and Yugntruf.

The DWYT remains an enduring site for Yiddish continuity in Montreal. Dora Wasserman's daughter, Bryna Wasserman, a participant in the original "Friday Night Group" of the 1950s and a graduate of New York's Tisch School of the Arts in theatre, assumed the role of artistic director of the DWYT from 1998 to 2011. She and subsequent directors continued her mother's tradition of staging innovative plays in Yiddish both in local performances and on international tours, and introduced English and French supertitles in order to reach broader audiences. Members of the theatre coach an increasingly diverse group of actors, including young newcomers with no previous exposure to the language. Edit Kuper (born 1944), a long-time associate of the DWYT as an actress, producer, translator, and promoter, notes the enduring attraction for younger cast members: in addition to the fun of performance and group camaraderie "Yiddish has very special meaning. Yiddish has a history, a link, a grounding. For us, it is the link to all of the generations, link to our past, to our past-past and not in an old-fashioned Hasidic style with the *peyes* and the *shtetl*. It is not only a chance to show their beautiful voices, it is meaningful for them. There is something in the language, the feeling that gets to peoples' hearts, even young people."[123]

The youth wing of the theatre remains an active site for exposing children and youth to Yiddish song and performance. Known as Young Actors for Young Audiences (YAYA), it has since the late 1970s created productions for young people while also reaching out to wider audiences and fostering intercultural understanding. In 2003 it staged a production of *No More Raisins, No More Almonds: Children's Ghetto Songs*, written by child survivor and Jewish educator Batia Bettman to sensitize Canadian youth to the lessons of the Holocaust. The cast of over forty high-school students played in Yiddish (with English and French supertitles) to thousands of their peers across the Montreal region, including Indigenous students at a Mohawk school; the YAYA troupe also toured schools in Toronto and Ottawa in 2007.[124] The play included a "talk back" component for the audiences following the performances to discuss issues raised by the play, such as racism and human rights. YAYA's other productions have included musicals and adaptations of Jewish-themed short stories and picture books, most recently in partnership with PJ Library, founded in December 2005 to produce and distribute Jewish children's books to families. Whereas previously, children who had been involved in YAYA often transferred into the regular theatre, YAYA has also come to function as a freestanding extracurricular activity and after-school programming for school-age children.[125] According to its website: "The YAYA course provides musical theatre training through theatre-based exercises and games from the perspective of Jewish heritage and Yiddish culture. The course focuses on storytelling, building trust within the ensemble, tactic and objective work, and status and character development. The students are introduced to the Yiddish language through song. Based on core Jewish values, the award-winning YAYA program forms the foundation of youth arts education at the Segal

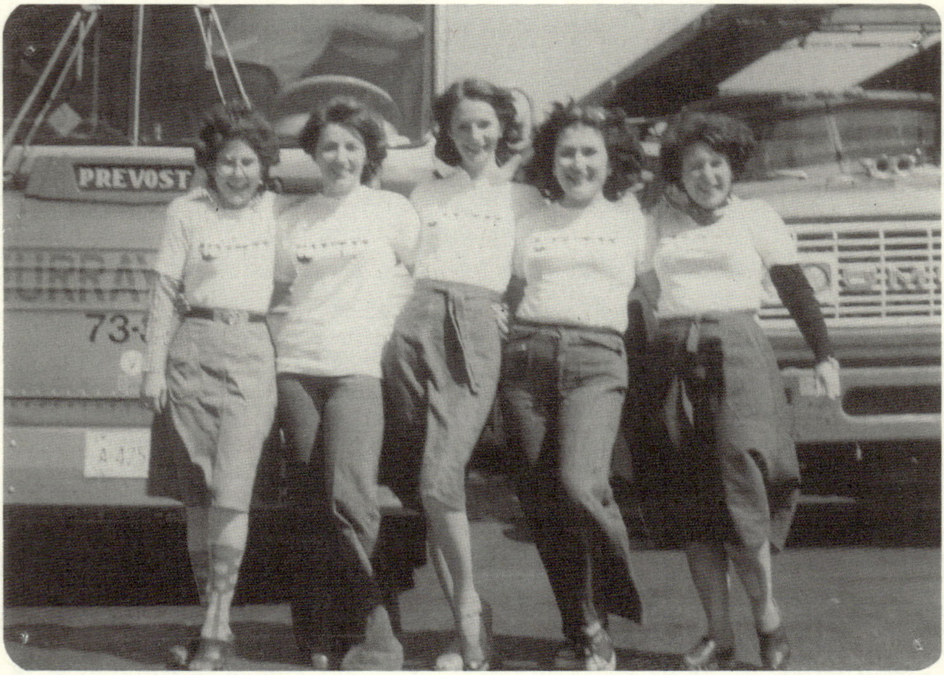
PREVOST

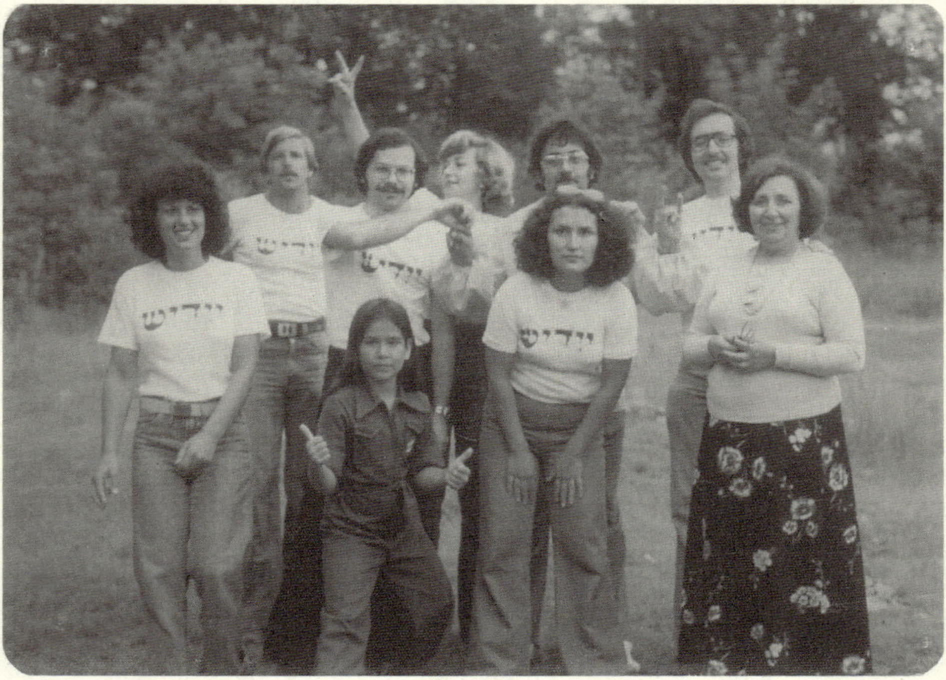
יידיש

Figures 3.2–4 Visit of Dora Wasserman and the Yiddish Drama Group to Pripstein's Camp, Summer 1974

Centre. Founded in the 1950s and inspired by the vision of Dora and Bryna Wasserman, YAYA is the cornerstone of the renowned Dora Wasserman Yiddish Theatre."[126]

The DWYT and YAYA have produced a new generation of leadership, with the YAYA executive including graduates whose parents were also involved. One example is the Fishman Gonshor family, which has been involved with both Montreal Yiddish theatre and formal Yiddish education as teachers and students. The family includes teacher Yena Fishman and her daughter, DWYT member Chana (Anna) Fishman Gonshor, and her family. Gonshor's husband, Aron Gonshor, a long-time member of the DWYT, points to the significance of Wasserman's promotion of performance as an avenue to Yiddish for young people: "This is how we began to live our lives out culturally in Yiddish. And what an exciting time it was!"[127] Their son, film producer Ben Gonshor, began his involvement with the DWYT at the age of six. With a degree in cinema, he is an accomplished playwright who in 2019 assumed the position of DWYT president, a role previously held by his father. "It's time to give back," he stated in an interview, noting the impact of his own life-long involvement with the theatre.[128] Significant overlap has evolved between the participants of YAYA and the DWYT and other sites of Yiddish such as the KlezKanada music festival.

This twenty-first century Yiddish educational and cultural activity has occurred despite a decline in formal Yiddish education within secular Jewish day schools. By the end of the twentieth century, JPPS and Bialik High School (Montreal) and Bialik Hebrew Day School (Toronto) had become some of the world's few schools outside of Hasidic communities where Yiddish study remained a compulsory component. However, by the turn of the twenty-first century, the commitment to teaching Yiddish was waning even in Montreal. With increasing student diversity and families from non-Ashkenazi backgrounds, Yiddish no longer functioned as a shared heritage language for the JPPS student body. Structural changes in the curriculum drastically reduced the hours of Yiddish education, and schools, parents, and students expressed increasing ambivalence around the study of both Hebrew and Yiddish.[129] By the end of the 2010s, Yiddish instruction within grades one through six of JPPS was being offered by a single teacher, Nancy Sculnik (born 1979). Whereas Sculnik's own Yiddish education in JPPS comprised five to six hours per week, including instruction in Jewish history, Holocaust Studies, poetry and prose, her curriculum as a teacher was limited to weekly sessions. Together with her associate, Sheila Witt (born 1941), herself a long-time Yiddish teacher in Montreal, Sculnik created an innovative program using simple Yiddish phrases to convey material in engaging ways: movement, stories, games, songs, and short conversation practice. One objective of her program is to help the children to learn to regulate their emotions as part of a broader pedagogy on mindfulness. By the end of sixth grade, the students know a variety of Yiddish songs and stories such as the folktales of Chelm; they are able to hold a short conversation in the language and understand that Yiddish is "alive and well."[130] Once at the core of the original school system, Yiddish instruction at JPPS hinges today on a single full-time teacher.

As a point of comparison, an alternative model of the engagement of school-aged children with Yiddish is offered in Australia by SKIF (Sotsyalistisher kinder farband/Socialist Children's Union, originally founded in 1926), the youth arm of the Bund. The Melbourne chapter was formed in 1950 with the establishment of a summer camp. In the 1960s and 1970s, SKIF expanded to provide a wide range of activities for youth – group meetings, choirs, camps – for children being raised in Yiddish-speaking homes and attending secular Yiddish schools.[131] SKIF members have become enduring activists for the promotion of the language. With the motto of *"chavershaft, doikayt, yidishkayt"* (equality and empathy, linking the struggles of Jews with others, and the shared heritage of the Jewish people),[132] SKIF provides programming for children aged eight to eighteen in weekly youth-led meetings and camps throughout the year. Although fluent knowledge of Yiddish is neither required nor produced by SKIF, its integration of Yiddish in its activities, notably singing, provides a youth-oriented space. Ongoing formal Yiddish children's education in Melbourne is offered by Sholem Aleichem College, a secular Jewish day school that offers Yiddish instruction several times a week through grade six, and also coordinates an after-school high school program to prepare students for state examinations in the Yiddish language.[133]

Yugntruf has continued to promote Yiddish as a spoken language within a transnational and increasingly diffuse community. Sandra Fox's recent study of youth Yiddishism traces the incarnations of Yugntruf activism across three generations in response to changing trends. Whereas in the 1960s, the emphasis was on elevating the status of Yiddish among its existing speakers, the 1970s reoriented its activities to include youth more broadly, for example in programming and lobbying for Yiddish courses on university campuses. Yugntruf activists picketed Yiddish newspapers to adopt a standardized system of spelling. As the number of speakers declined, Yugntruf increasingly emphasized the value of speaking Yiddish in addition to hosting reading groups and conferences. By the 1980s, Yugntruf had seeded a cohort of teachers, scholars, and artists.[134] One example is Sheva Zucker, born and raised in Winnipeg, and a graduate of the city's Peretz Shule. As a student at New York Teachers' Seminary and People's University in the 1970s, Zucker joined a circle of friends in Yugntruf who gathered regularly to socialize in Yiddish. A Yiddish teacher in university programs, author of Yiddish textbooks, and editor of Yiddish-language publications, Zucker has articulated the importance of Yugntruf in combination with new academic courses in producing a new generation of young people who did not come from Yiddish-speaking homes but who know the language well enough to hold formal lectures in the subject.[135] In addition to serving as an editor of *Yugntruf*, she coordinated the annual Yugntruf Yiddish Teachers Seminar at its annual retreat.[136] Like many Yugntruf

members, Zucker spoke to her own children in Yiddish while they
were growing up.

The 1980s and 1990s, which intersected with the "revival" of klezmer music and the development of subcultures such as Queer Yiddishkeit, brought a shift within Yugntruf to intergenerational continuity. As its original members began having families, the organization
oriented itself towards raising Yiddish-speaking children. Yugntruf's
Yidish-Vokh (Yiddish Week, founded 1975) expanded as an immersive
annual retreat for speakers from diverse backgrounds and ages within
driving distance of New York City. Via immersion in the language
while swimming, playing baseball, eating meals, singing, or attending
lectures and workshops, Yidish-Vokh has offered a site to cultivate
friendships, romances, and children's programming. In the 1980s,
Yugntruf parents formed a Yiddish playgroup in New York called
Pripetshik as well as a Sunday school program. In addition to the
journal, members formed a writing circle to cultivate new writing
and published an anthology (*Vidervuks*, 1989).[137] In 2000, Yugntruf
launched the Yiddish-Svives, where small groups of six to ten members would meet at least twice a month to speak Yiddish in a deliberate, sustained, and high-quality manner by discussing a text prepared
in advance, reading a play, playing games, and conversing; the initiative included support for such groups to be set up by anyone interested.[138] During this time, the organization's membership included
some one thousand households, a majority in the United States and
the rest spanning twenty-six countries worldwide, with members of
varying ages.[139]

At this time, the next generation – the children of the founding
Yugntruf generation raised in Yiddish – stepped in to lead the organization. While they continued to use Yiddish as a spoken language,
they were unable to sustain the *Yugntruf* journal, which ceased publication in 2008 after 104 issues. Fox observes the new focus away from
producing Yiddish writing to building a "new Yiddish social world"
in activities such as university "Yiddish Breaks" where Yiddish speakers could gather, and newcomers could be exposed to the movement.[140] An offshoot of Yugntruf was Yiddish Farm, a training farm
and community founded in 2012 where Yiddish was spoken and
taught in Goshen, New York. Attracting a new cohort of new learners
to an immersive environment, the leadership faced challenges in
propagating an "authentic" spoken Yiddish or determining what constituted one.[141] Entering the 2020s, Yugntruf maintains an active pres-

ence through its website as well as by coordinating physical gatherings such as the Yidish-Vokh retreat. Yugntruf's ongoing orientation towards young speakers is reflected in its *Kinder-Loshn* series of bilingual Yiddish-English books for children and youth.[142]

Scholars have positioned Yugntruf within a discourse around vernacularity versus postvernacularity. Jeffrey Shandler notes the singularity of Yugntruf within the Yiddishist activist world: "From its inception Yugntruf's commitment to Yiddish vernacularity has been conceived of as an act of cultural persistence, demanding vigilance and rigour on the part of its members."[143] As he suggests, "the nature of the activities [undertaken by Yugntruf] is of secondary importance; their ultimate value is that they are conducted in Yiddish." [144] Abigail Wood writes, "The purpose of Yugntruf's *svives* ... is not only recreational: rather, the meetings are an expression of rigorous devotion to language study, creating a space where, for an hour or two, Yiddish is no longer *post*vernacular."[145] Fox's study of youth Yiddishist activism suggests that "these postwar and contemporary Yiddishists have sought to *revernacularize* Yiddish in response to its postvernacularity, even as the very act of doing so exemplifies the postvernacular [italics in the original]."[146] She finds that the pockets of passionate young Yiddishists between their teenaged years and parenthood have had shifting priorities over time, while at the same time, new subcultures and organizations have proven accessible to a later generations who had not been exposed to Yiddish as a spoken language or who came from a non-Jewish background.[147]

The 1960s and 1970s models of activity created specifically for and subsequently by youth have been a powerful tool for the transmission of Yiddish. They have offered fluid spaces that shifted the locus of engagement to gatherings and experiences rather than buildings and institutions. Increasingly, activity would take place in festivals and camps, classrooms, and through the coming together of people connected to the language as activists, academics, learners, or performers. Thus, in 2019 in Toronto, the Workmen's Circle – a longtime centre of Yiddish culture – was selling its building while the Ashkenaz Festival continued to coordinate a variety of Yiddish activities around the city. The apolitical character of youth initiatives like Yugntruf is also emblematic of the ideological drift that would increasingly become a feature of the Yiddish world, with participants moving between secular Jewish organizations that might once have been politically opposed: for example, between the Socialist Workmen's Circle and the formerly Communist-affiliated Morris Win-chevsky Centre in Toronto.

The 1960s and 1970s marked a highpoint of the convergence of the European-born generation and the Canadian-raised generations. Three distinct movements worked in tandem to promote Yiddish: the network of formal and informal education, including the Dora Wasserman Yiddish Theatre; a cadre of youth activists in Yugntruf; and the established Jewish community as represented by the Canadi-an Jewish Congress. The forward-looking and collaborative strategies they devised and implemented spurred the continuity of the language and culture against ongoing decline of Yiddish as a spoken language within mainstream Jewish life.

The legacies of the youth activism of this era are extensive and far-reaching. For Canadian-raised activists, continuity encompassed Yiddish-speaking homes, networks of secular Jewish schools (*shuln*) and camps, Yiddish cultural activity and, in Montreal, the Dora Wasserman Yiddish Theatre. While these efforts could not stave off the decline of the cultural world erected by their immigrant parents – the daily newspapers and periodicals, popular theatre, book pub-lishing and bookstores, political and cultural organizations, and so on – they did mark a revitalization for a new generation as well as for increasing numbers of young people who would gravitate towards Yiddish in the decades to come. These newcomers would include those with an Eastern European Jewish heritage and those coming to Yiddish as an alternative form of Jewish or other identity.

The next chapter examines Yiddish publishing with a focus on the transitional period of the 1970s and 1980s. Here created language spaces are mediated by the medium of print, with access contingent upon literacy. However, these decades introduced enduring strategies of anthologizing and translation that have opened up vast reposito-ries of Yiddish literature to new audiences.

4

Yiddish Writing and Publishing
The 1970s and 1980s

Publishing has played a disproportionate role in the transmission of modern Yiddish culture in comparison with other minority or heritage languages, where radio and television have often played a larger role. From the 1880s to the 1920s, a transnational popular press comprising newspapers and journals spanned Eastern Europe and its immigrant centres in the Americas and elsewhere, to reach a highpoint in the interwar years. In the linguistic acculturation that took place in Canada and other newer centres of Yiddish life in the first half of the twentieth century, a mass readership thrived within a single generation whose children would increasingly produce and seek out reading material in other languages. While theatre and music remained accessible, published writing became less so as Yiddish literacy decreased.

By the 1950s the Yiddish press was in decline, whereas Yiddish books continued to be written, sponsored, published, and celebrated. In Canada, authors from the first wave of immigration and survivors of the Holocaust, along with a handful of second-generation writers, produced works that encompassed poetry, fiction, memoir, and non-fiction to include history, psychology, and traditional Jewish scholarship. Over two hundred books were published in Yiddish between 1950 and 2020, an astonishing total; a list of titles appears in an appendix to this volume. The 1970s and 1980s marked a pinnacle of Yiddish book culture due to a convergence of writers, community and state support, and new interest in ethnic writing as part of Canadian multiculturalism. Whereas the decreasing number of readers fluent enough to access the texts has ultimately constrained Yiddish publishing, this period saw a profusion of publishing projects

among new voices as well as an ingathering and anthologizing of a
Canadian literary tradition.

This chapter investigates the hopes for continuity associated with
book production combined with an expansive community apparatus
to support it. I examine the created language spaces associated with
this milieu, which include not only the books themselves but also
support for publishing programs as well as readings and book launches. I focus here on the history and wider implications of Yiddish book
publishing in Canada after the Holocaust: what kinds of works were
published after 1950, what strategies emerged to facilitate the process,
and how those strategies shifted over time. Rather than offer literary
analysis of this wide body of work, I examine the changing approaches within the careers and publications of its authors. Following an
overview of broader trends in the prewar and postwar periods, the
chapter will discuss the publishing outputs of the 1950s and 1960s,
the highpoint in the 1970s and 1980s, and a decline since the 1990s.
The chapter concludes with a brief discussion of contemporary Yiddish publishing in both the Haredi and non-Haredi worlds.

The chapter raises a question that can have no real answer: did the
Holocaust encourage work by Yiddish writers who might have otherwise opted to use other languages, or not become writers at all? For
example, Chava Rosenfarb's career, which was first formed in the
Łódź Ghetto and subsequently in Canada, expressed a lifelong imperative to record her experiences before, during and in the aftermath of
the Holocaust. In his book *Survivors and Exiles: Yiddish Culture after
the Holocaust,* Jan Schwarz characterizes the impetus behind Yiddish
cultural work for survivors such as Rosenfarb: "to commemorate and
bear witness to the destruction of Ashkenaz, and to continue to develop a modern Yiddish culture."[1]

THE CANADIAN YIDDISH WRITERS

Over four hundred Yiddish writers were published in Canada between 1910 and 2010 and they share a common profile. I offer some
tabulations based on *Hundert yor yidishe un hebreyishe literatur in
kanade* (A Hundred Years of Yiddish and Hebrew Literature in Canada), the biographical lexicon compiled by writer Chaim Leib Fuks
(Fox) in 1980 and Pierre Anctil's analysis in his introduction to its
French translation, *Cent ans de littérature yiddish et hébraïque au Canada*. Virtually all were immigrants, with the largest group (171) arriving

during the height of Jewish immigration between 1900 and 1918, followed by a slightly smaller group (142) in the interwar years, and a third group of some 70 Holocaust survivors between 1940 and 1960. A majority were born in Poland (151), followed by Ukraine (107); only 6 were Canadian-born. Yiddish writers were active in Canada's Jewish cultural life, including schools, libraries, and political organizations. They were affiliated with ideological movements such as the labour Zionist Poale Zion (82), religious Zionism (23), and the Bund (20). Their primary place of publication was the Canadian Yiddish press, notably the Montreal *Keneder adler/Canadian Eagle* (mentioned 284 times), Toronto's *Der Yidisher zhurnal/Daily Hebrew Journal* (mentioned 160 times), and Winnipeg's *Dos yidishe vort/Israelite Press* (mentioned 115 times). Before 1950, many of the authors also published in smaller local newspapers and journals that appeared from the 1920s through the 1950s (over 300 mentions). In terms of genre, the writers were active as any of the following, usually in some combination: journalists (163), fiction authors (55), researchers (46), poets (40), teachers (30), traditional Jewish scholars (28), activists (20), memoirists (17), translators (9), playwrights (3), and musicologists (3). A vast majority resided in the larger urban centres of Montreal (227), Toronto (106), or Winnipeg (60), while smaller numbers (fewer than 6) were active in the Jewish agricultural settlements or smaller cities such as Ottawa, Calgary, and Edmonton. While Yiddish is by far the dominant Jewish language of publication, a quarter of the group were bilingual writers who published in both Yiddish and Hebrew: 311 spent their literary careers exclusively in Yiddish across all genres; 101 published in both Yiddish and Hebrew. In comparison, only 17 published exclusively in Hebrew, and they did so in the genre of scholarly religious texts rather than modern Hebrew literature, which, unlike Yiddish, did not evolve its own Canadian tradition due to limited audiences and venues for publication.[2]

In exceptional cases, extensive literary activity occurred within a single, extended family. The most prominent example is Montreal's Shtern-Krishtalka family, which included three generations of published authors by 1960, including one born in Canada: Polish-born scholar Rabbi Abraham Shtern (1878–1955) in the first generation; Polish-born poet Sholem Shtern (1906–1991), prose writer Yaakov Zipper (1900–1983), poet Ish Yair (Dr Israel-Hersh Shtern, 1913–2000), and teacher Shifre Shtern Krishtalka in the second generation; and Canadian-born and -raised poet Aaron Krishtalka (1940–

present) in the third. The family's individual members will be discussed throughout this chapter. However, such intergenerational literary activity was rare.

The activities of these writers dispel any notion of an inevitable transition away from Yiddish. Schwarz and other scholars argue that the post-1945 period marked a "Silver Age" of the Yiddish book, "the culmination of the great achievements of a group of Yiddish literary artists who brought to fruition the cultural agendas, the visions, and the potential that originated in the golden age of Yiddish culture prior to World War II. The artistic triumphs of these writers are independent of the decline of vernacular Yiddish."[3] This last point is of particular significance as the afterlife of these works has exceeded the capacity of most readers to access them. Anita Norich's *Discovering Exile: Yiddish and Jewish American Culture during the Holocaust* reveals a renewed vibrancy in the Yiddish milieu; she argues that the widespread failure to acknowledge it has distorted a broader understanding of American Jewish culture.[4] Schwarz refers to "the myth of 'the Holocaust as the end of Yiddish,'" when there was, in fact, a marked increase in Yiddish cultural activity in the 1940s and 1950s that coincided with the earliest incarnations of Holocaust public memory more broadly.[5] In Canada, this activity concurred with the advent of English-language writers who emerged out of the Yiddish immigrant milieu to national and international acclaim; it was not supplanted by it. Prominent Anglo-Jewish writers – poet and novelist A.M. Klein (1909–1972), novelist Mordecai Richler (1931–2001), poet Irving Layton (1912–2006), poet and short story writer Miriam Waddington (1917–2004), poet and novelist Leonard Cohen (1934–2016), and many others – demonstrated various degrees of influence from the Yiddish milieu.[6] At the same time, post-1950 Canadian Yiddish writers rejected the model of Yiddish literature as simply the forerunner to new literary traditions in the majority language. Rather, they wrote and published in greater capacity than before, while exploring alternate avenues to disseminate their work to broader audiences. A community of writers published continuously into the twenty-first century in the wake of the annihilation of both their historic homeland and a significant portion of their readership base, and the steady attrition of their remaining audiences. They did so within a broader narrative of Yiddish creativity as both continuity and resistance.

CANADIAN YIDDISH PUBLISHING
BEFORE AND AFTER 1950: A COMPARISON

Yiddish literary production has historically spanned multiple major and minor centres. In the prewar period, main publishing centres were located in Poland, the United States, and the Soviet Union. In the postwar period, publishing activity followed the authors who had survived the Holocaust to cities where supporters were active or to countries where private or state financial support was available, with Canada emerging as a lively publishing centre. This section surveys some of the major changes to Canadian Yiddish publishing within a global context before and after the Holocaust.

As modern Yiddish literary culture crystalized in the late nineteenth century, a single book by a single author was not the typical mode of publication. For a global Yiddish readership that largely ranged from indigent to working class, newspapers were accessible, whereas books were too costly both to produce and to purchase. Publication in book form tended to come only after an author's work had been widely read and well received in other media. In Europe and its immigrant offshoots, literature expanded as a site for innovation as ideologies proliferated in political movements and literary schools. The Jewish masses sought out self-education via translations of world literature as well as from original Yiddish writing that ranged from technical manuals and textbooks to works of poetry. Literary journals formed a site of experimental, innovative, and avant-garde literature. Literary anthologies served to bring authors of a shared tradition or movement together. The history of Yiddish literature has seen few for-profit publishers outside of Poland and the United States, with most books published under the auspices of daily newspapers or political and cultural organizations, by short-lived private publishing houses, or by the authors themselves. Only in the interwar Soviet Union did Yiddish book publishing receive ongoing and extensive state support.[7]

The primary site for the development of modern Yiddish literature before 1950 was the international periodical press, including daily and weekly newspapers and specialty journals.[8] Nathan Cohen's study, "The Yiddish Press and Yiddish Literature: A Fertile but Complex Relationship," investigates how newspapers in the interwar period served as the initial forum for many writers and as the site where readers encountered Yiddish poetry and prose. The scope was vast: in 1950, when New York served as the world's largest literary centre, the city housed four Yiddish dailies with a combined circulation of 238,500,[9] down from 600,000 during the peak year of 1915–16.[10] Meanwhile, Yiddish periodical publishing flourished in other New World centres such as Buenos Aires and Montreal.[11] Canada was home to Yiddish-language newspapers in each of the three major centres of Jewish immigration: the Montreal daily *Keneder adler* (founded in 1907), the Toronto daily *Yidisher zhurnal* (founded in 1912), and Winnipeg's weekly *Dos yidishe vort* (founded in 1910 as *Der kurier/ Courier*). In addition, dozens of shorter-lived newspapers and journals representing diverse political and ideological orientations and interests featured literary texts.[12] In 1954, Canada was home to five Yiddish newspapers with an estimated total circulation of 50,000, the highest number after English, French, and Ukrainian; at that time, the only daily newspapers outside of English and French were in Chinese and Yiddish. 1951 Canadian census statistics – that 96 per cent of the Canadian Jewish population declared themselves able to speak English and more than 57 per cent were Canadian-born – suggest that a vast majority of readers of the daily Yiddish press could read English newspapers and accessed Yiddish newspapers as supplements, specifically for their Jewish news coverage or for their cultural content.[13] Despite a rapidly expanding readership, Yiddish publishing was rarely profitable outside of the daily newspapers. Whereas newspapers were a commercial enterprise, book publishing lacked enduring financial backing and stability.

Canadian Yiddish publishing changed both qualitatively and quantitatively in the wake of the Holocaust. Before 1950, Yiddish texts were produced for a target audience of Eastern European immigrant Jews and their descendants for whom the Yiddish proved more accessible than Hebrew, English, or other languages. These works included popular thrillers or romances, collections of hagiographic tales about rabbis, leftist political treatises, textbooks or manuals, and translations into Yiddish from sacred texts as well as world literature. Daring avant-garde and leftist poetry and prose also appeared in specialized literary journals or published volumes.[14] After 1950, Yiddish publishing was increasingly dominated by literary texts – in particular, collections of poetry – that appeared in book form. The post-1950 cohort of Yiddish writers, both major and minor, would be the last to experience modern Yiddish literature as a mass phenomenon and the genre of books shifted to reflect a changing authorship and readership. In place of the translations into Yiddish from world literature, serialized popular works or experimental literary works, one increasingly finds volumes of belles lettres with the vanished world of Eastern European Jewry as their point of reference. The change from periodical to books demonstrates a shift in the scope of literary activity from local to international; whereas newspapers such as the *Keneder Adler* were directed primarily at a Canadian readership, book distribution indicates the extent to which audiences for Yiddish writers were increasingly found beyond Canada's borders.

The corpus of Canadian Yiddish writing after 1950 is embedded in the aftermath of the Holocaust. Literature served to transmit Yiddish written by a last generation of European-raised authors. A majority of the works under discussion deal with Eastern Europe; far fewer are set in Canada. This corpus marked a break with prewar Yiddish culture in both format and content as books increasingly served to record a pre-Holocaust culture that existed only in the memories of their authors. An interconnected community of writers produced works that not only expressed their creative visions in innovative ways but served to perpetuate the language itself, even as its population of speakers was diminishing and not being replenished. The highpoint of this innovation took place in the 1970s and 1980s, when Chava Rosenfarb and Yehuda Elberg published semi-autobiographical novels depicting the Holocaust experience while Canadian-raised Leybl Botwinik authored a science fiction novel about time and space travel partially set in pre-Holocaust Vilna. This period coincided with the elevation of Yiddish letters globally with the 1976 awarding of the Nobel Prize for literature to Polish-born, Yiddish-language author Isaac Bashevis Singer.

The production of books became a mode of Yiddish transmission within the community: their publication paid for by a committee of supporters; launched, inscribed, and disseminated at public events; and – most importantly – celebrated. This form of book publishing did not depend on widespread fluency and literacy in the language or an actual or intended audience of readers. Rather, the physical books became objects in the material culture associated with Yiddish: sometimes discarded due to a lack of readers, sometimes cherished despite a lack of readers, and – more recently – showcased, exhibited, and digitized. In the concentric circles of secular Yiddish, this chapter is three circles removed from the middle as it entails transmission from

Yiddish-speaking writers to an imagined community of readers, as well as being a form of material culture accessible by means of digitization and online technologies to those who might not speak the language (see figure 0.1).

The vast majority of Yiddish writers active before 1940 can be considered minor, with their reputations not extending beyond their local circles. Their work has not been widely anthologized or translated and only a few achieved international acclaim during their lifetimes and after: Ida Maza (also Maze/Massey; born Zhukovsky, 1893–1962), J.I. (Jacob Isaac/Yankev Yitskhok) Segal (1896-1954), and Yaakov Zipper. By 1960, Canada was home to a group of Yiddish writers with international reputations who had arrived during and after the Holocaust, including Yehuda Elberg (1912–2003), Rokhl Korn (born Häring, 1898–1982), Peretz Miransky (1908–1993), Melech Ravitch (pseudonym of Zekharye-Khone Bergner, 1893–1976), and Chava Rosenfarb (1923–2011). These Holocaust survivors published critically acclaimed Yiddish poetry and prose, received international awards, and have been widely and internationally anthologized and translated. They galvanized the local landscape and made Canada a major centre of Yiddish literature. This period was accompanied by a shift from publication across all genres to primarily belles-lettres and memoirs, as well as a shift in geography so that a majority of Canadian Yiddish books were authored and published in Montreal.

Jan Schwarz characterizes the post-1945 generation of Yiddish writers as "trailblazers of the last blossoming of secular Yiddish culture."[15] He situates them within a "transnational Yiddish infrastructure" in geographic flux as Holocaust survivors relocated from Europe and adopted new priorities in an awareness of being the last of their generation. As a group, the writers tended to emphasize collective creation of a "virtual Ashkenaz" in their writing, and in the process "spearheaded the ingathering of Yiddish cultural treasures."[16] At the same time, a cadre of highly productive writers worldwide sought to contribute to the building of modern Yiddish culture. However, rather than prompting the experimental or ideologically aligned works (leftist or modernist) such as those that had characterized the interwar period, postwar innovation centred on the initiation of new collective publishing opportunities. For example, Mark Turkov (1904–1983) published 175 volumes of the Yiddish-language series *Dos poylishe yidntum* (Polish Jewry, 1946–66) in Buenos Aires under the sponsorship of the Central Union of Polish Jews in Argentina; the series, aiming for nothing less than "to rebuild Yiddish culture in the diaspora,"[17] was extremely well received. Schwarz posits that for the post-Holocaust "Ashkenazi dispersion," a global network encompassing "literary, musical, theatrical, and other artistic works that filled the void left behind after the destruction of Ashkenaz in Central and Eastern Europe" enabled Yiddish survivor writers to maintain their creativity, readership, and support.[18]

The Yiddish literary world offered Holocaust survivors a fertile meeting ground in Canada. Newly arrived writers were welcomed, their projects supported, and they found themselves part of a cultural life that included visits by many of the world's major writers in addition to an active local scene. Writers were encouraged to publish Holocaust-themed testimonials and memoirs, and were able to sustain long careers supported by the Yiddish cultural milieu.[19] This stands in contrast to the established Canadian Jewish community, which had immigrated in the decades prior to the Holocaust and adopted English as their main language. Frank Bialystok suggests this group "did not want to know what happened, and few survivors had the courage to tell them."[20] In Canada and elsewhere, the extent to which writers were supported is reflected in the prominence of Yiddish works published by a committee comprised of friends and supporters. Publishing increasingly came to hinge on support locally as well as internationally, not just for economic reasons but because of the significance of book production to a global community.

In Canada, as in other Yiddish centres worldwide, postwar book production tended to follow a given pattern. An author or committee fundraised for the publication of a book, which entailed extensive outreach within a local as well as an international community, including both readers and non-readers of Yiddish. The book was then edited, printed, and distributed to readers and supporters. The book was launched and celebrated in local literary circles, and it was critically reviewed in Yiddish periodicals by fellow authors in Canada as well as abroad. Ruth R. Wisse recalls her mother's innovation of *prenumerantn* (pre-publication subscriptions for Yiddish books): "Mother's truly creative effort was to sell customers preordered copies of books by local authors so that they could pay for their printing and publication. Fifty copies at ten dollars apiece would cover the advance to the publisher; some of her friends made additional contributions. Buyers then received their finished copies at a reception in our home where the authors read selections from their work and others praised it."[21] Nowhere in this process was a popular readership essential. This explains the frequent occurrence of signed first editions of Yiddish volumes, especially in the 1970s and 1980s: supporters of the project were thanked with an inscribed copy of the book, and many volumes were distributed this way.

Yiddish books published after the Holocaust transmitted the language as well as the culture it carried. Since each volume contained the author's particular idiom and local dialect, Yiddish books came to encapsulate ways of speaking and writing in a language nearly obliterated by the Holocaust and linguistic acculturation. The books thus fulfilled a dual function: to express the artistic vision of the individual author and to memorialize a vanishing or vanished culture. Schwarz expresses these contradictory impulses: "In addition to serving as the embodiment of continuity and the hope for the future of Yiddish culture, these writers felt a strong obligation to give voice to the nameless dead."[22] Yiddish authors wrote from the vantage point of a civilization ravaged by genocide and they wrote for declining audiences, yet they continued to experiment with content and form and actively seek out new readers even as the number of Yiddish speakers dropped. Further, as I discuss below, a number of authors were actively involved in the translation of their works in order to expand their readership.

EARLY POST-HOLOCAUST YIDDISH PUBLISHING

The late 1940s through the end of the 1960s marked a period of transition, during which some of the momentum of the "Golden Age" of the interwar period was carried over. Canada's Jews began to respond to the decimation of Yiddish civilization in the Holocaust. These changing dynamics are reflected in the post-1945 activity of Canada's most renowned prewar Yiddish poet, J.I. Segal. A literary modernist, pioneering editor of a series of Canadian avant-garde journals in the 1920s, and author of eight volumes of lyrical poetry from 1918 to 1944, Segal was deeply embedded in the Yiddish cultural milieu. The last volume of verse to appear before his sudden death in 1954, *Seyfer yidish* (The Book of Yiddish, 1950), expresses a deep sense of loss; words with the root ק–ד–ש (k-d-sh) appear frequently in many of the poems, with a variety of meanings: "holy," "sacred," "sanctity," "holy martyr," and "victim." Segal's poetry embodies what Anita Diamant and David Roskies call a "liturgical turn within secular Yiddish culture" in the wake of the Holocaust, where "Yiddish had become *loshn-hakdoyshim*, the language of martyrs" and writers created a new, sacred language to depict the cataclysmic destruction of European Jewry.[23] While Segal mourned the losses of the Holocaust and questioned what his legacy might be, his poetry would form part of a postwar commitment to creating educational materials for North American-raised youth. In this vein, a posthumous volume of Segal's collected works, published by the educational committee of the New York Workmen's Circle in 1961, contains his poetry for children, which had originally appeared in the Canadian Yiddish press.[24]

Support for Yiddish publishing increased in institutions whose mandates supported and fostered Yiddish literature and culture. Yiddish writers were hosted across the country in conjunction with secular Jewish schools and other cultural institutions. In Montreal, the Jewish Public Library provided both a physical home and an organizational hub for local literary activity. During the interwar period, the Library expanded into a major Jewish organization that promoted adult education and cultural programming including lectures, literature courses, readings, book launches, and other events featuring local and visiting writers and cultural figures. In the 1940s, the organization revived its People's University (Yidishe Folksuniversitet, formed 1914, disbanded 1917) with courses that included Yiddish literature, and in 1954 it erected a purpose-built building on the corner of Esplanade and Mount Royal in the heart of the Jewish immigrant quarter that included not only reading rooms but a large auditorium. Literary activity was also coordinated by a host of other local institutions, notably the network of secular Jewish schools that offered instruction in Yiddish.[25]

The Yiddish books published in Canada after 1950 form part of a global shift away from the periodical as the primary site of Yiddish publishing activity. Just three Yiddish literary journals appeared in Canada after 1950. In contrast to the ephemeral nature of many of the prewar periodicals – most of which only appeared once as a single, thin volume before the editors regrouped for a new project – the postwar magazines appeared in multiple volumes and in expansive issues more like anthologies.[26] The first of these was *Tint un feder: Literarisher khoydesh-zhurnal* (*Pen and Ink: Literary Monthly*, 1949–50), edited by Toronto printer Gershon Pomerantz, which appeared in four issues ranging from thirty-two to seventy-two glossy pages featuring the works of Canadian writers.[27] *Montreoler heftn: Shrift far literatur* (*Mont-

real Notebooks: A Publication for Literature, 1955–58), edited by local
writers N.J. Gotlib, M.M. Shaffir and A.Sh. Shkolnikov, appeared in
three volumes, with the contributors reading like a "who's who" of the
local Yiddish literati.[28] *Vidershtand* (*Resistance*, 1957–59), a periodical
for literature and cultural issues, edited by writer and essayist Yitshak
Goldkorn, appeared in Montreal over twelve issues, again spotlighting
the city's pre- and postwar Yiddish writers.[29] These three magazines
marked the last of the Canadian literary journals in Yiddish; when the
writers' work would appear together in the 1960s and thereafter, it
would be in anthologies. Just a handful of Yiddish journals continued
publication in the United States, Israel, and the Soviet Union. Among
these, *Di goldene keyt: Fertlyorshrift far literatur un gezelshaftlekhe
problemen* (The Golden Chain: A Quarterly for Literature and Social
Problems, 1949–95), published in Tel Aviv by acclaimed poet Avrom
Sutzkever (1913–2010), would emerge as the world's leading Yiddish
literary periodical and would publish the poetry, prose, and essays of
an international array of Yiddish authors, including the Canadians.[30]

The postwar era saw the publication of volumes of scholarship
whose contents had originally been serialized in the periodical press.
This points not only to the shift from newspapers to books, but also
to the accompanying ingathering of works into a more enduring
form. This period marks a maturing of the Canadian Jewish immigrant community, which was beginning to write its own history, first
in Yiddish, and subsequently in English. B.G. Sack (1889–1967), a pioneering historian and long-time contributor to the *Keneder adler*,
authored the first book-length study on the subject: *Geshikhte fun yidn
in kanade: Fun di friste onheybn biz der letster tsayt* (History of the Jews
in Canada: From their First Beginnings until the Present, 1948),
which appeared in English translation before the Yiddish as *History of
the Jews in Canada* (1945). Simon Belkin (1889–1969) wrote *Di poyle
tsien bavegung in kanade: 1904–1920* (The Poale Zion Movement in
Canada, 1956), a scholarly history of the Jewish left. These volumes
appeared with the assistance of committees of friends and the labour
Zionist movement respectively. Joseph Kage, long-time director of
social services with the Canadian Jewish Immigrant Aid Society, published *Tsvey hundert yor fun yidisher imigratsiye in kanade* (Two Hundred Years of Jewish Immigration, 1960), which appeared in English
translation two years later as *With Faith and Thanksgiving*. All three
books accessed archival and government sources and scholarly literature and remain trailblazing studies of their respective subjects.

Belkin's and Kage's volumes were published in English translation in the 1960s, which coincided with a rising interest in ethnic history as a precursor to Canadian multiculturalism.

As one of the handful of Jewish refugees who settled in Canada during the war years, Symcha Petrushka (1893–1950) produced a significant body of scholarship that marked the completion of projects begun in Europe. A renowned Polish journalist, Petrushka published monumental works of Yiddish-language scholarship that aimed to bring Jewish learning to the masses. Two projects occupied Petrushka after his arrival to Montreal in 1939: his *Yidishe folks-entsiklopedye* (1942), a Jewish people's encyclopedia in two volumes, and his magnum opus, *Mishnayes mit iberzetsungen un peyrush in yidish* (1945–49), a six-volume translation and interpretation of the Mishna into Yiddish. This work, which strove to transmit a centuries-old tradition of Jewish study in Poland annihilated in the Holocaust,[31] formed a model for a growing body of literature that aimed to make sacred text accessible to a wide readership, including the widely used multi-volume modern Hebrew commentary on the Mishna published by Pinchas Kahati in the 1950s (*Mishnayot Mevoarot*/Explained Mishnayot).

Studies of traditional Jewish texts and traditions marked an expanding field of postwar Yiddish book publication. Rabbi Abraham Shtern, a highly respected Montreal scholar and patriarch of the Shtern-Krishtalka family of Yiddish writers, published two bilingual volumes of Biblical stories and Hasidic legends in Yiddish and Hebrew.[32] Nachman Shemen (1912–1993), a Polish-born rabbi and scholar and prolific writer for the Toronto Yiddish press, published eight books on religious themes from the 1940s to the end of the 1980s, including volumes on biblical and rabbinic literature and portraits of Polish-Jewish religious figures and places. Meir Schwartzman (1901–1968), a Polish-born Winnipeg rabbi, published sermons, the history of the Ger Hasidic dynasty, and an account of his travels in Israel.[33] Outside of the rabbinic world, Shimshen Dunsky published the first of his award-winning series of Yiddish translations of the traditional homiletical biblical interpretations of *Lamentations*, *Esther*, *Ecclesiastes*, and *Song of Songs* (1956–73). All these books drew on the Eastern European system of traditional Jewish education. Straddling scholarship and folklore, each evokes a Jewish civilization uprooted in the Holocaust and transplanted to Canada by survivors.

The Montreal literary milieu was revitalized by the wartime arrival of Melech Ravitch, who settled in the city in 1941. One of Jewish Warsaw's most prominent essayists and poets, Ravitch became active in local cultural life, reviving the People's University at the Jewish Public Library and spearheading local literary projects.[34] He published prolifically in conversation with global intellectual and artistic trends. The multi-volume *Mayn leksikon* (1945–82), comprises vignettes and reminiscences about Jewish cultural figures Ravitch had known in Europe, the Americas, and elsewhere. He edited and published the pre-Holocaust memoir of his mother, Hinde Bergner, in 1946.[35] His collection of essays, *Eynems yidishe makhshoves in tsvantsikstn yorhundert* (On Jewish Thought in the Twentieth Century, 1949), examines Jewish continuity, including youth education. However, poetry remained his primary vocation and the three volumes published during this time point to Jan Schwarz's notion of the post-Holocaust "Ashkenazi dispersion" and its virtual community, with each published in a different Yiddish publishing centre: Buenos Aires, New York, and Montreal.[36] Ravitch was a linchpin in a translational Yiddish milieu by publishing, traveling, and reviewing newly published works. His edited projects are discussed below.

Holocaust testimonial literature in Yiddish in the postwar years encompassed various forms: memoirs, novels, collections of poetry, accounts of return to the sites of destruction, *yizkor bikher* (memorial books), and others. Within the Yiddish world, memorial Holocaust literature was not peripheral to, but rather a cornerstone of, literary and broader culture, as reflected in the 175 volumes that comprise the series *Dos poylishe yidntum* (Polish Jewry). The series included two survivors who would make Canada their home: Rokhl Korn, author of *Heym un heymlozikayt* (Home and Homelessness, 1948), and Yehuda Elberg, author of *Unter kuperne himlen* (Under Copper Skies, 1951). Testimonial literature appeared in various genres. Paula Frankel-Zaltzman's *Haftling numer 94771: Iberlebenishn in daytshe lagern* (Prisoner Number 94771: Experiences in German Camps, 1949) offers a harrowing account of survival,[37] as does Joseph Rogel's book of verse *Oyshvits: Lider* (Auschwitz: Poems, 1951).[38] Survivors also published memoirs of a pre-Holocaust Jewish life that was no more. For example, Paul Trepman's *A gesl in varshe* (A Street in Warsaw, 1950, translated as *Among Men and Beasts*, 1978), based on a series of articles he had written for the *Keneder Adler*, offers reminiscences of Warsaw and its inhabitants, while Benjamin Orenstein's *Der umkum un vidershtand fun a yidisher shtot, tshenstokhov* (The Destruction and Resistance of a Jewish City, Tshenstokhov, 1949), does so for the ghetto where he was incarcerated during the war. This Yiddish literary output coincided with the beginnings of English Holocaust-themed fiction by Canadian-raised writers A.M. Klein and Leonard Cohen.[39]

Publishing personal accounts of prewar life extended to members of the Canadian Yiddish community who had immigrated before the Holocaust. Memoirs that spanned Europe and immigrant experience in Canada included works by long-time affiliates of the Canadian Yiddish press, published under the aegis of their respective newspapers in 1945 and 1946 as the Canadian community was beginning to come to terms with the obliteration of European Jewry. Hirsh Wolofsky (1878–1949), founder and publisher of the *Keneder adler*, offered his reminiscences in *Mayn lebens-rayze* (My Life's Journey, 1946).[40] Veteran *Keneder adler* journalist Israel Medres (1894–1964) published his *Montreal fun nekhten* (Montreal of Yesterday, 1947), followed by a memoir of the interwar years, *Tsvishn tsvey velt milkhomes* (Between Two World Wars, 1964). Writers published memoirs of the Canadian Jewish agricultural settlements: Michael Usiskin's *Oksn un motorn: Zikhroynes fun a yidishn farmer-pioner* (Oxen and Motors: Memoirs of A Jewish Pioneer Farmer, 1945), and Falek Zolf (1896–1961)'s *Oyf fremder erd: bletlekh fun a lebn* (On Foreign Soil, 1945) and *Di letzte fun a dor: Heymishe geshtaltn* (The Last of their Generation: Familiar Figures, 1952). In each volume, the authors offered glimpses of their European childhoods and early immigrant experiences as well as personalities they had known. These works appeared at a time when Yiddish writers were taking stock, leaving a record of people and places that had been lost, or attempting to capture traces of a civilization that had been destroyed in the Holocaust. They were writing to a transnational audience and with broad support. Since the 1990s, in tandem with expanding academic and popular interest in the Canadian Jewish immigrant experience, these volumes have been translated into English as well as French (see appendix).

This period marks an increased participation of women writers, a trend that would grow after the arrival in Canada of Holocaust survivors Chava Rosenfarb and Rokhl Korn. The celebrated Toronto poet who wrote under the name of Yudika (born Yehudis Tsik, 1898–1988) published her third book, *Tsar un freyd: Lider un dramatishe poemen* (Pain and Joy: Poems) in 1949. In Montreal, two poets produced their first books after having previously had their poetry appear in newspapers or literary journals; these were Mirl Erdberg Shatan's *Nit fun keyn freyd: Lider* (Not from Joy: Poems, 1950) and Ida Maza's collected poems, *Vaksn mayne kinderlekh: Muter un kinder lider* (Grow My Little Children: Poems for Mother and Children, 1954). Sheyndl Franzus-Garfinkle's second novel, *Erev oktober* (The Eve of October, 1947), offers a rare example of a Yiddish novel published by a woman; women have historically been far more likely to produce and publish poetry than lengthy prose.[41]

Among the postwar literary volumes, Aaron Krishtalka's *Gut morgn dir, velt* (Good Morning, World, 1953) stands out as a work written by a Yiddish poet who grew up in Canada. Born in Montreal in 1940 into the Shtern-Krishtalka family of Yiddish writers, teachers, and activists, Krishtalka was a native speaker of Yiddish and a student in the Morris Winchevsky Yiddish day school. His father published the volume on the occasion of Aaron's bar mitzvah, and it was regarded by renowned New York critic Shmuel Niger and the wider literary world as a beacon of hope for the future of Yiddish literature. However, Krishtalka expressed ambivalence about the expectations associated with being a young Yiddish writer and *Gut morgn dir, velt* would be his only Yiddish book, though he continued to publish poetry, literary essays, and articles in the international Yiddish press into his thirties.[42] No other Yiddish book of poetry or prose would be published by a Canadian-born writer until 1980; only a handful of Yiddish volumes by second generation immigrant writers would appear worldwide. Unlike their immigrant parents, who came of age linguistically in pre-Holocaust Jewish Europe, almost all the Canadian-raised authors would write in English or French.

The 1960s marked the waning of the Yiddish press and the waxing of Yiddish book publishing in Canada. Montreal's *Keneder adler*, which had existed for over fifty years as a commercial venture, lacked both the readers and the writers necessary to sustain it. Once Canada's largest Yiddish daily and one of the city's highest circulation newspapers in any language, it was discontinued as a commercial enterprise in 1967 and revived as a weekly several months later, published by a committee with Polish-born journalist Joseph Gallay (1905–1988) resuming his previous role as editor.[43] By 1971, the *Keneder adler* was appearing as a weekly tabloid, with sections in Yiddish, English, Hebrew, and French, and was published by the Jewish Cultural Association on a non-profit basis until it folded in 1988.[44] Toronto's *Yidisher zhurnal* encountered financial problems in the 1950s and appeared sporadically into the 1980s; Winnipeg's *Dos yidishe vort* folded in 1967 and was resurrected by a group of supporters as a tabloid in 1969, finally ceasing publication in 1981.[45] Only in the Soviet Union did new periodicals emerge during this period as a forum for a young generation of Yiddish writers, with the establishment in 1961 of the literary magazine *Sovetish heymland* (Soviet Homeland, edited by Arn Vergelis) which, despite its ideological adherence to the Soviet party line, published notable works of Yiddish literature.[46]

One feature of Yiddish book publishing in the 1960s was an ingathering of sources from a vanished Jewish world, with Melech Ravitch spearheading a number of projects. The first was coediting *Almanakh yidish* (Yiddish Almanac, 1961) with New York writers Jacob Pat and Zanvel Diamant. Then, under the aegis of the Association of Warsaw Jews in Canada, he compiled a sweeping anthology of almost a thousand pages of poetry, prose, drama, essays, and other genres by Warsaw Jewish writers under the title *Dos amolike yidishe varshe, biz der shvel fun dritn khurbn 1414–1939* (Jewish Warsaw That Was, Until the Eve of the Third Destruction, 1966).[47] Ravitch also published the first of four volumes of his autobiography, *Dos mayse-bukh fun mayn lebn* (The Storybook of My Life, 1962), which detailed his experiences in prewar Europe. He made the following assessment in an article that appeared in the American Yiddish press in the mid-1960s: "Yiddish literature is not at an end – it is only concluding its earthly, temporal period, and it is moving to its heavenly period."[48] Ravitch was also among the first to frame Canadian Yiddish culture for both non-Yiddish and non-Canadian readerships in survey articles published in edited volumes in the 1960s.[49]

Other writers turned their attention away from Europe towards their adopted homeland. Polish-born writer Sholem Shtern, who settled in Montreal in 1927, produced a postwar body of literary work that was new in both theme and format. His poetry of the late 1920s and 1930s, published in literary journals, expressed his leftist orientation, while his three volumes of verse – *Noentkayt* (Nearness, 1929), *Es likhtikt* (It Grows Light, 1941), and *Inderfri* (In the Morning, 1945) – offered depictions of the traditional Jewish life he had left behind. In contrast, Shtern's works from the 1960s were novels-in-verse that explored themes related to the Jewish immigrant experience in Canada. The first of these, *In kanade* (In Canada, 1960–63), is a two-volume epic poem told from the perspective of a recently arrived immigrant writer named Yosl. *Dos vayse hoyz* (The White House, 1967), the most acclaimed of Shtern's works, offers a semi-autobiographical account of his stay in a tuberculosis sanatorium in the Laurentian Mountains not far from Montreal.[50] In an essay that discusses the creation of *In kanade*, Shtern recounts the transition in his writing as a result of a visit he took to Poland in 1949, where he witnessed the wholesale destruction of Jewish life: "I felt that I could not write about the great, wonderful past when everything was lying in ruins. I saw the destruction and the horror of the Holocaust and I sensed that I had to reorient myself elsewhere."[51] Shtern was not alone in turning his attention to his Canadian home at this time; poet N.J. Gotlib's 1968 volume, *Montreol*, is an epic poem dedicated to his adopted city.

CANADIAN YIDDISH PUBLISHING AT ITS HIGH POINT: THE 1970S AND 1980S

The largest number of Canadian Yiddish books was published with extensive community involvement during the 1970s and 1980s, a period that coincides with two developments. The first is significant attrition of Yiddish writers and readers due to the passing of the European-born generation and the linguistic acculturation of the younger generation. The second is the adoption of Canadian policies of multiculturalism to recognize, retain, and promote ethnic identity and exchange between the country's diverse cultural and heritage groups.[52] This transitional period introduced a new institutionalization of support for Yiddish publishing within the Jewish community, including the advent of national and international awards for Yiddish letters. In 1968, Montreal's Jewish Public Library created its J.I. Segal Awards, including a prize for Yiddish literature, to honour Segal's memory and promote Jewish creativity in Canada. It would be awarded to virtually all of Canada's active Yiddish writers from the 1970s through the 1990s (in order: Chava Rosenfarb, Yaakov Zipper, Yehuda Elberg, Melech Ravitch, Nachman Shemen, Chaim Leib Fuks, Peretz Miransky, M.M. Shaffir, and Simcha Simchovitch).[53] The J.I. Segal Award was established the same year as Israel's prestigious Itzik Manger Prize for Yiddish literature, which was awarded to several Canadian Yiddish writers – Rokhl Korn, Chava Rosenfarb, Shimshen Dunsky, and Yaakov Zipper – before its final year in 1999.

A voluminous body of Yiddish-language works appeared during this period, most self-published or published with the aid of local supporters. Several authors who were very active in local literary circles began to publish books after their work appeared in the press. Among them: Mordecai Husid (1909–1988) published volumes of poetry, prose, and youth fiction; Ish Yair (Israel Shtern, 1913–2000) published fables and poetry; journalist Jacob Grossman (1898–1982) published volumes of essays and memoirs. Poet M.M. Shaffir (Moyshe-Mordkhe Shaffir, 1909–1988), who had been active in the Montreal literary scene since his arrival in 1930, published no fewer than sixteen volumes of verse between 1963 and 1987 (see Appendix). Michael Greenstein alludes to the significance of these works as repositories of both language and memory, characterizing Shaffir as "known for the purity of his language and the rich use of East-European Jewish folklore in his writing."[54]

A new phenomenon was Holocaust literature in a genre that had not previously been well represented among Yiddish writers in Canada: the novel. Chava Rosenfarb settled in Canada in 1950 and joined a vibrant community of writers in Montreal, where she was welcomed, supported, and inspired by the city's Yiddish literary milieu.[55] Having previously published poetry and drama, she began a series of novels drawing on her experience as a survivor and witness of the Łódź Ghetto and Nazi concentration camps. Author of the critically acclaimed, award-winning trilogy Der boym fun lebn (The Tree of Life, 1972), Rosenfarb emerged as one of very few Yiddish women novelists. The trilogy was followed by its prequel, Botshani (Boaciany/ Storks, 1983), and Briv tsu abrashen (Letter to Abrasha, 1992). In his analysis of Rosenfarb, Jan Schwarz argues that "The trope of Yiddish literature as sacred text – a new Torah for the surviving remnant – is a defining feature of Yiddish culture after 1945 ... The fact that Rosenfarb's trilogy was published in three massive volumes, and not initially serialized in the Yiddish press as was common for novels and memoirs, indicates that she wanted to present the novels as standing apart from the daily Yiddish press. They were perceived as sacred books (sforim)."[56] Like Rosenfarb, Yehudah Elberg (1912–2003) was a Polish-born, award-winning novelist who interrogated the legacies of the Holocaust in the 1970s and 1980s. Having survived the Warsaw Ghetto as a partisan, Elberg in 1956 settled in Montreal, where he authored half a dozen novels and volumes of short stories including Afn shpits fun a mast (On the Tip of a Mast, 1974), which portrayed life in the Warsaw Ghetto, and Kalman kalikes imperye (The Empire of Kalman the Cripple, 1983), the story of a young Jew in a Polish town on the eve of the Holocaust.

The post-Holocaust arrivals introduced new themes and approaches to Yiddish literature to reconcile their European past with their

Canadian present. In the 1970s, as she was writing the first of her novels, Chava Rosenfarb articulated a sense of both freedom and alienation in Canada that would express itself in her writing.[57] In addition to recreating Jewish Poland in her novels, Rosenfarb published a series of short stories in the *Goldene keyt* literary journal that dealt with the psychological aftermath of the Holocaust for its survivors in Canada.[58] Her daughter and translator, scholar Goldie Morgentaler, observes that in her short fiction, Rosenfarb affects "a synthesis between her primary theme of the Holocaust and the Canadian milieu where she now finds herself, so that Canada becomes the land of the postscript, the country in which the survivors of the Holocaust play out the tragedy's last act."[59] One finds similar dynamics in the writing of Rokhl Korn, who survived the Holocaust in the Soviet Union and settled in Montreal in 1948. She published six volumes of poetry and a volume of short stories from 1949 to 1977, to international acclaim. Rachel Seelig's study of Korn observes, "It was within the 'third solitude' of postwar Montreal that Korn reconstructed the communal cohesion of the idealized past and grappled with her isolation in the present."[60] Seelig situates Korn's poetry, with its evocation of the creative experience, as a way back to a lost European home within the context of her adopted home in Canada. This body of writing coincided with the rise of Holocaust public memory, notably in the creation of Holocaust museums and education programs.[61]

Among Canada's established, European-born Yiddish writers, the 1970s and 1980s marked a time of taking stock. Several writers and critics published recollections that together offer a lens onto a vibrant world of Yiddish letters in Canada within a global milieu. A volume by Mirl Erdberg Shatan (1921–2000), *Regnboygn: Lider, eseyen, zikhroynes* (Rainbows: Poems, Essays, and Memoirs, 1975), offers a retrospective of her career as a writer and critic. Sholem Shtern's *Shrayber vos ikh hob gekent: memuarn un esayn* (Writers I Have Known: Memoirs and Essays, 1982),[62] followed by Yaakov Zipper's *Araynblikn in yidishn literarishn shafn* (Perspectives on Yiddish Literary Creativity, 1983), combine literary criticism and republished book reviews, memoirs of the immigrant experience and the literary scene in Canada, and portraits of other writers. With such volumes dedicated to reflecting on past accomplishments by its participants, the 1970s mark the beginning of a concerted showcasing of Canadian Yiddish writing.

The country's corpus of Yiddish writing was first anthologized outside of Canada, in a volume titled *Kanadish* (Canadian, 1974) as volume 75 of the literary series titled *Musterverk fun der yidisher literatur* (1957–84). Published by Shmuel Rozhanski/Rollanski in Buenos Aires, the series offered Yiddish literature in a new format to maximize both its visibility and accessibility. The hundred pocket-sized hardcover volumes – sometimes organized by author, other times by theme (e.g., women's writing) or geography (e.g., Canadian writing) – compiled Yiddish texts for the widest possible readership together with a Yiddish paratextual apparatus to each volume that formed an integral part of the book: a preface, afterword, bibliographical and biographical materials, and footnotes or glossaries with potentially unfamiliar vocabulary. As a recent study suggests, "*Musterverk* implied a process of transformation of the texts by virtue of their inclusion in the collection. What might be most innovative about the project is the conviction that Yiddish literature needed and deserved its ultimate collection or 'canon.'"[63]

Kanadish offers a first post-Holocaust canon of Canadian Yiddish writing. The volume includes excerpts of poetry, prose, and literary essays, as well as essays on Jewish life in Canada. The contributors are representative of Canada's Yiddish literary community of the previous twenty years, among them Mirl Erdberg Shatan, N.J. Gotlib, Mordecai Husid, Rokhl Korn, Aaron Krishtalka, Ida Maza, Peretz Miransky, Melech Ravitch, Chava Rosenfarb, J.I. Segal, M.M. Shaffir, Sholem Shtern, Paul Trepman, Yaakov Zipper, and Falek Zolf. In his introduction, "Yiddish Literature within the Atmosphere of Cultural Pluralism," Rozhanski situates Canadian Yiddish writing within a historical context to offer comparison with his native Argentina. While he notes the impact of the proximity of New York, he argues that Canada has created a distinct culture via its writers, literary organizations, newspapers, secular Yiddish day schools, and theatre. He concludes by noting the emergence of young academics in Jewish Studies from this milieu, writing: "Yiddish Canada marks a highpoint of [contemporary] Yiddish life."[64]

The documentation and memorialization of Yiddish cultural life intensified during the 1980s with the involvement of local and national organizations in tandem with Canadian programs to promote multiculturalism. For its writers and supporters, Yiddish literature came to form an integral part of multicultural Canada, and they became increasingly invested in collecting it. This trend was motivated not by a desire to spotlight writing bound by shared ideologies or the creation of a literary canon, but by a wish to broadcast the accomplish-

ments of a literary community as well as conserve them for posterity.
One model was the lexicon of Yiddish writers, an encyclopaedic bio-
graphic dictionary. Rather than a critical assessment of Yiddish letters,
the lexicon places prominent and lesser-known writers side by side.
The most comprehensive of these, the *Leksikon fun der nayer yidisher literatur*, edited by Shmuel Niger and others, appeared in New York in
eight volumes from 1956 to 1981 and included many of Canada's Yiddish writers.

Canada produced its own lexicon authored by poet, journalist,
and essayist Chaim Leib Fuks (Fox/Fuchs, 1896–1984): *Hundert yor
yidishe un hebreishe literatur in kanade* (One Hundred Years of Yiddish
and Hebrew Literature in Canada, 1980). Previously a prolific contributor to Niger's *Leksikon*, Fuks's *Hundert yor yidishe un hebreishe literatur in kanade* comprised 429 entries on virtually every Yiddish
and/or Hebrew writer active in Canada from 1870 through the
1970s. A recent immigrant to Montreal himself, Fuks gathered the
material for the volume over a period of six years by scouring newspapers, journals, archives, and other sources. Despite its inconsisten-
cies, the volume provides a sense of the depth and breadth of Yiddish
writing in the country and points to the web of substantial and
enduring connections between writers in Canada and other centres
worldwide: they published in each other's newspapers and journals,
reviewed each other's writing, and travelled extensively on book and
lecture tours. Its English translator, Vivian Felsen, hailed the volume
as "the most ambitious attempt to preserve Yiddish culture in Canada."[65] The work was deeply embedded in the local community: the
Chaim Leib Fuks Committee comprised three writers who had long
been active in the Yiddish cultural world – Yaakov Zipper, Joseph
Kage, and Chaim Spilberg – and was published with the assistance of
the Jewish Public Library, the Canadian Jewish Congress, the Multicultural Program of the Secretary of State of Canada, as well as a
committee of supporters; it received the J.I. Segal Award in 1979
when still in manuscript form.

A second large-scale project appeared in 1982, when Chaim
Spilberg and Yaakov Zipper produced the monumental Yiddish-
English-French *Kanader yidisher zamlbukh/Canadian Jewish Anthology/
Anthologie juive du Canada*. Published by the Canadian Jewish Congress's National Committee on Yiddish, the trilingual volume celebrates Jewish creativity in Canada, with three-quarters of the
contents in Yiddish. It underlines the shift from promoting innova-

tive Yiddish writing to gathering what has already been produced, with the involvement of both community agencies and Canadian granting agencies. Most of the volume consists of poems and stories alongside essays by and about Canada's Yiddish writers, with selected summaries in the English and French sections. The editors' introduction concludes, "We would like to believe that, despite the gaps and omissions mentioned above [a lack of material about certain topics such as education], we have succeeded in providing a representative selection of the Canadian Jewish cultural heritage as it has developed over the past century, and to acquaint the reader with the contributions achieved by the pioneers of Yiddish culture in Canada."[66] Organized by genre (literary essays, poetry, fiction, studies of the Jewish experience in Canada), the literature sections feature some two dozen writers and poets. A review of the volume by Eugene Orenstein, a professor of Jewish Studies at McGill University, begins: "Canada continues to be a visible point on the map of Yiddishland: the world of Yiddish literature. Attesting to this fact is the publication of *Kanader yidisher zamlbukh*."[67]

Unlike Rozhanski's efforts to assess what constitutes Canadian Yiddish writing, the inclusive approach of the *Kanader yidisher zamlbukh* editors celebrates the rich legacies of the Canadian Jewish experience. While praising the initiative, Orenstein's review suggests: "The editors seem to assume that anything written in Yiddish by a writer who was at some point a resident in Canada is a part of Canadian-Yiddish literature. No attempt is made to raise the question of what a Canadian-Yiddish writer is, let alone to distinguish between a Yiddish 'émigré writer' and a Yiddish writer who confronts some aspect of Canadian reality."[68] However, the aims of the *Kanader yidisher zamlbukh* – to bring together as many of its participants as possible – were in keeping with the larger objectives of the Canadian Jewish Congress's National Committee on Yiddish: to foster awareness and appreciation of Yiddish cultural activity across the country. It stands in sharp contrast to the first anthology of Canadian Yiddish poetry, *Yidishe dikhter in kanade* (Jewish Poets in Canada, 1934) published by Montreal literary critic H.M. Caiserman-Vital, which aimed to offer an assessment of this corpus, its participants, and its characteristics as a first step in what was widely seen as the beginning of a vibrant Canadian literary tradition.[69] In 1982, scholarly criticism of Canadian Yiddish writing was in its infancy, as was study of the Canadian Jewish experience as a whole. Orenstein had only recently published a first article, "Yiddish

Culture in Canada Yesterday and Today," in the groundbreaking
anthology *The Canadian Cultural Mosaic* (1981); Adam Fuerstenberg
would publish two studies of Canadian Yiddish literature in the mid-
1980s.[70] The thornier question of what distinguishes a Canadian Jewish writer working in non-Jewish languages remains a topic for debate
into the present.[71]

TRANSLATION OUT OF YIDDISH

The 1970s and 1980s also marked a time of increased translation as
a means of reaching broader audiences. As I discuss in my study "Yiddish Translation in Canada: A Litmus Test for Continuity," this has
long formed a significant component of Yiddish literary life, first
through the translation of texts from world literature into Yiddish,
and subsequently through the translation of Yiddish texts into other
languages. Whereas the former indicates an active engagement with
world culture, the latter is motivated by accessibility to a broader
audience, in particular because of the decline of readers in the original language. Translations can provide a gateway into the language
for readers who then study it in order to access the original texts,
while the process of rendering Yiddish texts into other languages also
forms its own site of engagement and creativity. While Canadian Yiddish writing has been rendered into multiple languages, notably
Hebrew,[72] this chapter focuses on translation into the country's two
official languages.

Beginning in the 1970s, translation into English and French
formed a site for the discovery of, and engagement with, Yiddish
belles-lettres in Canada. One dynamic within this trend has been
English-language poets translating works by Yiddish writers. The first
of these was Miriam Waddington, a celebrated poet who was born in
Winnipeg into a Yiddishist family. Waddington's translations of a
handful of J.I. Segal's poems appeared in the pioneering American
anthology edited by Irving Howe and Eliezer Greenberg, *A Treasury of
Yiddish Poetry* (1969).[73] Since the early 1970s, translator and scholar
Seymour Levitan has produced an extensive body of work by Canadian writers, notably of Rokhl Korn.[74] From her position as a professor of Yiddish literature at McGill University, Ruth R. Wisse was
instrumental in promoting the translation of Yiddish into English.
After working with Howe on two anthologies of literary translations

from the Yiddish in the 1970s,[75] she, Howe, and Chone Shmeruck collaborated on the 1987 bilingual anthology, *The Penguin Book of Modern Yiddish Verse*, which included poetry by Melech Ravitch and Rokhl Korn.[76] Wisse also served as the first editor-in-chief of The Library of Yiddish Classics beginning in the mid-1980s.[77]

Among the most fruitful translators of Canadian Yiddish verse, one finds Ottawa-based poet Seymour Mayne. Born into an immigrant family in Montreal in 1944, Mayne began his foray into Yiddish-English translation as a doctoral student in Canadian literature at the University of British Columbia in the early 1970s. Together with Seymour Levitan, who was a junior faculty member, Mayne joined a Yiddish reading circle. During his study of Canada's Jewish writers, Mayne noted how little Yiddish poetry had been translated into English. He began to translate some of the Montreal poets – Rokhl Korn, Melech Ravitch, Mordecai Husid, and J.I. Segal – and the poems were quickly published in *Jewish Dialogue* (edited by Joe Rosenblatt). Mayne recalls that the fostering of multiculturalism in the 1970s acted as "a stimulus to a younger Jewish Canadian like myself to retrieve or bring to light in English the body of excellent poetry written in Canada by Yiddish immigrant writers," which until that time had been largely unknown in English-language literary circles.[78] The nuances of the language presented a challenge: Mayne had grown up with Yiddish at home and learned the language until grade two at the Montreal Talmud Torah (while it was still taught there in the 1950s), but, like so many Anglo-Jewish writers of his generation, he did not know Yiddish as a literary language. As a result, he and one of Montreal's young native speakers, Rivka Augenfeld, would discuss the poems and their linguistic intricacies as part of the translation process. As a translator, Mayne gravitated towards shorter lyrical poetry where he could focus on the rhythm, sound, cadence, and imagery; his most successful translations emerged when "rhymes popped up along with images that made the Yiddish poem feel as if it had almost come alive in English."[79] In the 1980s and 1990s, Mayne published his collection of English translations of Avrom Sutzkever, Rokhl Korn, and Melekh Ravitch.[80] He considers his translation of Ravitch's poem "O gute shvester, az ikh vel shtarbn" (Good Sister, When I Die, 1961)" to be among his most successful renderings. Published in his 2017 collection, *In Your Words: Translations from the Yiddish and Hebrew*, it begins (original Yiddish in figure 4.1):

Good sister, when I die
quietly heeding the last call of my name –
wrap me up in soft green linen
and deliver my body to the flames.

Up through dark smoke to the blue heights
is the way I want to surrender
all my given limbs and parts –
and become one with the sky as I soar.[81]

In the 1970s and 1980s, Yiddish texts appeared in English-language anthologies of Canadian Jewish poetry, prose, and essays. The first was a volume comprised entirely of translations, *Canadian Yiddish Writings* (edited by Sarna and Boyarsky, 1976). It was followed by anthologies that included both English texts and English translations from the Yiddish: *The Spice Box: An Anthology of Canadian Writing* (edited by Wolfe and Sinclair, 1981), and *Mirror of a People: Canadian Jewish Experience in Poetry and Prose* (edited by Oberman and Newton, 1985). These anthologies intersect with a second, specifically Canadian, trend. Beginning in the 1970s, anthologies of literature translated from immigrant languages appeared with support from local ethnic organizations as well as Multiculturalism Canada, alongside the first scholarly works on these writings. For example, Jars Balan's *Identifications: Ethnicity and the Writer in Canada* (1982), emerged out of a 1979 conference that aimed to broaden the country's literature beyond its official languages. The volume, which includes chapters on Icelandic Canadian, Ukrainian Canadian, ethnic writing, and the "hyphenated Canadian," contains Seymour Levitan's study, "Canadian Yiddish Writers."[82] Since the late 1980s, a host of other anthologies including Yiddish writing in translation have appeared: *Essential Words: An Anthology of Jewish Canadian Poetry* (edited by Mayne, 1985), *The Canadian Jewish Outlook Anthology* (edited by Rosenthal and Berson, 1988), *Canadian Jewish Short Stories* (edited by Waddington, 1990), *Not Quite Mainstream: Canadian Jewish Short Stories* (edited by Ravvin, 2001), *Contemporary Jewish Writing in Canada: An Anthology* (edited by Greenstein, 2004), and *The New Spice Box: Canadian Jewish Writing* (edited by Panofsky, 2017). Jeffrey Shandler's study, "Anthologizing the Vernacular," suggests that "Anthologies of modern Yiddish literature rendered into English (the largest corpus of Yiddish belles-lettres rendered in a non-Jewish language) seek to

אַ גוטע שוועסטער, אַז איך וועל שטאַרבן —

אַ גוטע שוועסטער, אַז איך וועל שטאַרבן,
שטום־האַרקנדיק דעם לעצטן רוף —
אין מילדער, גרינער לייוונט היל־איין
און גיב די פלאַמען אַוועק מײַן גוף.

אַזוי אַ וויל איך איבערגעבן
מיט חשבון מײַנע רמ״ח און שס״ה,
דורך טונקעלע רויכן צו בלויע הויכן —
און ווערן אַליין ווי דער הימל בלאָ.

דעם גוף צוריקגעגעבן ערלעך
אין אָט דער שעה פון אַלע שעה,
וועט די נשמה ווידער פרײַ־זײַן
און ווידער אויף אַן אייביקייט דאָ.

און ווידער אין קרייז פון די גלגולים,
און ווידער צו נאָך אַ גלגול גרייט,
צו ווערן אַ ריננ אין ריננגען ווידער
פון דער אומענדלעך־קייט.

יאָ, ריננ אין ריננגען, ווידער, ווידער —
נאָר נישט קיין גלגול מענטש — נישט דאָס —
נאָר אַ סודות־פולער הירש אין וועלדער,
בײַ ווייטע ברעגעס — אַן אַלבאַטראָס.

אַ גוטער גאָט, אַז איך וועל שטאַרבן,
באַשווער איך דיך, איך שעלט, איך בענטש:
קער אום אין טויזנט מיך גלגולים,
נאָר נישט אין גלגול מענטש.

דו פרעגסט: פֿאַרוואָס? דו מיינסט — באַהאַלטן
וויל איך דאָ פֿאַר דיר אַ סוד?
ס׳איז פשוט — גאָט, מענטש איז דײַן גרעסטער
טעות — אַ דו אַן־טעותדיקער גאָט.

⧫ 115 ⧫

Figure 4.1 Original Yiddish text of the poem, "O gute shvester, az ikh vel
shtarbn," 1961

present the unique achievement of this modern secular literature to new audiences – not only to non-Jews and non-Ashkenazim, but to the growing number of descendants of Yiddish speakers who no longer speak or read Yiddish and who have a very different sense of linguistic and cultural vernacularity than did their recent forbears."[83] Given the increasingly precarious state of secular Yiddish, what is at stake in anthologization is far more than the exposure of literary works to new audiences; as Shandler notes, "the mission is ultimately extraliterary, imposing both on the works themselves and on their readers an onus of cultural, even communal survival."[84]

Declining Yiddish audiences prompted a number of Canadian Yiddish writers to become involved in the translation of their own works into English and French, either by creating translations or by working in close collaboration with other translators. In the 1980s, Sholem Shtern succeeded in having his literary corpus rendered into English and French with the aid of translators and government grants, both as a means of reaching a broader readership and as an expression of rapprochement within a multicultural Canada.[85] Chava Rosenfarb translated her works with her daughter Goldie Morgentaler, beginning with her trilogy, which appeared in English in 1985 as *The Tree of Life*. A long process of collaboration resulted in the publication of virtually all her Yiddish fiction in English as well as a recent volume of her nonfiction. The pair worked on Rosenfarb's prose over decades, with Rosenfarb producing a first draft in English and Morgentaler reviewing the translated text and recommending edits.[86] In her essay, "Confessions of a Yiddish Writer," she explains that "From the beginning, I was deeply immersed in the Yiddish language and, for much of my life, Yiddish was for me the only means of literary expression."[87] In another essay, "A Yiddish Writer Reflects on Translation," she observes:

I do not see myself primarily as a translator, although I have in fact, with the help of my daughter, translated much of my own work. Nevertheless, when I reflect more deeply on this subject, I realize that my entire life has been a process of translation. I have been translated from my birthplace in Europe to my present home in North America. I have written three novels, one collection of short stories, four books of poetry, three plays, many essays and travelogues. Yet without translation all of these would have been relegated to the graveyard of those few libraries that still contain books in my language, or to the bottom drawer of my own desk. This is because the language in which I write, Yiddish, has fewer and fewer readers and writers. Translation represents to me my literary future. It makes me think that not everything I write will be totally lost, even if things do inevitably get lost in translation.[88]

Yiddish writers at the turn of the twenty-first century recognized that their readers primarily relied on translation, and they grappled with the implications head on. Like Rosenfarb, Yehuda Elberg collaborated on the translation of his novel *Afn shpits fun a mast* (On the Tip of a Mast, 1974) into its English version, *Ship of the Hunted* (1997), and was closely consulted in the French translation of his novel *Kalmen kalikes imperye* (The Empire of Kalman the Cripple, 1983), which was published by Pierre Anctil as *L'empire de Kalman l'infirme* (2001). Canadian scholars have observed the dynamics of translation into both English and French in a multilingual city such as Rosenfarb and Elberg's Montreal.[89]

Self-translation is far more common among Yiddish authors than among those of most other languages. Translation scholar Rainier Grutman offers three categories of self-translators "whose linguistic repertoire is characterized by asymmetry as a result of power differentials between minority and majority languages": writers who belong to any linguistic minority group who opt to translate themselves into majority languages; colonial or postcolonial writers who alternate between their own languages and those of their colonizers; and immigrant or "ethnic" writers seeking to expand their reach in their adopted countries by translating themselves into its dominant language.[90] Postwar Yiddish writers blur these categories, sometimes translating their work out of necessity and, more recently, in deliberate and creative ways that play on the dynamics between the original and target languages.[91] Multilingual English-Spanish-Yiddish translator Ilan Stavans suggests that auto-translation can result in no less than a reinvention of one's literary work.[92]

In a contrast to the move away from Yiddish, some Canadian writers with Yiddish heritage have intentionally embedded the language in their writing. Régine Robin (1939–2021), a child survivor of the Holocaust and one of the leading figures in Québécois letters, integrated Yiddish into her French-language "autofiction" in order to address Holocaust themes. Her experimental novel *La Québécoite* (1983) features a narrator who speaks in French but writes Yiddish poetry.[93] Likewise, Norman Ravvin (born 1963), a graduate of Calgary's Peretz Shule, wove Yiddish into his short story collection, *Sex, Skyscrapers, and Standard Yiddish* (1997). A final example is Gary Barwin's award-winning satirical novel, *Yiddish for Pirates: Being an Account of Moishe the Captain, His Meshugeneh Life & Astounding Adventures, His Sarah, the Horizon, Books & Treasure, as Told by Aaron, His African Grey* (2016), which features an irreverent Yiddish-speaking parrot as narrator.[94]

A NEW GENERATION

Perhaps the biggest break with the dominant trends of this period was a native-born Yiddish writer who was a product of Montreal's secular Jewish schools. The *shuln*, which taught Yiddish composition and produced school magazines to showcase it, produced a handful of Canadian-born authors in addition to Aaron Krishtalka.[95] In the 1970s and 1980s, Leybl Botwinik (born 1959), a graduate of JPPS and Bialik High School, represented a singular exception: author of short Yiddish fiction and essays in the periodical press; editor and primary contributor to a multi-volume Yiddish magazine for youth; and author of a Yiddish science fiction novel.

Botwinik stems from a family in which secular Yiddish was – and remains – strongly promoted as a living language among multiple generations. Raised in a steadfastly Yiddishist home (see chapter 2), Botwinik graduated from Bialik fluent in spoken and written Yiddish to an extent that permitted creative expression in diverse genres, including poetry, prose, and incisive essays on contemporary themes. While a student, he made his literary debut in 1974 in *Yugntruf*, the Yiddish-language journal published by and for young people. In a short story titled "Tevye's Letter from New France in 1977," Botwinik offers a satirical commentary on language politics in a fictionalized Quebec that has recently declared political independence, written in the voice of one of Yiddish literature's most beloved characters, Sholem Aleichem's Tevye. In Botwinik's New France, the province's English speakers have been ousted and only Yiddish is permitted as a Jewish language: "They think that they will assimilate us but this shows that they are not as smart as they think. Yiddish is, after all, our culture. How can we be assimilated if we are allowed to maintain our culture?"[96] In this parodic work, whose rambling monologue indicates close familiarity with the original Tevye stories, one finds expressions of Botwinik's Yiddishist activism. For example, one of the story's footnotes observes that Jewish history has increasingly been taught in English rather than Yiddish at Bialik, despite protests by both Botwinik and his father.[97] The story indicates a young author closely attuned with Quebec's turbulent political times, coinciding with the election of the separatist Parti Québécois (1976) and preceding its referendum for the province's separation from Canada (1980). In 1976, the Canadian Jewish Congress awarded Botwinik a prize for his Yiddish fiction.[98]

Botwinik became editor of four issues of a magazine his father founded, *Der nayer dor* (The New Generation, 1978–82). The magazine's mandate was "A Jewish Educational medium for Young and Old, to develop and encourage Yiddish Culture and the widespread use of Yiddish as a living language."[99] With Botwinik as its main contributor, the magazine was produced by and for young people. Illustrated with hand-drawn cartoons throughout, the contents include short articles on local cultural activity, editorials commenting on the status of Yiddish in the community, manifestos, and original short poetry and prose – much of it science fiction – as well as special sections for novice learners of Yiddish, jokes, comics, science, sports, songs, and games. The message of the magazine is unequivocal: Yiddish can and must be used as a living language in multiple settings, not only within home, school, and community life but also for entertainment, amusement, and creative expression.

Botwinik's short novel, *Di geheyme shlikhes* (The Secret Mission, 1980), published when he was twenty-one years old, stands out for two reasons: it was written by a young adult born and raised in Canada, and it was one of a very few works of science fiction in the Yiddish language.[100] The novel tells the story of Neyekh, a young man living in Vilna in the 1930s who designs a time machine that sends him fifty years into the future. After he learns from his great-nephews about the Holocaust and its aftermath, they travel through time to assist a group of chroniclers of Jewish history in a technologically advanced repository of knowledge. The novel includes not only time travel but space travel, with the theoretical basis for both involving Einstein's theory of relativity explained in idiomatic Yiddish. The novel is dedicated to family members who perished in the Holocaust and its first chapter introduces Neyekh as seeking to avenge the six million *kdoyshim* (holy martyrs). At the same time, the novel suggests that an understanding of the past can be used to build a better future.

Di geheyme shlikhes expresses the belief of its author that the natural state for Yiddish is as a fully integrated language. Its universe functions fully in Yiddish, complete with linguistic nuances. Thus, the main characters speak Botwinik's home dialect of Vilna Yiddish (Northeastern or Litvish Yiddish); for example, they say "יע *yeh*" for "yes," instead of the Standard Yiddish "יאָ *yoh*"). In contrast, in the contemporary State of Israel, Neyekh meets a policewoman who speaks Standard Yiddish because she learned it in university. The beginning of the novel vividly portrays an immersive past: "Every one of them speaks Yiddish. This is Vilna, 1930, where the Jewish residents live their lives in Yiddish: on the street, at home, at school, in the synagogue, in the store, in the hospital, in the laboratory, on the sports field, in clubs, at gatherings. Yiddish here is the 'lingua franca'; Yiddish here is the language of children and youth, the language of every age."[101] (Original Yiddish text in figure 4.2.)

A bewildered Neyekh is given to understand the perilous state of Yiddish among the Jewish youth of the 1980s in a sharp indictment of the older generation: "There are many who are guilty among the immigrant generation: a lot of them live their lives in Yiddish but keep Yiddish for themselves, they hide it from their children ... And this is why the youth is not aware of our spiritual treasures, our modern literature, or that Yiddish is capable of everything – just like all other languages – whether in the fields of mathematics and physics, music, or sports and so on."[102] This is followed by cautious optimism: "But there are good people who are working on behalf of Yiddish and are doing a lot to fight assimilation. They are swimming against the tide but we will – we must – win!!"[103]

A comparison with Michael Chabon's novel *The Yiddish Policemen's Union* (2007), set in an imaginary Yiddish-speaking Jewish homeland in Alaska, underlines the singularity of Botwinik's novel. With no real knowledge of Yiddish, Chabon's post-Holocaust Yiddish-speaking world is portrayed through the intermediary of Yiddish-accented English and Yinglish. The novel was inspired by Chabon's discovery of a phrasebook titled *Say It in Yiddish*, authored in 1958 by linguist Uriel Weinreich and his wife, folklorist Bena Weinreich. Chabon was widely reviled in Yiddishist circles for an article he published characterizing the phrasebook as "an absurd, poignant artifact of a country that never was" and yet he employed phrases from the book as dialogue to provide comic relief in his novel.[104] In contrast, Botwinik's *Di geheyme shlikhes* features Yiddish as an idiomatic and muscular vernacular that

נח, וואָס שטייט צווישן עולם אויפן מכבי־
פּלאַץ, קוקט אַ צופֿרידענער ווי זייַן ייַנגערער
ברודער, בערל, שיסט אַרייַן אַ גאָל. מיט דעם
פֿאַרענדיקט זיך דער פוטבאָל־מאַטש. בייַדע
מאַנשאַפֿטן קומען זיך אַנטקעגן און גיבן זיך אײנע
די אַנדערע די העטנט. אַלע ריידן זיי ייִדיש. — דאָס
איז ווילנע, 1930, וואו די ייִדישע אײַנוואוינערס
לעבן זיך אויס אין ייִדיש: אין גאַס, אין דער היים,
אין שול, אין בית־מדרש, אין געשעפֿט, אין
שפּיטאָל, אין לאַבאָראַטאָריע, אויפֿן ספּאָרט־
פּלאַץ, אין קלובן, אויף פֿאַרזאַמלונגען, — —
ייִדיש איז דאָ די „לינגװאַ־פֿראַנקאַ"; ייִדיש איז דאָ
דאָס קינדער־לשון און יוגנט־לשון — די שפּראַך
פֿון יעדן עלטער.

Figure 4.2 Excerpt of original Yiddish text of *Di geheyme shlikhes* (The Secret Mission)

can be used to talk about anything, from complex scientific principles to sports. The language in the novel represents nothing less than a vehicle to combat assimilation. The introduction by David Botwinik, the author's father and the publisher of the novel, expresses the hope that this work will "inspire other talented young writers to create in Yiddish and attract people of all ages who are alienated from Yiddish culture to begin to read Yiddish books, newspapers and so on."[105]

Over the next fifteen years, Botwinik would go on to publish essays, transcribed speeches, and opinion pieces in *Yugntruf* employing a rich and fluent Yiddish. He wrote on a variety of topics: the place of the Holocaust in his life; calls for increased youth-led Yiddish activism; and reports of Yiddish youth gatherings. He also contributed original short fiction and poetry.[106] He has remained active, publishing in the periodical press: most recently, he was named a winner of the Yiddish Story Writing Contest for 2020 sponsored by Israel's National Authority for Yiddish Culture, for "*Fli, farbn-flaterl, fli* (Fly, Colourful Butterfly, Fly)."[107]

Botwinik's *Di geheyme shlikhes* appeared at a time of new opportunities for youth. In 1983, Montreal's Jewish Public Library created an annual anthology for teenagers called *First Fruits*. For twenty-five years, a committee gathered poetry and prose in English, French, Hebrew, and Yiddish from some twenty Montreal high schools and published the winning compositions. In addition, Yugntruf published an anthology titled *Vidervuks: A nayer dor yidishe shrayber* (Regrowth: A New Generation of Yiddish Writers, 1989), co-edited by Eugene Orenstein and two New York poets, Beyle Schaechter Gottesman and Moyshe Steingart. Published with two other New York-based Yiddish organizations (the Yidish-Lige/League for Yiddish and the Yidisher Kultur-Kongres/Congress for Jewish Culture), the book featured twenty young Yiddish writers, including one Montrealer, Leah Lipsky. The launch at Montreal's Jewish Public Library attracted over 150 people.[108] The 1980s also continued to offer opportunities for the generation born after the Holocaust to publish Yiddish work in journals, notably *Yugntruf*.

POST-HOLOCAUST YIDDISH PUBLISHING IN ITS DECLINE: 1990S AND BEYOND

Due to natural attrition and a dearth of younger writers, the 1990s marked a time of rapidly declining Yiddish-language publishing in Canada and globally. It increasingly became the purview of a handful of Holocaust survivors located mainly in Montreal and Toronto. Diamant and Roskies observe a dramatic shift in the status of Holocaust survivors during this period, with the authoring of firsthand testimonials to the events by its remaining witnesses.[109] In this vein, the last of the Canadian Holocaust survivors published volumes documenting prewar Eastern Europe in Yiddish. In order to reach wider audiences, English translations of these works often appeared before the original Yiddish, or soon after. For example, Toronto writer Ariel Koprov (1913–2007) offers anecdotes about family life in the Bessarabian region where he grew up in *Tsvishn tsvey velt milhomes* (Between Two World Wars, 1991, English translation 1995).

The 1990s also saw the publication of Yiddish poetry, prose, song, and pedagogical materials for use in secular Yiddish schools. Ukrainian-born writer Grunia Slutzky-Kohn (1928–2020) published children's poems, short stories, and songs, beginning with *Kinder lider* (Children's Poems, 1990). A long-time teacher, her project reveals the close connection between Yiddish writers and the schools that taught their language. Produced under the aegis of the JPPS, the volume opens with an introduction by a representative of the schools: "JPPS welcomes *Kinder Lieder* [*sic*] as a valuable contribution to our Yiddish curriculum, one that will fulfill the school's goal of fostering in our students a love for Yiddish language and literature." Shifre Shtern Krishtalka (1909–2003) – a devoted teacher of Yiddish to generations of JPPS students and mother of the poet Aaron Krishtalka – published *Yidish a lebedike shprakh: A lern-program far lerer* (Yiddish a Living Language: A Teaching Program for Teachers, 1992–97). In three volumes, the work comprises 1,500 pages of pedagogical materials developed over decades of teaching, including texts and activities as well as extensive model dialogues for teachers to use in the classroom. The life's work of David Botwinik appeared in *Fun khurbn tsum lebn: naye yidishe lider/From Holocaust to Life: New Yiddish Songs* (2010). Published by his son, Alexander (Sender) Botwinik, the weighty bilingual volume contains fifty-six original solo and choral works ranging from songs for children and the Jewish holidays to Holocaust commemorations, which were composed during Botwinik's thirty-five-year career as choir director at JPPS and the United Talmud Torah Schools. The book was launched in multiple sites in Canada, the United States, and Israel and released together with recordings of the songs.[110]

By the twenty-first century, Yiddish writing by the European-born generation was being produced by just a handful of survivors worldwide. With the passing of figures such as poet Avrom Sutzkever (Israel, 2010) and poet and songwriter Beyle Schaechter Gottesman (New York, 2013), Canada became home to some of the world's last Yiddish writers who came of age in pre-Holocaust Europe. One was Polish-born poet Simcha (Sam) Simchovitch (1921–2017), author of volumes of poetry and a semi-autobiographical novel, *A shtifkind bay der vaysl* (*Stepchild on The Vistula*, 1992, English translation 1990). Having settled in Montreal in 1950 and relocated to Toronto in the 1960s, Simchovitch was active in cultural milieus that encompassed both the secular Yiddish literary world and traditional Jewish learning. A multilingual writer, he authored nineteen volumes of poetry, prose, and non-fiction in Yiddish, Hebrew, English, and Polish; he also translated his own works as well as those of others from Yiddish into English. Simchovitch expressed an abiding and sacred sense of responsibility to immortalize the world that had been lost: "There were 3.5-million Jews in Poland then. There was an intensive Jewish life, religious and secular. There were youth organizations, political organizations, sports clubs – there was so much. All of this dispersed, all of this was

wiped out and there was no time for the writers of the new generation to appear and to tell their stories. So this I felt was my main task:
to re-create this life."[111]

At her death in 2020, Slutzky-Kohn was the last of these writers in
Canada. Born in Ukraine, where she survived the Holocaust and
remained until her departure for Canada in 1980, she began to write
Yiddish-language poetry and prose a few years after she settled in
Montreal. She published eleven books of award-winning poetry and
prose in Yiddish between 1987 and 2015. Her final multilingual volume, *Survivor* (2015), includes English-language poetry and memoirs,
excerpts of her Yiddish children's poetry, Yiddish-language Holocaust
memoirs, and a selection of Russian poetry and prose. In the introduction, she notes that she began to write in Yiddish in remembrance
of the family that she lost in the Holocaust, with each of her books
containing a chapter dedicated specifically to the Holocaust: "I feel I
have a special mission to fulfill – I have to write memories."[112]

Chava Rosenfarb most keenly expressed the awareness of being one
of the last. Morgentaler observes that Rosenfarb wrote almost entirely in Yiddish to portray her native Poland, despite having spent most
of her life in Canada; she did so "out of fidelity to the lost Jewish community of her youth."[113] In an essay titled "Harps on the St Lawrence,"
Rosenfarb offers the vantage point of a participant in the decline of
her Yiddish cultural world:

> There are no more Yiddish periodicals, or Yiddish daily newspa-
> pers appearing in Canada. The Jewish Public Library is no longer
> the Yiddish Public Library. In the span of the forty-four years since
> my arrival, a desert has replaced the forest.
>
> I am convinced that the treasure of our rich Yiddish literature
> will never perish. It bears witness to our people's spiritual tri-
> umph. Our poets and prose writers will be with us whenever we
> shall encounter their winged words between the covers of their
> books. Yet it fills me with nostalgia, and, yes, with grief, to cast my
> mind back to the images of my Canadian literary past. These
> memories make me aware of how dim the lights have grown in
> the garden of Yiddish literary creativity. We have lost almost all
> the dreamers and poets who sat with us by the waters of the St
> Lawrence and who never hung up their harps on the weeping
> willows, but instead transformed our alienation into a home of
> unimagined beauty and welcome. Now they themselves have
> become the weeping willows.

Rosenfarb expresses some optimism that Yiddish literature will survive both among younger writers and new audiences of readers: "Let us hope that the treasure of our sumptuous Yiddish literature will not be forgotten or dismissed as merely a curiosity, but will instead imbue new generations with vitality and riches for many years to come. Then perhaps the sound of Yiddish harps will once again be heard by the shores of the St Lawrence."[114] However, in an interview, Morgentaler suggests that although her mother concluded the essay on a note of optimism, "I don't believe she was really optimistic about the future of Yiddish. That was why she was so eager to be translated into English."[115] In 2006, at the age of eighty-three, Rosenfarb was awarded an honorary doctorate from the University of Lethbridge. At the convocation ceremony, she framed the honour as simultaneously conferred upon Yiddish, the language of her childhood, community, and vanished world. She stated, "Little did I realize that in a few short years, Yiddish itself would no longer exist – at least not as I knew it, not as a living and breathing language of day-to-day life … And so here I am – a Yiddish writer on the prairies. A Yiddish writer who must depend on translation in order to be read."[116]

In the 1990s, Yiddish translation in Canada formed a site of significant innovation. Pierre Anctil published the first French translations of the poetry of J.I. Segal to reach Québécois audiences.[117] Anctil suggests that rising interest in Yiddish as a minority language in the 1980s served as a catalyst to situate Yiddish immigrant writing alongside English and French as part of Montreal's twentieth-century literary legacy.[118] He has published a dozen French-language translations of poetry, prose, and non-fiction works by Canadian Yiddish writers, including the memoirs and early histories of Jewish Canada by Belkin, Medres, and Wolofsky discussed above. His French translations inspired the subsequent English translations by Medres's granddaughter, Vivian Felsen. Felsen has also rendered Anctil's French translation of Fuks's lexicon of Canadian Jewish writers into English along with scholarship on Fuks's legacy.[119] In translating Yiddish for Québécois readers, Anctil was joined by poet Chantal Ringuet, who edited a first collection of Canadian Yiddish writing in French translation as a under the title *Voix yiddish de Montréal* (2013). Canada also produced translations of Yiddish women's writing with the objective of bringing to light forgotten or unknown voices. The first, *Found Treasures: Stories by Yiddish Women Writers* (1994), was produced by a collective of translators in Toronto spearheaded by feminist academic and activist Frieda Forman; it was followed by a second volume also edited by Forman, *The Exile Book of Yiddish Women*

Writers: An Anthology of Stories That Looks to the Past So We Might See the Future (2013). *Arguing with the Storm: Stories by Yiddish Women Writers* (2008) emerged out of the Winnipeg Women's Yiddish Reading Circle, and began with reading and discussing the stories within the informal setting of a *leyenkrayz* (reading group). As pioneering works, *Found Treasures* and *Arguing with the Storm* contain introductions by prominent figures in feminist Yiddish literary scholarship: Irena Klepfisz and Kathryn Hellerstein respectively.

The pairing of verse with music, which was widespread throughout modern Yiddish culture, continues into the twenty-first century. As two Canadian examples among many, poet M.M. Shaffir was recorded in the 1970s singing musical renditions of poems from his 1940 collection, *A stezshke*[120] and David Botwinik's original compositions include lyrics taken from Yiddish poet Ida Maza and others.[121] A more recent example is Toronto writer Peretz Miransky, one of the longest-surviving members of the Yung Vilne (Young Vilna) group. His Yiddish fables, which had been widely disseminated in prewar publications, school textbooks, and in published volumes in the 1970s and 1980s, appeared in new volumes of English translation locally and abroad: *Selected Poems and Fables*, published in bilingual English-Yiddish format (Toronto, 2000, Toronto), and *Between Smile and Tear: Poems and Poetic Fables* (Vilnius, 2005). However, the greatest impact of Miransky's work today is through musical adaptations on two albums: Marilyn Lerner and David Wall's *Still Soft Voiced Heart: New Yiddish Lieder* (2002) and the Flying Bulgar Klezmer Band's *Sweet Return* (2003). Most recently, Canadian Yiddish writers had their poetry set to original melodies performed by renowned Montreal-based musicians on the album by French-born artist Henri Oppenheim, *Tur Malka: New Songs of Yiddish Montreal* (2016), which includes poems by Chava Rosenfarb, J.I. Segal, Ida Maza, Melech Ravitch, Rokhl Korn, and N.J. Gotlib.[122]

Another twenty-first-century Canadian development has been the publication of popular texts to introduce Yiddish language and culture to broad audiences. Michael Wex (born 1954), a native Yiddish speaker born in Lethbridge, Alberta, published the *New York Times* bestseller *Born to Kvetch: Yiddish Language and Culture in All Its Moods* (2005); this was followed by the phrase book *Just Say Nu: Yiddish for Every Occasion (When English Just Won't Do)* in 2008. While they are often lighthearted in tone and do not shy away from vulgarity, these volumes are erudite and grounded in Wex's longstanding involvement with culture as a translator, educator, writer, and performer. A review by Yiddish linguist Dovid Katz concludes, "The *untershte shure* (bottom line)? Besides being a pleasure for anyone, every Yiddish student should really – *mamesh* – have to read it."[123] Aviva Weintraub's article, "Bordering on 'Lehavdl': Michael Wex, Performing Yiddish, and a Discourse of Discomfort," raises broader issues around the presentation of these works to suggest that his performance of Yiddish expresses a profound sense of otherness, made even more glaring by their Canadian multicultural context.[124]

The twenty-first century has brought increased academic interest in Canadian Yiddish literature. Scholars have produced new studies of Rokhl Korn, Chava Rosenfarb, and J.I. Segal.[125] As one of the world's last remaining writers to have experienced prewar Yiddish civilization, Rosenfarb's awareness of her position and her enduring commitment to Yiddish have become the subject of particular scholarly attention. Norman Ravvin writes, "Rosenfarb's dual status as novelist and eyewitness provides us with an unparalleled view of the processes by which history is transformed into art."[126]

CONTEMPORARY YIDDISH-LANGUAGE PUBLISHING

Today's Yiddish literary world comprises two primary streams: writers who have deliberately adopted Yiddish, and Haredi writers. Publishing opportunities for Canadian writers exist in both realms, producing Yiddish-language books, periodicals, and other materials. A number of periodicals and anthologies have published original Yiddish writing in the twenty-first century authored by writers not raised in prewar Europe.

Outside of the Haredi world, anthologies, newspapers, magazines, and journals – in print and online – have become the main sites for the publication of new Yiddish literature. This marks a kind of return to the pre-1950 model of collaborative publishing while also offering a forum to cultivate Yiddish writing by younger authors, many of them new speakers of the language. Two notable New York-based Yiddish periodicals feature original writing by non-Haredi writers from across the world. The *Forverts* (*The Jewish Daily Forward*, established in 1897) is a site for new literary works as well as a growing library of original multimedia materials.[127] The magazine *Afn shvel* (On the Threshold, established in 1941) features new literature alongside articles and essays. It is published by the Yidish-lige/League for Yiddish, an organization that also produces dictionaries and educational materials.[128] Some magazines active in the twenty-first century have become dormant or ceased publication: *Tsukunft* (Future, New York, 1892–2013), *Yugntruf-zhurnal* (Call for Youth, New York, 1964–2007), *Naye vegn*

(New Paths, Jerusalem, 1992–2006), *Der nayer fraynd* (The New Companion, Saint Peterburg, 2004), *Yidishe heftn* (Yiddish Notebooks, Paris, 1996–2016), *Gilgulim* (Transformations, Paris, 2008–12), and *Toplpunkt* (Colon, Tel Aviv, 2000–06). Other new Yiddish literary publications offer fresh opportunities. Among these, Israel's National Authority for Yiddish Culture has funded the production of *Yerusholaymer almanakh* (Jerusalem Almanac, established in 1973 in the Former Soviet Union, now in Jerusalem), which published a new volume in 2020, and *Yidish-land* (Yiddish Land, established 2018).[129] Further, that organization launched a national Yiddish literature contest in 2019, with the three winning 2020 entries published in the *Forverts*.[130] Two anthologies showcasing original writing by the younger generation have also appeared. *Trot bay trot: Haynttsaytike yidishe poezye* (Step by Step: Contemporary Yiddish Poetry, Italy, 2009) presents writing by twenty-two contemporary Yiddish poets with English translations.[131] *A ring/Antologye* (A Ring/Anthology, Israel, 2017), which features twenty poets born between the late 1940s and the 1980s, marks the first Yiddish anthology to exclusively feature the generation born after the Holocaust.[132]

Within a transnational Haredi world, publishing has evolved alongside the expanding role of Yiddish as a daily, spoken vernacular. Hasidim – notably adherents of Satmar, the largest group – have produced media over the last seventy years that adheres to the community's worldviews including newspapers, guides to belief and practice, children's picture books, pedagogical materials, and fiction. A recent article cautions against applying a reductionist approach to Hasidic culture: although Haredim reject the trappings of mainstream culture, they still create their own cultural products and "scholars, students, and lovers of Yiddish lose a significant opportunity by overlooking Hasidic work because of a perceived lack of artistic quality."[133] A new addition to the Hasidic publishing scene is *Veker* (One Who Awakens), a print magazine published four times a year since 2016. The publication, which began as an online magazine affiliated with the Yiddish discussion forum Kave Shtiebel, offers a variety of content: articles, interviews, and works of contemporary Yiddish prose and poetry. According to its editor, the magazine is published in Yiddish not for ideological reasons but because that is the language spoken among Hasidim. *Veker* accepts submissions from both Haredi and non-Haredi writers that fit its worldview.[134] For example, the cover story of its July 2020 issue (number 17) discussed Arun Viswanath's translation of the novel *Harry Potter and the Philosopher's Stone*, under the title "*Der kishef in yidish* (Magic in Yiddish)." In terms of Canadian content, *Veker* featured an article on Jewish mysticism by Justin Jaron Lewis, a Jewish Studies professor at the University of Manitoba, who has characterized *Veker* as "the *New Yorker* [magazine] of the Hasidic Yiddish world."[135] As a smaller Hasidic centre, Montreal has intermittently been home to Yiddish-language periodicals that include literary texts. For example, a publication called *Der moment/The Moment* (2014–17) was published by Zvi Hershkovich, a Montreal-based Lubavitch Hasid. The bimonthly newspaper featured content in Yiddish and English: news from Montreal as well as New York, editorials, commentary on Jewish sacred text, a children's page with riddles, puzzles, and games, holiday-themed short fiction, and serialized novels with Holocaust themes.[136] While beyond the scope of this book, a literary tradition in the Yiddish-infused English dialect of "Yeshivish" is emerging as a possible outgrowth of Hasidic Yiddish literature, in particular among women.[137] Given the growth of the communities, Haredi publishing will certainly increase in importance as a site for Yiddish texts, for both insiders and secular readers and writers.

YIDDISH BOOKS RECOVERED

Publishing represented a core vehicle for Yiddish transmission among the European-born generation of speakers. Fluent in the language, they wrote in Yiddish as a means of literary expression, to record and transmit their experiences, and to chronicle and memorialize a vanished world. After the Holocaust, these writers were celebrated and supported within Yiddish cultural circles. They saw themselves – and were seen by others – as the final generation who had experienced Ashkenaz before the Nazi conflagration. While the transmission of Yiddish through books marked an unequivocal success in the volume of works published, by the 1970s physical books were being cast aside in alarming numbers as their owners passed away and the younger generation lacked the facility to read them.

Efforts to salvage and collect discarded Yiddish books began. Vancouver's Peretz Centre for Secular Jewish Culture expanded its circulating Yiddish library in 1979 and later integrated Yiddish book collections from defunct organizations across Canada, such as Calgary's Peretz Shule.[138] These efforts took place in tandem with efforts on a larger scope under the auspices of the Yiddish Book Center (founded 1980, Amherst, Massachusetts), which gathered well over a million discarded books worldwide over a period of decades. Its *zamlers* (book gatherers) included a sizable cohort of Canadians across the country who laboriously collected books from private homes and institutions.[139] More recently, the Yiddish Book Center has spearheaded the digitization of virtually all of Yiddish literature, comprising almost twelve thousand titles that are available open access, free of charge, for online reading or downloading. In November 2019, it added OCR (Optical Character Recognition) technology to render this literature fully searchable online. These titles include almost all of the Yiddish authors of the European prewar generation that appear in this chapter.

In the secular context that forms the heart of this study, Yiddish publishing has not sustained itself in terms of readers or writers, with the many descendants immigrants who became writers doing so almost exclusively in English or, less often, French. The model of widespread Yiddish literary production was not sustainable for future generations in Canada. Innovation in publishing helped to spur new projects but not readers, with the direct link between books and active language transmission largely severed. By the same token, the corpus of Yiddish books published by European-born authors has functioned to preserve the language; these books have come to serve as containers for a civilization that was lost in the rupture of the Holocaust. While most are accessible in digitized versions with open access, only the few that have been translated are likely to find a broad readership. Access to published works and the created language spaces associated with literary production – readings, book launches, and so on – tend to entail a high degree of literacy. However, the circle of Yiddish publishing is rendered porous by processes of translation and other modes of dissemination. As part of my discussion of new media in chapter 6, I present another model for Yiddish book as objects of study, reverence, or display within interactive exhibits, increasingly in conjunction with online components, to be discovered by a broad public.

The next chapter examines singing as a site of Yiddish transmission and as leading to the development of new created language spaces. Here Yiddish texts are set to music and performed in an embodied and participatory way that offers a gateway into the culture as well as a site for exchange with world music and diverse traditions and identities. In contrast to written texts, singing can draw in those without a Yiddish heritage and with varying degrees of literacy. As such, singing spans multiple circles of Yiddish, from the central ring of traditional native speakers raised in pre-Holocaust Europe to the outermost ring of the broad public.

5

Yiddish Singing
The 1990s and 2000s

With the locus for Yiddish transmission outside of the Haredi world overwhelmingly shifting from families to organizations, music has offered an accessible, participatory, and inclusive mode of engagement. A longstanding and integral part of Yiddish civilization, music has become both a significant point of encounter with the culture and an entry point into the language itself. Occasions for Yiddish singing form part of a radical redefinition of intergenerational transmission by creating shared sites of dissemination among people of diverse ages and backgrounds including teachers and students, musicians, researchers, and others committed to the continuity of the language.

Over the last century, Yiddish song has formed a resilient expression of Eastern European Jewish culture. A varied corpus – folksongs, political and workers' songs, theatre songs, art songs, Hasidic and other religious songs, and more – was transmitted in political and cultural gatherings, in community choirs, and in secular Jewish schools and camps. Singing was an essential activity at gatherings of all kinds and maintained its hold against the mid-century decline of Yiddish as a spoken language. In addition to its presence within secular Yiddish education or community choirs, Yiddish song has been embraced as part of a postwar revitalization that emerged in North America as an alternative to mainstream Jewish music. It has since expanded globally. Within a network of immersive programs to teach and promote Yiddish, singing has been integrated into both formal classroom and cultural enrichment programming. The first of these, New York's Uriel Weinreich Yiddish Summer Program in Yiddish Language, Literature, and Culture (hereafter YIVO Summer

Program) was created under the auspices of the YIVO in 1968. Since then, a cluster of intensive language programs worldwide have provided language training and cultural literacy to thousands of students, among them leading musicians. The klezmer revival (also called the klezmer revitalization) of the 1970s generated a global network of institutions encompassing intergenerational and immersive music festivals and retreats that include workshops, concerts, and performances. Further, since the 1980s, Yiddish musical creativity has come to be supported by an infrastructure of established organizations and transnational networks that promote concerts, festivals, annual camps, and other opportunities to perform, study, and disseminate Yiddish song. In Canada, these include the Ashkenaz Festival (founded 1995) at its biennial gathering as well as through events throughout the year, and KlezKanada (founded 1996), which promotes Yiddish culture through music and performance, notably in an annual summer retreat.

Over the last four decades, Yiddish song has become increasingly diverse, including the genres of jazz, heavy metal, hip hop, rock, and folk music, paired with lyrics from the folksongs of prewar Jewish Eastern Europe, cantorial music and other liturgical genres, the Hasidic world, political songs adopted by the Jewish left, the Yiddish theatre in Europe and America, and Yiddish poetry, whether traditional or contemporary. Yiddish music production and performance are geographically dispersed, with a repertoire that is widely available on music and video-sharing sites and other online venues. Those who sing in Yiddish are as diverse as the repertoire: Jews of Eastern European descent who grew up immersed in the culture; those with that heritage who are exploring their roots as well as new speakers of Yiddish; professional and amateur musicians; and Jews and non-Jews attracted to the Yiddish language and culture for artistic or ideological reasons. The growing corpus of Yiddish song has widened its reach dramatically to become associated not only with an Eastern European Jewish heritage but with contemporary subcultures.

In the Canadian context, Yiddish music has come to form a site of creativity and cultural exchange for artists as well as audiences. An early example was Finjan, a Winnipeg-based band (founded in 1982) that pioneered the fusion of traditional Eastern European Jewish music with swing and other genres, paired with Yiddish lyrics. Perhaps most famous is eclectic Montreal-based artist Josh Dolgin (born 1976). Under the stage name "Socalled," he spearheaded a klezmer-hip hop hybrid featuring Yiddish rap and other vocals in his albums *Hiphopkhasene* (2003), *The Socalled Seder* (2005), and *Ghettoblaster* (2007). A performer and workshop leader, he has worked on projects such as an original Yiddish musical, *Isaac Babel's Tales from Odessa* (created in 2013, recorded in 2017).[1] Scholars have interrogated the use of Yiddish in Dolgin's work and the impact of technologies such as sampling that fuse a recorded Yiddish past with the present in order to create new cultural forms.[2] Against a decline in communicative fluency and firsthand experience of Yiddish culture, artists such as Dolgin have attained increasing familiarity with Yiddish through music, notably at festivals such as KlezKanada. Singing also serves to bring diverse artists together to revitalize Yiddish literary texts. As one example, the 2016 album of music by French-born artist Henri Oppenheim, *Tur Malka: New Songs of Yiddish Montreal*, sets the poetry of immigrant writers to original melodies performed by local artists such as jazz vocalist Karen Young. Through musical adaptation of the poems, the project "aims to revive an important period of Yiddish culture in Canada."[3] In Canada and abroad, singing has increased cultural literacy among a younger generation, which may lack exposure to Yiddish at home but be more familiar with traditional Yiddish music than previous generations.

Around the turn of the millennium, the music scene expanded in tandem with a surge of academic interest, with participant-scholars investigating the transformation of Yiddish culture since the Holocaust. Both Jeffrey Shandler's studies of postvernacular Yiddish and Abigail Wood's concept of a heterotopic Yiddishland interrogate the implications of a contemporary music scene that may or may not intersect with the communicative functions of the language. Here Yiddish is reconstituted not as a language of everyday life but as a symbolic or separate space by and for an amorphous group of adherents. In "Yiddish as Performance Art," Shandler writes:

> Yiddish concerts and sing-alongs, as well as other anthological performances of Yiddish texts, function like museums, presenting a selection of cultural fragments whose juxtaposition enables attendees to experience a cultural expanse ranging over generations and across continents. In these performances, collections of songs (or of poems, stories, folktales, proverbs, jokes, etc.) limn the dimensions of Yiddish culture as a totalized "world." Elided in these enterprises are the nuances of Ashkenazic subcultures, the

dynamics of their history, and the complexities of their erstwhile multilingual and multicultural contacts. But what is gained is an ameliorating vision of Yiddish as constant and comprehensive.[4]

Wood, in turn, nuances Shandler's concept of the "postvernacular" by positing that transmission of cultural literacy is occurring through Yiddish song: "In focusing on language, Shandler's model of postvernacularity posits the end of fluency and the move towards a highly valued but atomised Yiddish. Such a Yiddish necessarily focuses on performance rather than creativity: the Yiddish language becomes an end rather than a means. Here, however, musicians point towards a new kind of vernacular use of Yiddish: aesthetic rather than ethnic or linguistic; embedded among rather than separated from other cultural forms."[5]

With the number of native speakers dwindling, the questions *by whom*, *when*, and *where* Yiddish is being spoken are overshadowed by *how* and *why*. If our understanding of the vernacular uses of the language expands to encompass creative engagement and the enthusiasm or connections that this activity evokes, singing can be framed as a site of continuity, to be encountered on its own terms, neither fragmented nor inchoate. The virtual absence of people outside of the Haredi communities having grown up exposed to Yiddish as an everyday vernacular is prompting a profound relocation and reinterpretation of cultural literacy and participation. In the two decades that have passed since Shandler and Wood conducted their fieldwork, many of their observations still hold true. Singing has become linked to identity and the formation of spaces for shared community experiences within a contemporary cultural milieu where Yiddish serves as a linguistic denominator but where fluency is not an essential feature. A new generation of young people has gravitated towards Yiddish within institutional settings where singing forms a focal point of participatory engagement. These newcomers have taken on leadership roles within the Yiddish music world as directors and coordinators of programs and as resources of cultural capital.

This chapter builds upon Shandler and Wood's theoretical models by examining the ways in which singing generates created spaces for Yiddish language transmission. I discuss music as an accessible and embodied point of access, with song offering a gateway into linguistic acquisition as well as an anchor for Yiddish speakers to maintain or strengthen their connections with the language. I provide a brief comparison with Scottish Gaelic to discuss singing as a strategy of language learning and revitalization. I also examine the subculture of Queer Yiddishkeit that emerged from the music scene as model for continuity. As in previous chapters, the particular focus is on Yiddish continuity among youth. I investigate singing as a site of continuity within two spaces: the klezmer music scene and its immersive camps, with a focus on Canada's KlezKanada retreat, and the community-based choir, with a focus on the Vancouver Jewish Folk Choir. The fieldwork for this chapter was conducted in 2019 and included my participation at the KlezKanada retreat and a concert of the Vancouver Jewish Folk Choir as well as interviews. In order to tease out the place of music within Yiddish continuity, I spotlight the perspectives of individuals who became involved with these organizations as young people (aged twenty-five to forty-five) around the turn of the millennium, have remained involved with them for ten years or more, and have deliberately studied Yiddish and remain engaged with its cultural milieu into the present. In the concentric circles of secular Yiddish, the focus of this chapter is four circles from the middle, encompassing people with a wide range of knowledge and backgrounds and where transmission occurs via a participatory activity that does not require fluency in Yiddish (see figure 0.1).

YIDDISH SINGING
AND LANGUAGE REVITALIZATION

Over the last fifty years, Yiddish singing has evolved any number of connotations for its practitioners: countercultural, progressive, radical, celebratory, heritage, memorializing, sacred, and devotional, among others. Singing in a minority language like Yiddish can be readily adapted to countless performative, educational, and social contexts and paired with diverse musical traditions, repurposed and reimagined. The very act of singing in a minority language can create community and connection. Writing about the role of singing as part of her fieldwork, Wood asserts: "The majority of those who identify with Yiddish language and culture are not specialist musicians, and most contexts for song are combined with other activities: the theatre, social events, education or commemoration. Song is constitutive of community: an enjoyable, sociable activity, and is a structural element that can be used and re-used in creating contexts for the performance of language. Singing is in itself a reason to get together, and a means of performing common purpose once gathered. In performance, songs become a concretized manifestation of culture and community."[6]

Wood posits that singing facilitates the creation of the counterspaces that transform the mundane and everyday into "heterotopic instantiations of Yiddishland."[7] In this formulation, singing together creates an inclusive community where imagined Yiddish worlds connecting past and present can be constituted, even if only briefly. Further, Yiddish song supports cultural exchange, notably among those who travel internationally to perform, research, study, or teach. This flexible cultural literacy is of particular significance in the wake of the massive dislocation of the Holocaust. Wood posits that post-Holocaust initiatives in salvage ethnography and publication of collected folklore have shifted the site of song transmission so that "mother to child becomes folklorist to public," while the publication of Yiddish songbooks has created a canon.[8] The professionalization of Yiddish culture combined with a disconnect between the historical contexts of the songs and their performers and listeners has shifted the dynamics of cultural authority. Wood writes, "Today's folklorists, academics, compilers and teachers play the roles of cultural representatives, standing in for a world lost to the observer, and providing an answer to which questions about Yiddish culture could be addressed given the lack of surviving family members."[9] These representatives bring their own values to the project: a recent ethnographic study of contemporary American Yiddish culture suggests that "most Yiddish devotees today are academics, artists, and other members of the 'creative class' who work in fields of cultural production in which criteria of newness and innovation are prized."[10] Other attributes attributed to Yiddish singing may include nostalgia and memorialization.

Within sites of learning – schools and camps for children, and adult education – Yiddish song has served to support fluency, functioning not only to increase linguistic competence but to build and teach cultural literacy. In recent decades, singing has become deeply ingrained in the teaching of Yiddish language and culture in workshops as well as in the classroom, in contexts both formal and informal. For example, Wood recalls that as a student in the YIVO Summer Program, she sang musical versions of poems studied in class; "While the texts formed the basis for language exercises, the message was clear: songs not only are an aid to language learning, but also help one to internalize and to perform a Yiddishist message: traditional Jewish

life, Yiddish literature and song and the survival of the language itself
are all bound up together."[11] Shared cultural literacy, with singing as
a core component, both builds and helps to define a Yiddishist community "shared across time and place."[12] Gathering around song in
secular educational and community settings builds an inclusive Yiddishland that and can bridge generations, diverse origins, and geographic distances.

Due to fundamental religious and ideological divides as well as
different cultural and aesthetic goals, singing in the non-Haredi and
Haredi worlds occurs largely in mutual isolation, as both spheres produce their own music with Yiddish lyrics. In the Haredi world, song
functions in tandem with religious observance and embodies its
norms.[13] However, some secular song practitioners look to the contemporary Hasidic world as carriers of the vocal tradition, while the
Hasidic world has given birth to an Orthodox pop music industry
that makes Yiddish singing accessible to a broader public.[14] This
genre, which has yielded crossover stars such as American Hasidic
singer Lipa Schmeltzer, is disseminated to the wider public via digital
music distribution platforms such as Spotify.

Children's singing is a particularly effective means to promote
intergenerational Yiddish transmission. Children's music facilitates
linguistic and cultural continuity beyond childhood, with these songs
having formed an integral part of Yiddish cultural literacy. An Australian 2013 study, "Music and the Continuity of Yiddish Language
and Culture in Melbourne," recommends teaching the language to
children through singing as a foundation for formal language acquisition.[15] Wood suggests that children's songs offer new speakers of the
language the opportunity to access the Yiddish childhood they did
not themselves experience; she writes, "Within a disrupted linguistic
society, learning children's songs at least allows this childhood to be
redeemed, enabling an illusion of cultural fullness."[16]

Innovative projects to transmit language and culture to children
via song have taken place in Canada. One example is a children's
play group at Montreal's Jewish Public Library called Yidishe Kinder
(Jewish children) held at the Norman Berman Children's Library in
the 1980s and 1990s. Founded in 1983, it evolved as a group for tod-
dlers and their caregivers in response to a request for more early
childhood programming in Yiddish by the Hasidic community; it
was soon overrun by secular families who sought a way to expose
their children to the language. With a Heritage Language Grant

from Multiculturalism and Citizenship Canada, Yidishe Kinder coordinators, librarian Eva Raby and children's musician Sandy Kogut, created an album of some two dozen songs for children and their families, *Kinder Klangen: Holiday and Play Songs for Children ... of All Ages* (1995). Accompanied by a booklet of song lyrics, the album has been widely used by parents and teachers worldwide. Eva Raby notes that it has enabled her to pass on elements of the Yiddish language to her own grandchildren.[17]

SCOTTISH GAELIC SINGING

As an endangered language with few native speakers whose revitalization is increasingly tied to new learners, the dynamics around Scottish Gaelic singing in Canada offer a revealing comparison with secular Yiddish. Song – both imported and local – has played a pivotal role in language transmission in Canada, alongside instrumental and dance traditions. Gaelic scholar Jonathan Dembling suggests: "[m]usic is almost always a central feature of language revitalization efforts. An endangered language's musical and dance traditions typically attract much larger audiences than language classes, and so events such as dances and concerts are a productive 'hook' to draw in potential learners and advocates for the language. Music also provides a vital cultural context in which language activity takes place; songs in particular are effective tools in language instruction, simultaneously providing lessons in linguistic and cultural competency."[18] Some of the same dynamics that exist around Yiddish music in terms of continuity and innovation are also found with respect to Scottish Gaelic in Canada. For example, linguistic erosion has meant that increasingly, the performers and their audiences do not speak the language or are new speakers, which has resulted in contested notions of agency and authenticity.[19] By the same token, singing has offered an important opportunity for social engagement among newcomers to Scottish Gaelic. For example, at the Colaisde na Gàidhlig/The Gaelic College on Cape Breton Island, singing opens a majority of classroom sessions to encourage a sense of community among the students as well as to improve pronunciation and vocabulary.[20] Writing about Cape Breton Island, where the language is spoken by just a few hundred people, ethnomusicologist Heather Sparling found that in the early 2000s, although native or fluent speakers were likely to dismiss the Puirt-á-beul (vocal dance music) as brief, repetitive and easy-to-learn, they were potentially "fundamental to the enculturation of 'new' Gaels."[21] A further study found that the production of "traditional music" fostered a sense of connection and shared identity as well as strong emotion ("heritage passions and convictions"), which benefited language learning.[22] Recent studies of Scottish Gaelic in Cape Breton affirm that with a shortage of formal learning settings, younger generations were exposed to the vibrancy of the language at intergenerational parties known as *ceilidhs* ("visits") or at concerts that combined singing, instrumental music, and dance. These settings offered "highly motivating slow experiences" that supported the students in their learning by deepening a sense of connection to the language.[23]

YIDDISH SINGING WITHIN KLEZMER MUSIC

The genre most often associated with "Yiddish music" is klezmer, which has come to refer to an eclectic category of world music with Eastern European Jewish roots. The term "*klezmer*" (plural: *klezmorim*) originally referred to a musician within a band that performed the celebratory instrumental tradition forming the cornerstone of Eastern European Jewish weddings. Over a period of some three centuries, their repertoire was also performed for audiences and to accompany dance, until its decline to near obscurity by 1950 in the wake of the Holocaust.[24] Among Jewish immigrants to America and their descendants, this style of music was supplanted by popular music, in which American Jews like Irving Berlin, Richard Rodgers, and Jerome Kern were prominent. Accounts by participant-scholars indicate that klezmer music emerged as a genre in the United States in the mid-1970s, when musicians began to explore specifically Jewish music within the American folk revival as an alternative to music associated with religious observance or Israeli culture.[25] 1970s klezmer musicians combined a return to the music's roots with new approaches; often unbeknownst to each other, they sought out recordings and mentorship from carriers of the prewar European tradition in order to create music that fused heritage with innovation. The overlap between the study, practice, performance, teaching, and academic research among the cohort of klezmer revivalists is high, with many of the same musicians in multiple roles: unearthing and expanding the repertoire; participating in ensembles and projects on stage or in recordings; sharing their knowledge in workshops and classes; and publishing scholarly studies. By and large, these musicians have remained active over decades as performers, researchers and teachers, a commitment to creativity, research, and teaching being a core feature of the klezmer scene. A second wave in the 1990s infused the genre with new hybridity as klezmer increasingly mixed with other musical styles and integrated Yiddish lyrics from new sources. For example, the Klezmatics (founded 1986) offered interpretations of Yiddish poetry from folklore, the labour movement, as well as composing original lyrics to reflect the band's progressive politics.[26]

Klezmer music has converged with a resurgence of interest in Yiddish language and culture in two main ways. First, since the klezmer revival of the 1970s, bands have featured vocalists who sing in Yiddish and often integrate spoken Yiddish into their onstage interactions with audiences (e.g., greetings, comments between songs). The process of pairing an instrumental melody with Yiddish lyrics entails exploration: selecting an existing Yiddish song that may be lesser known, setting a Yiddish poem to music, or composing original lyrics. Second, the culture that has evolved around the klezmer scene – in particular the expansion of multi-day music camps and festivals – has created an opportunity for Yiddish to reach broader audiences. Involvement in the klezmer scene has prompted musicians to learn Yiddish and produce their own creative work in the language. As one example among many: an article about American musician Daniel Kahn notes that an interest in learning and translating klezmer songs prompted him to study Yiddish.[27] Kahn's Yiddish-language translation of Leonard Cohen's song "Hallelujah," originally for a choral performance at KlezKanada, was posted on web-sharing sites and went viral after Cohen's passing in 2016.[28]

While, historically, singing did not form part of the klezmer repertoire, it became a core component of the genre in the 1970s and ever since, as its artists increasingly paired the instrumental music with Yiddish lyrics. Wood observes, "Not only is the klezmer revival the most prominent context for the performance of Yiddish song today, but, vice versa, song has become integral to the klezmer scene, providing an important medium for musical and cultural creativity."[29] Zev Feldman's 2016 *Klezmer: Music, History, and Memory* points to the tensions inherent in bringing together klezmer music and Yiddish song: "We must remember, however, the novelty of the combination … While at the start of the klezmer revitalization, some of its practitioners (like the present author) were adamant in maintaining the traditional distinction between instrumental music and Yiddish song, increasingly the first and especially the second generation of klezmer practitioners have sought to negotiate their relationship to Yiddish song without losing their primary identity as klezmer musicians."[30]

Yiddish song encompasses lyrics from a variety of sources, including folksongs, theatre songs, poetry, or original compositions in a creative process of pairing, production, and performance. This eclectic approach might yield, for example, an instrumental piece that originated as part of a traditional wedding ceremony being paired with a poem authored by a Yiddish poet of the 1920s. While the primary vernacular of the klezmer revival is English – the language musicians and scholars use to talk, write, or teach about the genre – the primary language of song remains Yiddish. One of the challenges lies in the communication boundaries between singers who choose to perform in Yiddish and audiences who rarely speak the language.

The role of the vocalist exemplifies the ways in which klezmer and the Yiddish cultural arts more broadly are bound up with collective traditions on the one hand, and contemporary individualism on the other. Klezmer singers eclectically draw on vocal repertories with origins in an Eastern European past. While few singers possess the linguistic fluency to compose their own lyrics, Yiddish has remained the genre's primary vehicle of vocal expression and a source for creativity through interpretations or arrangements of songs that reflect contemporary realities or identity politics. Further, Wood observes, "As the 'voice' of a band, singers are invested with cultural authority."[31] In performing the Yiddish lyrics of the past on their own terms, klezmer singers imbue them with new meaning.

Two discourses associated with klezmer transfer more broadly into the culture around Yiddish transmission: that of authenticity and continuity with a historical past and Old World tradition on the one hand, and innovation and openness on the other. Barbara Kirshenblatt-Gimblett posits that the klezmer scene emerged in the late 1970s as part of the radical youth counterculture in a "catalytic rupture" from previous traditions of Jewish wedding or heritage music in America. Encompassing diverse and fluid musical influences and ideologies not connected to political or religious movements, klezmer music offered fertile ground for innovation and shared characteristics with youth and countercultures.[32] Amanda Scherbenske posits two seemingly contrasting modes that emerged in klezmer: first, an "authentic" musical practice through study of the Eastern

European folk tradition and the involvement of veteran musicians as mentors; second, an "experimental" practice building upon the jazz background of many klezmer revivalists, in which a high value is placed on improvisation, creativity, and individual expression.[33] Mike Anklewicz suggests that because "klezmer" historically represents a category of – rather than a name for – an eclectic and changing repertoire of music adapted to the needs of the community, it can be understood as an inherently hybrid genre. He also argues that the rupture caused by the earlier marginalization of klezmer music in favour of Israeli culture within the Jewish mainstream ultimately freed it from ideological baggage and made it possible for musicians to generate their own styles.[34] Klezmer music emerged out of a cultural dislocation and was unclaimed by any single segment of American Jewish life, which resulted in tremendous freedom. At the same time, it remains bound to its Eastern European origins, musical traditions, and heritage.

As klezmer is a significant entry-point into Yiddish, many of its characteristics transfer into the culture around it: fluidity, hybridity, freedom from any single ideological orientation, and inclusivity. A cohort of younger, non-native, or new speakers – some of them descendants of Yiddish speakers, others with no heritage connection – has been steadily gravitating towards Yiddish culture as an alternative to the Jewish or broader cultural mainstream. Some enter through klezmer music and then become immersed in the language; others begin in the classroom and seek out other expressions of the culture. As Shandler suggests, for this cohort, this non-hegemonic language can offer a "Jewish signifier of the diasporic, politically progressive, culturally avant-garde, feminist or queer."[35]

QUEER YIDDISHKEIT AND INTERGENERATIONAL TRANSMISSION OF YIDDISH

A queer Yiddish subculture emerged in the 1980s as an outgrowth of the alternative politics of the klezmer revival. It has become known under the umbrella of "Queer Yiddishkeit" (also: Queer Yiddishkayt), which refers to the activities of musicians, artists, performers, and theorists involved in Yiddish cultural production that exposes or critiques socially established norms and imagines possible alternatives. The term "queer," an umbrella term for gender minorities who are not heterosexual or cisgender, challenges dominant, hegemonic, and heteronormative ways of thinking. For example: what constitutes success versus failure (other models than milestones such as marriage, biological reproduction, and career trajectory); the linearity of time and alternative possible futures; and identity as performed rather than predetermined. In *Like Everyone Else … but Different*, Morton Weinfeld asserts, "Any discussion of klezmer music would be incomplete without acknowledging the role of queer culture in the genre's revival… This affinity between klezmer and queer sensibilities is also true for the Canadian scene.[36]

Perhaps the most widely known example of Queer Yiddishkeit is the popular Yiddish song, "Ale Brider" (All Brothers). A folklorized version of a poem written by New York labour poet Morris Winchevsky (1856-1932), the song was featured by the Klezmatics on their debut album, *Shvaygn=Toyt* (Silence Equals Death, 1988). The album title, whose English version was a slogan of AIDS activism, identified the Klezmatics as the first klezmer band to associate with the surge in queer activism,[37] as did two new verses the band added to Winchevsky's poem. The song has been widely taught in Yiddish classes and has also come to function as a feminist and queer Yiddish anthem because of its inclusion of women's and gay voices within Jewish tradition. Wood considers the added lyrics emblematic of the "narrative of rebirth" at the core of the resurgence of Eastern European music in North America during the 1980s and 1990s. She quotes Winchevsky's original two verses (lines 1, 2 and 3, 4) followed by the two new verses the Klezmatics contributed (lines 5, 6 and 7, 8, English translation provided):

Un mir zaynen ale brider	And we're all brothers
Un mir zingen freylekhe lider.	And we sing happy songs.
Un mir haltn zikh in eynem	And we stick together
azelkhes iz nito bay keynem.	Like nobody else.
Un mir zaynen ale shvester	And we're all sisters
azoy vi rokhl, rus un ester.	Like Rachel, Ruth and Esther.
Un mir zaynen ale freylekh	And we're all gay
Vi yoynoson un dovid hameylekh.	Like Jonathan and King David.[38]

Klezmatics founding member, Alicia Svigals (born 1963), has been a voice of Queer Yiddishkeit for close to twenty-five years. In her 1998 article and manifesto "Why We Do This Anyway: Klezmer as a Jewish

Youth Subculture," Svigals recalls: "One of the most interesting new
developments in the Yiddishist movement and the klezmer revival is
a move towards a kind of twenty-something, in-your-face radicalism,
which carries a banner of Yiddish culture as a symbol of unapologetic
Jewish pride à la 'Queer Nation' ... The wider Yiddishist scene owes
this new trend in large part to the growing 'Queer Yiddishist' movement, made up of Queer Nation types who also identify as Yiddishist,
and who bring a queer radical sensibility to Yiddishism."[39] Revisiting
the topic in her 2021 article, "Whither Queer Yiddishkayt?" Svigals
observes the fruitful and fluid state of a movement she had initially
deemed "mostly aspirational" and that has since produced a rich array
of performance and publication that is alternately brazen, funny,
inclusive, sex-positive, and erudite. She concludes, "My brief follow-up
to my 1998 Manifesto is: let us always aim to expand beyond the best-
known vocabulary and easy Yinglish! Ever forward and ever deeper
with our beautiful Yiddish culture!"[40]

The image included with Svigals's article is the cover of a chapbook
titled *Schmutz* (Dirt, 2020) by Montreal writer Jess Goldman that
emblematizes many of the features of Queer Yiddishkeit. Goldman
explores the complex relationships between Jewishness and history,
heritage, politics, and culture in the project by "queering Yiddish folktales and through queer protagonists."[41] As Svigals points out, the
opening story, "Evelilith," which depicts a love affair between the biblical figures of Eve and Lilith, "brings queers into the tale of the very
creation of the world." [42] The stories are written in lively English that
incorporates some two hundred Yiddish words, which appear in a
glossary at the end. In the story, "Blumeh's Pleasure Quest," Goldman's
narrator says: "Tonight, I'd speak only Yiddish. At times it sounded
like a made-up language, a language of non-language, of gut and emotion, not speech. And though many Yids had tried to lift it out of its
pool of emotion and dry it off for the holy page – flicking off its flecks
of *matzoh*, carrot, onion, and dill, expunging its sweat and menstrual
blood with disinfectant – there was power in its immediacy. Yiddish
was like music: its notes hit you first, you felt it first."[43] In an interview, Goldman explained that the intent for the project was not to
have readers agree with the critiques or the uses of Yiddish suggested
by *Schmutz,* but to spur discussion about "a complicated reckoning
with history and with what it means to be Jewish, what it means to be
queer, the good and the bad, and the messy."[44] The book was written
at the beginning of Goldman's Yiddish journey, which has included

Figure 5.1 Cover of Jess Goldman's chapbook *Schmutz*, 2020

integrating more and more of the language into their work. Goldman is a self-directed new learner who has been studying Yiddish in private lessons with the Jewish Public Library's unofficial resident Yiddish expert, Moishe Dolman,[45] as well as in online courses; they have also attended KlezKanada.[46]A further example of a Queer Yiddishkeit text, this time from Australia and with Yiddish represented in its own alphabet, is *Kugel Western,* a graphic "sci-fi Western" by Mira Schlosberg that combines images with sparse Yiddish text to tell the story of a lesbian intergalactic erotic encounter between a cowgirl and an alien.[47] Both works reimagine genres and landscapes through a subversive queer lens that foregrounds the sounds of Yiddish.

In tandem with broader trends in queer theory, Queer Yiddishkeit is bound up with performativity. One frequent characteristic of contemporary Yiddish cultural production is camp, a mode that values the playful, the theatrical, and the ironically over-the-top. This sensibility, which emerged as part of queer culture in the 1960s, offers a significant point of intersection with Yiddish, in particular in performance such as drag.[48] The associations between non-hegemonic languages and campiness that characterize Yiddish also form a feature of other cultures with histories of hegemonic domination, for example the "camping" of Tagalog folklore in the Philippines.[49] Another facet of Queer Yiddishkeit entails bringing to light queer subtexts within existing works of literature, theatre, or film as well as using them as inspiration for contemporary performances.[50] For example, the classic Yiddish play *Der Dibuk: Tsvishn Tsvey Veltn* (The Dybbuk: Between Two Worlds, written by Sh. An-sky and first performed in 1920)[51] and its 1937 Yiddish film interpretation of the same name have prompted conversations about queer subtexts as well as novel interpretations. In her pioneering work in the 1990s, klezmer musician and film scholar Eve Sicular decodes queer subtexts in *Der Dibuk* and other classic Yiddish films of the 1920s and 1930s.[52] In a recent article identifying connections between Queer Yiddishkeit and *Der Dibuk*, Rokhl Kafrissen observes that "many of the most important Yiddish cultural spaces today have been built by queer artists and scholars, many of whom felt empowered to return to Jewish spaces not defined by the heteronormativity, and homophobia, of traditional Judaism."[53] Over the last decades, secular Yiddish has increasingly attracted queer-identified teachers, musicians, and activists.

The implications of an oppositional queer worldview extend beyond cultural material to a paradigm for Yiddish continuity more broadly. Queerness calls into question deeply rooted binary concepts of sexual or gender normativity and the idea of a fixed biological imperative, and by extension, interrogates social constructions of temporality and spaciality. As Jack Halberstam writes, "Queer uses of time and space develop, at least in part, in opposition to the institutions of family, heterosexuality, and reproduction. They also develop according to other logics of location, movement, and identification."[54] Lee Edelman's provocatively titled book, *No Future: Queer Theory and the Death Drive*, offers a radical polemic that "interrogates the politics that inform the pervasive trope of the child as figure for the universal value attributed to political futurity."[55] Concepts of queer temporality can also suggest a hopefulness or utopian potentiality.[56] José Esteban Muñoz's 2009 *Cruising Utopia: The Then and There of Queer Futurity*, proclaims: "The future is queerness's domain. Queerness is a structuring and educated mode of desiring that allows us to see and feel beyond the quagmire of the present."[57] Within Jewish studies in recent years, scholars like S.J. Crawsnow and Noam Sienna are positioning queerness as a site for resisting normativity as well as for innovative and creative renewal.[58] In their 2018 study, *Queer Expectations*, literary scholar Zohar Weiman-Kelman builds upon Halberstam's concept of "the queer art of failure" and the valuable process of discovering alternatives to conventional concepts of success.[59] Weiman-Kelman concludes:

> By treating Yiddish as an alternative past and an alternative passed, one avenue of Jewish history that did not come to fruition, it becomes a queer tool for the present. The value of bringing it into our current conversation by going back to its time of expectancy lies in understanding the present we are living in as but one of the many futures that Jewish history could have had. And it is opening that past potentiality that can make room for complexities that the present would have us obscure ... Rather than fighting for a national heteronormative future viability that leaves much of the Jewish past and present behind at the expense of actively oppressing many others, I turn backward in search of a queer history, in queer expectation of radical change now.[60]

Queer Yiddishkeit entails potentially subversive, transgressive, or non-conformist ways of thinking about questions of Jewish identity, gender, space, and time, and, of greatest significance to this study, concepts of transmission. Shandler suggests that Queer Yiddishkeit offers "an alternative to a biological model of conceptualizing intergenerational cultural transmission."[61] He explains: "The alternative model of Jewish continuity implicit in Queer Yiddishkeit contests traditional notions of cultural and communal continuity, which are rooted in heterosexual reproduction and family life, and which are assumed as normative in almost all discussions of the continuity of Yiddish ... Instead of the ideal image of culture as an enduring inheritance passed from parents to children, the queer paradigm of culture is that of a dynamic proving ground, its constancy comprising an ongoing breaking down and rebuilding of cultural practices and sensibilities among closely differentiated cohorts."[62] Within this queer model for cultural continuity, Yiddish transmission does not rely on a parent passing the language on to a child. Rather, it suggests alternative genealogies for transmission: among cohorts with shared interests, teacher to learner, singer to student, or among peers. The concept of generation can be very fluid, with transmission occurring in a variety of contexts. In the contemporary non-Haredi world, declining numbers of native speakers implies that Yiddish is not reproducing within biological families but is rather being chosen by new speakers, artists, and activists who are deliberately opting to engage with the language. In a 2016 interview, Weiman-Kelman suggests:

> The idea of language being chosen rather than inherited really offers a fundamental challenge to reproductive heteronormative cultural transmission. What I mean is that the way in which we imagine identity, family, and even history as structured based on blood-ties binding nuclear families for generations is fundamentally challenged when we think of a language being chosen. Because Yiddish is so intimately bound with reproduction, even in its being called "mother tongue," thinking of it as a choice makes us think about all the ways we queerly create other identities, families, and histories outside the norm.[63]

Weiman-Kelman explains in their introduction to *Queer Expectations* that Yiddish suggests "non-normative ways of looking forward" as a language that is largely no longer transmitted as a native language outside of the Haredi world. They write, "In order to have a future, it must be actively (queerly) chosen rather than (heteronormatively) produced and inherited. Turning away from the languages of my present (Hebrew and English) to Yiddish means adopting a past I did not inherit, making Yiddish itself a foundling language, rather than a normatively generative one."[64]

As a "foundling language," secular Yiddish offers opportunities for new learners in each generation to explore and build upon elements of a Jewish usable past, in particular its leftist, progressive heritage. The positioning of secular Yiddish within immersive environments such as intensive language programs, retreats, or music festivals – in remove from the mundane and everyday – has entrenched a utopian character in Yiddish transmission; in this vein, a 2017 article by two participants in an American Yiddish language program about their experiences is titled "Seeking and Queering Utopia."[65] The carrier of transmission becomes the teacher, researcher, or musician as cultural authority within chosen space such as a workshop or lecture hall.

Drawing on the leftist heritage of Yiddish and their own queer identities, organizers are building in-person and virtual spaces to come together to study, sing and actualize their activist politics. In a Canadian example, since 2015, writer, cultural organizer and activist freygl gertsovski has been actively building a Queer Yiddish community in person and virtually from their home north of Tkarón:to/Toronto. Drawing on grassroots activism around feminist, Queer/Trans, environmental justice, and disability issues and Yiddish learning, gertsovski is a co-organizer of Rad Yiddish, which offers Queer Yiddishist Shmueskrayzn (conversation groups) and other activities.[66]

The Yiddish music scene offers a space to enact the utopian subculture suggested by Queer Yiddishkeit. It brings together people of diverse ages and backgrounds to grapple with, reinterpret, create, and perform Yiddish-language texts. Within this process, the concept of generationality has thus become less about when and where one was born and more about attained knowledge of the language and culture. Concepts of expertise and authority have shifted significantly over the last three decades from native-born speakers to teachers, researchers, musicians, and others who have deliberately sought out ways to acquire fluency. A bidirectional gateway has evolved between singing and Yiddish language use to create new models for continuity. As an integral component of these activities that for many kindles a sense of joy as well as attachment to the language and culture, singing forms a scaffolding for Yiddish continuity.

KLEZMER AND IMMERSIVE MUSIC SPACES

Multi-day festivals dedicated to klezmer or Yiddish music provide a venue for immersive experiences that can facilitate a process of reconnection with or creation of a distinct and idealized Yiddish. Festivals can create miniature and portable ideal worlds that hinge on leftist, feminist, queer, or other ideologies as alternatives to the mainstream. Often physically removed from the distractions of the everyday, these programs allow participants to engage with Yiddish within a chosen community. Yiddish becomes associated with a particular physical location and group of people, with connections that can be nurtured virtually using mechanisms such as social media. Here Yiddish literacy and cultural capital can be propagated and ideological frameworks constituted in immersive created language spaces.

The first of the Yiddish music camps, KlezKamp, was founded as a winter gathering of Yiddish arts in the Catskill Mountains of New York in 1985 by two musicians integral to the klezmer revival: instrumentalist Henry "Hank" Sapoznik (born 1953) and vocalist Adrienne (Khana) Cooper (1946-2011). Its aim was to transmit the Yiddish folk arts – klezmer music, Yiddish song, Yiddish language and literature, and the culinary and visual arts – at a weeklong, annual, intergenerational retreat. In an interview, Cooper noted that from the beginning, the program fused the model of music camps, such as the Balkan Music and Dance Workshop (founded 1977), with that of the YIVO Summer Program and its immersion language component.[67] KlezKamp inspired other institutes worldwide to bring together practitioners to teach, workshop, and perform Eastern European Jewish music. Wood notes that these intergenerational camps have become "a primary context for Yiddish cultural life, challenging the linguistic focus of Shandler's 'vernacularity' by facilitating a community with a shared base of Yiddish cultural literacy."[68] She posits the deep significance of these music camps:

> At Yiddish music festivals, it is the outside world that is let go: music camps are a consummate form of heterotopia, secluded places of intensely enacted community life where physical distances between participants are virtually eliminated while the conceptual distance from the outside world is heightened. Set apart from the outside world, Yiddish culture becomes a lived norm, and ordered timetabling affords structured shared experiences. The concentrated production and consumption of music during these festivals creates a rich sensory environment, encouraging repeated experiences of emotional engagement and musical entrainment which occur on a much less frequent basis in "normal life." These experiences build a bank of community experiences, encapsulated and (re)experienced in the sensory act of

musical production. The ripples of these events pan into the future: recorded teaching sessions provide material to work on back home, emotional peaks are relived in conversation, and their energy is channeled into the beginning of new musical projects – a kind of recharging of creative batteries.[69]

Yiddish music retreats have emerged as part of a larger trend of festivals devoted to music – everything from rock to worldbeat – that have become increasingly popular since the 1960s. One study of the music festival phenomenon suggests that "festivals offer the opportunity to experience intra-personal existential authenticity through release and 'going free' and inter-personal existential authenticity through liminal communitas [community spirit] not apparently experienced in their everyday lives."[70] Researchers interrogate concepts of authenticity and the ways that culture is constructed, packaged, and consumed within the enclaves formed by music festivals.[71] This body of scholarship underscores some of the distinctive features of Klez-Kanada and other Yiddish festivals or retreats: unlike the expanding industry of transient commercial music festivals, the Yiddish music festivals attract participants who return annually – alone or with their families – and build strong and lasting networks. For their participants, Yiddish music festivals offer an intensive experience of activities that they engage in year-round and an opportunity for a portable, transnational slice of an imagined and often utopian Yiddishland. Wood observes the connections within these immersive experiences: "The structure of the week creates an illusion of cultural cohesion and nondisrupted traditions. Here there was no question of having to go to work, go shopping or go to the cinema on the Sabbath: for those for whom family traditions had fallen by the wayside, here was the real thing ... and far more, saturating the senses, with events usually found distributed across a family calendar condensed into one week. Whatever background an individual arrived from, and whatever their specialization, during the week they would be pulled into a contemporary version of Yiddish cultural life."[72]

KLEZKANADA, MONTREAL

Many activities take place at KlezKanada, but this chapter focuses on the role that singing plays at the world's largest multi-day immersive retreat devoted to Yiddish music and culture. KlezKanada meets annu-

ally for a week in August in the Laurentian Mountains north of Montreal. It started in the 1990s when founder Hy Goldman and his wife
Sandy, who were coordinating concerts and programs of Yiddish
music, joined forces with the Yiddish Committee of the Jewish Education Council of Montreal and the Foundation for Yiddish Culture
at the Canadian Jewish Congress.[73] Jack Wolofsky, a co-founder of
KlezKanada, identifies influences including Hankus Netsky's Klezmer
Conservatory Band playing at the Montreal Jazz Festival in 1982 alongside Québécois artists, and the activities of Montreal's Mame Loshn
Yiddish group under the leadership of Sara Rosenfeld. Given the success of KlezKamp in the United States, a Montreal-based group decided to create a Canadian counterpart.[74] With the tagline "Tradition,
Innovation, and Continuity," KlezKanada has become a site for a range
of activities that integrate Eastern European Jewish heritage under the
umbrella term of "klezmer." Like KlezKamp and other klezmer retreats
or institutes, the activities include not only musical instruction and
performance but other cultural arts such as dance, film screenings, lectures, and language courses.

KlezKanada has from its beginnings oriented itself towards youth.
In 2019 it attracted over four hundred participants, including many
families with parents who had been attending since they were children or young adults and whose own children were now participants;
in other cases, grandparents brought grandchildren. Young people
participate in the cultural life of the camp via a daily children's program and special performances, as well as in the communal singa-
longs and dance sessions, workshops, and classes. A scholarship program to support younger participants has been in place since
KlezKanada's inception, with education and active involvement of
youth identified as the future of Yiddish culture by its leadership.[75]
The scholarship program is presented as a badge of pride: "Our students – over 1,500 in number – have gone on to win major prizes, perform across the globe in prestigious venues, and lead major festivals
and other endeavours in Jewish culture."[76] An intensive for-credit
summer course offered by McGill University, titled Eastern European
Jewish Music (JWST 354), was conceived of in 2011 as a hybrid online
component with participation at KlezKanada.[77] The instructor, long-
time KlezKanada affiliate Hankus Netsky (born 1955), brings the perspective of an "instigator" of klezmer revitalization as a musician, ethnomusicologist, and educator.[78] In an interview about the pedagogy
of the course, Netsky noted how germane music is to Eastern Euro-

pean Jewish culture: "Yiddish is a singing culture. It is more potent to bring language and music together."[79]

KlezKanada's orientation towards youth has also shaped a new generation of leadership. Avia Moore (born 1982) offers the perspective of a long-time participant, coordinator, and teacher. Having attended sessions since 2003, she was invited by Michael Alpert and Jeff Warschauer to join the dance staff in 2006 and the following year became coordinator of the Youth Scholarship Program. In 2021, she was named artistic director. Outside of KlezKanada, Moore is active as a producer of festivals, events, and theatre, and (as of 2022), a doctoral candidate in Theatre and Performance Studies at York University, where her research focuses on the transmission of cultural practices using KlezKanada as a case study. Moore attributes her acquisition of Yiddish and sense of kinship in its cultural world to her KlezKanada experiences. Raised in Vancouver, she was first "dragged" to KlezKanada at the age of twenty-one by her father, a musician involved with klezmer music, and found a sense of community that was warm, welcoming, inclusive, and mentoring. She credits KlezKanada with sparking her interest in a discovery of Yiddish that was about "cultural transmission and bits and pieces of memory that felt right. It felt right to learn Yiddish." Moore characterizes klezmer music as a catalyst: "Listening to the music and feeling something shift inside me, this feeling that people often use to describe klezmer, of laughing and crying at the same time ... In theatrical speak, we often search for that moment ... a great artistic catalyst, that's the catharsis moment ... It felt like a moment where I needed to follow it."[80]

KlezKanada prompted Moore to engage in formal language acquisition when instructor Adrienne Cooper told her that if she wanted to really sing Yiddish, she would have to learn the language. "I extrapolated from this, coming to believe that if I want to engage with what I consider Yiddish cultural practices – from leading Yiddish dances to organizing Yiddish festivals – I should have at least some understanding of the language in which so many of these practices evolved."[81] Her initial exposure at KlezKanada led to an internship at the Yiddish Book Center (2006) and further study at the YIVO Summer Program (2007), as well as continued engagement with the language as a graduate student, event producer, and Yiddish dance leader. While Moore does not identify transmission of Yiddish as a vernacular language as a priority for KlezKanada, she observes that the retreat organizers have deliberately increased the number of language offerings so that participants would be able to engage in Yiddish-language activities for most of the day. She suggests, "I do think that KlezKanada has tremendous potential as a site that encourages first engagements with Yiddish as a language. My own experience is an example of this."[82] She identifies Klez-Kanada as offering a heterotopic space for Yiddish to "model or rehearse alternatives to the world outside the heterotopia. This might mean that participants are inspired by their experience to learn to speak the language or to find other ways of engaging with the language, culture, and/or community. How have the alternate possible realities Yiddish festivals model been carried forth outside the space of the festival?"[83] If heritage is considered as a process or performance rather than something static, Yiddish in the immersive environment of KlezKanada is fluid, to be experienced and formed by each participant.

Like Moore, KlezKanada's executive director, Sebastian Schulman (born 1984), forms part of a new generation of cultural activists. As a McGill student in the early 2000s, he participated in the internship program at the Yiddish Book Center (2004) and there discovered his connection to Jewishness: "Yiddish filled in all these gaps, the texture and the meaning behind all these things. This is where I came from … Once I learned Yiddish, I felt comfortable in all these Jewish contexts. I felt I fit in as a Jew."[84] As a scholar of Eastern European Jewish life and literary translator in Yiddish, Russian, and Esperanto, he directed the Yiddish Book Center's translation program before joining KlezKanada in 2017. A promoter of Yiddish as a living language, he is among a small cohort of young Yiddishists and new speakers of Yiddish who are opting to raise their children in the language.[85] He observes that, although language transmission represents a secondary goal at KlezKanada, Yiddish functions in varying capacities: as the object of language courses, as a language of instruction in classes or workshops, and as a language of communication among the participants. "There is a palpable sense at KlezKanada that here is a community that owns and creates in a living, vital and relevant Yiddish culture tradition." Further, KlezKanada offers an immersive experience for people seeking to expand their understanding of non-linguistic aspects of Yiddish culture once they have studied the language elsewhere. For the program's under-thirty participants, including its scholarship students, Schulman observes, "Whereas serious engagement in Yiddish 10 to 15 years ago seemed like it was a niche interest or subculture, the language and culture are gradually becoming more and more visible, better understood, and, incrementally, part of the palette of options available to North American Jews and others in terms of identification and Jewish cultural engagement."[86] He notes that attendance at KlezKanada's Yiddish events in 2019 was robust: a quarter of all participants took part in one of the three levels of Yiddish classes while the two lectures on literature or music that were conducted in Yiddish attracted well over a hundred audience members.[87]

As a faculty member and participant at the 2019 KlezKanada, I observed multiple structured and unstructured opportunities to engage with Yiddish in song lyrics, language study, and lectures in inclusive, intergenerational contexts. The weeklong workshops included a masterclass titled "Serving Schmaltz-free Yiddish Songs" that focused on issues such as diction. A KlezKinder Program organized for children aged four to eleven taught popular Yiddish songs, which the children subsequently performed for the camp. The intermediate language class that I taught attracted students between the ages of ten and ninety, including native speakers, musicians, children who heard Yiddish at home, and young language learners; about a third were under the age of thirty. In addition to formal programming, there were sessions on Yiddish literature and morning Yiddish-language nature walks. Outside of the programmed activities, a *Yidish tish* (Yiddish table) offered a designated space in the dining hall where mealtime conversations could take place. I heard Yiddish being spoken not infrequently, either in full conversation or in conjunction with English in a fluid back and forth (code switching) by a core group of fluent or near-fluent speakers. Yiddish-language knowledge carries cultural capital at KlezKanada and, as such, the event offers a site for initial encounter of the language, an incentive to learn or improve, and a meeting place for those wishing to use their Yiddish in varied contexts. The leftist legacies of Yiddish were foregrounded in a session titled "Bread and Roses: A Shabes Program Celebrating Labour Justice," which attracted a younger cohort. Yiddish also served to express feminist and queer perspectives at KlezKanada. For example, the opening concert by Tsibele – a Brooklyn-based ensemble led by women, queer, and non-binary musicians[88] – offered a rendition of the Hasidic song, "Vos iz Vikhtik" (What is Important) to express and affirm the value of hearing these voices onstage, where they are so often absent.

Figure 5.2 KlezKinder Program, coordinator Madeline Solomon with Bena Margolis singing her first Yiddish song on stage, 2019

Figure 5.3 Adah Hetko and Sadie Gold-Shapiro, program led by Sarah Gordon, "Bread and Roses: A Shabes Program Celebrating Labour Justice," 2019

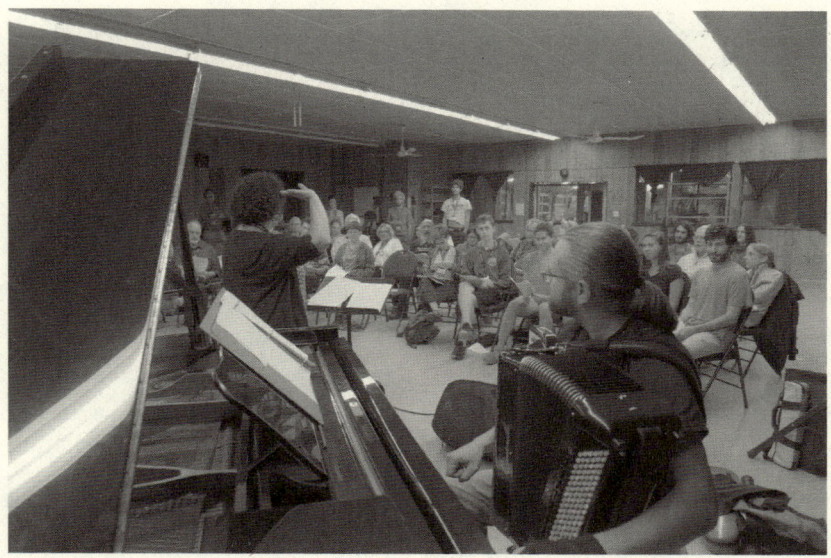

Figure 5.4 KlezKanada Yiddish Singalong led by Sarah Gordon, 2018

The heterotopic Yiddishland of KlezKanada was most fully enacted during the daily post-dinner session of "Lomir Ale Zingen (Let's all Sing) – A Yiddish Sing-along," which attracted upwards of fifty participants for a spirited forty-five minutes. Its facilitator, Sarah Mina Gordon, a faculty member since 2011, offers an example of the dynamic younger leadership. A 2018 magazine article titled "A New Generation Is Reclaiming Yiddish" tells Gordon's story: "A fourth-generation Yiddish singer, Gordon, 39, grew up going to KlezKamp, the New York klezmer festival co-founded by her mother, Adrienne Cooper. Like many non-Hasidic Yiddish-speakers today, Gordon learned the language as a curious adult. Like many of her fellow Yiddish innovators, she put her own spin on the culture: She's the founder and lead singer of Yiddish Princess, a heavy metal band that fuses Yiddish lyrics with vibrating synth chords."[89]

The singalong was remarkable in the range of ages and backgrounds represented, and the enthusiasm with which the group sang from the songbook Gordon compiled. The twelve-page songbook contains thirty-two songs from all segments of the Yiddish vocal repertoire: folksongs, Hasidic songs, drinking songs, anthems from the American labour movement, theatre songs, Soviet revolutionary

songs, children's songs, lullabies, and art songs. All appear in English
transliteration for those unable to read Yiddish, alongside brief translations into English. The songbook opens with the Klezmatics rendition of "Ale Brider," and its easy-to-follow melody and upbeat and
inclusive message were met with gusto by the crowd. A youth contingent sang songs with politically progressive overtones with particular
passion: "Hey Zhankoye," a Soviet-era song praising collective farm
labour popularized by American folksingers in the 1960s, and especially David Edelstadt's nineteenth-century anarchist anthem, "In ale
gasn/Daloy politsey" (In Every Street/Down with the Police).

The singalong created an intergenerational, inclusive created language space that expressed the utopian impulses of today's heterotopic Yiddishland. Sarah Mina noted in an interview that the singalong is her favourite activity at KlezKanada. She pointed out the
egalitarian arrangement of the room: while she and a musician lead
the event, Gordon does not act as teacher or performer but rather
offers some structure, when required; participants determine the
order of the songs by calling out the titles, and no individual singer
is featured. The songbook levels the playing field by making the
songs accessible to everyone. Group singing supports learners and
those who are less confident, as does the prevalence of repeated choruses and the repetition of the same pieces over the week. According
to Gordon, the repertoire comprises songs that are beloved and that
people enjoy singing together, with "no pretense, genius worship or
attempt at esoterica."[90] This open, accessible, and participatory structure allows it to belong fully to the KlezKanada community: "The
sing-along lets people own and share Yiddish song together. It's their
room, their commentary, their song choices, their voices, and the
words belong to them as they take their books home at the end of
the week."[91]

Yiddish is enacted in diverse modes at KlezKanada: verbally,
musically, bodily, and temporally, just as a broad, multisensory
experience of Yiddish has formed an integral part of the klezmer
revival. Shandler observes:

Translating Yiddish at postvernacular events not only entails code-
switching with other languages but also complementing or
replacing Yiddish with one or more other activities, such as
singing, dancing, or playing musical instruments. These heighten
the affective significance assigned to the language or provide

metaphors for its expressiveness via performance genres in which the audience has greater fluency. Sometimes this entails assigning "Yiddish-ness" to nonverbal genres of performance with only a tangential connection to the language – for example, "Yiddish dance" (i.e., traditional East European Jewish folk dance), which is both performed and taught (in English) at KlezKamp.[92]

Dance features prominently at KlezKanada in classes, workshops, a daily afternoon tea dance (*Tey-tants*), and a festival-wide dance ball which is a highlight of the week's schedule. At these events, dancing offers not only a physical accompaniment to klezmer but a bodily expression of Yiddish itself. Zev Feldman posits that it is only "within the context of East European Jewish dance" that "the genre system of klezmer music" can be understood.[93] Dance brings together individuals of all ages in a way that might not be possible for other activities; there is no requirement for linguistic fluency or familiarity with song lyrics. Movement, speech, and song are enacted within a rhythm where Yiddish can be experienced bodily, emotionally, intellectually, and creatively.

Offering both formal and informal learning, KlezKanada is a site for continuity among Yiddish musicians and cultural activists. The culture of the organization supports the widespread participation of families where Yiddish can be experienced by new speakers and native speakers alike. In a 2021 article, KlezKanada student intern and learner of Yiddish, Asa Brunet-Jailly, describes how the milieu offered a sense of intergenerational and international community where "belonging felt effortless."[94] This space is supported by several interconnected strands: the convergence of experts in Yiddish culture, the energy and excitement generated by both participation and performance, and the formation of relationships and lasting bonds.

A comparison with Canada's other major Yiddish cultural festival, Ashkenaz, highlights the kind of created language spaces immersive experiences like KlezKanada foster. Whereas KlezKanada is held in a remote country location, the Ashkenaz Festival takes place on Toronto's busy Harbourfront and other locations within the metropolis, which allows it to showcase Yiddish as well as other aspects of Jewish culture to the broadest of audiences. While KlezKanada participants sequester themselves for a week in an intensive schedule of workshops, courses, lectures, and concerts, thousands of Ashkenaz spectators wander through diverse cross-cultural offerings in an open-air festival, free of charge, but these are only some items among many on their weekly schedules. KlezKanada entails an engagement with Yiddish culture that is active, deliberate, and participatory; Ashkenaz exposes new audiences to music and performance in a way that is largely passive. Perhaps the best example of this difference is Klez-Kanada's Yiddish singalong, which unifies its participants in an embodied way only possible with shared cultural literacy and a strong sense of community.

JEWISH COMMUNITY CHOIRS

In their heyday in the 1920s and 1930s, Jewish communities in North America housed dozens of Yiddish choirs, some boasting hundreds of members. Offshoots of the Jewish labour movement, these choirs offered a shared social and musical space in tandem with a network of Jewish fraternal associations and other educational and cultural organizations. The choirs existed outside the mainstream, with members from an ethnic minority largely comprised of recent immigrants who were Yiddish-speaking, working class, and affiliated with revolutionary politics. They fulfilled multiple functions: rallying members to political causes or raising funds, providing an emotional and creative outlet for Jewish workers, emphasizing the Yiddish language while offering opportunities for cross-cultural exchange with other choirs and repertoires, and bringing together diverse and often polarized segments of the Jewish community.[95] With the end of mass immigration and the integration of the Jewish population into the mainstream, most choirs either closed or revised their orientation. Postwar changes within the Jewish world significantly impacted the choirs, the values associated with them, and the role of Yiddish. In the 1950s, alliances between the Jewish left and the American Civil Rights movement bolstered the universal, human rights orientation of the choirs. As the Jewish community reoriented its conception of the language within changing models of religiosity, "singing in Yiddish was constructed not only as a form of musical protest but as a sacred act and a Mitzvah (religious obligation)."[96] In the 1960s, most of the remaining choirs disappeared or merged, faced with aging memberships and the decline and dispersion of the Jewish left.

The handful of North American Yiddish community choirs that endured into the 1970s entered a new phase as part of the revival/revitalization associated with klezmer music and a new generation interested in Yiddish. Over the decades, the choirs became increasingly diverse and intergenerational, with decreasing Yiddish fluency among the singers. A study of New York's Yiddish choirs at the turn of the twenty-first century notes the elimination of the last vestiges of ideological or political rivalries between choirs, with singers "in pursuit of a common reverence and affection for Yiddish music."[97] A shared feature of these choruses is their accessibility: they are open to all, with recruitment to attract new members and special strategies to work with choristers with varying vocal styles and degrees of singing experience. The choirs have continued to perform primarily in Yiddish with a diverse musical repertoire comprising folksongs, labour songs, Holocaust songs, and art music performed in multiple settings, notably annual concerts and commemorative events such as Holocaust remembrance ceremonies. Marion Jacobson's study of Yiddish community choirs observes: "For the younger people who choose to sing these songs (instead of or in addition to other musical pursuits), their involvement with choruses and singing gives way to a more powerful involvement with a constructed, idealized Yiddish world. More than simply a reminder or emblem of identity and history, the repertory and its performance have been the primary medium for Yiddish singers' creation of community and alternative spaces. Their spaces – and the objects that fill them – are real and symbolic."[98]

The Toronto Jewish Folk Choir, the country's longest-enduring Yiddish community choir, reveals these transitions within a Canadian context. Formed in 1925 in close association with the Labour League (subsequently the United Jewish People's Order, UJPO), the choir had an avowedly secular and politically progressive worldview in the 1920s and 1930s. Yiddish folk song occupied a place of primacy in the repertoire to express a Jewish identity that was working class and revolutionary in its politics.[99] In the 1950s, the choir incorporated a more varied repertoire to promote the positive contributions of Jewish Canadians to the country's fabric. In both its repertoire and discourse around ethnicity, the choir formed a kind of precursor to the multiculturalism that would emerge in the 1960s and 1970s.[100] Housed at Toronto's Morris Winchevsky Centre, a leftist organization for secular Jewish culture and home to the UJPO, the choir performed in an annual concert, local community functions, and festivals such as Ashkenaz with a varied repertoire that included Yiddish folksongs, workers' songs, and art songs as well as works from other traditions. After closing in 2015, the choir was reconceived as a less formal and more accessible monthly drop-in called Zing!Zing!Zing! (Sing!Sing!Sing!).[101]

Community choirs across diverse ethnic and religious groups have formed the subject of extensive research in connection with community building, group identity formation, and positive health outcomes.[102] Yiddish choirs offer what Jacobson terms "a utopian vision centred on the effective performance of Yiddish music."[103] As of 2020, the website of New York's oldest continuing Yiddish community choir (founded 1922), speaks to the profile of the North American twenty-first century Yiddish choir as an inclusive created language space: "The Jewish People's Philharmonic Chorus (JPPC) is a multigenerational forty-voice ensemble. We're students, professionals, and robust retirees, all in love with singing and committed to promoting Yiddish language and culture through beautiful four-part harmony. Few of us are fluent, but we all learn together from the Yiddish vocal literature – traditional folk songs, settings of classic and contemporary poetry, labour anthems, theater works, holiday standards, and modern pieces in translation."[104]

THE VANCOUVER JEWISH FOLK CHOIR

Today, Canada is home to one enduring Yiddish community choir: the Vancouver Jewish Folk Choir, which celebrated its fortieth anniversary in 2019. It differs from its counterparts in Toronto or New York in terms of geography and history. Vancouver is home to a midsized Jewish community that was boosted in the postwar years by an influx of former soldiers, many of whom brought their experience in Yiddish organizational life from other places, as well as the immigration of Holocaust survivors. The home of the Vancouver Jewish Folk Choir is the Peretz Centre for Secular Jewish Culture, founded in 1945 as a supplementary school to provide children with politically progressive Jewish education. The Peretz Centre expanded into a community organization for all ages, with members of wide-ranging backgrounds and ideological orientations bound together by the common denominator of Yiddish. Housed in its own purpose-built building erected in 1961, it encompasses a diverse group of members, Jewish as well as non-Jewish, to "provide an alternative, secular humanist approach to Jewish life through the appreciation of Jewish history and culture within the context of world history, and through the celebration of Jewish traditions."[105] A period of growth in the 1970s expanded its Yiddish programming to encompass language courses; lecture series and holiday celebrations; the Yiddish language Kirman Library (founded 1976); and the Vancouver Jewish Folk Choir (founded 1979).

Faith Jones (born 1965) offers the perspective of a long-time active member, librarian, Yiddish scholar and translator, and singer as well as resident Yiddish expert with the Vancouver Jewish Folk Choir. Her trajectory to Yiddish differs from many whose gateway was via music; she joined the choir in order to maintain the connections to the culture she had acquired as a young adult. Although she heard Yiddish as a child, her encounter with the language began with reading works of lesbian Jewish thought, notably the writings of Irena Klepfisz, as part of a journey to determine the place of Jewishness within her own life. In the early 1990s, when a fellow member of a queer Jewish women's group announced that she would be attending a weekly Yiddish course at the Peretz Centre, Jones joined the class and found a welcoming, relaxed, and queer-friendly community. The Kirman Library, where she devoted countless hours cataloguing books, would form the subject of her thesis, "The Vancouver Peretz Institute Yiddish Library: The Social History of a Jewish Community Library" (1994). Jones's study underlines the ties between Yiddish, marginality, and secular identities: "It is impossible to imagine Yiddish as a neutral entity: its meanings are never simple, and very often it conveys contradictory messages. Yiddish culture resists any normative reading. It disrupts categories, creates uncertainty, and urges reconsideration of held positions."[106] She characterizes Yiddish as "ideologically malleable, personally invested, open to subversive readings, and available without adherence to a particular political or religious credo."[107] In her thesis Jones expresses an optimistic, forward-looking view of the intersections between Yiddish, politics, and identity. She ends her study with these words: "In looking at the nexus of secular identity, the left, women, lesbians and gays, and Yiddish, it has occurred to me that what these strands have in common is the belief in the power of human beings to alter the course of history. In left political life, in feminist theory, in the movement for lesbian and gay equality, in the political culture of secular humanism, it is not the past which is romanticized, but the future. Yiddish does not offer the path to the past as much as to a collective future which is linked with the past: a better future, but better because of human endeavour."[108]

Four years after completing her thesis, Jones left for New York to enroll in the YIVO Summer Program, where she first encountered the city's extensive secular Yiddishist milieu. While she had established close relationships with native Yiddish speakers in Vancouver – her teacher at the Peretz Centre, Chaya Fuks, as well as the founder of the Centre's Yiddish library, Polina Kirman – she did not know anyone of her generation who spoke the language. She soon relocated to New York City, where she immersed herself in Yiddish language classes, cultural events, and a weekly *leyenkrayz* (reading group). When she moved back to Vancouver, she set about creating a version of that world. She returned to the Peretz Centre as a natural home and took part in a Yiddish reading group led by scholar and translator Seymour Levitan. Once she completed a master's degree on Yiddish print culture in Winnipeg (2014),[109] she joined the Vancouver Jewish Folk Choir, where she has been an active member ever since.

The choir was formed under the leadership of conductor and long-time Peretz Centre activist Searle Friedman, previously director of the Toronto Jewish Folk Choir. The choir's webpage notes, "The largest, best, and ONLY Yiddish choir in Canada, the Vancouver Jewish Folk Choir performs the music of the Jewish people in Yiddish, Hebrew, Ladino and English, as well as other languages of countries where Jews have lived." Within this multilingual and multicultural repertoire, the centrality of Yiddish is underlined by the major works the choir has performed in recent years: classic works of the Yiddish theatre, adaptations of Yiddish literature, and ambitious translations of world theatre into Yiddish.[110] In their 2019 study and online exhibit to mark the choir's fortieth anniversary, titled *"Un mir zingen freylekhe lider*: The Vancouver Jewish Folk Choir as Alternative Jewish Space,"*[111] members Faith Jones and Cynthia Ramsay observe that the goal of the choir has remained stable: "Its purpose, which has been articulated in slightly different ways over the years, is still to contribute to the perpetuation of Yiddish culture, while also trying to reach a broader community."[112]

Like many of the leftist-oriented Yiddish choruses, the choir has worked to spotlight political issues and commemorate injustice while also embracing a repertoire that includes material from other languages and cultures. Yet, Jones and Ramsay add, "Yiddish has been at the core of the choir's purpose since the beginning. This goal is frequently asserted in the choir's written materials, from its inception until the present. Broadly speaking, the choir seems to articulate any use of Yiddish as a contribution to continuity, and appears particularly interested in demonstrating the existence and persistence of Yiddish culture to both Jews and non-Jews."[113] For example, a 1989 planning document states, "We specialize in perpetuating the Yiddish language in song," while a concert program from 2016 proclaims "the aim of keeping Yiddish music alive and educating both Jewish and non-Jewish audiences to a world cultural treasure." As Jones notes in her 1994 thesis, "The choir's music allowed Yiddish to remain a part of Peretz [Centre] events even though Yiddish language instruction in the school had ceased."[114] Membership in the multi-generational choir requires no previous singing experience or knowledge of Yiddish and many of the choir's members are not Jewish; its longstanding conductor of twenty-five years, David Millard, is a church musician who began his career with the choir as a member.

The linguistic composition of the choir has shifted over the years, with the choir having lost all its native Yiddish speakers (the last, Richard Rosenberg, passed away in 2019). In its early years, when the choir's members were predominantly Yiddish speakers whose familiarity with the repertoire dated from their youth, the rehearsals were punctuated by arguments about dialect and pronunciation as well as which songs to feature.[115] As newcomers joined, they increasingly learned the lyrics phonetically and were coached by members of the choir.[116] Jones, its only fluent Yiddish speaker in 2019, has increasingly become a resource within the choir. In this collaborative role, she has assisted Millard in finding music for the repertoire, helped the choir to understand what they were singing, and written English translations for the program. Jones has also occasionally penned Yiddish lyrics for tunes, such as her own trans-inclusive lyrics of "Ale Brider." Jones and Ramsay connect the choir's location in Vancouver to its enduring success: "We posit that the choir fills a role that is not easy to come by otherwise in the Vancouver Jewish community. While Toronto offers a multitude of Yiddish musical experiences – such as the Ashkenaz Festival and a half-dozen resident klezmer bands – Vancouver has no other outlet for Yiddish music ... It may be that the very paucity of Yiddish culture in Vancouver gives the choir a unique niche that it wouldn't have in a larger Jewish community."[117] For the non-Yiddish speaking members, the choir is a Yiddish space that is relaxed and does not require language knowledge; for Jones, it offers a space where she can engage with Yiddish in a participatory and meaningful way.[118]

The choir offers a mode of community engagement that is Jewish, socially engaged, and a site for queer Yiddishkeit. In a 2019 interview, Jones suggested that while a generation earlier Vancouver Yiddish activists could seamlessly live their cultural, professional, and political lives at the Peretz Centre, this is no longer possible. Rather, younger people with an affinity for Yiddish or seeking that connection gravitate towards Yiddish spaces such as the choir. She noted that with roughly a third of the current eighteen members on the LGBTQ (lesbian, gay, bisexual, transgender, and queer or questioning) spectrum, the choir offers a space to sing in Yiddish as well as a site to practice, perform, translate, and shape a repertoire of Yiddish song from a queer vantage point: "If you are marginal, you like marginal and Yiddish in Vancouver is very marginal. There is some kind of natural affinity."[119]

A performance by the choir in June 2019 reflected both the Yiddish and socially engaged character of the choir. The all-Yiddish contents were eclectic, with roots in different spheres of musical culture. The opening piece, "Giter Brider Nisht Gekhapt" (Buddy Don't Grab), a Yiddish penny song first published in New York in 1907, deals with the topic of sexual harassment: the singer threatens to retaliate brutally against men who commit sexual assault.[120] The choir programme called it "A Yiddish #metoo song," situating the piece within a contemporary movement to promote awareness of sexual violence. The choir also presented a recent composition by Millard: his musical setting of a Yiddish version of Lewis Carroll's nonsense poem, "Jabberwocky."[121] The final number on the program was a rousing rendition of Leonard Cohen's "Hallelujah" in Yiddish. The concert reflects the extent to which the worlds of Yiddish music intersect, and reveals how song can offer contemporary meaning, political expression, and creativity.

Yiddish community choirs form created language spaces embedded into the fabric of daily existence, in contrast to immersive music festivals, which require suspending one's regular life for the duration. Coro Mordje Guebirtig, founded in Buenos Aires in the aftermath of the 1994 bombing attack on the Asociación Mutual Israelita Argentina, demonstrates the abiding role that Yiddish singing can play; a 2008 study of the choir identifies it as a proactive communal response for positive social change, not just within the Jewish community but within the broader Argentinian society.[122] While singing in a choir does not engender fluency in Yiddish, it offers point of collective engagement with the language. Even less formal groups such as Toronto's drop-in choir Zing!Zing!Zing! can yield an experience of embodied connection. Choirs can support those who speak or have learned Yiddish in maintaining and expanding their language skills and can offer a broader context for its use, particularly for those without families or communities where the language is spoken on a regular basis.

YIDDISH CONTINUITY IN SONG AND BEYOND

As Canadian Jewry left the immigrant working class, the Jewish mainstream increasingly gravitated towards religious observance, Israel, or both as cornerstones of identity. In the postwar era, secular Yiddish increasingly became associated with ethnicity within the rubric of Canada's "multicultural" identity. It also became, as the decades passed, a chosen alternative to the mainstream: marginal, countercultural, imbued with a rich literary and musical heritage. Since the klezmer revival of the 1970s, pockets of young people, some with Yiddish heritage and others without, have been finding their way to Yiddish as a form of chosen identity. The 1990s and the first decades of the twenty-first century have increasingly marked the entry of newcomers into the world of secular Yiddish as active participants and builders. Individuals who are attracted to Yiddish for different reasons – heritage, academic study, political ideology, identity, art – form an amorphous, borderless, and dynamic community. Yiddish can offer any of the following: a rich site of creativity that draws on literary texts and song to combine the past with a reimagined present; a locus for social activism that draws upon the Yiddish heritage of leftist political engagement; a site for exploring countercultural identities under the rubric of Queer Yiddishkeit; and so on.

Singing offers a gateway into the language, not only by using lyrics in Yiddish but by creating an impetus for further study and reinforcing existing linguistic competency. Wood notes that "singing in Yiddish encompasses more than just performance of an externalized identity: if language classes and dictionaries supply the nuts and bolts of linguistic fluency, song is a medium for *becoming* Yiddish. As a participatory medium, song draws participants to reimagine themselves as cultural insiders. Participation opens a space for training and re-forming the self, for embedding Yiddish into bodily habitus. Song allows a re-envisioning of self, a way to insert oneself into a culture, vicarious *becoming* through uttering a lullaby, through singing in a choir representing the Yiddish body politic, or through stepping out of everyday life into a new Yiddishland."[123] A vast corpus of Yiddish song – gathered, annotated, and elucidated by generations of folklorists and ethnomusicologists – is interpreted by musicians, who transmit their knowledge at festivals and workshops. Yiddish texts can be mined for feminist or queer subtexts to be reinterpreted and performed.

Today's authorities in the secular Yiddish world are increasingly those with cultural literacy gained in classrooms, through self-study, and via participation in festivals and other organized Yiddish activities. If intergenerational continuity is separated from a biological reproductive context and instead implies transference from teacher to student or workshop leader to singer, singing offers a highly participatory vehicle for Yiddish to be transmitted among the generations. The next chapter examines the impact of new online and digital technologies and the creation of created language spaces for Yiddish via social media, websharing, and other tools.

6

Yiddish in New Media and Cinema
2000 to 2020

New technologies have historically served to promote Yiddish in
Canada both locally, underlining the specificity of the Canadian experience, and transnationally, underlining the global connections
between Canada and other Yiddish centres. This has been the case
since the first Yiddish-language newspapers documented Canadian
Jewry while also connecting Canada to the wider world of Yiddish
internationally. In the twenty-first century, new media – digital and
communication technologies, notably the internet – have the same
dual role. For example, the digitization of archival materials and their
dissemination on websites or online exhibits highlight the Canadian
experience, while the promotion of projects over social media connects Canada's Yiddish milieu to a global community. Online sites
include the active participation of Canadians as contributors and consumers: instructors of Yiddish draw on digital technologies in their
classrooms alongside their colleagues worldwide, while readers access
and contribute to digitized texts in online repositories and publications, as well as via social media. These online activities form created
language spaces that support a virtual community.

The advent and application of new media have been shaped – and
continue to be shaped – by the ways in which people use Yiddish: as
a lingua franca for a transnational population of speakers, as a language of literary creation, as a heritage tongue associated with collective memory, as an idiom of progressive politics, or as a vehicle for performance, among others. During the height of modern Yiddish
culture in the first half of the twentieth century, innovators produced,
promoted, and disseminated Yiddish-language content using the latest technologies to express their creative and ideological visions or to

create a commercial product, and often both. Yiddish products were diffused to, and consumed by, millions of speakers worldwide: a multifaceted print culture (newspapers, journals, and published books); recordings of music, sketches, and other audio entertainment; feature-length and shorter films; and commercial radio. These often came into being collaboratively across geographic borders, with partnerships between artists in the major Yiddish centres in Poland and the United States, as well as smaller hubs. In some cases, their reach extended beyond the Yiddish world, notably in the area of film. For example, the 1936 musical comedy *Yidl mitn Fidl/Yiddle with His Fiddle* (1936) was directed by Polish-born American Joseph Green, filmed in Poland, and starred the beloved American-born actress Molly Picon; it screened worldwide and was the third-top grossing film in Poland that year.

Media technologies that emerged after 1950, when Yiddish began its steep decline as a Jewish vernacular in the secular world, developed in very different ways. A notable example is television, which evolved in the 1950s as a form of mass media and where Yiddish-language programming is virtually absent. In contrast, a resurgence of interest in Yiddish culture in the 1970s, notably in klezmer music, led musicians to discover recordings of Eastern European Jewish instrumental music and songs, and to issue their own, often featuring Yiddish lyrics. As discussed in the previous chapter, musical recording in Yiddish has continued to evolve. Likewise, the advent of digital technologies has coincided with institutional support for new avenues to access products in the language. These include the digitization and online publication of Yiddish literature in a searchable format; online dictionaries and reference works, and recordings of radio shows, music, audio books, and oral histories; interactive internet exhibits; video sharing; social media sites devoted to Yiddish or in the language; educational websites and online courses; and other web-based media. In the third decade of the twenty-first century, much of this material is accessible via the internet at no cost, with online Yiddish audiovisual material paired with English subtitles. In addition, a growing corpus of film and television with Yiddish-language dialogue is providing access in ways that that do not rely on the fluency of its producers, its actors, or its audiences.

If, as this book suggests, each generation corresponds to a particular form of Yiddish transmission, then the first decades of the new millennium belong to digital technologies. New media allow speakers with varying degrees of fluency to engage with the language in fresh ways; for example, parents can expose their children to Yiddish-language music videos produced for young people in Sweden; readers of an online New York-based Yiddish newspaper can hover over unfamiliar terms to find their definitions; viewers can hear Yiddish dialogue spoken in new films, television shows and web series produced in Europe, Israel, or North America. Technology also makes it easy to create and share new products such as videos in Yiddish.

This chapter builds upon scholarship in Jewish new media studies, which investigates how changing technologies impact, refract, or reflect the Jewish experience. A recent survey of the field suggests, "As film mutates into digital and new media plays an increasingly prominent role in our lives, the relationship between us and what we are consuming will change in unexpected ways."[1] After briefly discussing the intersections between Yiddish and twentieth-century technologies such as radio and television, I investigate the impact on Yiddish of new media and explore opportunities for study, research, exploration, and virtual community building. I then examine new applications of technology around Yiddish-dialogue filmmaking mediated by processes of translation. Like the rest of the study, the focus is on Canada, in tandem with developments in the Yiddish world more broadly. In terms of the model of concentric circles of Yiddish that underpins this study, Yiddish in cyberspace and new Yiddish cinema are both located at the outermost rim in the fifth circle, where the language is accessible to the widest possible group (see figure 0.1). Here Yiddish is transmitted virtually as mediated by digital technology, or as part of a subtitled audiovisual experience on screen. Both can offer a gateway to language acquisition, an opportunity to deepen linguistic proficiency, and a means to create new narratives that integrate the language.

YIDDISH RADIO AND TELEVISION BROADCASTING IN TWENTIETH-CENTURY NORTH AMERICA

Beginning in the 1920s and in tandem with the wider development of radio broadcasting, Yiddish radio formed an integral part of popular culture in North American Jewish immigrant communities. With its golden age in the 1930s and 1940s, radio offered opportunities for musical innovation, a mirror of the immigrant experience in the newly adopted home, and exposure to mainstream consumer products through sponsorships and advertisements. During its peak years, Yiddish radio in the United States formed "an acoustic community," appearing in virtually every major Jewish population centre and offering content to suit all tastes.[2] In New York, station WEVD (purchased in 1932 by the *Forverts*) broadcast dramas, advice shows, talent shows, and variety shows.[3] While data on Yiddish radio is difficult to produce due to a lack of extant recordings, what has survived indicates a rich and varied content, musical and otherwise.[4] The appeal of community radio can be explained, in part, by its accessibility: unlike other media such as newspapers, radio did not depend on literacy or fluency in the language, and could be shared within families whose members had varying degrees of comprehension. Yiddish radio plummeted in popularity in the 1950s with the end of Yiddish-speaking immigration to America and the advent of television, with WEVD Yiddish radio enduring in diminished form until the 1980s. Yiddish community radio programs have broadcast from locations in the United States and abroad; a number of program remain accessible online.[5] As part of wider patterns of language shift, echoes of Yiddish have remained embedded in popular English-language radio and television shows in the form of individual loanwords, phrases, and intonation (Yinglish).[6]

While on a far smaller scale than the neighbouring United States, Canada evolved its own tradition of Yiddish radio. Again, a lack of recordings permits only partial knowledge of the scope and content. Canadian Jewish radio shows, like their American counterparts, were often sponsored by newspapers. One of the more enduring was a weekly show sponsored by Toronto's *Kanader nayes* (Canadian News) beginning in 1936; it survived the wartime ban on radio in non-official languages and lasted until the demise of its sponsor newspaper in 1954.[7] In Montreal, the private ownership of radio delayed the creation of programs in languages other than English or French until the 1960s. Nachum Wilchesky (1920–2009), an advocate for the Yiddish language, teacher, and long-time director of education for the Jewish People's and Peretz Schools, was hired to produce Jewish radio broadcasts when CFMB opened as Montreal's first multilingual station in 1962.[8] The show, which broadcast in Yiddish for about half of the ninety-minute weekly program and in English and Hebrew for the remainder, allowed him "to carry the torch for the language he loves."[9] Wilchesky's program, which opened with his trademark Yiddish greeting, *"khosheve fraynt* (dear friends)," ran for over fifty years until it went off the air soon after his death in 2009.[10] In Montreal, the last remnant of Yiddish radio endured in Radio Shalom (CJRS/CKZW 1650 AM), a non-profit Jewish community station, which broadcast occasional Yiddish content until it went off the air in 2016; later that year, it returned to offer Jewish programming in English and French only.[11]

Two Canadian innovations in Yiddish audio recording technology were pioneered in Montreal. Beginning in the 1950s, Wilchesky adopted the recent invention of reel-to-reel recording to capture nearly every one of the cultural programs that took place at Montreal's Jewish Public Library from 1953 until 2005. These eight hundred recordings feature almost every Yiddish cultural figure in the city, as well as visitors from abroad. They have been remastered and digitized in collaboration with the Yiddish Book Center, and are posted online and available free of charge for download.[12] A second area of innovation is in talking books, which began when the Jewish Public Library recorded works of Yiddish literature as a service to its clients in the 1980s and 1990s. The resulting audio recordings of some 150 books include novels, short fiction, nonfiction, memoirs, essays, and poetry. Eva Raby, former director of the Jewish Public Library, recalls the origins of the project, when a member lost her eyesight and her husband and other volunteers began to read the books onto audio cassettes for her; as demand grew due to an aging Yiddish readership, so did the scope of the project. Most readers were native speakers who received special training, including some of Montreal's Yiddish writers (e.g., Mordecai Husid); others were actors in the Yiddish theatre.[13] The recordings were conducted in a specially equipped studio at the Library, with volunteers monitoring pronunciation errors.[14] These recordings have also been remastered and digitized through the partnership between the Jewish Public Library and the Yiddish Book Center; the Yiddish Book Center's Sami Rohr Library of Recorded Yiddish Books can be accessed free of charge.[15]

While television has served to promote some lesser-spoken languages with state support – such as Welsh in Wales – Yiddish-language television has lacked such resources. While individual words or phrases appear in many popular television shows, notably American sitcoms, shows with dialogue primarily in Yiddish have been few. One exception is the legendary comedic duo Shimen Dzigan and Yisroel Shumacher's political satire broadcast on Israeli television in the 1970s.[16] Despite large potential audiences, the Yiddish-speaking Haredi world has not produced television or radio programming accessible to a broad public due to a reticence to engage with mainstream culture. Select audio and visual recordings such as adaptations of biblical stories or talks by rabbis have been disseminated within the communities. These offerings are, as discussed below, increasingly being posted online for wide accessibility.

An instructive comparison can be made with Scottish Gaelic. In its native Scotland, where the population is overwhelmingly English-speaking, Scottish Gaelic has declining numbers of speakers and is characterized by low intergenerational transmission. However, sustained state support has translated into an abundance of public broadcasting, for both radio and television. A BBC Gaelic radio service, Radio nan Gàidheal (launched 1985), broadcasts more than ninety hours per week. A digitally available Scottish Gaelic television station established in 2008 was accessed by some 16 per cent of Scottish viewers by 2011. These media ventures consume a majority of the state budget allotted to the promotion of the language. In contrast to the prevalence of print culture in Yiddish, there has never been a Scottish Gaelic daily newspaper in Scotland, and other periodicals in the language have appeared only sporadically due to low literacy rates and a lack of funding.[17]

As discussed in more depth below, Canada's Indigenous broadcast media offers a point of comparison closer to home. The Oka Crisis of 1990[18] led to the Royal Commission on Aboriginal Peoples, whose 1996 report contained wide-ranging recommendations of changes to government policy that included the creation of the Aboriginal Peoples Television Network (APTN). APTN was launched nationally in 1999 as an independent cable television network, the first of its kind in the world.[19] In addition to offering cable programming, the network's website (aptn.ca) streams dozens of shows, with news programs, documentaries, dramas, sports, comedy, soap operas, and children's programming appearing in English or French as well as Indigenous languages such as Inuktitut and Cree. With growing interest and demand, television producers and filmmakers from First Nations, Métis, and Inuit communities are creating a variegated audiovisual culture to reflect the perspectives of their members. Most recently, in early 2020, the Nunavut Independent Television Network (NITV) launched a new channel called Uvagut TV.

Television programming in Scottish Gaelic in Scotland and in Indigenous languages in Canada are state-sponsored ventures that recognize the cultural specificity of groups indigenous to their geographic regions that have undergone repression. While the eight-hundred-year history of Yiddish in Polish lands might have claimed indigenous status for Jews in the 1930s, in Canada – as in other centres worldwide – the language forms one among scores of immigrant or ethnic languages. In Sweden, where Yiddish exists as an official minority language that receives state support to promote its use, the country has evolved its own Yiddish-language media, including children's literature and television programming on the Swedish Educational Broadcasting Company.[20]

The diffusion of Yiddish via technology outside of the Haredi world has occurred largely through community-based media: the publication of newspapers, collaborative journals, and anthologies, or books produced with the aid of committees of supporters and, more recently, radio. In recent years, new technologies have opened avenues for the diffusion of Yiddish in mainstream culture. These technologies have also made inroads into the Haredi world.

YIDDISH, THE INTERNET, AND DIGITAL TECHNOLOGY

Digital communication technologies have supported contact, interaction, and community-building among Yiddish speakers worldwide, beginning with listservs in the 1990s. A recent body of scholarship on digital sociality investigates connections between such technologies and community building, and explores ways in which subcultures enact their identities online.[21] Within the Jewish context, scholarship points to the negotiation of use of internet or social media platforms within Jewish Orthodoxy, as well as innovative religious models within Judaism.[22] For secular Yiddish, the role of digital technologies in the building of virtual and face-to-face community and the formation of identities has become increasingly significant. A 2011 scholarly article, "Yiddish on the Internet," proposed the advent of a new "cyber-vernacular" stage in the sociological development of the language. Tsvi Sadan's analysis of Yiddish and computer-mediated communication (CMC) worldwide concludes:

The Internet, especially websites and mailing lists, has a greater potential for diaspora languages like Yiddish than for non-diaspora languages for forming virtual communities, as the former have few non-virtual communities, while the latter already have communities outside the Internet. Yiddish has not fully used this potential, so the virtual community in Yiddish remains rather small. The main use of Yiddish on the Internet is symbolic, or cyber-postvernacular, i.e., one communicates about Yiddish but not so often in Yiddish, in comparison with other languages with a similar population size. In this respect, there is no essential difference between the use of Yiddish on the Internet and outside it: the symbolic use of the language as postvernacular and cyber-postvernacular is an (increasingly) dominant one.[23]

The Yiddish cybervernacular as a virtual space to bring together enthusiasts, teachers, learners, and musicians has evolved in the decade since the publication of Sadan's article. The following offers a small sample of digital resources made available free of charge in 2020. Since the early 2010s, the increased ease of typing in the Yiddish alphabet across platforms has allowed for more effective written communication.[24] New and expanded dictionaries – the *Comprehensive Yiddish-English Dictionary* (2013) and the *Comprehensive English-Yiddish Dictionary* (2016)[25] – as well as corresponding online platforms[26] facilitate the processes of reading and writing as well as translation. The *Forverts*, which as of 2019 exists entirely online, includes articles, new literary works, an interactive crossword puzzle, and subtitled videos.[27] *In geveb: A Journal of Yiddish Studies* (launched 2015) posts academic articles, texts and translations, pedagogical resources, blog entries, reviews, and interviews.[28] A consortium of researchers has created a repository of scholarship and documentation available at the Digital Yiddish Theatre Project.[29] A dozen online radio programs with Yiddish content worldwide can be accessed via the internet,[30] as can *Vaybertaytsh: A Feminist Podcast, In Yiddish* (launched 2016).[31] YiddishPOP offers animated interactive online modules suitable for learners of all ages,[32] while the DuoLingo website launched a Yiddish course developed by a team of former American Hasidim as well as speakers raised in Yiddishist homes.[33] The Digital Library and Collections of the Yiddish Book Center offers online access to a vast collection of digitized materials available for download, including books, audiobooks, recorded lectures, interviews, and a growing collection of oral histories.[34] With new technologies ever evolving, existing projects in the digital humanities mark only the beginning of what may be possible in the fields of theatre, literature, music, and education.[35] Shandler suggests that on the one hand, digitized audio and video projects are valuable resources for the study of Yiddish as well as understanding its history; on the other, this "Yiddish afterlife" creates an immutable repository for the language. He suggests that recordings "fix speech acts, the most evanescent and mutable of cultural productions, in suspended time. Even as they provide incomparable access to Yiddish orality of the past, these collections of recordings also serve as reminders of its loss, bringing the listener speech acts that can be audited, but not joined."[36] The array of digital resources provide scaffolding for Yiddish continuity, in particular for new learners seeking to hear the language. However, without engaged viewers and listeners, such resources are mere phantoms of Yiddish continuity.

Social media has become a significant site for diffusing Yiddish content, notably among the younger generation that has grown up with the technology. In 2020, Facebook was hosting diverse groups that promote Yiddish ranging from a few hundred to a few thousand members each; for example, Events IN Yiddish (originally YiddishLIVE) is a clearinghouse for events that take place in (rather than about) Yiddish or that offer learning opportunities such as language classes, while Yiddish Research is a site that promotes scholarship related to Yiddish and connects researchers.[37] A Facebook project based in Toronto is Ontario Yiddishkayt, a virtual community of young people that both shares content and organizes events.[38] The YouTube video-sharing website hosts videos with Yiddish content and offers tremendous diversity, including native speakers from diverse political and ideological backgrounds, students, performers, and members of Hasidic communities. Video sharing technologies are also employed free of charge on the websites of institutions.

With the classroom forming a major site of Yiddish transmission today, educational institutions were increasingly making online platforms part of the student experience in the 2010s, with some courses being offered entirely online.[39] A 2016 article by Agnieszka Legutko, provocatively titled "Yiddish in the 21st Century: New Media to the Rescue of Endangered Languages," explores the ways in which "recent developments in new media integration within the Yiddish language classrooms have provided Yiddish language and culture a new life online."[40] She cites new digital tools such as YiddishPOP; the integration of collaborative digital projects such as online archives, videos on shared platforms (YouTube), online sound archives, and educational resources such as the Yiddish Book Center's digitized Yiddish library and pedagogical materials; and opportunities for distance learning. She goes on to suggest that the integration of new media in the teaching of Yiddish offers a model for other less commonly taught languages (LCTLs). Distance Yiddish learning became increasingly accessible around the world; for example, the New York-based Workers Circle/Arbeter Ring (formerly the Workmen's Circle) offered a wide array of online offerings from beginner through advanced levels. A 2017 "Pedagogy Forum" on the integration of digital technologies into the classroom organized by *In geveb* posits "Yiddish is at home on the web ... the web is a natural home for Yiddish, which may seem surprising to those who think of Yiddish primarily as an artifact of the past. If all that is true, then, Yiddish pedagogy should be right at home with digital methodologies, and digital Yiddish pedagogy should be the currency of all Yiddish teachers."[41]

Trends towards integrating digital technologies and new media have been accelerated by the coronavirus pandemic that began in late 2019. The global social restrictions that moved classrooms, workplaces, and social spaces online prompted a widespread turn to technologies such as the Zoom video-conferencing platform. As I discuss in my study, "Forays into a Digital Yiddishland: Secular Yiddish in the Early Stages of the Coronavirus Pandemic," the normalization of virtual modes of engagement has spurred fresh possibilities for community building.[42] Receptivity to virtual created language spaces has heightened the sense of a shared, global Yiddishverse.

The relationship between the Haredi world and new media has also been rapidly evolving. As Nathaniel Deutsch suggests in his 2009 study, "The Forbidden Fork, the Cell Phone Holocaust, and Other Haredi Encounters with Technology," a traditionalist worldview that rejects mainstream culture but has embraced some new technology has resulted in a complicated relationship with the internet. Deutsch writes, "Despite their profound ideological commitment to the past, many Haredim are highly sophisticated users – and often purveyors – of cutting-edge media and information technologies, including cell phones, video equipment, and computers, which have come to symbolize and, in practical terms, actualize the radical transformation of contemporary society ... The question, therefore, is not whether contemporary Haredim have an intimate relationship with 'modern culture,' including technology, but the nature and contours of this relationship."[43] The single Hasidic-made action film, *A Gesheft/The Deal* (2005, discussed below), offers a case in point: despite being produced and marketed as a "kosher" film that observes community norms – "No foul language, no sexual content, and no females"[44] – it was soundly condemned by Hasidic authorities in posters and newspaper advertisements cautioning against the implications of mainstream moviegoing and mixed-gender seating.[45] A mass rabbinic gathering held in New York in 2007 produced a denunciation of the internet as an unmediated sphere of communication that is potentially dangerous to Haredi communities, with the rabbis at the gathering forbidding their followers to make private use of the internet.[46] As Deutsch notes, despite this ban, many sites indicate continued internet use in Yiddish as well as English.[47] In fact, online technology has expanded within the Hasidic world. For example, the Satmar-affiliated newspaper, *Der Yid: The View of American Orthodox Jewry* has a website (deryid.org) that includes sample pages in Yiddish; from 2002 to 2018, Hasidic blogger Katle Kanye posted Yiddish satire and commentary, as well as his own original poetry (katlekanye.blogspot.com). Since 2006, the online Yiddish forum iVelt (ivelt.com/forum) has offered a moderated site for participants to post Hasidic news anonymously. Another site, kaveshtiebel .com (Coffee House, founded in 2012), is a forum promoting open and uncensored dialogue in Yiddish between all members of the Hasidic community, who post anonymously to exchange information and ideas, and find news otherwise difficult to locate.[48] The online magazine called *Der veker* (The One Who Awakens) that emerged out of Kave Shtiebel was transformed into a print publication simply called *Veker* in 2015 (discussed in chapter 4). Geographically diverse writers and readers access and contribute to these Hasidic sites. While most, like Kave Shtiebel, have emerged from New York, content can be found relating specifically to Canadian Hasidic life.

With its great abundance of Yiddish offerings – digitized books, audiobooks, oral histories, online publications and exhibits, podcasts, language learning apps, and social media sites, and others – the internet theoretically offers infinite potential as a site for both accessing and producing the language. The impact is more difficult to measure. As a point of comparison, Welsh speakers have been perceived as forerunners in the use of digital technologies for lesser-used languages. However, a case study of blogs and Twitter in Welsh found that neither were widely used, and that the promotion of the language did not appear as a goal for most who use them. The internet can both support and undermine minority language promotion, the study found: because the dominant language of the internet is English, it can discourage the use of other languages; at the same time, the internet can provide opportunities to both use and create content for users who seek to promote minority languages.[49] The role that online technologies can play in the promotion of minority languages hinges on their users' voluntary production and consumption of materials in those languages.

Strategies developed by Canadian Indigenous communities suggest the applications of new media for transmitting vulnerable or endangered languages. With over fifty Indigenous languages in existence in Canada today, a majority endangered, young activists are developing innovative ways of combatting linguistic attrition using social media. One model is a social media campaign that originated with the Sami language in Northern Europe, where the hashtag #SpeakSamiToMe is used to share images alongside the term in that language and a translated caption (e.g., a photograph of people laughing with the word for "laughter" in Sami as well as in translation). In Canada, young people have created their own versions of this grassroots movement. For example, at the age of twenty-one, Jacey Firth-Hagen, who was learning the severely endangered Gwich'in language (one of the Dene languages of northern Canada and Alaska) with elders, created the hashtag #SpeakGwichinToMe to teach the language one word at time using images as well as short instructional videos.[50] Motivational speaker Savvy Simon began employing Facebook and Twitter as well as YouTube to teach the Mik'maq language in her early twenties.[51] Further, an interactive app that offers instruction in multiple Dene languages is being accessed by young people who have not been able to learn the language of their elders.[52] The internet offers one means of beginning to combat and heal the intergenerational rupture of language transmission among Canada's Indigenous peoples. The Indigenous Languages Act passed in 2019, which explicitly supports initiatives to promote such languages, will likely increase the availability of, and access to, these types of resources.

These applications of social media to create online hubs for sharing, asking questions, and encouraging language learning and usage are a youth phenomenon, motivated by a powerful search for identity. Secular Yiddish is beginning to move into that space. One indication is the popularity among youth of the short-form video-sharing social media app TikTok, where Yiddish is well-represented.[53] Further, with materials from the Hasidic world also accessible online, the internet offers both a theoretical and practical meeting place for adherents of secular Yiddish globally as well as between secular and Hasidic Yiddish.

A speculative point of discussion is the potential for connections between Yiddish and virtual reality (VR) technology, which was developing rapidly by 2020, and which offers infinite possibilities for establishing virtual meeting places for language learning and practice. For example, in 2019 AltspaceVR hosted a series of "Let's Speak" events to bring together speakers of different languages in a virtual environment, such as a café, as personalized avatars (characters with customizable features such as gender, skin colour, hair, etc.) who can interact and speak to each other during a designated time period.[54] There are other language-learning apps with which learners can engage with avatars in interactive and realistic, immersive environments (for example a taxi or a hotel) to improve their skills.[55] A final virtual space is created by video games with Yiddish dialogue; for example, a game named *The Shivah* includes a Yiddish dictionary and integrates some Yiddish vocabulary.[56] In this vein, multiplayer online role-playing games offer another possible venue for a virtual Yiddishland, which still await their developer.

CANADIAN YIDDISH IN THE DIGITAL AGE

Yiddish is broadening its reach among the mainstream Canadian public using a combination of video sharing and social media. For example, the 2017 performance of a Yiddish version of Canada's national anthem created in honour of the country's 150th birthday elicited considerable interest as a result of online technologies. The brainchild of Hindy Nosek Abelson, a Toronto-based translator, the anthem was performed by 150 multigenerational and multicultural choristers for television, widely disseminated via ZoomerMedia, and promoted on social media, where it went viral.[57] An expanding function of digital technology lies in the dissemination of Yiddish cultural products produced by Canadians to new audiences, with one example being *Yiddish Glory: The Lost Songs of World War II*. Two decades ago, in Kiev's Vernadsky National Library, University of Toronto professor of Yiddish studies Anna Shternshis came across an archive of handwritten Yiddish songs that had been penned during the Holocaust by Soviet Jews – Red Army soldiers and civilians – and collected by ethnomusicologist Moisei Beregovsky. Shternshis's analysis of this previously

unknown body of material included setting the lyrics to music in collaboration with Psoy Korolenko (the pseudonym of Russian songwriter and performer Pavel Eduardovich Lion) and an international
group of musicians. Shternshis describes the essential role digital
technologies played in this process, beginning with her own virtual
communication with a research assistant working in Ukraine while
she was in Toronto: "The biggest effect of the technology was during
the publicity. I was interviewed by media outlets from all over the
world – by Skype, phone, electronically – and as a result the publicity
went beyond one language, one country or the Yiddish World. Social
media was just a start, but the real publicity actually came from the
digital platforms of 'real' media – newspapers, radio stations and TV –
who all accessed the project via internet."[58] The resulting performances and the release of a Grammy Award-nominated album in
early 2018 have generated international coverage in print, radio, and
television, and online articles in a dozen languages.[59]

New websites are rendering historical materials available. For example, the Canadian Jewish Heritage Network offers access to the data-
bases and digitized holdings of archives that include significant Yiddish
content.[60] Virtual exhibits offer a growing site for interactive Yiddish
learning with a Canadian focus. For example, in 2017, two graduate students in the University of Toronto's recently established master's degree
in Yiddish Studies, Miriam Borden and Jessica Pollock, curated an
exhibit of the university's extensive collection of Yiddish books. Titled
"Discovering the Mame-loshn: The Hidden World of Yiddish at Robarts,"
the exhibit showcased a selection of the library's extensive holdings in
five glass display cases on the Robarts Library's main floor, with each
case dedicated to a theme: the Yiddish press, texts by and for women,
sacred text, great Yiddish literary works, and reference works such as dictionaries. Pollock remarked, "First and foremost, the goal of this exhibit is to bring Yiddish into the spotlight. We want to show people what
Yiddish is, what we do with it and all sorts of cool things about it." She
also hoped that the exhibit might inspire others to study the language.
Borden commented on the question of whether Yiddish is a dying language: "Definitely not! However, I think one of the main problems facing Yiddish is that people are stuck on the image of what Yiddish used
to be, instead of considering what it is now."[61] Due to the significant
attention the exhibit received, including record numbers of visitors,
Borden created a website including photographs of each of the exhibit's five cases. The welcome page of "Discovering Yiddish" offers visitors

this introduction: "The 20th century was an unprecedented time of movement and relocation for the Jews of Eastern Europe. And in near-ly every new place Jews re-established themselves, whether in small or great numbers, they brought Yiddish with them. Today, Yiddish contin-ues to exist in many of these communities, often in muted tones, sitting quietly in a box, on a bookshelf, or in a display case. It is the goal of Dis-covering Yiddish to locate these precious materials from the past and return them to the spotlight, to demystify the past they hold, and to dis-play them proudly as pieces of local history."[62]

Yiddish-related items such as books, newspapers, and photographs are given a second life by being digitized and made available to a wide public, which allows for accessibility far beyond what has ever been possible. Using interactive tools, digital technology can help to bridge the deep chasms generated by time and geographic distance. When asked about the future of the Yiddish book, Borden suggests a model of digital and interactive maps that is being applied to medieval man-uscripts, which are also increasingly becoming digitized.[63] Borden created a second and more ambitious exhibit at the Robarts Library involving Yiddish books, this time with an online component built in from the outset. "*Komets-alef: o!* Back to School at the Yiddish *Kheyder*" (2018) invites its viewers to become student participants in an imag-ined school.[64] Online participants can download a Yiddish worksheet and open related images as well as audio files. The exhibit offers a model for accessible and engaging interactive encounters with Yid-dish. Borden has further explored theoretical questions in the second incarnation of her exhibit, held at the Canadian Language Museum in the summer of 2019. The website page about the exhibit notes:

> Built into the concept of a Yiddish *kheyder* is a theoretical chal-lenge that encourages us to think about space. As we know, learn-ing and teaching Yiddish was not the express purpose of the tradi-tional *kheyder*, where instruction instead largely emphasized liturgical and Biblical texts; as Max Weinreich wrote, "No one was ever flogged for not knowing Yiddish." This Yiddish *kheyder*, then, is a new creation. It is a Yiddish space rooted in history, but not found in historical space or time. Rather, this Yiddish *kheyder* is a creation for this space and this time, inviting visitors to reflect on the fact that increasingly, 21st century Yiddish spaces have moved from the street, the home, and the *shul* into the classroom, the library, and the museum.[65]

Borden's vision dramatically alters concepts of place in relation to what Yiddish is and what it can be. Here Yiddish books exist as material culture, and as such represent objects in an evolving relationship with people over time and space.

NEW YIDDISH CINEMA

The audiovisual realm of film and television reveals significant twenty-first-century Yiddish innovation. A new corpus of projects has appeared since 2005 that integrates significant dialogue in Yiddish; that is, Yiddish appears in a communicative function in full sentences in exchanges between characters rather than as isolated words or phrases, or in songs. Although these productions show some continuity with prewar Yiddish cinema, this twenty-first incarnation marks a radical departure in terms of its production and consumption, with most of the dialogue produced via a process of translation for largely non-Yiddish-speaking audiences, who access it via subtitles in another language.

Yiddish cinema is experiencing a second life after almost seventy years of virtual silence. Films produced prior to 1950 encompassed multiple countries – notably Poland and the United States – for a mass Yiddish-speaking audience. Cinema formed an integral part of a flourishing Yiddish culture that spanned Europe and immigrant settlements worldwide. Over one hundred full-length Yiddish films – popular dramas, melodramas, and musical comedies – were produced between the First World War and 1950, with their heyday in the 1930s.[66] Employing cutting-edge technologies and drawing on a pool of talented directors, cinematographers, writers, composers, and actors, these works range from serious drama to light musical comedy to the avant-garde supernatural. A number were commercial successes, both among Jewish and non-Jewish audiences. Aptly termed by one scholar "Films Without Borders,"[67] Yiddish cinema reflected the linguistic reality of its speakers with dialogue that was "heterolingual," a term from translation studies that refers to the juxtaposition of multiple languages within a single work.[68] Thus, while the dialogue of pre-Holocaust Yiddish cinema is primarily Yiddish, one also finds Russian, Polish, English, and other languages as its speakers increasingly adopted the vernaculars of the countries in which they lived. While in some cases production staff included non-Yiddish speakers, casts were generally composed of actors from the Yiddish theatre who spoke the language fluently.

This first generation of Yiddish cinema came to an abrupt end due to the decimation of the Yiddish heartland in Poland in the Holocaust and the linguistic assimilation of Jews in the United States. In the State of Israel, the language of the cinema – like other expressions of cultural life – was Israeli Hebrew. The interest in Yiddish culture of the 1970s and 1980s that generated the klezmer revival also yielded a desire to preserve and restore Yiddish films. The National Center for Jewish Film (founded in 1976)[69] has rescued, remastered, and rereleased some forty Yiddish feature films with new English subtitles, including many that had been lost or forgotten.[70] These formed a canon of Yiddish cinema as scholars published pioneering studies on the subject beginning in the 1980s.[71] The rerelease and viewing of these films and their distribution in the film festival mode falls into a postvernacular mode, with the subtitled Yiddish functioning as a nostalgic "acoustic landscape" for audiences who do not speak the language.[72] One notable exception was Joan Micklin Silver's turn of the century immigrant drama, *Hester Street* (USA, 1975), which featured extensive subtitled dialogue in Yiddish. While films with occasional dialogue or song lyrics in Yiddish appeared in the 1970s, 1980s, and 1990s, especially in Europe, it was only after 2000 that a body of film with extended scenes in Yiddish appeared.

Yiddish cinema in the new millennium includes full-length features, short films, and television programs released for mainstream audiences and receiving both critical acclaim and media attention. From 2005 to 2020, over twenty fiction productions with significant Yiddish dialogue appeared in Canada, the United States, Europe, and Israel, despite the fact that a majority of their creators and audiences do not speak the language. I situate this new cinema in a mode that I term the "transvernacular": spoken Yiddish achieved through translation out of another language.[73] While a complex and labour-intensive process, this transvernacular mode allows for the realization of a creative vision in a language in which the producers, actors, and audiences often lack fluency but in which Yiddish plays an essential role. This mode, which characterizes almost all twenty-first-century Yiddish movie, sets this new cinema apart from the earlier body of Yiddish film. The artistic visions of a new generation of creators, changes in film culture – notably an openness to subtitles in American cinema – and new technologies to facilitate production and distribution have yielded a robust body of twenty-first-century Yiddish-language film.

The first full-length feature film entirely in Yiddish appeared in 2005, produced by and for Haredi audiences under the title *A Gesheft/The Deal*. The film was directed by Yakov Kirsh and produced by Mendel Kirsh, two brothers from Monsey, New York who were raised as Vishnitzer Hasidim and established Kosher Entertainment Productions to make commercial films for Haredi consumption. With its story about a corrupt Hasid who ultimately achieves moral redemption, the film features Hasidic Yiddish speakers and deliberately abides by Haredi norms of behaviour and morality. The film was marketed to members of the community, where it initially sold well until Hasidic authorities censured it.[74]

In contrast, the other twenty-first-century films to feature sustained Yiddish dialogue have emerged in a transvernacular process whereby the Yiddish represents a translation and is heard by audiences who rely on subtitles to understand it. The Yiddish dialogue production in this cinema most often falls under the category of "vehicular matching," whereby the language used matches what the storyline demands; for example, a Jewish character in a *shtetl* or a recent immigrant on New York's Lower East Side would naturally speak in Yiddish. Unlike traditional subtitles, which are generated after the completion of a project, the creators of the new Yiddish cinema have envisioned subtitled dialogue from the outset. These subtitles are generated by a process of reverse translation, where the dialogue is constituted or reconstituted based on an original script composed in another language, which film scholar Carol O'Sullivan terms "pseudo-subtitling."[75] Dror Abend-David suggests that Yiddish dialogue on the mainstream screen amounts to "non-translation" since it does not serve any real or prospective speech community or the communication of a verbal text. Rather, the fluent delivery serves a dramatic function in the emotional associations the language may hold for audiences; the use of Yiddish dialogue rather than a dominant language can also serve to undercut or subvert hegemonic norms on screen.[76]

This new cinema allows mass audiences – a vast majority of whom are not conversant in Yiddish and may never have heard the language spoken before – to encounter fluently spoken Yiddish. The dialogue is delivered by actors with a range of Yiddish knowledge, including Haredim, long-time cast members in the Yiddish theatre, North American speakers raised in Yiddishist homes, and actors with no previous exposure to the language. These actors engage in their own translation processes, whether as co-creators of the dialogue or in memorizing dialogue that they do not understand. One example of the latter is Vancouver-born and -raised Seth Rogan, who plays a Yiddish-speaking immigrant in the prologue to the film *An American Pickle* (USA, 2020). While Rogan is Jewish and was recently honoured for his involvement with Vancouver's Workmen's Circle – a secular Jewish organization with strong Yiddish roots – he did not come to the project as a Yiddish speaker. He said of learning the film's dialogue: "I had to just memorize it basically by sound because I'd have, like, two words to say in English, and it would turn into, like, three sentences in Yiddish and I was, like, I don't even understand the one to one ratio of this stuff, but I did my best.[77] As in prewar Yiddish cinema, the Yiddish cinema is heterolingual, with Yiddish dialogue delivered alongside other languages. The Yiddish appears in prologues to English films or television episodes, in the mouths of specific characters, or in a process of fluently switching between languages (code switching).

New Yiddish cinema can be divided into three main categories. The first and largest entails mainstream film and television representing the Haredi world, in particular narratives that portray Hasidim struggling against repressive norms in their communities. Among these are the dramas *Mendy: A Question of Faith* (USA, 2003), *Romeo and Juliet in Yiddish* (USA, 2010), *Félix et Meira* (Canada, 2015), and *Menashe* (USA, 2017); the horror films, *Shehita* (Canada, 2018) and *The Vigil* (USA, 2019); the hit Israeli television soap opera *Shtisel* (three seasons, 2013–21); and the Netflix miniseries *Unorthodox* (USA/Germany, 2020). Because of their subject matter, the casts of these films often feature actors that are former members of Haredi communities, who are sometimes also involved in crafting the dialogue. The second category comprises Yiddish-speaking characters in Holocaust-themed dramas. The short feature film, *Homeland/Beit Avi* (Israel, 2009), which portrays two Holocaust survivors during Israel's War of Independence in 1948, and the full-length feature war drama *Di Shpilke/The Pin* (Canada, 2014) stand out for dialogue that is almost entirely in Yiddish; both include actors without prior knowledge of the language. In this category, one also finds Yiddish dialogue within multilingual dramas set during the Holocaust such as *Son of Saul* (Hungary, 2015) or in its aftermath, for example, the horror films *Demon* (Poland, 2016) or *The Vigil* (2019), which both employ Yiddish dialogue to signify possession by a malevolent spirit. The third category consists of films in which Yiddish is the language of a prologue portraying a distant *shtetl* or immigrant past, setting the scene for a narrative set in contemporary America. Here one finds the black comedy-drama *A Serious Man* (USA, 2009), whose prologue is set in an Eastern European *shtetl*, Adam Sandler's comedy *The Cobbler* (USA, 2015), with an opening scene set in New York's Lower East Side at the turn of the last century, and the *shtetl* prologue to *An American Pickle* (USA, 2020). Unlike the pre-Holocaust body of Yiddish film, in which musical comedies were prevalent, this new cinema falls primarily into the category of drama. Despite deep associations between Yiddish and humour, comedy is notably missing from the new Yiddish cinema. The Canadian web series *YidLife Crisis*, discussed below, offers a marked exception. A full filmography is found in the bibliography of this book.

The new Yiddish cinema arose within broader trends bucking the historical unpopularity of subtitles. In an overwhelmingly monolingual American industry, subtitled films have historically accounted for less than 1 per cent of the domestic box office.[78] Subtitles were deemed by critics to be unfaithful or incorrect; too much work to read; or to take away from the film experience.[79] In addition, conventions dating to the Hollywood studio system in the 1930s – an average of 750 subtitles in a ninety-minute feature film, eight subtitles per minute, thirty-two characters per line – place constraints on translators as well as viewers. Expanding interest in, and tolerance of, vehicular matching for the sake of authenticity has facilitated the inclusion of Yiddish dialogue in twenty-first century cinema. Audiences have also become accustomed to seeing subtitles on their screens and mobile devices. Further, scholars suggest that whereas historically hegemonic languages such as English have been used to represent marginal or disempowered languages, heterolingualism can address the inequality that may arise when a dominant language – and the experiences associated with it – is used to represent a marginalized group. As O'Sullivan's study *Translating Popular Film* suggests, "subtitled heterolingual dialogue must be considered a condition necessary, even if not sufficient, for representing the other."[80] Subtitled dialogue in lesser-spoken languages such as Yiddish can reinforce the experiences of historically disadvantaged groups while giving those groups a voice. Further, the nostalgic or symbolic relationship to the language that is particular to the postvernacular mode can contribute to the success of Yiddish-language films, as audiences seek out opportunities to hear the language spoken. It is certainly not coincidental that the two films with almost completely Yiddish dialogue – *Homeland*

and *The Pin* – were made in Israel and Canada respectively, two countries whose Jewish communities include a high proportion of people
who are descended from Holocaust survivors and have passive knowledge of the language. These films also share a feature of cinema produced in lesser-spoken or non-spoken languages via processes of
translation: "visual storytelling." In both films the dialogue, which
is particularly laborious to produce and for audiences to take in, is
reduced and transcended by visual elements such as landscape, which
are foregrounded to tell the story.[81]

CANADIAN NEW YIDDISH CINEMA

Canada has emerged as a leading site of new Yiddish cinema production across its three categories, with a number of ground-breaking
projects, some mentioned above: the world's first non-Haredi full-
length Yiddish-language feature film produced since 1950, *Di Shpilke/
The Pin* (2014); the world's first sitcom/first web series in Yiddish,
YidLife Crisis (2014–19), the first all-Yiddish horror movie, *Shehita*
(2018); and an original animated short narrative film, *Der Fus Tort/
Angel's Foot Cake* (2001, revised 2005 and 2016). The discussion that
follows briefly examines each of these projects.

Yiddish cinema forms part of a growing Canadian corpus of full-
length films with significant dialogue in a non-official language. As
Canada is an officially bilingual nation, heterolingual film is more
common and better tolerated there than in the United States. For
example, *Bon Cop, Bad Cop* (2006), a bilingual film made in Quebec,
was highly successful in the province among both English- and
French-speaking audiences but far less so abroad, according to Canadian film critic Jim Leach, "presumably because of audience resistance to even partially subtitled movies."[82] Beginning in the 1990s, in
the wake of policies of Canadian multiculturalism and despite the
challenge of raising funds to create films in languages other than English or French, filmmakers exploring ethnicity chose to include dialogue in non-official languages. These films, which span multiple historical contexts, languages, and genres, include: *A Bullet in the Head*
(drama/war, 1990, invented language), *La Sarrasine* (family drama,
1992, Italian, French, English), *Calendar* (drama/romance, 1993,
Armenian, English, and others), *Double Happiness* (comedy/drama,
1994, Cantonese, English), *Bollywood/Hollywood* (romantic comedy,
2002, Hindi, Spanish, English), *Water* (drama/romance, Hindi, San-

skrit, 2005), *Incendies* (tragedy, 2010, Arabic, French, English), and *Rebelle* (drama/war, French, Lingala, 2012). As independent films created by auteurs who were involved in their writing, directing, and production, these works express artistic visions that include a linguistic component. The films have been critically acclaimed and include several Academy Award nominees for Best Foreign Language Film.

Rare are Canadian feature films shot entirely in a non-official language. The first feature-length film made entirely in an Indigenous language, *Atanarjuat: The Fast Runner* (2001, Inuktitut), by Inuk director Zacharias Kunuk, ushered in a new era. Shot outdoors on location near Igloolik, Nunavut, the award-winning thriller is based on an Inuit legend and set in a distant past before European contact. The film's website explains: "Our film *Atanarjuat* is part of this continuous stream of oral history carried forward into the new millennium through a marriage of Inuit storytelling skills and new technology ... *Atanarjuat* gives international audiences a more authentic view of Inuit culture and oral tradition than ever before, from the inside and through Inuit eyes."[83] The screenplay was written collectively in Inuktitut and English, based on recordings of eight elders telling the legend as it had been passed down to them. The elders were regularly consulted during the film's production in a meticulous reconstruction of the past, "particularly about the authentic details of the period we were bringing to life": clothing, weapons, and the Inuktitut language itself, which would have been very different from that spoken in the 1990s when the film was being made.[84] *Atanarjuat* offers an example of what one scholar terms "rhetorical sovereignty," in which Indigenous voices tell their own tales, with the Inuktitut dialogue simultaneously serving to evoke an "authentic view" of another culture and a sense of disorientation and disconnect for non-Inuit viewers.[85] In its painstaking efforts to produce authentic dialogue, and the experience of mainstream viewers briefly entering a cinematic world that is utterly foreign to them, *Atanarjuat* shares features with the new Yiddish films. The film also resembles other films in lesser-used languages in that it minimizes dialogue and emphasizes visual storytelling instead.

While demanding in resources, production of Canadian cinema with Yiddish dialogue is expanding. With auteurs whose vision includes Yiddish dialogue as an integral part of the narrative, translators who can render the text into Yiddish and coach the actors, actors willing to memorize dialogue in a foreign language, and audiences prepared to accept the subtitles, the corpus has grown. For example, the critically acclaimed French-English-Yiddish drama *Félix et Meira* (Maxime Giroux, 2015), contains Yiddish dialogue in several short scenes where Hasidic characters – members of Meira's family and community – are conversing amongst themselves. The Hasidic Yiddish is delivered both by actors who learned the dialogue phonetically (including the film's protagonist, Meira, played by Israeli actress Hadas Yaron) and by Hasidim who have left the community (for instance, Meira's husband, played by Brooklyn-born Luzer Twersky, who also served as an advisor to the film). What follows is an analysis of Canadian cinema with dialogue predominantly in Yiddish. All citations from the Yiddish are offered in English transliteration to approximate the sound of the dialogue.

Di shpilke/The Pin (2014)

The Pin is almost entirely in Yiddish. Set in an undisclosed location during the Holocaust, the film tells the story of Jacob (Grisha Pasternak) and Leah (Milda Gecaite), who fall in love while hiding in a barn and then are tragically separated. The story is framed by scenes of the now-elderly Jacob (David Fox) in a Toronto morgue, fulfilling the Jewish custom of Shmira (attending to a body before burial), who discovers that the corpse he is watching belongs to his lost wartime love. Except for a few brief sentences in Russian and English, all the dialogue between the two main characters is in Yiddish. The film received critical acclaim, with the extensive media coverage noting the unusual fact of the film's Yiddish dialogue.[86] Although the director, Naomi Jaye, is neither a Yiddish speaker nor from a Yiddish heritage background, her concept for the dialogue matched her vision for the film: that it be in that language "for the sake of authenticity."[87] An American review suggested that Jaye being a Canadian who speaks both English and French contributed to her openness to creating a film in Yiddish.[88]

The Pin offers a highly visual experience in which Yiddish functions as an aural anchor. As one reviewer put it: "Although the Yiddish sounds very natural, the experience of watching *The Pin* is much closer to watching any subtitled foreign-language art film than it is to immersing yourself in Yiddish or Jewish culture. Jaye's camera establishes a languid, sensual rhythm, punctuated by moments of high tension, and the images do most of the storytelling."[89] Shot in and around

Toronto, long segments of the film – including its opening nine minutes – unfold with little or no speech, relying instead on sweeping
landscapes of forests and skies accompanied by the sounds of birds,
rain, or silence to forge its narrative. By the same token, the minimized
Yiddish dialogue occupies important functions. For example, the
opening scene depicts the young Jacob running in the forest until he
seeks shelter in a barn. He is wakened by Leah, who is attempting to
treat his wound, and jumps up to address her aggressively in Russian,
letting her know that he has a gun and will shoot, ordering her not to
move, and bombarding her with questions about who she is and how
long she has been there watching him. She answers in Russian that she
is hiding, and when he asks why he should believe her, she responds
that he might turn her over "to them." She then adds, in a quieter voice
and in Yiddish, *"un ikh veys, du host nit keyn revolver"* (subtitle: And I
know you don't have a gun). Here Leah's switch to Yiddish emphasizes
the characters' shared identity and experiences while also underscoring
these elements for the viewers, who are explicitly informed in the subtitles that the language has turned to Yiddish. This use of language
marked a core element of Jaye's vision: "This film is a Yiddish film! …
they would be speaking to each other, once each figured out the other
was Jewish, in Yiddish."[90] Jacob and Leah go on to share their stories of
escape from the Nazis and their collaborators, as well as elements of
their previous lives, such as their first romantic experiences. The intimate relationship they build unfolds in Yiddish, and language
becomes a protective cocoon for the young couple until they are
abruptly torn apart.

Jaye went to great lengths to create *The Pin* in Yiddish, including
challenges in fundraising to produce a film in the language.[91] The
English script was translated by York University Yiddish instructor,
Gloria Brumer. The film's two young stars, both recent immigrants
from Eastern Europe, worked with two Toronto Yiddish speakers, Ana
Kuper Berman (discussed in chapter 2) and Chaimie Muncher, who
reviewed the script with them phonetically and coached them on their
pronunciation.[92] Jaye noted that due to the actors' Slavic backgrounds,
"I figured they would be able to get their mouths around the Yiddish
words."[93] In consultation with her team of translators, Jaye expressed
her vision for the universality of the love story depicted in the film,
rather than the specificity of representing a particular place, by delivering the dialogue in *klal-shprakh* (Standard Yiddish) rather than a
dialect associated with a particular group of speakers. This not only

avoided adding complexity to the project but fit with Jaye's artistic vision of not revealing the geographic location of the film's events in order to augment the viewers' sense of displacement.[94] According to Brumer, "Young love in a terrible time is a universal theme. Having the young pair speak Litvish Yiddish would have immediately 'located' the film. That would have been contrary to Naomi's vision and intent. Because *klal* Yiddish is nobody's Yiddish, it is everybody's Yiddish."[95]

Even without the use of a specific regional dialect, the dialogue in *The Pin* acts as an expression of the Eastern European Jewish identity of its characters. Serving as both a "signifying code" and an object of representation, the dialogue in a film identifies the characters with other speakers of that language and signals to the audience the culture being represented.[96] In *The Pin*, the language of the marginalized group – the Jewish victims of the Holocaust – is prioritized. This use of Yiddish further indicates to the audience that these characters possess a cultural identity distinct from that of most of the viewing audience and allows viewers a greater appreciation of their experiences. This function may take on additional significance as feature films are increasingly being used to transmit Holocaust memory and teach the subject to students.[97] It also expands the potential for more authentic aural representation of the Holocaust within a recent scholarly literature that examines representations of trauma as well as the creation of cultural memory in cinema.[98]

YidLife Crisis (2014-19)

YidLife Crisis stands out as a work of new Yiddish cinema in Canada and globally in key ways. First, it employs the language to explore and express issues related to Jewish identity rather than for the sake of reproducing a particular present in the contemporary Haredi world, or representing a past in an imagined *shtetl* or Jewish immigrant quarter. Rather than vehicular matching, *YidLife Crisis* uses Yiddish to create a world on screen in which characters are speaking the language contrary to – not because of – what the story demands. *YidLife Crisis* focuses on two young, secular Jews who speak Yiddish in present-day Montreal. Its creators and stars, Eli Batalion and Jamie Elman, employ provocative comedic dialogue to address contemporary issues around Jewish identity. Whereas twenty-first-century subtitled films with Yiddish dialogue tend to reduce the number of lines in favour of visual storytelling, talking forms the core of *YidLife Cri-*

sis and is regularly punctuated by puns and other jokes. The show was introduced in 2014 with the tagline "YidLife Crisis: Sex, drugs, milk & meat. In Yiddish." The synopsis on the *YidLife* website expresses the contradiction at the show's core: "Drinking in the very best that Montreal's multicultural Mile End has to offer, Chaimie and Leizer, best friends and debating adversaries, tackle life, love, and lactose intolerance in this foodie-centric web series done entirely in their grandparents' Yiddish."[99] The show's slogan was later updated to "Yiddish. Kosherish. Blasphemish" (figure 6.1).

Yiddish, stereotypically a language of the past, is the vehicle for dialogue in the present between the two characters of Leizer (Batalion) and Chaimie (Elman) about what it means to be a Jew in today's world, with Leizer assuming a more traditional stance and Chaimie a more liberal one. *YidLife Crisis* is a sitcom with recurring protagonists who find themselves in amusing situations. In this sense, the show is akin to the Yiddish duo Dzhigan and Shumacher, who performed their witty satirical sketches in front of mass audiences in interwar Poland and postwar Israel as well as on Israeli television. *YidLife Crisis* deliberately references the interplay between the Yiddish-language dialogue and subtitles as part of its quirky brand of humour. The show's primary vehicle for dissemination is the internet: having premiered at Toronto's Ashkenaz Festival in 2014, it has received hundreds of thousands of views of episodes posted to its website via YouTube. *YidLife Crisis* also evinces a continuity that is singular among new Yiddish cinema today, with three seasons spanning 2014–19. The show's success partly hinges on its format: as a series of videos five to fifteen minutes in length, it can be accessed at any time and at no cost to the viewer. Free of the constraints of network television, which depends on commercial success and the sustained devotion of audiences, the creators can deliver offbeat sketches that feel like a series of in-jokes. Rather than being dazzled by elaborate sets or plot development, viewers share moments of offbeat comedy in a language that carries deep-rooted comedic associations. Viewers who opt to watch the show are coming to it with interest in the content, and possibly familiarity with Yiddish.

YidLife Crisis is a wholly Montreal production. Batalion and Elman are natives of the city who learned Yiddish at Bialik High School and were exposed to the language through their families and the Dora Wasserman Yiddish Theatre. Further, almost all of the episodes are

Figure 6.1 *YidLife Crisis* tagline

filmed on location in recognizable settings as a visual representation of the creators' experiences of their city. The sites include iconic eateries in the old Jewish immigrant neighbourhood of Mile End, Mount Royal Park, the performing arts centre of Place des Arts, the McGill University campus, the Jewish General Hospital, and private homes, streets, and parks within the Jewish neighbourhood of Côte Saint-Luc. In addition, the episodes are deeply rooted in the idiosyncrasies of Montreal culture, with jokes that play on quirks such as the city's potholes and the never-ending summer construction holiday.

The fact that the first season of the show is almost entirely in Yiddish is a focus for the extensive media attention that *YidLife Crisis* received in Canada and abroad. Prominent is a characterization of Yiddish as a humorous language: an interviewer for Israeli television announced, "Get ready for some funny, funny, Yiddish jokes!"[100] while a Québécois journalist commented, "L'humour juif sonne beaucoup mieux en Yiddish" (Jewish humour sounds much better in Yiddish).[101] Batalion and Elman state in an interview that "Jewish comedy stems from a Yiddish sensibility"[102] and they repeatedly cite the influence of the 1990s American sitcom *Seinfeld*. They recount that when the pilot episode was performed first in English and then in Yiddish, the French-Canadian staff on site laughed most at the Yiddish episode because it sounded funny, "like *Seinfeld*."[103] This "sounding funny" can be attributed to profound connections between humour and Jewishness, and the Yiddish language specifically.[104] Thus, the report of a 2018 Canadian Jewish population survey, which identifies Yiddish as "Jewish humour's richest reservoir," connects the decrease of humour as an identity marker to the language's decline among younger generations.[105] In *YidLife Crisis*, these associations are reinforced by the distinctive Yiddish intonation employed by Chaimie and Leizer, notably the telltale "rise-fall contour" of the voice to indicate a transition between phrases and to echo questions.[106] This intonation and associated Yiddish speech patterns, which transferred to North American Jews, became pervasive among English-language Jewish comedians such as Jerry Seinfeld, Jackie Mason, and Fran Drescher.[107]

In *YidLife Crisis*, Yiddish is presented as funny in spoken dialogue that was generated via a collaborative process of translation from English into Yiddish and back again. The subtitles – or pseudo-subtitles – represent the original script with which the Yiddish is painstakingly paired to meet the vision of the show's writers: to make the show as accessible as possible to general audiences. In addition to Yiddish phrases being selected to match the time it takes viewers to read the subtitles, the creators opted for cognates or terms likely to be recognized by the average viewer. Overall, the Yiddish pronunciation is closer to Standard Yiddish than to a dialect. In response to criticism about the quality of the Yiddish in season 1, Batalion and Elman explained that the goal of the dialogue, which was collectively translated into Yiddish by Batalion, his father, and a formerly Hasidic friend, was "not linguistic perfection but a tribute to what Yiddish represents culturally, comedically and Jewishly."[108]

Chaimie and Leizer punctuate their speech with novel Yiddish formulations, profanity in particular. For example, the pilot episode, "Breaking the Fast," opens with Chaimie, shown as a young man wearing casual clothes, eating poutine (French fries smothered in gravy and cheese) with great gusto in a restaurant on Yom Kippur. Leizer, of the same age but wearing a black suit and *yarmulke* (skullcap), sits across from him, shaking his head (figure 6.2).

> Leizer: *Es lozt zikh nisht gloybn az du kenst esn itst.*
> Subtitle: I can't believe you're eating right now.
> Chaimie: *Es lozt zikh nisht gloybn az du est nisht.*
> Subtitle: I can't believe you're *not*.
> Leizer: *Shvayg man, s'iz farkaktn yonkiper!*
> Subtitle: Chaimie, it's f—ing Yom Kippur!

While the first two lines of Yiddish dialogue match the English subtitles, the third one comprises two separate streams, each of which consists of profanity particular to its language. Although Yiddish has no exact equivalent of "fuck" as an invective, the Yiddish is equally vulgar, with "*farkakt*" meaning "to be shat upon." "*Farkakt*" also forms part of the Yinglish lexicon and thus more likely to be familiar to viewers from its contemporaneous use on American television (e.g. *The Big Bang Theory*). Rather than adhere to the tendency among subtitlers to decrease profanity because of its stronger effect in writing,[109] *YidLife Crisis* revels in the deliberate use of expletives and vulgarity in both the dialogue and subtitles. In "The Schmaltz" (season 1, episode 2), Leizer sits down in front of his smoked meat sandwich and asks, "*Mmm. Vos far a fak is dos?* (subtitle: What the *f–k* is this?)." While "*fak*" is not a Yiddish vocabulary word, the meaning of this borrowed word would be clear to any English speaker. That episode also features the neologism proudly coined by the show's creators: "*Nakete selbie*" (naked selfie).[110]

Figure 6.2 *YidLife Crisis*, pilot episode, "Breaking the Fast," 1 January 2014

The *YidLife Crisis* subtitles form an integral part of the production and are deliberately employed to add commentary or humorous effect, as opposed to standard subtitles, which aim to offer a direct translation. The subtitles do not serve to convey the simple meaning of the Yiddish; rather, they are pseudo-subtitles used in deliberate and creative ways. Whereas Batalion and Elman's characters swear, question core elements of Jewish practice, and speak in graphic terms about sex, their transgressiveness is mitigated by the use of dialogue in the internal Jewish language of Yiddish. Their use of Yiddish as the basis for their humour has yielded live performances at mainstream Jewish cultural institutions across the globe.[111]

YidLife Crisis unequivocally challenges the representation one finds elsewhere in new Yiddish cinema, in which Yiddish belongs to a distant or invented past, or to today's Hasidim. The show's creators draw a deliberate distinction between their project and "authentic" Yiddish speakers of the past: "We're not speaking the Yiddish from Second Avenue during the 1920s, or from Tevye the dairyman."[112] In "Great Debates" (season 1, episode 3) Chaimie and Leizer interrogate their identities as Montrealers and Yiddish-speaking Jews in relation to today's Hasidim: *"mir hobn gevolt zayn … zey, neyn?"* (subtitle: We would be … these guys, no?). When Chaimie inquires what they would talk about, Leizer answers, *"di narishste kleynikaytn fun talmudishn gezets, yedn tog un yede nakht"* (subtitle: Talmudic nonsense, all day and night), after which they lapse into a mock Talmudic debate

Figure 6.3 *YidLife Crisis*, "Great Debates," 1 March 2014

as the screen fills with English text evocative of a page of Talmud, with a box in the centre that reads, "(Passover-influenced gibberish)." After concluding, "*Oy, mishige*" (subtitle: Ridiiiiiculous), they apply the identical logic – with the sing-song intonation associated with traditional Talmudic study – to conversation about their bagels as the screen fills up with more layers of "Talmudic" text. The scene serves to underline the extent to which *YidLife Crisis* is carving out a new locus for Yiddish within contemporary Jewish life. In the words of the show's creators: "We are reclaiming Yiddish for secular, multicultural, democratic people."[113] The show subverts the practice of using vehicular matching, with Yiddish as an integral part of its brand of humour.

A particular dimension of the show's humour lies in its context within Quebec, where language politics between French and English have a long and complex history. Local media reviews in both languages point out parallels between Yiddish and the Québécois experience, with the theme being particularly prominent in French-language interviews with the show's creators. [114] Batalion notes similarities between the Yiddish vernacular and *joual* (a working-class dialect of Québécois French), and characterizes the show as a "projet de rapprochement" to educate others about Jewish heterogeneity.[115] Most often cited in the French media is the pilot episode, set during the holy fast day of Yom Kippur, in which Leizer orders his poutine at the famed La Banquise restaurant with "*la sauce à coté*" (gravy on the side) in order to conform to a selective version of the Jewish dietary law separating milk and meat. Chaimie calls him a "poutine separatist," a tongue-in-cheek reference to Quebec's sovereignty movement that has advocated political independence for the province over the last four decades. This scene integrates Quebec's particular culture of comedy, with the waitress in this scene played by a deadpan Léane Labrèche-Dor of the sketch comedy series SNL *Québec*,[116] who also translated the French subtitles for the show. This use of Yiddish – associated in Quebec with a working-class Jewish immigrant generation of the past – allows the show a unique platform from which to build understanding between the Jewish and Québécois communities through humour. Self-declared Canadian Comedian Peacekeepers, in 2019, the YidLife Crisis duo were named Ambassadors for Peace in Montreal.[117]

The show challenges common stereotypes regarding Yiddish that it exists only as a series of individual vulgar or emotive terms, or that it exists solely as a secret language among elders. The episode "YidLife Crisis Versus Howie Mandel" (season 2, special episode) interrogates the stereotype of Yiddish as an expressive, emotional language. When Chaimie and Leizer go to meet their hero, the real-life Canadian comic Howie Mandel, he overhears their conversation and exclaims, "Yiddish!" An awkward exchange with Mandel switches from English to Yiddish when Leizer accidentally sneezes on him, and a germophobic Mandel releases a barrage of Yiddish insults – "Oh *shmendik*" (subtitle: moron), "you *putz*" (subtitle: dick), "*yots*" (subtitle: idiot), "*shlemiel*" (subtitle: dumbass), "*shlemazl*" (subtitle: numbnuts), "*shmekl*" (subtitle: little prick), "*gey kakn afn yam*" (subtitle: GO SHIT IN THE SEA) – and then says, "The gala's off, I gotta be hosed down, thank you." This list of slang, profanity, and curses represent some of the most familiar Yiddish loanwords and offers what a viewer might expect from Yiddish in a mainstream setting: a series of vulgar terms.[118] However, this hackneyed presentation of the Yiddish is flipped on its head by the way in which the scene is framed by the fluently spoken Yiddish of Chaimie and Leizer. After receiving a "*gezundheit*" ("bless you" in German) from Mandel, Leizer and Chaimie return the language of the scene back to fluent Yiddish: "*Dos iz a mentsh*" (subtitle: *That* is a gentleman), "*An emeser mentsh!*" (subtitle: I *know*, right?!).

The episode "Off the Top" (season 2, episode 1) subverts the stereotype of Yiddish as a secret language. At a party, Leizer is approached at a buffet table by a young woman who has overheard him speaking with Chaimie:

> Evelyn: I have to ask. Was that Yiddish?
> Leizer: Ya.
> Evelyn: That's amazing! I thought it was a dead language.
> Leizer: I'm resurrecting it.
> Evelyn: Ah. My grandparents used to speak it to tell secrets in front of me.
> Leizer: Mine too. That's why I learned it. Now they only insult me in English.
> Evelyn: [Laughs] Is that what you guys were doing: telling secrets?

Here Leizer reveals for the first time an awareness of speaking Yiddish and its popular use as a secret language. When later in the episode Chaimie hears an older woman at the party, Chavah, speaking in Yiddish to the rabbi, it functions as an insider language: she openly complains about the lack of traditional Jewish food and questions whether "a little snip" (i.e., the circumcision) can make "*a yidishe neshome*" (Jewish soul). When Chaimie interjects in Yiddish, he inspires the following exchange:

> Rabbi: *Er redt yidish!*
> Subtitle: Oh, a Yiddish speaker!
> Chavah: *Zeyer sheyn. Khotsh dayn gramatish hinkt a bisl.*
> Subtitle: Very nice! Although your grammar [literally: grammatically] is a little off.

Here the joke is that it is that one of the "authentic" speakers of the older generation makes a grammatical error, whereas the young Chaimie is able to express himself flawlessly. Chavah's slip was deliberately left in the episode as a small inside joke.[119]

This nuanced humour in season 2 was facilitated by the involvement of Rivka Augenfeld, who has been involved in Montreal's Yiddish cultural life since childhood (see chapter 3), as the show's new translator. The result is a rich, idiomatic, and nuanced Yiddish, with Augenfeld identifying Chaimie and Leizer as "two intelligent *shmendriks*" speaking the language at the same level at which they speak English – in full sentences, with word play, puns, and inside jokes – at a time when so much of the language has been, and continues to be, lost.[120] For example, "Off the Top" opens with Chaimie offering Leizer a marijuana cigarette on Rosh Hashana (the Jewish new year), licking it with a smile and chanting, *"Bapisht!"* (subtitle: Baptized!). Augenfeld recalls that when she came across Elman's term "to baptize a joint" in the script, she made the link to a joke from her own Yiddish summer camp experience at Camp Hemshekh in the Catskill Mountains, where the campers from Montreal imported a local pun that conflated Saint John the Baptist, a prominent figure in the city's Catholic heritage,[121] with *"bapishn,"* meaning "to urinate on."[122] For Augenfeld, *YidLife Crisis* places the language in a modern, secular context replete with humour and cultural references that appeal to younger people and, in the process, brings the language to a public that may never have thought about it: "Wow, Yiddish is not just some funny words, it's a language. You can say anything in it."[123]

The potential exposure of this rich Yiddish to new audiences is not to be underestimated: "Double Date" (season 2, episode 3) attracted over 400,000 hits on YouTube during the first week of its release. The episode guest-stars Mayim Bialik, made famous by her roles in the American sitcoms *Blossom* and *Big Bang Theory*, playing the Yiddish-speaking Chaya.[124] An observant Jew with a Yiddish family background and a student of the language in university, Bialik was able to convincingly deliver the lines that Batalion and Elman wrote for her.[125] Much of the humour in the show's third season derives from the interplay between the Yiddish dialogue and its recognizable cadence, intonation, and gesturing on the one hand, and the English subtitles on the other. For example, in "Sukkanabis" (season 3, episode 1), Chaimie persuades Leizer to desecrate the holiday by smoking a little cannabis (*a bisl cannabis*), which Chaimie persuasively calls *a cannabisl*. In "Jewish General Hospital" (season 3, episode 3), a squirming Chaimie in the hospital waiting room utters: *"Oy, es brent a fayer!"* (subtitle: It's burning!). Leizer responds, *"Afn pripetshik?"* (subtitle: In your groin?). Both lines evoke a repertoire of popular Yiddish music. The first comes from a beloved twentieth-century Hannukah song, "Fayer, Fayer" (Fire, Fire), about the potato pancakes (*latkes*) that are traditional to the holiday: *"oy es brent a fayer, oy s'iz heys, fayerdike, brenendike, heyse latkes!"* (Oh, a fire burns, oh, it's hot, fiery, burning, hot latkes). The second comes from perhaps the most recognizable of Yiddish songs, Mark Warshavsky's popular nineteenth-century song, "Afn Pripetshik" (On the Hearth), which opens with *"Afn pripetshik brent a fayer!"* (On the hearth a fire burns) and nostalgically recounts a rabbi teaching his young students the alphabet in the traditional schoolhouse, the *kheyder*. Here, even a viewer with extremely limited knowledge of Yiddish might catch the reference and be part of the in-joke, which subverts the most beloved of tunes to refer to sexually transmitted infections.

Asked in an interview after the show's first season whether *YidLife Crisis* forms part of a wider revival, Batalion and Elman responded, "Yes, it feels like it's part of a movement of some sort, part of a small community of 'hip' events associated with things Yiddish" in what they term the "nouveau Yiddish world."[126] Batalion and Elman also situate *YidLife Crisis* within the independent television and video movement, where "authentic voices" are being distributed on web-based platforms such as YouTube.[127] The show points to the impact of new digital technology and existence of free online forums on which to share audiovisual works as new vehicles for Yiddish-language creativity.

TWO SHORT YIDDISH FILMS: *DER FUS TORT* AND *SHEHITA*

Canada has also produced two short Yiddish films: one animated and one live action. Both are original stories created in English by filmmakers who have been exposed to Yiddish but do not speak it. In both cases, the dialogue was rendered by native speakers with long histories of involvement in the secular Yiddish cultural milieus of Montreal and Toronto respectively.

The animated short is a genre of particular importance in Canada due to its prominence at the National Film Board, the country's public film producer and distributor.[128] In 2001, Ottawa-based artist and animator Sharon Katz wrote, directed, and animated an original short titled *Der Fus Tort/Angel's Foot Cake*, which was revised and re-released in 2016.[129] The film has been screened at festivals and is posted for public viewing on the Vimeo video-sharing site. It offers a modern folktale in the guise of a "zany animated tale [that] combines 21st century Yiddish storytelling with the hottest of new media."[130] Billed as "Slapstick comedy in Yiddish with English subtitles,"[131] whimsical black-and-white line drawings with occasional colour are accompanied by instrumental klezmer music performed by Yale Strom and his band, Zmiros. The film tells its story via visual storytelling, punctuated by minimal all-Yiddish dialogue.

Figure 6.4 Still from *Der Fus Tort/Angel's Foot Cake*, 2001, revised 2016

Der Fus Tort opens with a comical character named Drinkeleh Fresserkeh (from the Yiddish terms for "drink" and "gorge," respectively). Drinkeleh is munching a piece of cake when he spies playing cards fluttering down from above and a giant hand reaching down to pick them up; his eyes rest on the pair of large feet poking down out of the clouds. His thoughts, in English, appear in writing on the screen, "Angels' feet?" And then, taking another bite of cake, the words appear on the screen: "Angel's foot cake!" After this point, Drinkeleh is silent and only the angels speak. They wriggle their toes and comment to each other: "*a fus tort? ver vil kukn af a fus tort? a fus tort is mies, a fus iz nisht sheyn*" (subtitle: A foot cake? Who wants to see a footcake? A foot cake is ugly, a foot is not nice). Drinkeleh prepares to bake the giant "angel's foot cake" – making a foot-shaped pan, mixing the ingredients, and putting the cake in the oven – while the angels above attempt to sabotage the project. The angels are present only through their opinionated voices and their large feet and hands, cropped by the edge of the video frame. We see a giant hand slamming the kitchen door on Drinkeleh, "*vart a minut, me tor nisht esn keyn fis, dos iz farbotn*" (subtitle: Wait a minute, it's not permitted to eat feet, it's forbidden) and, as a smiling Drinkeleh gathers his ingredients, "*shoyn vider a fus cake! vos kumstu mir mit a fus cake? shoyn vider a fus cake! Kh'hob dokh gezogt* NISHT *keyn fus cake! a fus cake iz oysgeshlosn*" (subtitle: Again with a foot cake! Why come with a foot cake? Again with a footcake? I said NO foot cake! A foot cake is out of the question). A pair of giant hands empties entire cartons of eggs into the batter: "*a bisl kolesterol*" (subtitle: A little cholesterol). Paying no attention to the angels, Drinkeleh continues his labours and the cake is baked and distributed to friends. But then, a giant hand descends from above, "*vu iz a shtikl far mir?*" (subtitle: Where is a piece for me?). Drinkeleh, now dressed for an old-fashioned standoff, pulls a piece of cake from his holster and tosses it at the angels. They respond with the line, "*dakht zikh az undzer strategye toyg nisht*" (subtitle: Our strategy is not working), which is accompanied by laughter. The angel's hands descend once again, this time with an upside-down springform pan, and they shake a cherry cheesecake onto the town below, exclaiming, "*zol zayn tsum gezunt*" (subtitle: To your health), which is followed with them saying, in English, "That's it, that's the last line." In the 2016 revised ending, Drinkeleh is shown walking determinedly back into the frame with an umbrella and rain boots, sloshing through the cheesecake slush.

The film offers a personal narrative on multiple levels. In an interview, Katz shared that she first wrote the story about the frustrations of the creative process and the "constant circularity of creative endeavours: 1% inspiration, 99% exasperation, yet always coming back for more."[132] As an artist, she imagined her muses as angels who are both loving and interfering. Katz wanted the angels to speak Yiddish to reflect her experiences as someone born in the 1950s who grew up in Montreal with parents who spoke the language amongst themselves but did not pass it on. She said that for her, "Yiddish was a familiar foreign language of great intimacy, mystery, and humour."[133] In the film, Drinkeleh does not understand the angels' words, only their actions.

While the original story had no spoken words, as Katz's project evolved, the animated version had to have dialogue in Yiddish. This exchange between the angels was the product of a process of improvisation that involved two close friends prominent in Montreal's secular Yiddish milieu, Rivka Augenfeld (*YidLife Crisis* translator) and her mother, Liba Augenfeld. Katz describes the process: "I brought Rivka and Liba together in a make-shift sound recording studio and directed them in the storyline but let them invent the dialogue as we went along. We did multiple takes and while I had almost no idea what they were saying, I knew when a phrase was right by Rivka and Liba's uproarious laughter."[134] Ultimately, *Der Fus Tort* is both a twenty-first-century tale in Yiddish, and an artistic work about Katz's relationship with Yiddish: "It's about my most familiar foreign language, a nod to my Yiddish speaking ancestors, and my Yiddish speaking, poker-playing angel muses. My generation is only one removed from a long standing, incredibly rich culture, and I'm asking through this film what my relationship to that culture is (beyond the sentimental) and how Yiddish can be so important to me even though I don't understand it."[135]

The short film *Shehita* also has a non-Yiddish-speaking creator who draws on fluent speakers from Montreal and Toronto to produce the idiomatic dialogue. The *Shehita* website contains the following synopsis: "A Yiddish-speaking Jewish community in Quebec begins to unravel after a horrific discovery stirs up demons of the past."[136] Directed and written by Dean Gold, a Toronto-based, Israeli-born filmmaker, the twenty-six-minute film began as a Ryerson University thesis project under the title *Shehita: A Yiddish Horror Tale* and expanded into an award-winning film that has been screened to acclaim at multiple festivals. It tells the story of a Hasidic man and his wife (Max Sterling and Nina Iordanova) on an isolated dairy farm in rural Quebec whose cows mysteriously begin to produce blood instead of milk. The mashgiach (kosher supervisor, played by Avi Hoffman) is brought in, followed by the Hasidic rabbi (Sam Stein), and much of the film devoted to a heated dialogue between the two men about the theological implications of how to handle the situation. They represent two distinct perspectives: the mashgiach, who joined the Hasidic fold as an adult, appeals to the value of science and a belief in the tolerance of mainstream society; the Hasidic rabbi, a survivor of the Holocaust, invokes divine providence and expresses a profound mistrust of outsiders. Gold, who developed a fascination with Yiddish as a young adult in Israel, sought to combine two existing film genres against a specifically Canadian backdrop: videos made by and for Hasidim addressing issues of concern to the community, and the horror movie. In the process, the film could interrogate the collision of two cultures within what Gold terms "Canada's multicultural experiment": contemporary secular Quebec society and a traditionalist Haredi world that rejects what that mainstream represents. Having the Haredi characters speaking only in Yiddish would serve as an articulation of their worldview.[137]

The production of the Yiddish dialogue in *Shehita* entailed multiple steps. A casting call for one of the roles states: "The film will be in Yiddish, a language spoken by most Hasidic communities, though dialogue is minimal and the role contains mostly action so pronunciation can be worked out."[138] In the end, the four cast members included two seasoned actors with long associations with the Yiddish theatre: Sam Stein with Montreal's Dora Wasserman Yiddish Theatre, and Avi Hoffman with New York's National Yiddish Theatre Folksbiene. Having written the script in English, Gold invited Hindy Nosek Abelson (the author of the Yiddish rendition of "O Canada," discussed above), to join the project as translator and Yiddish coach to the two non-Yiddish speaking younger actors (Nina Iordanova and Max Sterling). For Nosek Abelson, the film's use of Yiddish evokes its emotional strength as well as adding authenticity. Her approach to the translation was to use a Yiddish that was not pedantic and academic but rather a daily and "*folkstimlekh*" (folky, popular) language belonging to contemporary Hasidim. She created an idiomatic dialogue in her native Ukrainian dialect with prominent use of linguistic markers from traditional Jewish observance such as the frequent interjection of *khasvesholem* (heaven forbid). Nosek Abelson treated the film like a translation of a lyrical poem or song by "painting the same picture in the translated version as in the original." She noted in an interview, "I think it's important that when showcasing Yiddish in any form, that we do justice to the authentic beauty of the language, regardless of what dialogue we use."[139]

Unlike many of the new Yiddish films – and films in lesser-spoken languages more broadly – *Shehita* does not limit dialogue to prioritize visual storytelling. Cinematographically, the film provides visually compelling images around blood, snow, and fire to express the primal emotions of fear or anguish. At the same time – with two stars who are fluent speakers – much of the film is taken up with dialogue in complex and nuanced discussion that raises deep-rooted questions about identity and belonging in contemporary multicultural Canada.

YIDDISH FILM DISSEMINATION

While *YidLife Crisis* and *Der Fus Tort* are available for public viewing online,[140] Yiddish film currently lacks a shared forum for dissemination. Whereas the genre of animated Yiddish shorts is well represented on video sharing sites like YouTube or Vimeo, dramas, especially full-length feature films, are more difficult to access. While the Yiddish Cinematheque Facebook group posts occasional links to newer material,[141] Yiddish cinema lacks a clearinghouse. One step forward is the forthcoming collection, *Kurtse Animirte Films af Yidish/Animated Yiddish Shorts*, produced by American professor and translator, Ilan Stavans and edited by Israeli animator Yoni Salmon.[142]

In contrast, Canadian Indigenous film and television have state-funded systems in place for dissemination. This has been the case since the 1999 launch of the national Aboriginal Peoples Television Network, whose multiple channels feature programs for children, youth, and adults in Indigenous languages.[143] The result has been a variety of original shows. For example, *Urban Native Girl* (2016), a biographical documentary series that follows Lisa Charleyboy, "an Aboriginal fashionista," offers subtitled narration in the Tsilhqot'in language, which Charleyboy learned as a student in Toronto.[144] The comedy *Qanurli?* (2011–19) features two Inuktitut-speaking comedians, "Inuk Qablunaaq" and "Nipangi Huittuq," hosting skits, parodies, and other materials from a tent in the Arctic.[145] These shows interrogate complex issues of language identity and revitalization, while making them accessible to wide audiences. A large selection of children's programming in Indigenous languages is offered commercial-free on APTN Kids.[146] In 2020, the selection included *Amy's Mythic Mornings*, which features traditional legends in Coast Salish; *Anaana's Tent*, which teaches new songs, words, and stories in Inuktitut; and *Louis Says*, which teaches words in Cree by showing the adventures of a young boy as he helps an elder in his community. Some of these shows offer enrichment activities in accompanying websites: the website "Welcome to Anaana's Tent" offers portals in both English and Inuktitut, with information about the show as well as interactive games, songs, and activities to teach new words; the website "Louis Says" offers resources such as a guide to the show, as well as additional games that can be played in Dene, Inuktitut, Plains Cree, and Woodland Cree.[147] The Nunavut Independent Television Network (NITV), which has been broadcasting since 2010, launched a channel of 24/7 Inuktitut programming called Uvagut TV (Our TV) in 2021. This includes five hours for children daily as well as archived content from community elders, available via online streaming through the website uvagut.tv.[148] A more community-based model is offered by the streaming company IsumaTV (established 2008), "a collaborative multimedia platform for indigenous filmmakers and media organizations," in which each user is invited to design their own channel and post publicly accessible materials.[149] Among many others, filmmaker Zacharias Kunuk has posted his *Atanarjuat: The Fast Runner* trilogy: "Three unique award-winning Inuit films express the dramatic history of one of the world's oldest oral cultures from its own point of view."[150] A model comparable to IsumaTV in Yiddish, even on a far more modest scale, could bring together existing films and encourage future audiovisual projects.

YIDDISH FUTURES IN CYBERSPACE AND ON SCREEN

Cyberspace transcends geographic borders, with Canada as one point on a transnational Yiddish map. When it comes to language promotion, the underlying question regarding new media is how the tools that could promote Yiddish continuity and revitalization or attract new speakers are being used, and what their impact might be. With the accessibility of digital communication software, web-based Yiddish can mimic at least some of the vibrancy of an in-person gathering. What is unquestionable is that the cyber-vernacular space offers potential for created language spaces that has barely been tapped. At present, the internet offers a wealth of material for those interested in learning, improving, or otherwise engaging with the Yiddish language: a digitized literature, thousands of hours of recorded books and other audio materials, oral histories, and films, not to mention formal online courses. Online and digital technologies offer a space in which to revisit and reinvent what the language and culture mean to new generations. Interactive exhibits invite the uninitiated public in to experience the language and culture; online tools mitigate inequalities caused by different levels of linguistic competence; social media offers a means of connecting speakers worldwide. New media offer opportunities for Canadians to both access their own Yiddish history and form part of a global cybercommunity.

The two streams of new Yiddish films that have emerged in a trans-vernacular mode – those that employ the language as an expression of authenticity and those that employ it as an expression of their creators' artistic vision – offer vast and untapped possibilities. For Yiddish speakers, hearing full dialogue as opposed to the more common interjection of individual words into English represents a validation of the malleability and potency of Yiddish. Film and television with Yiddish dialogue can enhance the experiences of emerging as well as more advanced learners, with studies in applied linguistics indicating the important role that subtitled films can play in language learning.[151] For audiences more broadly, this new cinema offers an immersion experience of the language, even if fleeting. These films offer fresh opportunities to hear spoken Yiddish in diverse settings and genres, be it casually or in a formal classroom.

In the new transvernacular mode, the trend to produce Yiddish dialogue is only at its beginning. Given the longstanding prominence of Yiddish in Jewish and in broader European and American history, there are no shortage of stories that call for Yiddish dialogue for authenticity's sake or as an expression of a creative vision. With far greater acceptance than ever before of subtitled dialogue, including its prominent use in the popular genres of fantasy and science fiction, increasing numbers of Yiddish-language projects will surely emerge. Methodologies to overcome a lack of fluency among filmmakers include collaborative or individual translation as well as dialogue coaches drawn from a diverse pool of Yiddish speakers, including native speakers, academics, new speakers, and former members of Hasidic communities. The transvernacular mode, with its creative and collaborative translation process, allows for non-fluent speakers to embrace Yiddish with infinite possibilities for creative exploration and expression. Just as the projects discussed in this chapter give voice to the particular perspectives and experiences of their creators, the transvernacular process invites other voices to contribute their own. Given the success of *YidLife Crisis* and the academic and performative activity around Queer Yiddishkeit, one can anticipate other web series offering feminist or queer perspectives. What remains to be created to enhance Yiddish cinema as a created language space is a collaborative multimedia platform to facilitate distribution as well as bring interested filmmakers, translators, and actors together.

Afterword

This book has presented multiple strategies for developing created language spaces as a vehicle for secular Yiddish transmission. For a lesser-used and less-commonly-taught language, continuity can take multiple forms over time and among those who engage with it. The more options, entry points, and modes of engagement with the language that are available, the more dynamic its transmission into the future will be. Continuity can occur across multiple modes in a participatory way: use within families; formal and informal education for all ages; performance; community activism; publishing and translation; singing; new media; and the production and viewing of cinema. Each has enriched Yiddish transmission and has built fluidity and resilience into the language; in tandem, they augment its continuity for a broad base of native and new speakers.

This book argues that linguistic continuity is best served with multiple points of entry and access across the concentric circles; for a lesser-used language, one cannot rely exclusively on transmission from parents to children or on education in a formal classroom (see figure 0.1). Each generation evolves its own approaches to transmission that incorporate the ideas, trends, and technologies of that time; some will survive into the future, while others may change or disappear. This process keeps languages vibrant and pertinent to subsequent generations, even if the languages are not fluently spoken on a daily basis. Ghil'ad Zuckermann's 2020 study of language reclamation, *Revivalistics*, notes that the "reinvigoration of Yiddish as a secular language" faces a challenge; although the twenty-first century has marked the advent of "somewhat enhanced/even creativity in Yiddish," the young people opting to study the language in immersive programs world-

wide do so in relatively small numbers: an estimated one to two thousand people under the age of forty, augmented by a small number of
Haredi native speakers who have become involved in secular Yiddish
culture.[1] His observations about the relative paucity of sites for young
people to engage with secular Yiddish underlines the extent to which
its transmission relies on multiple vehicles. The classroom, even in a
highly effective intensive format, must work in tandem with other
sites if lesser-used or less commonly taught languages like secular Yiddish are to maintain their hold on future generations.

This story of Yiddish in Canada between 1950 and 2020 points to
myriad models of continuity. A language and culture can be transmitted in multiple ways other than intergenerationally, in particular
in the wake of rupture caused by mass trauma or acculturation. Yiddish offers a slate upon which to write new identities and build collective spaces in Jewish as well as non-Jewish realms. If continuity is
separated from a biological context and replaced with the concept of
generational cohorts, then Yiddish is indeed being transmitted among
the generations. Accessible, inclusive, and participatory approaches to
cultural life via the creative arts represent an expanding feature of continuity. Alongside language courses offered in university classrooms
and community centres, wide-ranging initiatives to foster engagement with Yiddish have been pioneered for and by younger people
over the last seventy years and counting.

The strategies to preserve, transmit, and promote secular Yiddish
worldwide in 2020 and beyond are increasingly inclusive and
transnational. With heritage speakers, new learners, artists, and other
adherents of secular Yiddish coming together in real as well as virtual, online spaces, the flow between organizations that offer Yiddish
materials or programming has truly created a global milieu, one
where Canada features prominently. As this book has demonstrated,
Canada has produced secular Yiddish culture in the areas of theatre,
youth activism, publishing, music, and film as part of this web of
interconnected activity. Ultimately, the most effective modes of transmission involve an active, engaged, and participatory culture that
encompasses youth. With the passing of the last European-born pre-
Holocaust generation of Yiddish speakers, and with transmission taking place in the classroom or at festivals rather than in the home, the
culture associated with secular Yiddish has increasingly become comprised of new speakers. The book demonstrates how the trajectories
of language transmission can change. For example, individuals who

have studied Yiddish in university are transmitting the language to their children as a mother tongue, making them new native speakers.

To flourish, Yiddish requires multiple and intersecting created language spaces that are forward-looking and dynamic, embracing new technologies and approaches. The narrative about Yiddish as dead or dying needs to be replaced by one recognizing that a language lives by being used, whether in daily communication or in shorter encounters within created language spaces. The massive and immeasurable losses to Yiddish over the last century – the Holocaust, linguistic assimilation, persecution, exclusion – must be mourned, just as the resilience of Yiddish must be celebrated. This book argues that spaces created as sites for the language to be deliberately encountered can be formed anywhere – in person, online, or via other technologies – be it for a short time or for a lifetime. These spaces span the concentric circles of Yiddish, from raising children as native speakers to a virtual Yiddishverse. As the examples in this study indicate, created language spaces can exist in diverse contexts that meet the needs of their speakers in a particular time and place. ייִדיש לעבט *Yiddish lebt* – the language lives on – by virtue of those who proclaim, practice, explore, or perform in it, in ways that are ever-evolving in Canada and the world.

Yiddish Books Published by Canadian Resident Writers, 1945–2020

Aronoff, Joseph. *A gebet tsu der yu-en*. Montreal, 1955.

– *Gezangen un dertseylungen: Lider mit muzik.* Montreal: J. Aronoff, 1946.

– *Der mamen a brivale: Eynaker*. Montreal, 1962.

– *Der mentsh un di levone*. Montreal, 1959.

– *Oysgevigt di kinder: Eynakter*. Montreal, 1964.

Bas-Meltzer, Esther. *In di negl fun umkum.* Translated from Polish by Arn Zshukhovitski. Montreal: Aroysgegebn fun a grupe nay-gekumene khelmer, 1950.

Becker, Jacob Leib. *Dertseylungen un zikhroynes*. Montreal, 1956.

Belkin, Simon. *Di poyle tsien bavegung in kanade: 1904–1920.* Montreal: Aktsyons komitet fun der tsiyonistisher arbeter bavegung in kanade, 1956.

Bergner, Hinde. *In di lange vinternekht: Mishpokhe-zikhroynes fun a shtetl in galitsiye, 1870–1900*. Montreal: Moyshe Harari, Melech Ravitch, and Herts Bergner, 1946.

Bergner, Yosl. *59 ilustratsyes tsu ale geshikhtn folkstimlekhe geshikhtn fun yitshak leybush perets*. Introduced by Shmuel Niger and Y.Y. Sigal. Montreal: Farlag fun herts edelshtayn, 1950.

Birstein-Podoliak, Chaia. *Dos ershte lid: Lider, poemes un kurtse dertseylungen fun beyde zaytn yam*. Toronto, 1991.

Botwinik, David. *Fun khurbn tsum lebn: Naye yidishe lider*. New York: League for Yiddish, 2010.

Botwinik, Leybl. *Di geheyme shlikhes: Fantastishe dertseylung*. Montreal: D. Botwinik, 1980.

Bronshteyn, Yehezkel, ed. *Dray froyen poetn fun modernem yapan: Antologye*. Montreal, 1952.

Dunsky, Shimshen. *Midrash Rabbah. Ester, Rus: Targum yidish*. Montreal: S. dunsky medresh fond komitet, 1962.

– *Midrash Rabbah. Eykhah: Mit yidisher iberzetsung, derklerungen un araynfir.* Montreal: S. dunsky medresh fond komitet, 1956.
– *Midrash Rabbah. Koheles: Targum yidish.* Montreal: S. dunsky medresh fond komitet, 1967.
– *Midrash Rabbah. Shir ha-shirim: Targum yidish.* Montreal: S. dunsky medresh fond komitet, 1973.
– ed. *Shloyme vaysman bukh/Shloime Wiseman Book.* Montreal: Yidishe-folks-shuln, 1961.
Elberg, Yehuda. *Afn shpits fun a mast: Roman.* New York: Brider shulzinger, 1974.
– *In leymene hayzer: Roman.* Tel Aviv: Farlag yisroel-bukh, 1985.
– *Kalmen kalikes imperye: Roman.* Tel Aviv: Farlag yisroel-bukh, 1983.
– *Mayses.* Tel Aviv: I.L. Peretz Publishing House, 1980.
– *A mentsh iz nor a mentsh: Roman.* Tel Aviv: I.L. Peretz Publishing House, 1983.
– *Tsevorfene zangen: Dertseylungen.* Montreal: Shule publikatsyes, 1976.
– *Tsvishn morgn un ovnt: Roman.* Tel Aviv: Farlag yisroel-bukh, 1987.
– *Unter kuperne himlen: Dertseylungen.* Buenos Aires, AR: Tsentral-farband fun poylishe yidn in argentine, 1951.
Finkelstein, Leo. *Dortn un do: Vegn dem dertseyler un dramatiker f. bimko.* Toronto: Farlag gershon pomerants esey-bibliyotek, 1950.
– *Loshn yidish un yidisher kiyem.* Mexico City: Shlomo Mendelson, 1954.
– *Megilas poyln.* Buenos Aires, AR: Tsentral-farband fun poylishe yidn in argentine, 1947.
– *Pidyen-ha-shem.* Toronto: Farlag Gershon Pomerants esey-bibliyotek, 1948.
Frankel-Zaltzman, Paula. *Haftling numer 94771: Iberlebenishn in daytshe lagern.* Montreal: Aroysgegebn fun a komitet, 1949.
Franzus-Garfinkle, Sheyndl. *Erev oktober: Roman.* Montreal: Aroysgegbn mit der hilf fun dem dr. hayim zshitlovski leyen krayz, 1947.
Fuks, Chaim Leib. *Der akhter himl.* New York, 1974.
– *Hundert yor yidishe un hebreyishe literatur in kanade.* Montreal: Kh. l. fuks bukh-fun, 1980.
– *Lodzsh shel mayle: Dos yidishe gaystike un derhoybene lodzsh.* Tel Aviv: I.L. Peretz Publishing House, 1972.
– *Di teg neygn di kep: Lider, poemes, un balades.* New York: Cyko, 1969.
– *Tsu di himlen aroyf.* New York: Cyko, 1982.
– *Zunfargang.* Haifa, IL: Farlag hefah bay der hefaher opteylung fun yidishn literatn-un zshurnalistn-farayn in yisroel, 1972.
Giladi-Gelbfarb, Joshua. *Fun toyre oytser: Geklibene perl fun talmud, midrashim, zohar un gedole yisrael oyf hamishah humshe torah un pirke oves.* Montreal and New York: Gotlib bukh-komitet, 1949.

Goldkorn, Yitshak. *Epigramatish*. Montreal: Aroysgegebn fun a grupe fraynt, 1954.

– *Der farkishufter yarid: Naye mesholim*. New York, 1976.

– *Fun velt kval: Kleyne eseyen vegn groyse shrayber*. Tel Aviv: Hamenorah, 1963.

– *Heymishe un fremde: Literarishe etyudn*. Buenos Aires, AR, 1973.

– *Kurts un sharf: Epigram*. Toronto, 1981.

– *Literarishe siluetn*. Munich, DE, 1949.

– *Lodzsher portretn: Umgekumene yidishe shrayber un typen*. Tel Aviv: Hamenora, 1963.

– *Mesholim*. New York: Eigens, 1975.

Green, Tovia. *Di oyfgabe fun undzer dor vi azoy mir kenen makhn medines yisroel ekonomish shtark, zikher un zelbstshtendik*. Montreal: S.N., 1954.

– *Di tsukunft fun medines yisroel*. Montreal: Northern Printing and Lithographing Co., 1953.

Grossman, Jacob. *Eseyen un zikhroynes: Mit bilder un ilustratsyes*. Montreal: Northern Print and Lithographing, 1974.

– *Monografyes un eseyen*. New York: Grosman, 1977.

Heilik, Shimshen. *Dos lebedike folk: Undzer alte un naye geshikhte*. Winnipeg, MB: Peretz Publishing, 1974.

– *Di muser-literatur: Fun a kultur-historisher perspektiv*. Tel Aviv: I.L. Peretz Publishing House, 1999.

Hirschprung, Pinchas. *Fun natsishen yomertol: Zikhroynes fun a polit*. Montreal: Keneder adler, 1944.

Husid, Mordecai. *Chaim nakhman bialik*. Montreal: Jewish School Publishing House, 1973.

– *Doyres shrayen mikh ariber*. Montreal, 1969.

– *A shotn trogt mayn kroyn*. Montreal: M. Hosid bukh-fond komitet, 1975.

– *Shtoyb un eybikayt*. Montreal, 1981.

Ish Yair (Israel Shtern). *Fablen*. Montreal, 1986.

– *Vayehi biyemey*. Montreal, 1975.

Kage, Joseph. *Tsvey hundert yor fun Yidisher imigratsiye in kanade*. Montreal: Eagle Publishing, 1960.

Katz, Sholom. *Fun folks moyl: Zamlung fun yidishe shprikhverter*. Toronto: Farlag Amkha, 1947.

Koprov, Ariel. *Moral, mut un gloyn*. Toronto: Aroysgegebn fun a komitet, 1993.

– *Tsvishn tsvey velt milhomes*. Toronto, 1991.

– *A velt mit khokhmes*. Toronto, 1995.

Korn, Rachel. *9 dertseylungen*. Montreal, 1957.

– *Bashertkayt: poems*. Montreal, 1949.

– *Farbitene vor*. Tel Aviv: Farlag Yisroel bukh, 1977.

– *Fun yener zayt lid*. Tel Aviv: I.L. Peretz Publishing House, 1962.
– *Di gnod fun vort*. Tel Aviv: Hamenorah Publishing House, 1968.
– *Heym un heymlozikayt*. Buenos Aires, AR,1948.
– *Lider un erd*. Tel Aviv, 1966.
– *Oyf der sharf fun a vort*. Tel Aviv: Hamenorah Publishing House, 1972.
Krant, Miriam. *Geflekht fun tsvaygn: Eseyen un lider*. Montreal, 1995.
– *Oyf a tsvayg: Mayses un kinderlider*. Montreal: Adler Publishing, 1989.
Krishtalka, Aaron. *Gut morgn dir, velt!* Montreal, 1953.
Kuplik, Avraham. *Blut un fayer: Proze un khurbn lider*. Montreal, 1991.
Lubetkin, Zivia. *Farn koved fun unzer folk: Zamlung vegn geto-oyfshtand in varshe, april–may, 1943: Di letste teg in der varsheyer geto*. Toronto: Organizatsye fun yidn fun poyln in toronto, 1961.
Maza, Ida. *Dinah: Oytobiografishe dertseylung*. Montreal, 1970.
– *Vaksn mayne kinderlekh: Muter un kinder lider*. Montreal: Aroysgegebn mit der mithilf fun kanader yidishn kongres, 1954.
Medres, Israel. *Hundert yor baron de hirsh institut in montreal*. Montreal: Keneder adler, 1963.
– *Montreal fun nekhtn*. Montreal: Keneder adler, 1947.
– *Tsvishn tsvey velt milkhomes*. Montreal: Keneder adler, 1964.
Miransky, Peretz. *A likht far a groshn*. Montreal, 1951.
– *Nit derzogt: Lider*. Tel Aviv: I.L. Peretz Publishing House, 1983.
– *Shures shire*. Tel Aviv: I.L. Peretz Publishing House, 1974.
– *Tsvishn shmeykhl un trer: Mesholim*. Toronto, 1979.
– *A zemer fun demer: Lider un mesholim*. Toronto: P. Miransky, 1991.
Orenstein, Benjamin. *Koved di gefalene heldn in varshever geto: Tsum tsvelftn yor-tog fun varshever geto-oyfshtand*. Montreal: Farband fun varshaver yidn un umgegnt in montreol, 1955.
– *Sotsyale problemen bay yidn in der natsi epokhe*. Montreal: Yidisher kultur klub, 1964.
– *Tshenstokhover landsmanshaft in Montreal*. Montreal: Czenstochover Society of Montreal, 1966.
– *Der umkum un vidershtand fun a yidisher shtot, tshenstokhov*. Montreal, 1949.
Osovsky, A. *Tsvey veltn, dray doyres*. Winnipeg, MB: Dos idishe vort, 1946.
Petrushka, Symche. *Mishnayes mit iberzetsungen un peyrush in yidish*. 6 vols. Montreal, 1945–49.
– *Yidishe folks-entsiklopedye: Far yidishe religiye, geshikhte, filozofiye, literatur, biographiye, lender-kibutsim and andere inyonim*. Montreal: Keneder adler, 1943.

Ravitch, Melech. *67 lirishe, satirishe, natsyonale, sotsyale un filozofishe lider fun di letste finf-zeks yor.* Buenos Aires, AR: Dovid Lerman, 1946.

- *Dos amolike yidishe varshe, biz der shvel fun dritn khurbn 1414–1939 in lid, balade, poeme, drame, dertseylung, roman, humoreske, glaykhvort, folkslid, geshikhte, zikhroynes, esey, publitsistik, zshornalistik, rede, reportazsh, khronik, fun 13.* Montreal: Farband fun varshever yidn in kanade, 1966.
- *Eynems yidishe maskhshoves in tsvontsikstn yorhundert: Eseyen.* Buenos Aires, AR: Dovid Lerman, 1949.
- *Hamishim shirim.* Tel Aviv, 1969.
- *Iker shokhakhti: Lider un poemes fun di yorn 1954–1969.* Montreal: M. Ravitch Committee at the Jewish Public Library, 1969.
- *Di kroynung fun a yungn yidishn dikhter in amerike: Poeme.* New York: D. Ignatov Literatur Fund, 1953.
- *Di lider fun mayne lider.* Montreal: M. Ravitch bukh-komitet, 1954.
- *Mayn leksikon: Yidishe shraybers, kintslers, aktiorn, oykh klal-tuers in di amerikes un andere lender.* Tel Aviv: I.L. Peretz Publishing House, 1980.
- *Dos mayse-bukh fun mayn lebn.* Tel Aviv: I.L. Peretz Publishing House, 1975.

Rogel, Joseph. *Oyshvits: Lider.* Montreal: Aroysgegebn durkh a komitet fun shrayber, 1951.

Rosenfarb, Chava. *Aroys fun gan-eyden.* Tel Aviv: I.L. Peretz Publishing House, 1965.

- *Di balade fun nekhtikn vald.* Montreal: H. Hershman, 1948.
- *Botshani.* 2 vols. Tel Aviv: I.L. Peretz Publishing House, 1983.
- *Der boym fun lebn.* 3 vols. Tel Aviv: Hamenora, 1972.
- *Briv tsu abrashen.* Tel Aviv: I.L. Peretz Publishing House, 1992.
- *Der foygl fun geto: Tragedye in drey aktn.* Montreal: H. Morgentaler, 1958.
- *Geto un andere lider: Oykh fragmentn fun a tog bukh.* Montreal: H. Hershman, 1948.

Rozhanski, Shmuel, ed. *Kanadish: Antologye. Musterverk fun der yidisher literatur 62.* Buenos Aires, AR: Literatur-gezelshaft bam yivo in argentine, 1974.

Sack, Benjamin Gutelius. *Geshikhte fun yidn in kanade: Fun di friste onheybn biz der letster tsayt.* Montreal: Aroysgegebn durkh a komitet fun fraynt, 1948.

Segal, J.I. *"Bazunder" lider.* Montreal: Farlag Montreal, 1921.

- *Di drite sudeh: Lider.* Montreal: Keneder adler, 1937.
- *Fun mayn velt.* Montreal: Farlag Montreal, 1918.
- *Dos hoyz fun di poshete: Lider.* Montreal, 1940.
- *Letste lider.* Montreal: J.I. Segal komitet, 1955.

– *Lider far yidishe kinder*. New York: Bildungs komitet fun arbeter ring, 1961.
– *Lider fun Y.Y. Segal*. New York, 1926.
– *Lider un loybn*. Montreal: J.I. Segal komitet, 1944.
– *Lyric*. Montreal: J.I. Segal komitet, 1930.
– *Mayn nign*. Montreal: J.I. Segal komitet, 1934.
– *Seyfer yidish: lider un poemen*. Montreal: J.I. Segal komitet, 1950.
Shaffir, M.M. *Bay der kholem-multer*. Montreal, 1983.
– *Boyre mine khaloymes*. Montreal, 1971.
– *Fir eyln elntkayt*. Montreal, 1980.
– *Di fleyt fun mayne beyner*. Montreal, 1978.
– *Ikh kum aheym*. Montreal: M.M. Shaffir, 1963.
– *In mayn gefalnkeyt*. Montreal, 1975.
– *Di lipn fun mayn troyer*. Montreal, 1979.
– *Mit der lider-torbe*. Montreal, 1973.
– *Mit tsugeneygte reyd*. Montreal, 1977.
– *Oyf mayn fidele*. Montreal, 1966.
– *A rege dakhtenish*. Montreal, 1969.
– *Rege ru gefinen*. Montreal, 1981.
– *Der shtern-vogn*. Montreal, 1968.
– *A stezshke*. Montreal, 1940.
– *Tropns trayst in der bide*. Montreal, 1987.
– *Unter der shtern-khupe*. Montreal: M.M. Shaffir, 1984.
Shatan, Mirl Erdberg. *Nit fun keyn freyd: Lider*. Montreal, 1950.
– *Regnboygn: Lider, eseyen, zikhroynes*. New York: C.F. Shatan, 1975.
Shemen, Nachman. *Batsiung tsu arbet un arbeter*. 2 vols. Toronto, 1963.
– *Batsiyung tsu der froy loyt tanakh, talmud, yahadus un literature-shtudyes*. Buenos Aires, AR: YIVO, 1968.
– *Batsiyung tsu mentsh loyt tanakh, talmud, yahadus un literature-shtudyes*. Tel Aviv: I.L. Peretz Publishing House, 1989.
– *Di batsiung tsum fremden loyt tanakh, Talmud and rabonishe literatur*. Toronto, 1945.
– *Di biografye fun a varshever rov: Tsvi yehezkol mikhlzon*. Montreal: Keneder adler, 1948.
– *Dos gezang fun khasides*. 2 vols. Buenos Aires, AR: Unino Israelita Polaca en la Argentina, 1959.
– *Kdushe in yidishn familye-lebn*. Tel Aviv: I.L Peretz Publishing House, 1977.
– *Lublin: Shtot fun toyre, rabones un khsides*. Toronto: Gerhson Pomerantz esey-bibliotek, 1951.
Shtern, Abraham. *Khasidishe mayses*. Tel Aviv, 1960.

– *Kvutses kitve agode*. Montreal, 1947.

– *Sefer hutim ha-meshulashim*. Montreal, 1953.

Shtern (Krishtalka), Shifre. *Yidish a lebedike shprakh: A lern-program far lerer*. 3 vols. Montreal: Jewish People's and Peretz Schools, 1992–97.

Shtern, Sholem. *In kanade*. 2 vols. Montreal: Sholem Shtern bukh-komitet, 1960–63.

– *Di mishpokhe in kanade un dos hoyzgesind fun profesor sidni goldstin: Tsvey noveln*. Montreal, 1975.

– *Shrayber vos ikh hob gekent: Memuarn un esayn*. Montreal: Adler Printing, 1982.

– *Dos vayse hoyz*. New York: YKUF, 1967.

Shtern, Yehiel. *Kheyder un besmedresh*. New York: YIVO, 1946.

Shvartsman, Meir. *Der yidisher flam*. Winnipeg, MB, 1958.

Simchovitch, Simkhe. *Azoy iz a yugnt fargangen*. Montreal: Komitet fun shrayber, 1950.

– *Blendiker harbst*. Toronto: Adler Printing, 1990.

– *Funken in zshar*. Toronto: Aroysgegebn durkh a komitet, 1997.

– *In shoh fun tefileh: Lider*. Montreal: Aroysgegebn durkh a komitet, 1958.

– *Dos likht fun khesed*. North York, ON, 2005.

– *A shtifkind bay der vaysl*. Toronto: Aroysgegebn durkh a komitet, 1992.

– *Tsar un treyst: gezamlte lider*. Montreal: Adler Printing, 1989.

Slutzky-Kohn, Grunya. *In shpigl fun der velt*. Montreal: Grunya Slutzky-Kohn, 2009.

– *Kinder lider*. Montreal: Farlag yidisher shul bay di montreaoler folks shuln un peretz shuln, 1990.

– *Kuk nit troyerik azoy in fenster*. Montreal, 1994.

– *Lider un mayses far kinder*. Montreal, 2010.

– *Lider un proze*. Montreal, 1987.

– *Opgebrente tsangen*. Montreal: Grunya Slutzky-Kohn, 2009.

– *A shtral fun hofn: Lider un mayses far kinder*. Montreal: Grunya Slutzky-Kohn, 2004.

– *Shtumer geshrey*. Montreal: Grunya Slutzky-Kohn, 2008.

– *Tsvantsikster yorhundert*. Montreal: Grunya Slutzky-Kohn, 2013.

Slutzky-Kohn, Grunya, and Sharon Chazan. *Zingt kinder*. Montreal, 1993.

Spilberg, Chaim, and Yaakov Zipper, eds. *Kanader yidisher zaml-bukh/Canadian Jewish Anthology/Anthologie juive du Canada*. Montreal: National Committee on Yiddish, Canadian Jewish Congress, 1982.

Trepman, Babey, and Elly Trepman. *Paul Trepman: Bikher, publikatsyes, arkhivn*. Montreal: Di fundatsye fun der yidisher kehileh fun Montreol, 1999.

Trepman, Paul. *A gesl in varshe*. Montreal: Aroysgegebn fun a komitet in montreol, 1950.

– *Di tsavoe*. Montreal: Farband fun varshaver yidn un umgegnd in Montreal, Kanade/Association of Warsaw Jews, 1954.

Usiskin, Michael. *Oksn un motorn: Zikhroynes fun a yidishn farmer-pioner (di geshikhte fun idnbridzsh)*. Toronto: Farlag Vokhnblat, 1945.

Viderman, Hanah. *Alte heym un kinder yorn*. Montreal, 1960.

– *Umetiker shmeykhl: Derinerungen, dertseylungen, briv, monologen, humoreskes, felyetonen*. Montreal: A. Viderman, 1946.

Weissenberg-Akselrod, Perl. *Y.M. vaysenberg: Zayn lebn un shafn, 1878–1938*. Montreal: Y.M. Weissenberg bukh-fond, 1986.

Wolofsky, Hirsh. *Mayn lebens-rayze*. Montreal: Keneder adler, 1946.

Yudika. *Shplinters*. Toronto: YKUF, 1943.

– *Tsar un freyd: Lider un dramatishe poemen*. Toronto, 1949.

– *Vandervegn*. Montreal: Shrayber-grupe, 1934.

Zipper, Yaakov. *Araynblikn in yidishn literarishn shafn, in guter demonung fun khaverim un tuer*. Montreal: Adler Printing, 1983.

– *Fun nekhtn un haynt*. Montreal: Yaakov Zipper bukh-fond komitet, 1978.

– *Geven iz a mentsh*. Montreal, 1940.

– *In di getseltn fun avrom*. Montreal: Yaakov Zipper bukh-fond komitet, 1973.

– *Kh'bin vider in mayn khorever heym gekumen*. Montreal, 1965.

– *Leyzer zuker gedenk bukh*. Montreal, 1968.

– *Oyf yener zayt bug*. Montreal, 1946.

– *Pinkes tishevits*. Tel Aviv: Irgun yotse tishevits be-yisrael, 1970.

– *Tsvishn taykhn un vasern*. Montreal, 1960.

Zolf, Falek. *Di letste fun a dor: Heymishe geshtaltn*. Winnipeg, MB: Israelite Press, 1952.

– *Oyf fremder erd: Bletlekh fun a lebn*. Winnipeg, MB: Israelite Press, 1945.

– *Undzer kultur hemshekh: Eseyen*. Winnipeg, MB: Universal Printers, 1956.

Notes

PREFACE AND ACKNOWLEDGMENTS

1 Zuckermann, *Revivalistics*, 202–3.
2 YIVO Institute, "Basic Facts about Yiddish," 2014, https://www.yivo.org/cimages/basic_facts_about_yiddish_2014.pdf.
3 Kuznitz, "Yiddish Studies"; Shandler, *Adventures in Yiddishland.*

INTRODUCTION

1 Hornsby, *Revitalizing Minority Languages*, 64.
2 1937 marked the creation of a Jewish State in the remote Russian city of Birobidzhan, whose official language remains Yiddish. See Shneer, *Yiddish and the Creation of Soviet-Jewish Culture.*
3 See Nathan Cohen, "The Jews of Independent Poland," 172.
4 The figure of eleven million is from YIVO Institute, "Basic Facts about Yiddish" while the larger figure is from Katz, "Yiddish."
5 In 1999, due to its unbroken history of transmission in the country, Yiddish was declared one of five minority languages along with Finnish, Sami, Romani, and Meänkieli, with a law ratified in 2010 that provided official recognition and protection. The country has some 1,200 Yiddish speakers in a total population of 9.5 million. In practice, this translates into state funding to promote Yiddish. Heikkilä, "The Language Situation in Sweden."
6 See Chaver, *What Must Be Forgotten*, Halpern, *Babel in Zion*, and Rojanski, "Ben-Gurion and Yiddish after the Holocaust," and *Yiddish in Israel.*
7 Weinfeld, Morton. *Like Everyone Else … but Different*, 189.
8 Ibid., 193.

9 These include black suits, wide-brimmed hats, beards, and *peyes* (side-locks) for men; long skirts, stockings, and head coverings or wigs for the women.

10 Katz, "The Yiddish Conundrum," 554–5.

11 Judy Maltz, "Nearly One Out of Every Four Jews will be Nearly One in Four Jews Will be Ultra-Orthodox by 2040, New Study Says," *Forward*, 30 May 2022, https://forward.com/fast-forward/501328/nearly-one-in-four-jews-will-be-ultra-orthodox-by-2040-new-study-says.

12 Ibid.

13 Friedman, "Serious Jews," 154.

14 Trifonas and Aravossitas, *Rethinking Heritage Language Education*, xiii.

15 See Levin, *While Messiah Tarried*.

16 For example, Brossat, Klingberg, and Fernbach, *Revolutionary Yiddishland*, which offers an idealized account of the leftist heritage of Yiddish, has come to serve as a source text for some new Yiddishists.

17 See Rad Yiddish, https://m.facebook.com/RadYiddish.

18 Davids, "Hebrew and Yiddish in Canada," 48.

19 See David Lazarus, "Yiddish Speakers Drop by 10,000 in Five Years," *Canadian Jewish News*, 21 February 2008.

20 Rosenfarb, *Confessions of a Yiddish Writer*, 179.

21 Wisse, *Free as a Jew*, 41–5, 338.

22 David Roskies, oral history recording, interview by Jayne Guberman, 2–3.

23 See Wisse, *The Schlemiel as Modern Hero, A Little Love in Big Manhattan, I.L. Peretz and the Making of Modern Jewish Culture*, and *The Modern Jewish Canon*. Wisse's involvement in anthologization and translation is discussed in the chapter on Yiddish publishing.

24 See, for example, Wisse, "The Politics of Yiddish," and "Shul Daze."

25 Roskies, "A City, a School, and a Utopian Experiment," and "Yiddish in Montreal: The Utopian Experiment."

26 On the meanings attributed to the *shtetl*, see Shandler, *Shtetl*.

27 See Hornsby, *Revitalizing Minority Languages*, and Costa, "New Speakers, New Language."

28 Kadimah: Jewish Cultural Centre and National Library, https://www.kadimah.org.au.

29 League for Yiddish, http://www.leagueforyiddish.org.

30 Maison de la culture Yiddish Bibliothèque Medem, http://www.yiddishweb.com/medem.

31 Yiddish Book Center, https://www.yiddishbookcenter.org.

32 YUNG YiDiSH, http://yiddish.co.il/en/about.

33 See Robinson, Anctil, and Butovsky, *An Everyday Miracle*, Anctil, *Tur Malka*, Simon, *Translating Montreal*, and Margolis, *Jewish Roots, Canadian Soil*.

34 For example, Olko and Sallabank, *Revitalizing Endangered Languages*.

35 For example, Desmoulins et al., "Imagining University/Community Collaborations," Dudgeon, "Third Spaces within Tertiary Places," and Lotherington, "Creating Third Spaces."

36 For example, the model Braj Kachru proposed in the 1990s suggests that English is disseminated by users in three concentric circles based on geographical location. Kachru, Kachru, and Nelson, *Handbook of World Englishes*, 178–9.

37 Harshav, *The Meaning of* Yiddish, 8. See also Matisoff, *Blessings, Curses, Hopes, and Fears*.

CHAPTER ONE

1 Rosenberg, *Canada's Jews*, 12.

2 Ibid., 19–20; and Kage, *With Faith and Thanksgiving*, 259–61.

3 See Margolis, *"Ale Brider."*

4 On Canada's changing immigration policies, see Kelley and Trebilcock, *Making of the Mosaic*.

5 Rosenberg, *Canada's Jews*, 27, 31, 33, 34. They included Toronto's Kensington Market and Winnipeg's North End. See Speisman, *Jews of Toronto*, 81–95, and Gutkin, *Worst of Times*, 5–12.

6 On Jewish farming colonies, see Friedgut, "Jewish Pioneers on Canada's Prairies," and Kats and Lehr, *The Last Best West*.

7 This ideal was most clearly expressed by one of the architects of the new open-door policy, Sir Clifford Sifton, minister of the interior from 1895 to 1905. Cited in Friedgut, "Jewish Pioneers on Canada's Prairies," 387.

8 Mendelson, *Exiles from Nowhere*.

9 An Order in Council is an administrative decision that the Cabinet of Canada originates and the Governor General of Canada issues.

10 Zimmerman, "'Narrow-Minded People.'"

11 Abella and Troper, *None Is Too Many*. For a revised analysis, see Comartin, "Opening Closed Doors."

12 See Betcherman, *The Swastika and the Maple Leaf*.

13 Bialystok, *Delayed Impact*, 18.

14 See Tulchinsky, *Canada's Jews*, 242–82.

15 For more on the Jewish settlement of Montreal within the context of

Jewish culture, see Tulchinsky, "The Third Solitude," 96–112, and Baker, "Montreal of Yesterday," 39–52.

16 On the history of Anglophone domination of the Montreal economy, see Levine, *The Reconquest of Montreal*, especially 9, 18–19, 35.

17 Cited in Greenstein, *Third Solitudes*, 15. The term alludes to the title of Hugh MacLennan's 1945 novel *Two Solitudes*; there it refers to the two separate European nations that comprised colonial Canada.

18 Robinson and Butovsky, *Renewing Our Days*, 18.

19 See Gilbert, "We Long for a Home," Myers Feinstein, "Re-imagining the Unimaginable," and Isaacs, "Yiddish in the Aftermath."

20 See Draper, "Canadian Holocaust Survivors," and Goldberg, *Holocaust Survivors in Canada*.

21 Bialystok, "'Greener' and 'Gayle,'" 33, 43.

22 See Bialystok, *Delayed Impact*, and "'Greener' and 'Gayle.'"

23 See Gerber, "Opening the Door," Giberovitch, "The Contributions of Holocaust Survivors to Montreal Jewish Communal Life," and Sheftel and Zembrzycki, "We Started Over Again, We Were Young."

24 Rosenberg, "A Study of the Changes in the Population Characteristics," 3.

25 On the pre-Holocaust Hasidic communities of Canada, see Lapidus, "The Forgotten Hassidim."

26 Rosenberg, *Golem and Wondrous Deeds*.

27 Robinson, "'Letter from the Sabbath Queen.'" One of Rosenberg's grandsons was the profoundly secular English-language novelist Mordecai Richler.

28 In 1944, the *Keneder adler* both serialized the memoir of the Hassidic rabbi Pinchas Hirschprung and printed it in book form, *Fun natsishen yomertol* (recently translated by Vivian Felsen as *The Vale of Tears*). See the special volume dedicated to this book, *Canadian Jewish Studies* 26 (2019).

29 Shaffir, "Safeguarding a Distinctive Identity."

30 Lacasse, "À la croisée de la révolution tranquille et du judaïsme orthodoxe," 422. See also Shaffir, "Separation from the Mainstream in Canada."

31 Bialystok, *Delayed Impact*, 57.

32 See, for example, Yolande Cohen, "The Migrations of Moroccan Jews to Montreal," Elbaz, "Les héritiers. Générations et identités chez les Juifs sépharades à Montréal," and Lasry, "Essor et tradition."

33 See Stein, "Asymmetric Fates."

34 Rosenberg, "Population Characteristics of the Jewish Community of Montreal," 45.

35 Davids, "Hebrew and Yiddish in Canada," 48.

36 Rosenberg, "Population Characteristics of the Jewish Community of Montreal," 41–9.

37 Grossman, *Our Library 1914–1957*, 113.

38 Davids, "Hebrew and Yiddish in Canada," 51.

39 Rosenberg, "A Study of the Changes in the Population Characteristics," 12.

40 Thiessen, *Yiddish in Canada*, 89.

41 Lansky, *Outwitting History*, 228.

42 Ibid., 230–1.

43 From 1991 to 2016, *Der Bay* and the International Association of Yiddish Clubs, under the leadership of Philip Kutner, hosted an annual gathering and published an Anglo-Yiddish newsletter to serve as a North American clearinghouse for Yiddish club activity. The gatherings included prominent Canadian contingents. See *Der Bay* Anglo-Yiddish Newsletter and the International Association of Yiddish Clubs, http://www.derbay.org.

44 Friends of Yiddish, accessed 13 December 2020, https://www.friends ofyiddish.ca.

45 Ibid.

46 Friends of Yiddish, "About," accessed 13 December 2020, https://www.friendsofyiddish.ca/about.html.

47 Rena Godfrey, "Group Celebrates Yiddish Language and Culture," *Canadian Jewish News*, 5 April 2012.

48 Blaik Kirby, "Cable TV Companies Plunge Ahead with Ambitious Programming Ideas," *Globe and Mail*, 1 August 1970, 5.

49 Full-page advertisement for a Ford dealership, *Globe and Mail*, 12 October 1970, 7.

50 Herbert Whittaker, "Ida Kaminska: Frail, Flexible and Dazzling," *Globe and Mail*, 25 May 1970, P4.

51 Ron Csillag, "Yiddish, Anyone?" *Toronto Star*, 24 March 1988, M1.

52 Sheldon Kirshner, "Yiddish Gets a New Lease on Life," *Canadian Jewish News*, 28 August 1997, 11.

53 Elena Cherney, "Director Refuses to Let the Curtain Fall on Yiddish: Dora Wasserman Uses the Theatre to Help Save a Language," *National Post*, 9 July 1999, A8.

54 Leo Davids, "Yiddish and Hebrew in Canada: The Latest Word, Examining the Data from the 2011 Census," *Canadian Jewish News*, 6 November 2012, 9. Davids also presented these findings in "Hebrew and Yiddish in Canada."

55 Joe Friesen, "Colourful Language Still Has a Voice," *Globe and Mail*, 8 December 2012, A10. See also Joe Friesen, "Yiddish Finding a Way to Survive in Canada," *Globe and Mail*, 7 December 2012.

56 Mireille Silcoff, "On a Tongue with No Land and the (J)oys of Speaking Yiddish," *National Post*, 22 September 2012.

57 Ben Spurr, "Last Vestige of Jewish Enclave to Survive New Store Ownership," *Toronto Star*, 13 July 2015, GT2.

58 Stacey Stein, "Handing Down a Spritz of Yiddish to the Tots," *Globe and Mail*, 10 March 2007, M6.

59 Navneet Pall, "Lyrics and Latkes Sing-along Gears Up for 4th Edition at Segal Centre," *Global News*, 6 December 2016.

60 Josh Dehaas, "Yiddish Lives on Canadian Campuses: As the Jewish Tongue Dies at Home, Scholars Step Up," *Maclean's*, 22 December 2011, https://www.macleans.ca/education/uniandcollege/yiddish-lives-on-canadian-campuses.

61 Yanofsky, "What's the Yiddish Word for Comeback?"

62 Martin Zeilig, "Yiddish in Western Canada, Notably Winnipeg: Ancient Language Appears in Most Unexpected Places," *Winnipeg Free Press*, 30 July 2003, 8.

63 Michael Fraiman, "Inside the Burgeoning Yiddish Renaissance," *Canadian Jewish News*, 22 August 2018.

64 Michael Berger, "Yidd-ish," Squadcasts, http://www.empathysquad.ca/main, 6:04.

65 See Fox, "The Passionate Few."

66 My thanks to Professor Robert Dunbar, University of Edinburgh, for his invaluable input on this section.

67 See Dunmore, "Emic and Essentialist Perspectives on Gaelic Heritage."

68 Colaisde na Gàidhlig / The Gaelic College, accessed 25 October 2019, www.gaeliccollege.edu.

69 Kenneth MacKenzie, email to the author, 28 October 2019.

70 See Dunbar, "The Gaelic Language (Scotland) Act 2005."

71 "What We Do," Gaelic Affairs, https://gaelic.novascotia.ca/work.

72 *Gaelic Nova Scotia: A Resource Guide*, Nova Scotia, 2017. https://gaelic.novascotia.ca/sites/default/files/inline/documents/gaelic-nova-scotia-a-resource-guide.pdf.

73 Gaelic Nova Scotia Month, https://gaelic.novascotia.ca/gaelic-nova-scotia-month.

74 Dembling, "Joe Jimmy Alec Visits the Gaelic Mod and Escapes Unscathed."

75 See Dunmore, "Emic and Essentialist Perspectives on Gaelic Heritage."

76 Baker, "A Social Psychological Approach."

77 Dunmore, "Emic and Essentialist Perspectives on Gaelic Heritage," and "Transatlantic Context for Gaelic Language Revitalisation."

78 Nance et al., "Identity, Accent Aim, and Motivation in Second Language Users," 185.

79 Dunmore, "Emic and Essentialist Perspectives on Gaelic Heritage."

80 Dunmore, "Transatlantic Context for Gaelic Language Revitalisation."

81 Dunmore, "Language Policy and Prospects," 76.

82 See Friedan, *Classic Yiddish Fiction*; Miron, *A Traveler Disguised*.

83 See Slucki, *The International Jewish Labor Bund*.

84 See Gilman, *Jewish Self-Hatred*.

85 See Fogel and Weiser, *Czernowitz at 100*.

86 See Kuznitz, YIVO *and the Making of Modern Jewish Culture*.

87 Schaechter, *The Standardized Yiddish Orthography*.

88 See Kleine, "Standard Yiddish."

89 Howe, *World of Our Fathers*, 16.

90 See Biale, *Hasidism*, section 3, "The Twentieth and Twenty-First Centuries."

91 Michael Levy, "Vizhnitzer Rebbe," *Israel National News*, 25 October 2016, http://www.israelnationalnews.com/News/News.aspx/219319.

92 Benor, *Becoming Frum*.

93 Shandler, *Yiddish*, 185.

94 Isaacs, "Haredi, *haymish* and *frim*," 10–15.

95 Soldat-Jaffee, "Yiddish without Yiddishism," 3.

96 Fader, *Mitzvah Girls*.

97 See Fishman, "Planning and Standardization of Yiddish."

98 Nove, "Erasure of Hasidic Yiddish."

99 Krogh, "How Satmarish Is Haredi Satmar Yiddish?," and Nove, "Social Predictors of Case Syncretism in New York Hasidic Yiddish."

100 See Igartua, "Loss of Grammatical Gender and Language Contact."

101 Isaacs, "Haredi, *haymish* and *frim*," 27–8.

102 Krauss, *Language Diversity Endangered*, 2.

103 Endangered Languages Project, http://www.endangeredlanguages.com/lang/ydd.

104 Hadda, "Imagining Yiddish," 15.

105 Endangered Languages Project; Katz, *Words on Fire*, 349; Assouline, "Linguistic Outcomes of a Hasidic Renewal," 141.

106 Beider, "Yiddish in Eastern Europe," 227.

107 Katz, "The Yiddish Conundrum," 555.

108 Glinert, *The Story of Hebrew*.

109　Zuckermann, *Revivalistics*, 32.

110　Ibid., 179.

111　Zaritt and The Editors, "Yiddish Lives! *Loshn* of the Living Dead."

112　Norich, "Yiddish Literary Studies," 298.

113　See Suchoff, *Kafka's Jewish Languages*.

114　Katz, *Words on Fire*, 349.

115　Abley, *Spoken Here*, 201–28.

116　Esther Singer makes this point in her MA study, "Yiddish Melbourne: A Community in Transition," 18.

117　Wisse, "Shul Daze," 19.

118　See Peltz, "A Researcher Writes for His People"; Fishman, *Yiddish: Turning to Life*.

119　See Fishman's introduction to his 1981 bilingual anthology, *Never Say Die! A Thousand Years of Yiddish in Jewish Life and Letters*, which documents the resilience of the language in its history of ideologies, institutions, and language planning.

120　Boyarin, *Thinking in Jewish*, 1.

121　Shneer and Aviv, *New Jews*, 8.

122　Kuznitz, "Yiddish Studies."

123　Shandler, *Adventures in Yiddishland*, 22.

124　Ibid.

125　Shandler, "The Cultural Politics of Yiddish in the United States after the Holocaust."

126　Shandler, *Adventures in Yiddishland*, 21, 28.

127　Ibid., 190.

128　Avineri, "Yiddish Endangerment as Phenomenological Reality and Discursive Strategy," 19–20.

129　Ibid., 21–3.

130　Glaser, "The Idea of Yiddish," 259.

131　Ibid., 268.

132　This concept stems from historian Pierre Nora, who suggests that places or objects can signify a group's national or collective memory. See Nora and Kritzman, *Realms of Memory*.

133　Wood, *And We're All Brothers*, 13.

134　Ibid., 7.

135　Ibid., 20.

136　Ibid., 21.

137　Shandler, *Yiddish*, 189.

138　Ibid., 102.

139　Ibid., 182–3.

140 Ibid., 186. "Alterity" refers to the state of being other or different. "Hegemony" refers to political or cultural dominance over others. "Heteronormativity" is the assumption that everyone is heterosexual.

141 See Stein, "Asymmetric Fates."

142 Naar, "On Words Reclaimed and the Fate of Ladino," 143.

143 See Jacobs, "Ladino and Yiddish Classes Boom Online."

144 Zuckermann, *Revivalistics*, 201.

CHAPTER TWO

1 Estraikh, "On the Acculturation of Jews," 217.

2 Ibid., 222.

3 Rosenberg, "A Study of the Changes in the Population Characteristics."

4 Davids, "Hebrew and Yiddish in Canada."

5 Census Profile, 2016 Census, https://www12.statcan.gc.ca/census-recensement/2016/dp-pd/prof/details/Page.cfm?Lang=E&Geo1=PR&Code1=01&Geo2=&Code2=&Data=Count&SearchText=Canada&SearchType=Begins&SearchPR=01&B1=All&GeoLevel=PR&GeoCode=01.

6 Margolis, *Jewish Roots, Canadian Soil*, 28.

7 Davids, "Hebrew and Yiddish in Canada," 53.

8 Census Profile, 2016 Census, https://www12.statcan.gc.ca/census-recensement/2016/dp-pd/prof/details/Page.cfm?Lang=E&Geo1=PR&Code1=01&Geo2=&Code2=&Data=Count&SearchText=Canada&SearchType=Begins&SearchPR=01&B1=All&GeoLevel=PR&GeoCode=01.

9 Isaacs, "Haredi, *haymish* and *frim*."

10 Brym, Neuman, and Lenton, *2018 Survey of Jews in Canada*, 6. Survey respondents were over the age of eighteen, living in the four largest Jewish population centres of Toronto, Montreal, Winnipeg, and Vancouver, and identified as either Jewish or part-Jewish.

11 Ibid.

12 Brym and Lenton, "Young, Canadian and Jewish."

13 Ibid., 16.

14 Ibid., 20.

15 Ibid., 68.

16 Ibid., 6, 21.

17 Brym notes that the results are highly tentative due to the small numbers involved. Email to the author, 8 April 2019.

18 Ibid.

19 Ibid.
20 Hobart, "Adjustment of Ukrainians in Alberta."
21 Weinfeld, "Myth and Reality," 88.
22 Fishman, *Reversing Language Shift.*
23 Clyne, *Community Languages,* 113.
24 See, for example, Eriksson, "Societal, Community, Family, and Individual Factors," Caneva and Pozzi, "Transmission of Language and Religion," Hua and Costigan, "Familial Context of Adolescent Language Broker-ing," and Iqbal, "Mother Tongue and Motherhood."
25 Houle, "Recent Evolution of Immigrant-Language Transmission."
26 Ibid., 12.
27 Brym, Neuman, Lenton, "2018 Survey of Jews in Canada," 8.
28 Jedwab, "Canada's 'Other' Languages," 251.
29 Ibid., 252.
30 Ibid.
31 Margolis, "Yiddish and Multiculturalism."
32 Statistics Canada, 2006 Census, Data Products, Topic-Based Tabulations, Detailed Mother Tongue.
33 Davids, "Hebrew and Yiddish in Canada," 159.
34 See Lapidus, "The Forgotten Hasidim."
35 See, for example, Assouline, Krogh, Nove.
36 See Assouline, "English Can Be Jewish but Hebrew Cannot"; Fader, *Mitzvah Girls.*
37 See Burdin, "New Notes on the Rise-Fall Contour."
38 Margolis, *"Ken men tantsn af tsvey khasenes? A.M. Klein and Yiddish."*
39 Waddington, *Apartment Seven,* and Waddington, *Canadian Jewish Short Stories.*
40 Margolis, *Jewish Roots, Canadian Soil,* 33.
41 Piller, "Private Language Planning," 61–80.
42 Venables et al., "One-parent-one-language (OPOL) Families."
43 Ibid., 62.
44 Taft and Markus, *A Second Chance,* 283.
45 Piller and Gerber, "Family Language Policy between the Bilingual Advantage and the Monolingual Mindset."
46 Little, "Whose Heritage? What Inheritance?"
47 Ingrid Piller discusses Little's model in a blog entry, "Bilingual Children Refusing to Speak the Home Language," *Language on the Move,* 15 August 2018, http://www.languageonthemove.com/bilingual-children-refusing-to-speak-the-home-language.
48 Farr et al., "It's My Language, My Culture, and It's Personal!"

49 David Botwinik, *Fun khurbn tsum lebn*, xxiv.

50 On the concept of the Yiddish maximalist, see Lansky, "The Maximalist's Daughter."

51 David Botwinik, *Fun khurbn tsum lebn*, xxiv–ix.

52 David Botwinik, oral history recording. English translation taken from the subtitles that accompany the interview.

53 Ibid.

54 Botwinik, *Chicken Soup with Chopsticks*, 21–3.

55 Ibid.

56 See Margolis, *Jewish Roots, Canadian Soil*, 154–8.

57 Botwinik family (Yankl, Bina Ester, Leybl, Nathaniel), interview.

58 Botwinik, *Fun khurbn tsum lebn*, and "Music and the Holocaust," http://holocaustmusic.ort.org/memory/yiddish/david-botwinik.

59 Botwinik family interview.

60 Berman, oral history recording.

61 Email from Ana Kuper Berman to author, 24 May 2018.

62 Email from Ana Kuper Berman to author, 14 January 2018.

63 I have published an analysis of the survey in Margolis, "*In der heym*: Yiddish in Canada Today."

64 My thanks to Celia Brauer and Vivian Felsen for their invaluable help in the dissemination of the survey.

65 Hornsby, *Revitalizing Minority Languages*, 64.

66 Costa, "New Speakers, New Language," 129.

CHAPTER THREE

1 Rosten, *The Joys of Yinglish*.

2 Taft and Marcus, *A Second Chance*, 226.

3 See Menkis, "Jewish Communal Identity."

4 Jewish Labour Committee, "J.L.C. telegram to Premier Jean Lesage asking the Quebec Government to permit the teaching of Yiddish in Montreal public schools 1965," *Correspondence, clippings, drafts:* volume 26, file 20, Jewish Labour Committee Collection, Library and Archives Canada.

5 Resolutions Adopted at the 16th Plenary Session of the Canadian Jewish Congress Held in Montreal, 13–16 November 1971, CJC Collection, Series AB (Plenary records), 5–6.

6 Read, "The Precarious History of Jewish Education."

7 Lacasse, "A Curse or a Blessing?" 6.

8 Lacasse, "Jews of the Quiet Revolution."

9 J. Glatstein, "A Fascinating Ferment," *Canadian Jewish Chronicle*, 15 June 1962, 6, 12.

10 Ben Taube, "The Number of Canadian Jews," *Canadian Jewish Chronicle*, 3 August 1962, 6.

11 For example, as part of an anti-Communist police campaign in Quebec, Montreal's Morris Winchevsky Schools closed their doors in the early 1950s after the United Jewish People's Order (UJPO) community centre was raided. Within this Cold War climate, the organized Jewish communities of Toronto and Vancouver terminated funding to their UJPO schools. See Srebrnik, "Chasing an Illusion," and Reiter, "Canadian Jewish Left," and *A Future without Hate or Need*.

12 Irwin Cotler, "Yiddish Language and Literature Is Indispensable to Jewish Life," *Canadian Jewish Chronicle*, 1 April 1955, 4.

13 A.A. Roback, "Yiddish: Foundation of Jewish Culture," *Canadian Jewish Chronicle*, 26 May 1955, 5, 13.

14 Lacasse, "À la croisée de la révolution tranquille et du judaïsme orthodoxe," 422.

15 Freidenreich, *Passionate Pioneers*.

16 Canadian students would also attend the New York Teachers' Seminary and People's University Seminary (founded 1918), which trained teachers raised in North America for much of the secular Jewish school movement and also offered graduate studies in Yiddish language and literature.

17 See Reiter, *A Future Without Hate or Need*.

18 For a list of Jewish communities and their corresponding schools and teachers, see Freidenreich, *Passionate Pioneers*, 246–338.

19 Two Jewish teachers' seminaries established in Montreal in 1946 were united in 1949 to form the Yidisher lerer seminar (United Jewish Teachers' Seminary).

20 These included a Socialist Arbeter Ring/Workmen's Circle Shule and a Marxist-Socialist Arbeter Ring Freiheit Temple Shule that offered a kindergarten, a day school, a supplementary school, a high school, a magazine, and adult education programming; and a left-wing Sholem Aleichem Shule that became affiliated with the communist-oriented UJPO. Freidenreich, *Passionate Pioneers*, 293.

21 These included (in chronological order): Camp Kindervelt and Camp Naivelt (Children's World/New World), in Brampton, Ontario (1925–present), later sponsored by the UJPO; Camp Yungvelt (Young World), Canada's largest secular Yiddish camp, sponsored by the Arbeter Ring/Workmen's Circle, in Pickering, Ontario (1925–50s); and Camp

Kinderland (Children's Land) with Nit Gedayget (No Worries) for adults in Shawbridge, Quebec, sponsored by UJPO (1930s–60s). The Farband-sponsored Camp Kindervelt (Children's World) and Unzer Camp (Our Camp) for adults in the Laurentian Mountains in Préfontaine, Quebec (1930–62) served as the summer home of Montreal's Labour Zionist movement, with many of the counsellors and campers affiliated with Montreal's Peretz Shule or Yidishe Folks Shule.

22 Freidenreich, *Passionate Pioneers*, 365.
23 Reiter, "The Canadian Jewish Left," 82.
24 Freidenreich, *Passionate Pioneers*, 195.
25 See Margolis, "Choosing Yiddish in the Classroom."
26 Raby, oral history recording.
27 Ibid.
28 Rivka Augenfeld, interview.
29 Jones, "Vancouver Peretz Institute Yiddish Library."
30 See Freidenreich, *Passionate Pioneers*, 260–4.
31 O'Bryan, Reitz, and Kuplowska, *Non-Official Languages*, 16.
32 Fox, "Laboratories of Yiddishkayt," 279.
33 Cited in Freidenreich, *Passionate Pioneers*, 400.
34 Rosenfeld, oral history recording.
35 Ibid.
36 Edit Kuper, "Youth in Yiddish Theatre," 2008, promotional text provided via email to the author, 15 May 2018.
37 Larrue, *Le théâtre yiddish à Montréal*, 149.
38 See Margolis, "Yiddish at a Crossroads."
39 Margolis, "Holocaust and Post-Holocaust Yiddish Theatre in Montreal."
40 Kuper, "Youth in Yiddish Theatre," 2008.
41 M. Lauter, letter, undated [performance dated 23 June 1964], David Roskies Scrapbook 2, Yiddish Book Center.
42 Kuper, "Youth in Yiddish Theatre," 2008.
43 Ibid.
44 A.J. Arnold, "Graduates of Jewish People's School present 'Uncle Moses,'" *Canadian Jewish Chronicle*, 23 March 1962, 3.
45 A.N. Eigener, "Confidentially Yours" (editorial), *Canadian Jewish Chronicle*, 2 March 1962, 5.
46 Chayele Thalenberg, "Der montrealer yidisher yugnt teater," *Yugntruf* 2 (1965): 12–13.
47 Larrue, *Le théâtre yiddish à Montréal*, 123.
48 Ibid., 127.
49 Ibid., 127–9.

50 "Yiddish Drama for Children," letter dated 30 August 1979, CJC, DA 17, Box 15, File 16.

51 Pritz, "Ukrainian Cultural Traditions," 71–93.

52 Ibid., 95.

53 See Margolis, "Les belles-sœurs and Di shvegerins."

54 Gold, "Study of Three Montreal Children's Theatres," 43.

55 Ibid.

56 Janice Arnold, "Yiddish Theatre Giant Dora Wasserman Memorialized in Montreal," *Canadian Jewish News*, 3 July 2019, https://www.cjnews .com/news/canada/yiddish-theatre-giant-dora-wasserman-memorialized-in-montreal.

57 Margolis, "Montreal Yiddish Theatre."

58 Chana Fishman Gonshor, "Di yidishe dramatishe grupe in montreol," *Yugntruf* 22 (September 1971): 10.

59 Fox lists David Roskies and Sheva Zucker among them, both discussed below. Fox, "The Passionate Few," 6.

60 Ibid., 7.

61 See Bleaman, "Uriel Weinreich."

62 The Havurah movement emerged in the 1960s to promote a model of informal and egalitarian Jewish communities that gathered to pray or study. Neo-Hasidism marked the incorporation of Hasidic texts into contemporary Jewish workshops. See Ariel, "Walking Together, Walking Apart."

63 Roskies, *Against the Apocalypse*, 1.

64 These are currently housed at the Yiddish Book Center, where Roskies donated them in 2019 when he was interviewed as part of the Wexler Oral History Project.

65 David Roskies, oral history recording, interview by Jayne Guberman, 9.

66 Roskies, *Yiddish Lands*, 125–6.

67 D[avid] R[oskies]. "A briv fun a 15-yorikn leyener," *Afn Shvel*, March-April, 1964. At his parents' request, the letter was published with only Roskies's initials.

68 Schaechter, *The Standardized Yiddish Orthography*.

69 David Roskies, oral history recording, interview by Jayne Guberman, 10.

70 David Roskies, letter, 24 April 1964, David Roskies Scrapbook 2.

71 David Roskies, letter to Avrom Sutzkever, [June?] 1964, David Roskies Scrapbook 2.

72 David Roskies, letter/press release, 15 June 1964, David Roskies Scrapbook 1.

73 Rokhl Rotenberg, undated letter [1964?], David Roskies Scrapbook 1.

74 David Roskies, "A kurtse geshikhte fun yugntruf," *Keneder Adler*, 10 September 1964, 3, 5.

75 Yugntruf, typewritten document, [June?] 1964, David Roskies Scrapbook 2.

76 Yugntruf alveltlekher yidisher zhurnal, 13 August 1964, David Roskies Scrapbook 2.

77 Typewritten text on index cards, David Roskies Scrapbook 2.

78 Roskies, *Yiddish Lands*, 129–30.

79 "Di konstitutsye fun der yugntruf bavegung," *Yugntruf* 2 (Winter 1965): 6–7, https://yugntruf.org/zhurnal/zhurnal.php?ui=embed&numer=2#page/7/mode/1up. See also Shandler, *Adventures in Yiddishland*, 147–9.

80 Roskies, *Yiddish Lands*, 129–30.

81 L[eybl] Z[ilbershtrom], "Mir zaynen do!" *Yugntruf* 1 (Fall 1964), 2.

82 Sore Apelboym, "Tsveyshprakhikayt baym yidishn folk," *Yugntruf* 1 (Fall 1964), 4.

83 Elye Palevsky, "Vuhin geyen di dervaksene," *Yugntruf* 1 (Fall 1964), 5.

84 *Yugntruf* 1 (1964), 10–11.

85 "Diskusye arum di takones fun yugntruf," *Yugntruf* 2 (Winter 1965): 5–6.

86 Rukhl Schaechter, oral history recording clip, "The Beginnings of Yugntruf," Wexler Oral History Project, https://www.youtube.com/watch?v=hcTXScURI_M.

87 Bela Zinger, "'Yugntruf' in sidni," *Oystralisher yidisher nayes/Australian Jewish News*, 23 April 1965, 2.

88 Rivka Augenfeld, letter, 8 October 1964, David Roskies Scrapbook 2.

89 "Montreoler yugntruf-komitet," *Yugntruf* 1 (November 1964), 15.

90 Raizel Fishman, "Barikht fun montreoler yugntruf komitet," *Yugntruf* 2 (Winter 1965), 10.

91 Melech Ravitch, "Bamerkungen vegn a 'yugntruf yizker ovnt,'" *Keneder Adler*, 26 May 1965, 4.

92 Thalenberg, "Der montrealer yiddisher yugnt teater."

93 Fishman Gonshor, "Di yidishe dramatishe grupe," 10.

94 Roskies, "Der amerikaner yiddisher teater: vos tut men?," 12.

95 Margolis, "Montreal Yiddish Theatre."

96 Roskies, oral history recording, interview by Christa Whitney, 2:15.

97 "National Conference for Yiddish Opening Session Part 1 (May 17th–18th, 1969) with Abraham Fuks, Raizel Fishman, Chana Fishman, Rivka Augenfeld, Pearl Levy, Chava Rosenfarb and Jacob Glatstein," Jewish Public Library, Montreal, https://archive.org/details/National

ConferenceForYiddishOpeningSessionPart2may17th-18th1969; and
"Part 2," https://archive.org/details/NationalConferenceForYiddish
OpeningSessionPart1may17th-18th1969.

98 Jacob Beller, "Who Is Responsible for the Decline of Yiddish – Two
Views," *Canadian Jewish Chronicle Review*, December 1972, 30–1.

99 Victor Topper, "Who Is Responsible for the Decline of Yiddish – Two
Views," *Canadian Jewish Chronicle Review*, December 1972, 32–4.

100 "Jewish Peretz School Campaign Opens," *Canadian Jewish Chronicle*, 30
September 1960, 15.

101 David Schwartz, "Yiddish Culture Marches On," *Canadian Jewish Chronicle*, 30 September 1960, 15.

102 S.J. Goldsmith, "Yiddish in Our Days," *Canadian Jewish Chronicle*, 4 January 1962, 2.

103 S.J. Goldsmith, "Yiddish in Jewish Life," *Canadian Jewish Chronicle*, 25
February 1965, 2.

104 Lappin, "Rehabilitation or Renaissance," 181.

105 Rosenberg, "Canada," *American Jewish Year Book* 65 (1964), 172.

106 Wisse, *Free as a Jew*.

107 Canadian Jewish Congress, "Resolution on Yiddish and Hebrew
Adopted at the Plenary Session of the Canadian Jewish Congress,"
Canadian Jewish Chronicle, 6 July 1962, 12.

108 Canadian Jewish Congress 15th Plenary Session Report, Convention
Newsletter, no. 2, 17 May 1968, CJC Collection, Series AB (Plenary
records), 1968, 4.

109 Kage authored the study, *Tsvey hundert yor fun yidisher imigratsiye in
kanade* (1960), published in English translation as *With Faith and
Thanksgiving*.

110 "National Conference to Probe Decline of Yiddish Language," *Canadian Jewish Chronicle*, 25 April 1969, 3.

111 Ibid.

112 Jedwab, "Politics of Dialogue," 42–74.

113 "National Yiddish Committee," Canadian Jewish Congress, 17th Plenary Assembly, Royal York Hotel, Toronto, CJC Collection, Series AB
(Plenary records), 1974, 68.

114 Michael M. Solomon, "Canada," *American Jewish Year Book* 72 (1971),
285.

115 Resolutions Adopted at the 16th Plenary Session of the Canadian Jewish Congress Held in Montreal, 5–6.

116 "National Yiddish Committee," Canadian Jewish Congress, 17th Plenary Assembly, 68.

117 "Yiddish," Resolutions Adopted at the Fourth Annual Plenary Session, Jewish Public Library, Montreal, CJC Collection, Series AB (Plenary records), 1974, 14.

118 Arthur Lermer, "Interest in Yiddish Capitalized by CJC National Committee," *Canadian Jewish News*, 14 June 1974, Congress Edition, 6, 16.

119 Ibid., 6.

120 Sharon Chazen, Alan Farkus, Ava Kanner, Eli Kogut, Evelyn Rosenfeld, and Sam Stein.

121 "Summer Camp Program," DA12-02-24, Alex Dworkin Canadian Jewish Archives, 2.

122 "Yiddish Summer Camp Laurentians," PC01-15-001A, B, and C, Alex Dworkin Canadian Jewish Archives. It includes photos from the performances.

123 Edit Kuper, interview.

124 Allison Lampert, "Mohawks See Selves in Ghetto Drama," *Montreal Gazette*, 17 September 2003.

125 Kuper, interview.

126 Young Actors for Young Audiences, Dora Wasserman Yiddish Theatre, accessed 15 December 2018, https://www.segalcentre.org/en/yayam.

127 Aron Gonshor, oral history recording.

128 Ben Gonshor, telephone conversation with the author, 12 September 2018.

129 Fishman Gonshor and Shaffir, "Commitment to a Language" and Feuerverger, "Jewish-Canadian Identity and Hebrew Language Learning."

130 Nancy Sculnik, interview.

131 Taft and Markus, *A Second Chance*, 258, and Slucki, *The International Jewish Labor Bund*, 142–72.

132 "What Is SKIF," https://www.skif.org.au/what-is-skif.

133 Singer, *Yiddish in Melbourne*, 19.

134 Fox, "The Passionate Few."

135 Zucker, oral history recording.

136 Yiddish Teachers Seminar, *Yugntruf*, https://yugntruf.org/yiddish-vokh/teachers-seminar/?lang=en.

137 Orenstein, Schaechter Gottesman, and Steingart, *Vidervuks*.

138 Announcement printed in Shandler, "The Yiddish-'Svives,'" 32.

139 Shandler, *Adventures in Yiddishland*, 146–7.

140 Fox, "The Passionate Few," 17.

141 Ibid., 21.

142 Solomon Simon's *The Clever Little Tailor*, Jenny Kjaerdbo's *Uh Oh!*, and

Jacob Glatstein's *Emil & Karl*. See Kinder-Loshn Publications, https://kinderloshn.org.

143 Shandler, *Adventures in Yiddishland*, 147.
144 Ibid, 149.
145 Wood, *And We're All Brothers*, 20.
146 Fox, "The Passionate Few," 4–5.
147 Ibid., 15.

CHAPTER FOUR

1 Schwartz, *Survivors and Exiles*, 12.
2 Fuks and Anctil, *Cent ans de littérature yiddish et hébraïque au Canada*, 437–42.
3 Zachary Baker, "1000 Essential Yiddish Books." Yiddish Book Center, Digital Library and Collections; Schwartz, *Survivors and Exiles*, 245.
4 Norich, *Discovering Exile*.
5 Schwarz, *Survivors and Exiles*, 244. See also Baron, "The Holocaust and American Public Memory," and Diner, *We Remember with Reverence and Love*.
6 See Greenstein, *Third Solitudes*. On Klein, see Caplan, *Like One That Dreamed*, and Ravvin and Simon, *Failure's Opposite*. On Richler, see Posner, *The Last Honest Man*. On Waddington, see the introduction to Waddington and Panofsky, *The Collected Poems of Miriam Waddington*. On Layton, see Beissel and Bennett, *Raging Like a Fire*.
7 See Shneer, "Who Owns the Means of Cultural Production?"
8 The Yiddish Periodicals Index (http://yiddish-periodicals.huji.ac.il), an exhaustive online database, includes over eight hundred titles from the end of the nineteenth century through the 1950s, including publications from Czarist Russia, the Soviet Union, Poland, the United States, and Palestine/Israel.
9 Schwarz, *Survivors and Exiles*, 126.
10 Hillel Halkin, "Press," *Encyclopaedia Judaica*, vol. 13 (New York: Macmillan, 1971): 1055.
11 See Margolis, "The Yiddish Press in Montreal, 1900–1945."
12 For a discussion of these newspapers in the Montreal context before 1945, see Margolis, *Jewish Roots, Canadian Soil*.
13 Rosenberg, "The Eagle and the Foreign Language Press: Dedicated to Israel Rabinovitch on His 60th Birthday," *Canadian Jewish Chronicle*, 24 December 1954, 4.

14 See Margolis, "Negotiating Jewish Canadian Identity."

15 Schwarz, *Survivors and Exiles*, 3.

16 Ibid., 6–14.

17 This was part of the title of an article published by Schwarz, "A Portable Library for Polish Jews."

18 Ibid., 244.

19 Ibid., 55.

20 Bialystok, *Delayed Impact*, 7.

21 Wisse, *Free as a Jew*, 44.

22 Schwarz, *Survivors and Exiles*, 63.

23 Roskies and Diamant, *Holocaust Literature*, 119.

24 Segal, *Lider far yidishe kinder*.

25 See Margolis, "Yiddish at a Crossroads."

26 See Margolis, "Negotiating Jewish Canadian Identity."

27 *Tint un feder: Literarisher khoydesh-zhurnal* (*Pen and Ink: Literary Monthly*), ed. Gershon Pomerantz, Toronto: Pomer Publishing & Printing. See the first four issues: no. 1 (January 1949), no. 2 (February 1949), no. 3 (September 1949), and no. 4 (September 1950).

28 To view the cover of the first volume, see the Joe Fishstein Collection of Yiddish Poetry, http://digital.library.mcgill.ca/fishstein/prepresent.php?catname=Canada.

29 *Vidershtand* (*Resistence*), ed. I. Goldkorn, nos. 1–12 (December 1957–September 1959), Montreal.

30 See Bar-Am, "Our Shtetl, Tel Aviv, Must and Will Become the Metropolis of Yiddish."

31 See Margolis, "Translating Jewish Poland into Canadian Yiddish."

32 *Kvutses kitve agode* (1947) and *Sefer hutim ha-meshulashim* (1953).

33 Robinson, "Canadian Jews Engage with Hasidism in Yiddish in the Mid-Twentieth Century."

34 On Ravitch's role in the Montreal Yiddish milieu, see Margolis, "Melekh Ravitch as Yiddish Catalyst."

35 See the introduction to Justin Cammy's translation of Bergner, *On Long Winter Nights*.

36 *67 lirishe, satirishe, natsyonale, sotsyale un filozofishe lider fun di letste finf-zeks yor* (Buenos Aires, 1946); *Di kroynung fun a yungn yidishn dikhter in amerike: Poeme* (New York, 1953); and *Di lider fun mayne lider* (Montreal, 1954).

37 Roskies and Diamant, *Holocaust Literature*, 102. http://migs.concordia.ca/memoirs/frankel_zaltzman_paula/frankel_zaltzman_paula_intro.htm.

38 The volume was published in translation by the author as *Confessions of An Auschwitz Number (A-18260)*.

39 See Brenner, "A.M. Klein and Mordecai Richler," and Ravvin, *House of Words*, 22–31.

40 The work was penned in Yiddish but published earlier in book form in an abridged English translation by A.M. Klein as *Journey of My Life: A Book of Memoirs* (1945).

41 See Hellerstein, *A Question of Tradition*.

42 On Krishtalka and the publication, see Margolis, *Jewish Roots, Canadian Soil*, 156–7.

43 Rosenberg, "Canada," *American Jewish Year Book* 68 (1967), 392.

44 Ibid., and Michael M. Solomon, "Canada," *American Jewish Year Book* 73 (1972), 404.

45 Levendel, *A Century of the Canadian Jewish Press*, 28–36.

46 See the section "After the Holocaust" in Krutikov, *Yiddish Literature*.

47 The "third destruction" points to a traditional Jewish sense of continuity between the events of the Holocaust and previous catastrophes. See Roskies, *The Literature of Destruction*.

48 Schachter, *Diasporic Modernisms*, 154.

49 See Ravitch, "Yiddish Culture in Canada," and "Kanadisher tsvayg fun shtam."

50 Margolis, "Sholem Shtern: Bridging the Gaps."

51 Sholem Shtern, "Vegn mayn poeme 'in kanade,'" in *Shrayber vos ikh hob gekent*, 203. Cited in Margolis, "Sholem Shtern: Bridging the Gaps," 95.

52 See Margolis, "Yiddish and Multiculturalism: A Marriage Made in Heaven?"

53 Barbara Wisnoski, Jewish Public Library, email to the author, 27 November 2019.

54 Greenstein, Anctil, and Orenstein, "Canadian Literature," 427.

55 See Margolis, "Chava Rosenfarb's Yiddish Montreal."

56 Schwarz, *Survivors and Exiles*, 54.

57 Morgentaler, "'I Am Still There.'"

58 Seven of these stories were published in English translation in Rosenfarb, *Survivors*.

59 Morgentaler, "Land of the Postscript," 169.

60 Seelig, "Like a Barren Sheet of Paper," 366.

61 See Bialystok, *Delayed Impact*, Chatterley, "Canada's Struggle with Holocaust Memorialization," and Hollenberg, "At the Western Development Museum."

62 The volume has been partially translated into French by Pierre Anctil under the title *Tristesse et nostalgie: Mémoires littéraires du Montréal yiddish*.

63 Chinski and Fiszman, "A biblyotek vos felt," 147.

64 Rozhanski, "Yidisher literature in der atmosfer fun kultur-pluralism," *Kanadish*, 62, 22.

65 Felsen, "Preserving Yiddish Culture in Canada," 9.

66 Spilberg and Zipper, *Kanader yidisher zamlbukh*, 14.

67 Orenstein, Review of *Canadian Jewish Anthology*, 496.

68 Ibid.

69 See Margolis, *Jewish Roots, Canadian Soil*, 70.

70 Fuerstenberg, "From Yiddish to '*Yiddishkeit*,'" and "Faithful to the Dream."

71 See, for example, the introduction to Panofsky, *The New Spice Box: Canadian Jewish Writing*, and Margolis, "Across the Border."

72 Yaakov Zipper's *Oyf yener zayt bug* (1946) appeared as *Me'ever le-nahar bug* (1957) and Sholem Shtern's *Dos vayse hoyz* appeared as *Ha-bayit ha-lavan be-harim* (1972).

73 Howe and Greenberg, *A Treasury of Yiddish Poetry*," 151–60.

74 Korn, *Paper Roses*.

75 Howe and Greenberg, *Voices from the Yiddish* (1972) and Howe and Wisse, *The Best of Sholom Aleichem* (1979).

76 Wisse, *Free as a Jew*, 242–5.

77 The series was sponsored by the Fund for the Translation of Jewish Literature launched by author Lucy Dawidowicz in 1986 to commission translations of works in Yiddish and Hebrew for publication with Schocken Books. Aviva Cantor, "Major Effort Under Way to Retrieve and Reclaim Yiddish Literature," *Jewish Telegraphic Agency*, 7 February 1986, 3.

78 Seymour Mayne, email to the author, 3 December 2019.

79 Seymour Mayne, interview.

80 Sutzkever, *Burnt Pearls*; Korn, *Generations*; Ravitch, *Night Prayer and Other Poems*.

81 Ravitch, *Iker shokhakhti: lider un poemes fun di yorn 1954–1969*, 115. Translation in Mayne, *In Your Words*, 24–5.

82 Balan, *Identifications: Ethnicity and the Writer in Canada*.

83 Shandler, "Anthologizing the Vernacular," 304.

84 Ibid., 317.

85 See Margolis, "Sholem Shtern: Bridging the Gaps."

86 Goldie Morgentaler, conversation with the author, Vancouver, 3 June 2019.

87 Rosenfarb, *Confessions of a Yiddish Writer*, 3.

88 Ibid., 180. See Margolis, "Chava Rosenfarb's Yiddish Montreal," and Morgentaler, "Land of the Postscript."

89 See Simon, *Translating Montreal*.

90 Grutman, "Beckett and Beyond," 201–2.

91 For example, American Yiddish poet Zackary Sholem Berger (born 1973) offers intentionally different versions of his "self-translated" poems in Yiddish and English in his 2014 bilingual volume *Eyn folk aroysgenumen fun tsveytn/One Nation Taken Out of Another*.

92 Stavans, *On Self-Translation*.

93 See Margolis, "French Canada as a Site of Holocaust Representation."

94 See Ball, "Shouldering the Burdens of History."

95 See Margolis, *Jewish Roots, Canadian Soil*, 154–8.

96 Leybl Botwinik, "Tevye's a briv fun nay-frankraykh fun yor 1977," *Yugntruf* 31 (September 1977), 14.

97 Ibid.

98 *Forverts* Staff, "Israel's National Yiddish Story Writing Contest Announces the Three Winners," *Forward*, 20 October 2020, https://forward.com/yiddish/457210/israels-national-yiddish-story-writing-contest-announces-the-three-winners.

99 Title page, *Der nayer dor*, 4 (1982), 1.

100 An online listserv discussion about science fiction in Yiddish resulted in a list of about a dozen items, none of them more recent than 1960. "Mendele: Yiddish Literature and Language," vol. 10.004, 2 June 2000, http://www.columbia.edu/~jap2220/Arkhiv/vol10%20(2000-1)/vol10004.txt.

101 Botwinik, *Di geheyme shlikhes*, 16. All translations from this text are mine.

102 Ibid., 52.

103 Ibid., 54.

104 Simon Swartzman, "Chabon Pens World from 'Exile,'" *Yale News*, 28 February 2008, https://yaledailynews.com/blog/2008/02/28/chabon-pens-work-from-exile. On the controversy surrounding Chabon's article, see Shandler, *Imagining Yiddishland*, 123–4.

105 Botwinik, *Di geheyme shlikhes*, 10.

106 Botwinik, "Khurbn mizrekh eyrope: a yugntruf symposium," *Yugntruf* 35:4; "Reyd vos hobn oyfgerisn," *Yugntruf* 36–7:4; "Drey mir nit keyn kopeyk: yugntruf aroysfor," *Yugntruf* 50:3; "Fun nekhtn, haynt un morgn," *Yugntruf* 57–8:11, *Yugntruf* 60:8; "Far a dor vos farshteyt (nokh) nit," *Yugntruf* 63:8; "A bekher mit vayn," *Yugntruf* 63:12.

107 *Forverts* Staff, "Israel's National Yiddish Story Writing Contest Announces the Three Winners," *Forward*, 20 October 2020,

https://forward.com/yiddish/457210/israels-national-yiddish-story-writing-contest-announces-the-three-winners.

108 "In der bavegung: Vidervuks in montreol," *Yugntruf* 71 (December 1990), 21.

109 Diamant and Roskies, *Holocaust Literature*, 163.

110 "From Holocaust to Life," http://botwinikmusic.com/old/index.htm.

111 Bill Gladstone, "Poet and Author Sam Simchovitch Dead at 97," *Canadian Jewish News*, 14 July 2019, https://www.cjnews.com/news/canada/poet-author-sam-simchovitch-dead-97.

112 Slutzky-Kohn, *Survivor*, 8.

113 Morgentaler, "I Am Still There," 189–90.

114 Rosenfarb, *Confessions of a Yiddish Writer*, 208–9.

115 Johnson and Allardice, *Confessions of a Yiddish Writer* (interview).

116 Chava Rosenfarb, Convocation address, University of Lethbridge, 31 May 2006, https://chavarosenfarb.com/convocation-address.

117 Anctil, *Poèmes Yiddish, Jacob Isaac Segal (1896–1954)*.

118 Anctil, "1992: Translating Montreal's Yiddish Poet Jacob Isaac Segal into French," 247.

119 See Felsen, "Preserving Yiddish Culture in Canada."

120 "Khidesht zikh nisht," Archive for M.M. Shaffir, The Jewish Song of the Week, presented by the An-Sky Jewish Folkore Research Project, https://yiddishsong.wordpress.com/tag/m-m-shaffir.

121 Botwinik, "Music and the Holocaust," *From Holocaust to Life*, http://holocaustmusic.ort.org/memory/yiddish/david-botwinik.

122 Tur Malka, l'Institut Européen des Musiques Juives (IEMJ), https://www.iemj.org/en/tur-malka.

123 Katz, "Born to Kvetch: Yiddish Language and Culture in All Its Moods: Yiddish, Without the Inhibitions," *The Jewish Chronicle*, 8 October 2009, https://www.thejc.com/culture/books/born-to-kvetch-yiddish-language-and-culture-in-all-its-moods-1.11721?highlight=Dovid+Katz.

124 Weintraub, "Bordering on 'Lehavdl.'"

125 See Anctil and Felsen, *Jacob Isaac Segal*; Margolis, "Chava Rosenfarb's Yiddish Montreal"; Morgentaler, "I Am Still There"; Morgentaler, "Land of the Postscript"; Panofsky, "Chava Rosenfarb's Early Life Writing"; Seelig, "Like a Barren Sheet of Paper"; Valencia, "Yidishe Dikhterins."

126 Ravvin, *A House of Words*, 86.

127 *The Yiddish Daily Forward*, http://yiddish.forward.com.

128 "League for Yiddish," *Afn Shvel*, http://www.leagueforyiddish.org/afnshvel.html#english.

129 See Rojanski, *Yiddish in Israel*, 271–3.
130 *Forverts* staff, "Israel's National Yiddish Story Writing Contest Announces the Three Winners."
131 Bemporad and Pascucci, *Trot bay trot*.
132 Chernin and Felsenbaum, *A ring/antologye*.
133 Waldman, "Seizing the Means of Cultural Production." See also Waldman, "New York's Yiddish Press Is Thriving."
134 Bleaman, "Der *Veker*: A yoytse-min-haklal in der khsidish-yidisher peryodik."
135 Lewis, "A New Yiddish Renaissance."
136 The Yiddish serialized novel in 2017 was titled "The Butcher of Riga: The gripping story of a group of Jews that tracked down and liquidated a brutal Nazi-murderer twenty years after the War." In 2017, when it ceased publication, it was delivering about three thousand copies per issue in the Hasidic neighbourhoods of Greater Montreal and had about two thousand online subscribers. Steven Lapidus, email to the author, 19 April 2017.
137 See Chaya Sara Oppenheim, "Where Are the Yeshivish Writers?" *Tablet Magazine*, 22 December 2021, https://www.tabletmag.com/sections/arts-letters/articles/where-are-the-yeshivish-writers.
138 See Jones, "The Vancouver Peretz Institute Yiddish Library."
139 See Lansky, *Outwitting History*, especially 219–40.

CHAPTER FIVE

1 Socalled, https://www.socalledmusic.com.
2 See Wood, "(De)constructing Yiddishland," with an updated version in *And We're All Brothers*, Margolis, "*HipHopKhasene*," and Smulyan, "The SoCalled Past."
3 Tur Malka, l'Institut Européen des Musiques Juives (IEMJ), https://www.iemj.org/en/tur-malka.
4 Shandler, *Adventures in Yiddishland*, 145.
5 Wood, *And We're All Brothers*, 103. See also Wood, "Yiddish Song in Twenty-First Century America."
6 Wood, *And We're All Brothers*, 20.
7 Ibid., 21.
8 Ibid., 62.
9 Ibid., 80.
10 Friedman, "Yiddish Returns," 208.
11 Wood, *And We're All Brothers*, 26.

12 Ibid., 33.

13 For example, Vaisman's study, *Being Heard: The Singing Voices of Contemporary Hasidic Women*, examines the important role that singing plays in the lives of women in communities where they are barred from singing in public by Jewish religious law.

14 Wood, "Pop, Piety and Modernity."

15 Kornhauser, "Music and the Continuity of Yiddish Language and Culture in Melbourne."

16 Wood, *And We're All Brothers*, 23.

17 "Flash from the Past: Kinderklangen," Jewish Montreal of Yesterday, Jewish Public Library Archives, http://www.jewishpubliclibrary.org/blog /?p=1613; "How I Came to Record Kinder Klangen Children's Music Tapes," Yiddish Book Center's Wexler Oral History Project, https://www .yiddishbookcenter.org/collections/oral-histories/excerpts/woh-ex-0001829/how-i-came-record-kinder-klangen-children-s-music-tapes; Raby, "If You Build It, They Will Come": The Norman Berman Children's Library, 1983–2013."

18 Dembling, "Instrumental Music and Gaelic Revitalization in Scotland and Nova Scotia," 245.

19 Ibid.

20 Kenneth MacKenzie, email to the author, 28 October 2019.

21 Sparling, "Music Is Language and Language Is Music," 156.

22 McDonald and Sparling, "Interpretations of Tradition: From Gaelic Song to Celtic Pop."

23 Macintyre et al., "Heritage Passions, Heritage Convictions, and the Rooted L2 Self," and "Flow Experiences and Willingness to Communicate."

24 See Feldman, *Klezmer: Music, History, and Memory*.

25 See Slobin, "Klezmer Music," Netsky, "An Overview of Klezmer Music and its Development in the U.S.," and "Klez Goes to College," and London, "An Insider's View."

26 The Klezmatics 2002 album, *Possessed*, includes an ode to cannabis called "Mizmor Shir Lehanef" (Reefer Song) with original lyrics by *Born to Kvetch* author Michael Wex.

27 See Larry Yudelson, "A New and Very Yiddish Hallelujah," *The Jewish Times*, 17 November 2016, https://jewishstandard.timesofisrael.com/a-new-and-very-yiddish-hallelujah.

28 Ibid.

29 Wood, *And We're All Brothers*, 85.

30 Feldman, *Klezmer: Music, History and Memory*, 372–3.

31 Wood, *And We're All Brothers*, 87.

32 Kirshenblatt-Gimblett, "Sounds of Sensibility," 53.

33 Scherbenske, "From Folksmentshn to Creative Individuals," 230.

34 Anklewicz, "Extending the Tradition," 91.

35 Shandler, *Adventures in Yiddishland*, 87.

36 Weinfeld, *Like Everyone Else ... but Different*, 192.

37 See Astmann, "*Freylekhe Felker*: Queer Subculture in the Klezmer Revival."

38 Wood, *And We're All Brothers*, 1.

39 Svigals, "Why Do We Do This Anyway," 48.

40 Svigals, "Whither Queer Yiddishkayt?"

41 Orly Zebak, "'Great and Powerful' Schmutz: An interview with Jess Goldman," *Niv Magazine*, 18 September 2020, https://nivmag.com/gross-great-powerful-schmutz-interview-jess-goldman.

42 Svigals, "Whither Queer Yiddishkayt?"

43 Goldman, *Schmutz*, 31. A pdf of the chapbook is available here https://museemontrealjuif.ca/wp-content/uploads/2020/08/Schmutz FinalDraft.pdf.

44 Zebak, "'Great and Powerful' Schmutz."

45 In addition to working with Jess on her Yiddish, Dolman also advised on some of the phrasing in *Schmutz*. On Dolman's relationship to Yiddish, see Dolman, oral history recording.

46 Jess Goldman, email message to the author, 20 January 2022.

47 Schlosberg, *Kugel Western*.

48 See Shandler, "Queer Yiddishkeit," and Blitz, "Translated and Improved."

49 See Lim, "Queer Aswang Transmedia."

50 See Shandler, "Queer Yiddishkeit," and Hoffman, *The Passing Game*.

51 A *dybbuk* is a figure from Eastern European Jewish folklore, a dislocated human spirit who wanders until it possesses the body of a living person. The play has been translated into multiple languages and is among the most performed Jewish plays in history. See Neugroschel, *The Dybbuk and the Yiddish Imagination*.

52 Sicular, "A yingl mit a yingl hot epes a tam."

53 Kafrissen, "Queer Yiddishkeit."

54 Halberstam, *In a Queer Time and Place*, 12.

55 Edelman, *No Future*.

56 See Dinshaw et al., "Theorizing Queer Temporalities."

57 Muñoz, *Cruising Utopia*, 1.

58 Crasnow, "I Want to Look Transgender," and Sienna, *A Rainbow Thread*.

59 Halberstam, *The Queer Art of Failure*.

60 Weiman-Kelman, *Queer Expectations*, 136.

61 Shander, "Queer Yiddishkeit," 111.

62 Ibid., 112.

63 Fruchter, "Embracing the Multiple."

64 Weiman-Kelman, *Queer Expectations*, xxiv–v. See also Fruchter's interview with Weiman-Kelman, "Embracing the Multiple."

65 Green and Benjamin, "Seeking and Queering Utopia."

66 freygl gertsovski, email message to the author, 27 January 2022. See Rad Yiddish, https://m.facebook.com/RadYiddish.

67 Cooper, oral history recording.

68 Wood, *And We're All Brothers*, 8.

69 Ibid., 40–1.

70 Szmigin et al., "Socio-spatial Authenticity," 11.

71 For example, see Laing and Mair, "Music Festivals and Social Inclusion."

72 Wood, *And We're All Brothers*, 46–7.

73 Charlie Fidelman, "'Jewish Jazz' Steps Up: KlezKanada Concert Tops Four-day Festival in Laurentians." *Montreal Gazette*, 20 August 1998, D11.

74 Wolofsky, oral history recording.

75 Eric Stein, "KlezKanada Yiddish Festival Proves a Success," *Canadian Jewish News*, 23 September 1999, 25.

76 KlezKanada Programme, 2019, 5.

77 McGill Course at KlezKanada, accessed 1 March 2019, https://youtu.be/UwS9huyzp7c; Summer McGill/Klezkanada course, JWST 354 Eastern European Jewish Music, Jewish Studies, McGill University, accessed 1 March 2019, https://www.mcgill.ca/jewishstudies/undergraduates/summer-mcgillklezkanada-course.

78 Hankus Netsky, "Another Kind of 'Return' by Dr. Hankus Netsky," *Huffpost*, 22 March 2016, https://www.huffpost.com/entry/another-kind-of-return-by_b_9517000.

79 Hankus Netsky, Skype conversation with the author, 28 March 2019.

80 Moore, oral history recording.

81 Avia Moore, email to the author, 22 March 2019.

82 Ibid.

83 Ibid.

84 Maureen Turner, "Alumni Profile: Sebastian Schulman," *Pakn Treger* 71 (2015), https://www.yiddishbookcenter.org/alumni-profile.

85 Janice Arnold, "Yiddish Is Alive and Well for New KlezKanada Director," *Canadian Jewish News*, 14 May 2018, https://www.cjnews.com/news/canada/yiddish-is-alive-and-well-for-new-klezkanada-director.

86 Sebastian Schulman, email to the author, 25 February 2019.

87 Sebastian Schulman, email to the author, 23 October 2019.

88 "Tsibele," Philadelphia Folksong Society, https://pfs.org/folkies/tsibele.

89 Hilary Danailova, "A New Generation Is Reclaiming Yiddish," *Hadassah Magazine*, November 2018, https://www.hadassahmagazine.org/2018/11/01/new-generation-reclaiming-yiddish.

90 Sarah Mina Gordon, email to the author, 29 October 2019.

91 Ibid.

92 Shandler, "Postvernacular Yiddish: Language as a Performance Art," 28–9.

93 Feldman *Klezmer: Music, History and Memory*, 165.

94 Asa Brunet-Jailly, "Revitalizing Yiddish Culture: KlezKanada Bolsters Communal Creativity and Cultural Vitality," *Niv Magazine*, 13 June 2021, https://nivmag.com/klezkanada-communal-creativity-cultural-vitality.

95 Jacobson, "With Song to the Struggle," 90–2.

96 Ibid., 118.

97 Ibid.

98 Ibid., 162.

99 Wolters-Fredlund, "We Shall Go Forward with Our Songs."

100 Wolters-Fredlund, "We Shall Be Better Canadians."

101 "Zing!Zing!Zing," UJPO/Morris Wincehvsky Centre, https://www.winchevskycentre.org/zing-1.

102 For example, see Dabback, "A Community of Singing."

103 Jacobson, "With Song to the Struggle," 372, cited in Wood, *And We're All Brothers*, 39.

104 The Jewish People's Philharmonic Chorus, https://www.thejppc.org.

105 Peretz Centre for Secular Jewish Culture, www.peretz-centre.org,

106 Jones, "Vancouver Peretz Institute Yiddish Library," 128.

107 Ibid., 134.

108 Ibid., 140.

109 Jones, "The Autobiography of Esther Shechter."

110 In recent years, these have included: "Rozhinkes mit mandlen," "Yomer-vokhets" (Jabberwocky), "In Amerike," "Benyomin der driter," "Ikh bin a Yid," "Oyb nit nokh hekher," and excerpts from "Di yam gazlonim" (*Pirates of Penzance*, translated into Yiddish). Vancouver Jewish Folk Choir, https://peretz-centre.org/vancouver-jewish-folk-choir.

111 "And We Sing Happy Songs," the second line of the song "Ale Brider."

112 Jones and Ramsay, "Un mir zingen freylekhe lider."

113 Ibid.

114 Jones, "The Vancouver Peretz Institute Yiddish Library," 73.

115 "Origins," *Mir zingen: The Vancouver Jewish Folk Choir Turns 40*, online exhibit of the Jewish Museum, https://jewishmuseum.ca/exhibit /yiddish-folk-choir.

116 Jones, "Vancouver Peretz Institute Yiddish Library," 73.

117 Jones and Ramsay, "Un mir zingen freylekhe lider."

118 Faith Jones, emails to the author, 14–15 October 2019.

119 Ibid.

120 Jane Peppler, *Yiddish Penny Songs*, 16 October 2017, http://www.yiddish pennysongs.com/2017/10/guter-bruder-nit-gekhapt-yiddish-song.html.

121 The work had been translated by Raphael Finkel as "Yomervokhets," which Millard recalled hearing about and in 2016 decided to set to music as a fresh addition to the choir's repertory. Yomervokhets (David Millard), CPDL (Choral Public Domain Library)/ChoralWiki, http://www2.cpdl.org/wiki/index.php/Yomervokhets_(David_Millard).

122 Zaretsky, "Singing for Social Change."

123 Wood, *And We're All Brothers*, 47.

CHAPTER SIX

1 Abrams, "Film, Television and New Media Studies," 118.

2 Kelman, *Station Identification*, 128–9.

3 "The Stations That Spoke Your Language: Radio and the Yiddish American Cultural Renaissance," Symposium, 6–7 September 2012, American Folklife Centre, Washington, DC, https://www.loc.gov/folklife/Symposia/yiddishradio/program.html.

4 "The Yiddish Radio Dial," Yiddish Radio Project, http://yiddishradioproject.org/exhibits/history.

5 The Yiddish Voice/Dos Yidishe kol, WUNR 1600 AM in Brookline, MA, can be accessed at www.yv.org.

6 This trend began with *The Goldbergs*, a domestic comedy serial featuring beloved housewife Molly Goldberg that ran from 1929 to 1949, was one of the most successful radio serials to feature Yiddish vocabulary and syntax, and popular across America. The show continued as a television sitcom. See Smith, *Something on My Own*. Since that time, the sounds of Yiddish have been heard in sitcoms such as *The Nanny*, *Seinfeld*, and more recently, the musical dramedy series *Crazy Ex-Girl-friend*.

7 Mandel, *The Jewish Hour*.

8 Ibid., 37.

9 "Living a Language: Yiddish Advocate's Radio Show in 35th Year (Nahum Wilchesky)," *Montreal Gazette*, 27 December 1996.

10 David Lazarus, "Future of the Jewish Program to Be Decided Next Month," *Canadian Jewish News*, 29 July 2009, https://www.cjnews.com /news/canada/future-jewish-program-decided-next-month.

11 Janice Arnold, "After Fifteen Years, Radio Shalom Goes off the Air," *Canadian Jewish News*, 4 April 2016, http://www.cjnews.com/news /canada/after-fifteen-years-montreals-radio-shalom-goes-off-the-air. Its schedule in 2021 included a variety of programing: https://radio-shalom.ca/horaire.

12 Sherman, "Voices from the Vault."

13 Raby, oral history recording.

14 Hubner, oral history recording.

15 Yiddish Audiobooks, The Yiddish Book Center's Sami Rohr Library of Recorded Yiddish Books, https://www.yiddishbookcenter.org /collections/yiddish-audiobooks

16 Rotman, "The 'Tsadik from Plonsk' and 'Goldenyu.'"

17 McLeod, "Gaelic in Contemporary Scotland."

18 The Oka Crisis was a standoff between Mohawk protesters, Quebec police, the RCMP, and the Canadian Army that lasted for almost three months.

19 Aboriginal People's Television Network, "Who We Are," http://aptn.ca/corporate2/about/who-we-are. On the history of the APTN, see Roth, *Something New in the Air*.

20 See Ingall, "How Sweden Became the Epicenter of Yiddish Children's Media," Anonymous, "A Yiddish TV Show from Sweden, Inspired by Star Wars," *Tate-Loshn: The Adventures of a Young Father Raising His Son in Yiddish*, blog post 2 July 2016, https://tate-loshn.weebly.com/home/a-yiddish-tv-show-from-sweden-inspired-by-star-wars. The Swedish television offerings in Yiddish can be accessed under "Jiddisch," Sveriges Utbildnings radio AB, https://urskola.se/Produkter?ur_subject_tree=modersm %C3%A5l+och+minoritetsspr%C3%A5k%2Fjiddisch.

21 See, for example, Parigi and Gong, "From Grassroots to Digital Ties," and Ragusa and Ward, "Caught in the Web."

22 See Campbell, *Digital Judaism* and Abrams, "Film, Television and New Media Studies."

23 Sadan, "Yiddish on the Internet," 105–6.

24 These resources include a Yiddish online keyboard at Lexilogos (https://www.lexilogos.com/keyboard/yiddish.htm), as well as extensive Yiddish language functionality in computers and handheld devices.

25 Beinfeld and Bochner, *Comprehensive Yiddish-English Dictionary*, and Schaechter-Viswanath et al., *Comprehensive English-Yiddish Dictionary*.

26 Yiddish Dictionary Online, http://www.Yiddishdictionaryonline.com; Comprehensive Yiddish Dictionary Online, www.verterbukh.org.

27 *Forverts/Yiddish Daily Forward*, http://yiddish.forward.com.

28 "About *In geveb*: Mission," https://ingeveb.org/about.

29 Digital Yiddish Theater Project, https://web.uwm.edu/yiddish-stage.

30 See "Yiddish Radio Links," *Der Bay*, http://www.derbay.org/radio links.html.

31 "Vaybertaytsh: A Feminist Podcast in Yiddish," http://www.vaybertaytsh.com.

32 YiddishPOP: An Animated Educational Site for Yiddish, http://www.yiddishpop.com.

33 Duolingo incubator, Course Status, https://incubator.duolingo.com/courses/yi/en/status.

34 Yiddish Book Center, Digital Collections, http://www.yiddishbookcenter.org/collections.

35 Caplan, "Notes from the Frontier," 347.

36 Shandler, *Yiddish*, 184–5. See also Shandler, "The Savior and the Survivor."

37 Events IN Yiddish, https://www.facebook.com/groups/199054598206104; Yiddish Research, https://www.facebook.com/groups/yidforsh/about.

38 Ontario Yiddishkayt, https://www.facebook.com/groups/Ontario Yiddishkayt/about.

39 Kirzane et al., "Online Yiddish Language Instruction."

40 Legutko, "Yiddish in the 21st Century," 236.

41 Zarrow, "Digital Yiddish Classroom."

42 Margolis, "Forays into a Digital Yiddishland."

43 Deutsch, "Forbidden Fork," 4.

44 Shana Liebman, "Chooray for Chollywood! All-Yiddish Indie Film," *New York Magazine*, 13 February 2006, http://nymag.com/news /intelligencer/15752.

45 Anthony Weiss, "Trailblazing Yiddish Action Flick Makes Waves," *Forward*, 24 February 2006, http://forward.com/news/israel/1103 /trailblazing-yiddish-action-flick-makes-waves.

46 Deutsch, "Forbidden Fork," 4–5.

47 Ibid., 5n6, for a sample of URLs. Most of these no longer operate for various reasons, technological and other; this is characteristic of the transient nature of the internet.

48 Bleaman, "Der *Veker*: A yoytse-min-haklal in der khsidish-yidisher peryodik."

49 Honeycutt, "Examining the Diffusion of CMC Technologies in Minority Languages."

50 "Aboriginal Woman Using Social Media to Save Dying Language," *APTN News*, 25 August 2015, http://aptn.ca/news/2015/08/25/aboriginal-woman-using-social-media-to-save-dying-language.

51 Amanda Sage, "Savannah Simon, Motivational Speaker-Entrepreneur-Visionary," Kickass Canadians, 9 February 2017, https://kickass canadians.ca.

52 "Want to Learn Dene? There's an App for That," 16 May 2012, http://aptn.ca/news/2012/05/16/want-to-learn-dene-languages-theres-an-app-for-that-2.

53 Zach Golden, "Cameron Bernstein: TikTok Yiddishist," *Forward*, 24 December 2021, https://forward.com/news/479946/cameron-bernstein-tiktok-yiddishist.

54 Email to the author from Yunji Johanning, associate producer/community support, AltspaceVR, 11 April 2019.

55 Steven Wesley, "Learn a Language in Realistic VR Scenarios with These Apps," 29 February 2018, VirtualSpeech, https://virtualspeech.com/blog/learn-language-vr-scenarios-apps.

56 Dave Gilbert. *The Shivah*. V.2, Wadjet Eye Games, 2013. See Abramson, "Film, Television and New Media Studies," 116.

57 "The Making of Yiddish O Canada," Zoomer TV, 29 June 2017, http://www.visiontv.ca/shows/Yiddish-o-canada.

58 Email from Anna Shternshis to the author, 11 May 2019.

59 "Press: Yiddish Glory," Dan Rosenberg, http://danrosenberg.net/press_yiddish_glory.

60 Canadian Jewish Heritage Network, https://www.cjhn.ca. These holdings include the Alex Dworkin Canadian Jewish Archives (formerly CJCCCNA), the Jewish Public Library Archives of Montreal (JPL-A), the Montreal Holocaust Memorial Centre (MHMC), the Ottawa Jewish Archives, and others.

61 "Yiddish Texts on Display at University of Toronto," *Canadian Jewish News*, 10 August 2017, 29.

62 "Discovering Yiddish: Welcome," https://www.discoveringyiddish.com.

63 For example, John Wyatt Greenlee's "Mapping Mandeville" project at Cornell University, http://historiacartarum.org/john-mandeville-and-the-hereford-map-2.

64 "Komets-alef: o!," Robarts Library, Canadian Language Museum, May-

September 2018, https://www.discoveringyiddish.com/the-yiddish-kheyder.

65 "The Yiddish Kheyder," Discovering Yiddish, www.discoveringyiddish .com/the-yiddish-kheyder.

66 The last European Yiddish-language feature film was *Undzere Kinder* (*Our Children*, Poland, 1948, dir, Natan Gross and Shaul Goskind). Starring the duo Shimon Dzigan and Israel Shumacher, with Jewish children who had survived the Holocaust, it was prevented by the Polish Communist Party from being screened in Poland. The last American film was *Catskill Honeymoon* (1950, directed by Joe Berne), which combined a series of musical variety acts into a film. On the classic Yiddish cinema, see Goldberg, *Laughter through Tears*; Goldman, *Visions, Images, and Dreams;* Hoberman, *Bridge of Light.*

67 Koos, "Films Without Borders," 8.

68 Grutman, "Refraction and Recognition."

69 See National Center for Jewish Film, "Yiddish Film Restored by NCJF," http://www.jewishfilm.org/Catalogue/yiddish.htm.

70 These include *Der Dibuk/The Dybbuk* (Michal Waszynski, 1937), *Tevye* (Maurice Schwartz, 1939), four dramas by renowned director Edgar G. Ulmer (*Grine Felder/Green Fields*, 1937, *Fishke der Krumer/The Light Ahead*, 1939, *Yankl der Shmid/The Singing Blacksmith*, 1938, and *Amerikaner Shadkhn/American Matchmaker*, 1940), and Molly Picon's musical comedies *Yidl mitn Fidl/Yiddle with His Fiddle* (Joseph Green, 1936) and *Mamele* (Joseph Green and Konrad Tom, 1938).

71 Three book-length studies appeared in the United States in the 1980s and early 1990s: Goldberg, *Laughter through Tears: The Yiddish Cinema*, Goldman, *Visions, Images, and Dreams: Yiddish Film, Past and Present*, and Hoberman, *Bridge of Light: Yiddish Film between Two Worlds*. See also, Paskin, *When Joseph Met Molly: A Reader on Yiddish Film,* and Joseph Cohen, "Yiddish Film and the American Immigrant Experience."

72 Carol O'Sullivan uses these terms to refer to the use of foreign languages in general in the early Hollywood era in *Translating Popular Film*, 93–9.

73 Margolis, "New Yiddish Film and the Transvernacular," 3.

74 Weiss, "Trailblazing Yiddish Action Flick."

75 O'Sullivan, *Translating Popular Film*, 118–23.

76 Abend-David, "The 'Non-Translation,'" and "Louis Zukofsky and The West Wing." See also Shohat and Stam, "The Cinema after Babel."

77 Shira Hanau, "Seth Rogan Talks about Jewish Humor, Learning Yiddish

and His Most Jewish Role Yet," *New York Jewish Week*, 26 November 2019, https://jewishweek.timesofisrael.com/seth-rogen-talks-about-jewish-humor-learning-yiddish-his-most-jewish-role-yet.

78 Béhar, "Cultural Ventriloquism," 80.

79 See, for example, Sinha, "The Use and Abuse of Subtitles," 172.

80 O'Sullivan, *Translating Popular Film*, 104, 112–15. See also Shohat and Stam, "The Cinema after Babel."

81 For example, Mel Gibson's *Passion of the Christ* (2004), which features subtitled Latin, Aramaic, and Hebrew dialogue in a graphic depiction of the last hours of Jesus, represents one of a very few blockbuster subtitled films. O'Sullivan, *Translating Popular Film*, 126.

82 Leach, *Film in Canada*, 94.

83 *Atanajuat*, http://www.isuma.tv/atanarjuat.

84 Gauthier, "Speaking Back with Similar Voices," 111–12.

85 Siebert, *Indians Playing Indian*, 69.

86 For example, Miriam Bale, "Finding Love in a Cruel Time: 'The Pin,' a Romance Set in World War II," *New York Times*, 24 October 2013, http://www.nytimes.com/2013/10/25/movies/the-pin-a-romance-set-in-world-war-ii.html.

87 Justin Skinner, "Filmmaker Naomi Jaye to Debut First Yiddish-Language Feature Ever Filmed in Canada," *Inside Toronto*, 26 April 2014, http://www.insidetoronto.com/news-story/4484971-filmmaker-naomi-jaye-to-debut-first-yiddish-language-feature-ever-filmed-in-canada.

88 Miriam Rinn, "The Pin," *New Jersey Jewish Standard*, 25 October 2013, http://jstandard.com/content/item/the_pin/28850.

89 Ibid.

90 "The Pin – Naomi Jaye," question and answer streamed live on 11 January 2014, https://www.youtube.com/watch?v=4t7YouuqJaU.

91 Renee Ghert-Zand, "First Canadian Drama in Yiddish Debuts in NY," *Times of Israel*, 22 October 2013, http://www.timesofisrael.com/first-canadian-narrative-drama-in-yiddish-debuts-in-ny.

92 Ibid.

93 Ibid.

94 Jordan Kutzik, "How to Make a New Yiddish Film," *Forward*, 31 October 2013, https://forward.com/culture/film-tv/186546/how-to-make-a-new-yiddish-film.

95 Gloria Brumer, email to the author, 13 November 2016.

96 O'Sullivan, *Translating Popular Film*, 217.

97 Rauch, "Understanding the Holocaust through Film," 155.

98 For example, Frodon, *Cinema and the Shoah*, Hedges, *World Cinema and*

Cultural Memory, Grainge, *Memory and Popular Film*, and Kerner, *Film and the Holocaust*.

99 YidLife Crisis, IMDb online database, https://www.imdb.com/title/tt4035864.

100 "Eli Batalion and Jamie Elman Sit Down with i24news in Tel Aviv," i24 News, 29 December 2014, https://www.youtube.com/watch?v=KMziPLXt5Dw.

101 ("Jewish humour sounds much better in Yiddish.") Émilie Dubreuil, "YidLife Crisis: Fascinantes capsules web," *Radio Canada*, 3 October 2014, http://ici.radio-canada.ca/emissions/medium_large/2011-2012/chronique.asp?idChronique=351070.

102 Renee Ghert-Zand, "Jews on the Verge of a 'YidLife Crisis,'" *Times of Israel*, 16 September 2014, http://www.timesofisrael.com/jews-on-the-verge-a-YidLife-crisis.

103 Brigit Katz, "Spotlight On: Eli Batalion and Jamie Elman of 'YidLife Crisis,'" *Jewcy*, 27 October 2014, http://jewcy.com/jewish-arts-and-culture/spotlight-on-eli-batalion-jamie-elman-YidLife-crisis-montreal.

104 See, for example, Rosten, *The Joys of Yiddish*, and Wex, *Born to Kvetch*.

105 Brym, Neuman, Lenton, "2018 Survey of Jews in Canada," 6.

106 Weinreich, "Notes on the Yiddish Rise-Fall Intonation." See also Jacobs, *Yiddish: A Linguistic Introduction*, 153, Newman, "The Jewish Sound of Speech," and Burdin, "New Notes on the Rise-Fall Contour."

107 See Stratton, "Seinfeld is a Jewish Sitcom, Isn't It?"

108 "Sex, Sandwiches and Talmud," TLV1, 11 April 2015, http://tlv1.fm/weekend-edition/2015/04/11/sex-sandwiches-and-talmud.

109 O'Sullivan, *Translating Popular Film*, 121.

110 "The Big Falafel with Molly Livingstone," *Voice of Israel*, 2 April 2015, https://www.youtube.com/watch?v=qr9iv2lTGGo.

111 For example, "YidLife Crisis Launches Edmonton United Jewish Appeal with Irreverent Humour," *Edmonton Jewish News*, 22 September 2015, http://www.edmontonjewishnews.com/yid-life-crisis-launches-edmonton-united-jewish-appeal-campaign-with-irreverent-humour. The duo has performed in synagogues, community centres, and theatres across Canada, the United States, and Australia.

112 Kustanowitz, "Talking Tachlis with 'YidLife Crisis.'"

113 Ghert-Zand, "Jews on the Verge of a 'YidLife Crisis.'"

114 *Federation* CJA, "YidLife Crisis: Can Yiddish Comedy Be the New Rapprochement?" and "YidLife Crisis on CJAD News Talk Radio," CJAD 800 AM, 23 December 2014, https://www.youtube.com/watch?v=RQks94zfUv4.

115 "Montréalité," MA/tv, 9 December 2014, http://matv.ca/montreal/mes-emissions/montrealite/videos/3930928517001.

116 SNL *Québec* was a version of the sketch comedy series *Saturday Night Live* that aired on the Télé-Québec public television network in 2014–15.

117 "What's Nu?" *YidLife Crisis*, https://www.yidlifecrisis.com/whatsnu; Jamie Elman and Eli Batalion, "YidLife Crisis Does … Antisemitism?" *Canadian Jewish News*, 19 September 2019, https://www.cjnews.com/perspectives/features/yidlife-crisis-does-anti-semitism.

118 Gold, "Yiddish Words in Canadian English: Spread and Change," 216.

119 Rivka Augenfeld, telephone conversation with the author, 15 November 2015.

120 Ibid.

121 Quebec's national holiday, 24 June, is the feast day of St John the Baptist.

122 Rivka Augenfeld, telephone conversation with the author, 15 November 2015.

123 Ibid.

124 Jordan Kutzik, "Nayer episod fun 'yidlife crisis' mit mayim bialik," *Forverts*, 9 February 2016, http://yiddish.forward.com/articles/194603/new-episode-of-yidlife-crisis-stars-mayim-bialik.

125 Judie Jacobson, "Q&A with Mayim Bialik: An Observant Jew in Hollywood," *Jerusalem Post*, 18 August 2012. http://www.jpost.com/Arts-and-Culture/Entertainment/Q-and-A-with-Mayim-Bialik-An-observant-Jew-in-Hollywood.

126 Eli Batalion and Jamie Elman, email to the author, 9 November 2015.

127 Ibid.

128 For a selection of National Film Board animated shorts, see the NFB's animation channel at https://www.nfb.ca/channels/Animation/

129 Sharon Katz, *Der Fus Tort*, http://www.sharonkatz.net/animated_films.

130 "Der Fus Tort (2005)," IMDb, http://www.imdb.com/title/tt1486633.

131 Sharon Katz, *Der Fus Tort*.

132 Sharon Katz, email to the author, 11 December 2019.

133 Ibid.

134 Ibid.

135 Ibid.

136 Dean Gold, *Shehita*, http://www.dean-gold.com/portfolio#shehita.

137 Dean Gold, interview.

138 "Shehita: A Yiddish Horror Story–Film–Union & Non-Union May

Apply," eBOSS Canada, 29 November 2016. The posting was taken down from the site after the positions were filled.

139 Hindy Nosek Abelson, telephone conversations with the author, 11 and 13 December 2019.

140 Sharon Katz, *Der Fus Tort*, http://www.sharonkatz.net/fustort/index.html; YidLife Crisis, www.YidLifeCrisis.com.

141 Yiddish Cinematheque, https://www.facebook.com/YiddishCinema.

142 The 2022 collection includes Stavans's 2019 animated Yiddish short, *Dos Shvaygn fun profesor tosla/The Silence of Professor Tosla*, as well as Sharon Katz's 2001 short, *Der Fus Tort/Angel's Foot Cake*.

143 Aboriginal People's Television Network, http://aptn.ca.

144 "About Urban Native Girl," APTN, https://aptn.ca/urbannativegirl.

145 "About Qanurli," APTN, https://aptn.ca/qanurli.

146 APTN Kids, https://aptn.ca/kids.

147 "Welcome to Anaana's Tent," http://www.louissaystv.com; and Louis Says, http://www.louissaystv.com.

148 Beth Brown, "Nunavut Television Network Launches Inuit-language Channel," *CBC News*, 15 January 2021, https://www.cbc.ca/news /canada/north/nunavut-television-network-launches-inuit-language-channel-1.5875534.

149 IsumaTV, https://www.mqup.ca/isuma-products-9780773533783.php.

150 "The Fast Runner: Download Pay-What-You-Can," http://www.isuma .tv/fast-runner-trilogy-pay-what-you-can-vod-download-starting-december-1st.

151 For example, Gambier et al., *Subtitles and Language Learning*.

AFTERWORD

1 Zuckermann, *Revivalistics*, 202–3.

Bibliography

This Bibliography contains only those Yiddish works referenced in the book.
A complete list of Yiddish books published by Canadian resident authors is found
in the appendix.

ORAL HISTORY RECORDINGS

Augenfeld, Rivka. Interview by Rebecca Margolis, Montreal, Canada, 9 July 2017.

Berman, Ana Kuper. Interview by Christa Whitney. The Yiddish Book Center's Wexler Oral History Project, Toronto, Canada, 11 May 2016. https://archive.org/details/AnaKuperBerman11May2016YiddishBookCenter.

Borts, Joanne. Interview by Christa Whitney. The Yiddish Book Center's Wexler Oral History Project, KlezKanada, Quebec, Canada, 21 August 2014. https://www.yiddishbookcenter.org/collections/oral-histories/interviews/woh-fi-0000606/joanne-borts-2014.

Botwinik, David. Interview by Jordan Kutzik. The Yiddish Book Center's Wexler Oral History Project, KlezKanada, 13 December 2011. Video recording. https://www.yiddishbookcenter.org/collections/oral-histories/interviews/woh-fi-0000215/david-botwinik-2011.

Botwinik family (Yankl, Bina Ester, Leybl, Nathaniel). Interview by Rebecca Margolis, Ottawa, Canada, 30 October 2016.

Cooper, Adrienne. Interview by Pauline Katz. The Yiddish Book Center's Wexler Oral History Project, KlezKamp 2010, 28 December 2010. Video recording. http://archive.org/details/AdrienneCooper28dec2010YiddishBookCenter_821.

Dolman, Moishe. Interview by Christa Whitney. The Yiddish Book Center's Wexler Oral History Project, Montreal, Canada, 12 July 2020. Video recording.

Gold, Dean. Interview by Rebecca Margolis, Skype, 26 September 2019.

Gonshor, Anna. Interview by Sara Israel. The Yiddish Book Center's Wexler Oral History Project, Montreal, Canada, 13 December 2011. Video recording. http://archive.org/details/AnnaGonshor13dec2011Yiddish BookCenter.

Gonshor, Aron. Interview by Sara Israel. The Yiddish Book Center's Wexler Oral History Project, Montreal, Canada, 15 December 2011. Video recording. http://archive.org/details/AronGonshor15dec2011Yiddish BookCenter.

Hever-Chybowski, Tal. Interview by Allie Brudney. The Yiddish Book Center's Wexler Oral History Project, Berlin, Germany, 8 February 2014. http://archive.org/details/TalHeverChybowski8Feb2014YiddishBook Center.

Hubner, Malca Sussman. Interview by Christa Whitney. The Yiddish Book Center's Wexler Oral History Project, Montreal, Canada, 15 December 2011. Video recording. http://archive.org/details/MalcaSussmanHubner 15december2011YiddishBookCenter.

Kuper, Edit. Interview by Rebecca Margolis, Montreal, 14 May 2018.

Mayne, Seymour. Interview by Rebecca Margolis, Ottawa, Canada, 2 December 2019.

Moore, Avia. Interview by Christa Whitney. The Yiddish Book Center's Wexler Oral History Project, Montreal, Canada, 14 December 2011. Video recording. http://archive.org/details/AviaMoore14dec2011Yiddish BookCenter.

Orenstein, Eugene. Interview by Pauline Katz. The Yiddish Book Center's Wexler Oral History Project, KlezKanada, 16 August 2011. Video recording. http://archive.org/details/EugeneOrenstein26august2011Yiddish BookCenter.

Raby, Eva. Interview by Christa Whitney. The Yiddish Book Center's Wexler Oral History Project, Montreal, Canada, 10 July 2012. Video recording. https://archive.org/details/EvaRaby10july2012YiddishBookCenter_546.

Rosenfeld, Moishe. Interview by Hankus Netsky. The Yiddish Book Center's Wexler Oral History Project, New York City, USA, 13 June 2012. Video recording. https://archive.org/details/MoisheRosenfeld13june2012 YiddishBookCenter.

Roskies, David. Interview by Jayne Guberman. Jewish Counterculture History Project, Oral Histories 32, 12 December 2016. https://repository .upenn.edu/jcchp_oralhistories/32.

– Interview by Christa Whitney. The Yiddish Book Center's Wexler Oral History Project, New York City, USA, 28 January 2019. Video recording. https://archive.org/details/DavidRoskies28Jan2019YiddishBookCenter.

Rubinek, Saul. Interview by Christa Whitney. The Yiddish Book Center's Wexler Oral History Project, Hollywood, California, USA, 29 November 2017. Video recording. https://archive.org/details/SaulRubinek29 Nov2017YiddishBookCenter.

Schaechter, Rukhl (Sore-Rukhl). Interview by Christa Whitney. The Yiddish Book Center's Wexler Oral History Project, Yidish-Vokh, Reisterstown, Maryland, USA, 14 August 2014. Video recording. https://archive.org /details/RukhlSoreRukhlSchaechter14Aug2014YiddishBookCenter.

Sculnik, Nancy. Interview by Rebecca Margolis, Amherst, Massachusetts, USA, 11 November 2019.

Wasserman, Bryna. Interview by Christa Whitney. The Yiddish Book Center's Wexler Oral History Project, Museum of the City of New York, New York City, USA, 8 April 2016. https://archive.org/details/Bryna Wasserman8Apr2016YiddishBookCenter.

Wolofsky, Jack. Interview by Christa Whitney. The Yiddish Book Center's Wexler Oral History Project, KlezKanada, 22 August 2013. Video recording. https://archive.org/details/JackWolofsky22aug2013YiddishBook Center.

Zucker, Sheva. Interview by Christa Whitney. The Yiddish Book Center's Wexler Oral History Project, Reisterstown, Maryland, USA, 17 August 2013. Video recording. https://archive.org/details/ShevaZucker17 aug2013YiddishBookCenter.

FILMS AND TELEVISION

An American Pickle. Directed by Brandon Trost. USA: Warner Max and Point Grey Pictures, 2020. 89 minutes.

Bet Avi/Homeland. Directed by Dani Rosenberg. Israel: Sam Spiegel Film and Television School, 2008. 40 minutes.

The Cobbler. Directed by Tom McCarthy. USA: Image Entertainment, 2014. Prologue. 10 minutes.

Demon. Directed by Marcin Wrona. Poland: The Orchard, 2016. 94 minutes.

Félix et Meira. Directed by Maxime Giroux. Canada: Funfilm, 2014. 105 minutes.

Der Fus Tort/Angel's Foot Cake. Directed by Sharon Katz. Canada: Vimeo, 2016 [2001, 2005]. https://vimeo.com/140581156. 6 minutes.

A Gesheft/The Deal. Directed by Yakov Kirsh. USA: Kosher Entertainment Productions, 2005. 90 minutes.

Hester Street. Directed by Joan Micklin Silver. USA: Midwest Films, 1975. 89 minutes.

Kurtse Animirte Films af Yidish/Animated Yiddish Shorts. Produced by Ilan Stavans and edited by Yoni Salmon. USA: Quixote Productions, 2022. 51 minutes.

Menashe. Directed by Joshua Z Weinstein. USA: A24, 2017. 81 minutes.

Mendy: A Question of Faith. Directed by Adam Vardy. USA: Vanguard Cinema, 2003. DVD. 90 minutes.

Romeo and Juliet in Yiddish. Directed by Eve Annenberg. USA: Nancy Fishman Film Releasing, 2010. DVD. 90 minutes.

A Serious Man. Directed by Ethan and Joel Coen. USA: Feature Films, 2009. Prologue. 8 minutes.

Shtisel. Entire series. Created by Ori Elon and Yehonatan Indursky. Israel: 2013–21.

Son of Saul. Directed by László Nemes. Hungary: Mozinet, 2015. 107 minutes.

Di Shpilke/The Pin. Directed by Naomi Jaye. Canada: Search Engine Films, 2014. 85 minutes.

Unorthodox. Entire series. Directed by Maria Schrader. USA/Germany: Netflix, 2020.

The Vigil. Directed by Keith Thomas. USA: Blumhouse Productions, 2019. 98 minutes.

YidLife Crisis. Entire web series. Directed by Eli Batalion and Jamie Elman. Canada: 2014–19. www.yidlifecrisis.com.

BOOKS AND ARTICLES

Abella, Irving, and Frank Bialystok. "Canada." In *The World Reacts to the Holocaust*, edited by David S. Wyman, 749–81. Baltimore, MD: Johns Hopkins University Press, 1996.

Abella, Irving, and Harold Troper. *None Is Too Many: Canada and the Jews of Europe, 1933–1948*. Toronto: Lester and Orpen Dennys, 1982.

Abend-David, Dror. "Louis Zukofsky and the West Wing: Metaphors of Mentorship, Yiddish, and Translation at Street Level." *FORUM* 8, no. 1 (2010): 1–35.

– "The 'Non-Translation': Editor's Introductory Note," "Yiddish, Media and the Dramatic Function of Translation – or What Does It Take to Read Joel and Ethan Coen's film *A Serious Man*?" In *Representing Translation: The Representation of Translation and Translators in Contemporary Media*, edited by Dror Abend-David, 199–234. New York and London: Bloomsbury Academic, 2019.

Abley, Mark. *Spoken Here: Travels among Threatened Languages*. Toronto: Vintage Canada, 2004.

Abrams, Nathan. "Film, Television and New Media Studies." In *Routledge*

Handbook of Contemporary Jewish Studies, edited by Laurence Roth and Nadia Valman, 108–20. New York: Routledge, 2017.

Adelman, Howard, and John H. Simpson, eds. *Multiculturalism, Jews and Identities in Canada*. Jerusalem: Magnus Press, 1996.

Anctil, Pierre. "1992: Translating Montreal's Yiddish Poet Jacob Isaac Segal into French." Translated by Deborah Shadd. In *Translation Effects: The Shaping of Modern Canadian Culture*, edited by Kathy Mezei, Sherry Simon, and Luise von Flotow, 239–51. Kingston and Montreal: McGill-Queen's University Press, 2014.

– "À la découverte de la literature yiddish montréalaise." In *Traduire le Montreal Yiddish/New Readings of Yiddish Montreal*, edited by Pierre Anctil, Norman Ravvin, and Sherry Simon, 19–30. Ottawa, ON: University of Ottawa Press, 2007.

– *Jacob Isaac Segal (1896–1954): A Montreal Yiddish Poet and His Milieu*. Translated by Vivian Felson. Ottawa, ON: University of Ottawa Press, 2017.

– *Jacob-Isaac Segal (1896–1954): Un poète yiddish de Montréal et son milieu*. Quebec, QC: Presses de l'Université Laval, 2012.

– *Tur Malka: Flâneries sur les cimes de l'histoire juive montréalaise*. Sillery, QC: Éditions du Septentrion, 1997.

Anctil, Pierre, Norman Ravvin, and Sherry Simon, eds. *Traduire le Montreal Yiddish/New Readings of Yiddish Montreal*. Ottawa, ON: University of Ottawa Press, 2007.

Anklewicz, Mike. "Extending the Tradition: KlezKanada, Klezmer Tradition and Hybridity." *MUSICultures* 39, no. 2 (2012): 83–102.

Ariel, Yaakov. "Walking Together, Walking Apart: Conservative Judaism and Neo-Hasidism." *Jewish Culture and History* 21, no. 2 (2020): 172–87.

Assouline, Dalit. "English Can Be Jewish but Hebrew Cannot: Code-Switching Patterns among Yiddish-Speaking Hasidic Women." *Journal of Jewish Languages* 6 (2018): 43–59.

– "Linguistic Outcomes of a Hasidic Renewal: The Case of Skver." *Language and Communication* 42 (2015): 141–6.

Astmann, Dana. "Freylekhe Felker: Queer Subculture in the Klezmer Revival." *Discourses in Music* 4, no. 3 (2003). http://library.music.utoronto.ca/discourses-in-music/v4n3a2.html.

Avineri, Netta. "Yiddish Endangerment as Phenomenological Reality and Discursive Strategy: Crossing into the Past and Crossing Out the Present." *Language and Communication* 38 (2014): 18–32.

Baker, Susan. "A Social Psychological Approach to Preserving Heritage Languages: The Survival of Gaelic in Nova Scotia." PhD diss., University of Ottawa, 2005.

Baker, Zackary M. "Montreal of Yesterday: A Snapshot of Jewish Life in Montreal During the Era of Mass Immigration." In *An Everyday Miracle: Yiddish Culture in Montreal*, edited by Ira Robinson, Pierre Anctil, and Mervin Butovsky, 39–52. Montreal: Véhicule Press.

Balan, Jars, ed. *Identifications: Ethnicity and the Writer in Canada*. Edmonton: Canadian Institute of Ukrainian Studies, University of Alberta, 1982.

Ball, John Clement. "Shouldering the Burdens of History: The Parrot as Postcolonial Satirist in Gary Barwin's 'Yiddish for Pirates.'" *Journal of Jewish Identities* 13, no. 1 (2020): 1–16.

Bar-Am, Gali Drucker. "'Our Shtetl, Tel Aviv, Must and Will Become the Metropolis of Yiddish': Tel Aviv – a Center of Yiddish Culture?" *AJS Review* 41, no. 1 (2017): 111–32.

Baron, Lawrence. "The Holocaust and American Public Memory, 1945–1960." *Holocaust and Genocide Studies* 17, no. 1 (2003): 62–88.

Barwin, Gary. *Yiddish for Pirates*. Toronto: Random House Canada, 2016.

Béhar, Henri. "Cultural Ventriloquism." In *Subtitles: On the Foreignness of Film*, edited by Atom Egoyan and Ian Balfour, 79-86. Cambridge, MA: Alphabet City Media, 2004.

Beider, Alexander. "Yiddish in Eastern Europe." In *Languages in Jewish Communities, Past and Present*, edited by Benjamin Hary and Sarah Bunin Benor, 276–312. Boston, MA: De Gruyter, 2018.

Beinfeld, Solon, and Harry Bochner, eds. *Comprehensive Yiddish-English Dictionary*. Bloomington: Indiana University Press, 2013.

Beissel, Henry, and Joy Bennett. *Raging Like a Fire: A Celebration of Irving Layton*. Montreal: Véhicule Press, 1993.

Belkin, Simon. *Di poyle tsien bavegung in kanade: 1904–1920*. Montreal: Aktsyons komitet fun der tsiyonistisher arbeter bavegung in kanade, 1956.

– *Di poyle-tsien bavegung in kanade, 1904–1920/Le Mouvement ouvrier juif au Canada, 1904–1920*. Translated by Pierre Anctil. Sillery, QC: Éditions du Septentrion, 1999.

Bemporad, Elissa, and Margherita Pascucci, eds. *Trot bay trot: Haynttsaytike yidishe poezye/Step by Step: Contemporary Yiddish Poetry*. Florence and Macerata, IT: Verbarum/Quodlibet, 2009.

Benor, Sara. *Becoming Frum: How Newcomers Learn the Language and Culture of Orthodox Judaism*. New Brunswick, NJ: Rutgers University Press, 2012.

Berger, Zackary Sholem. *Eyn folk aroysgenumen fun tsveytn/One Nation Taken Out of Another*. Baltimore: Apprentice House, Loyola University of Maryland, 2014.

Bergner, Hinde. *In di lange vinternekht: Mishpokhe-zikhroynes fun a shtetl in galitsiye, 1870–1900*. Montreal: Moyshe Harari, Melech Ravitch, and Herts Bergner, 1946.

– *On Long Winter Nights: Memoirs of a Jewish Family in a Galician Township*. Translated by Justin Cammy. Cambridge, MA: Harvard University Press, 2005.

Betcherman, Lita-Rose. *The Swastika and the Maple Leaf: Fascist Movements in Canada in the Thirties*. Toronto: Fitzhenry & Whiteside, 1975.

Biale, David, et al. *Hasidism: A New History*. Princeton, NJ: Princeton University Press, 2018.

Bialystok, Franklin. *Delayed Impact: The Holocaust and the Canadian Jewish Community*. Kingston and Montreal: McGill-Queen's University Press, 2000.

– "'Greener' and 'Gayle': Relations between Holocaust Survivors and Canadian Jews." In *Remembering for the Future: The Holocaust in an Age of Genocide*, vol. 3, edited by John K. Roth and Elisabeth Maxwell, 32–46. Basingstoke, UK: Palgrave Macmillan, 2001.

Bleaman, Isaac L. "Der *veker*: A yoytse-min-haklal in der khsidish-yidisher peryodik." *Afn shvel* 382–3 (2019): 20–5, 62.

– "Uriel Weinreich: Contact Linguist, Historical Linguist, and Yiddishist Par Excellence." *Journal of Jewish Languages* 5, no. 2 (2017): 131–43.

Blitz, Avi. "Translated and Improved: Yiddish Pop Culture in Israel." *In geveb*, 26 November 2018. https://ingeveb.org/blog/translated-and-improved-yiddish-pop-culture-in-israel.

Botwinik, David. *Fun khurbn tsum lebn: Naye yidishe lider*. New York: League for Yiddish, 2010.

Botwinik, Jack. *Chicken Soup with Chopsticks: A Jew's Struggle for Truth in an Interfaith Relationship*. Ottawa, ON: Paper Spider, 2005.

Botwinik, Leybl. *Di geheyme shlikhes: Fantastishe dertseylung*. Montreal: D. Botwinik, 1980.

Boyarin, Jonathan. *Thinking in Jewish*. Chicago, IL: University of Chicago Press, 1996.

Brenner, Rachel Feldhay. "A.M. Klein and Mordecai Richler: Canadian Responses to the Holocaust." *Journal of Canadian Studies* 24, no. 2 (1989): 65–77.

Brossat, Alain, Sylvia Klingberg, and David Fernbach. *Revolutionary Yiddishland: A History of Jewish Radicalism*. Translated by David Fernbach. London, UK: Verso, 2017.

Brym, Robert, and Rhonda Lenton. "Young, Canadian and Jewish: The Shift from Religious to Cultural Identity." *The Conversation*. 29 March 2019. https://theconversation.com/young-canadian-and-jewish-the-shift-from-religious-to-cultural-identity-113326.

Brym, Robert, Keith Neuman, and Rhonda Lenton. *2018 Survey of Jews in Canada: Final Report*. Toronto: Environics Institute for Survey Research, 2018. https://www.environicsinstitute.org/docs/default-source/project-documents/2018-survey-of-jews-in-canada/2018-survey-of-jews-in-canada-—final-report.pdf.

Burdin, Rachel Steindel. "New Notes on the Rise-Fall Contour." *Journal of Jewish Languages* 5, no. 2 (2017): 145–73.

Campbell, Heidi, ed. *Digital Judaism: Jewish Negotiations with Digital Media and Culture*. London: Taylor and Francis Group, 2015.

Caneva, Elena, and Sonia Pozzi. "The Transmission of Language and Religion in Immigrant Families: A Comparison between Mothers and Children." *International Review of Sociology* 24, no. 3 (2014): 436–49.

Caplan, Debra. "Notes from the Frontier: Digital Scholarship and the Future of Theatre Studies." *Theatre Journal* 67, no. 2 (2015): 347–59.

Caplan, Usher. *Like One That Dreamed: A Portrait of A.M. Klein*. Toronto: McGraw-Hill Ryerson, 1982.

Chaver, Yael. *What Must Be Forgotten: The Survival of Yiddish in Zionist Palestine*. Syracuse, NY: Syracuse University Press, 2004.

Chernin, Velvl, and Michoel Felsenbaum, eds. *A ring/antologye: Yidishe poezye. Der nokhn-khurbn-dor*. Tel Aviv: Bibliotek fun der haynttsaytiker yidisher literature, 2017.

Chinski, Malena, and Lucas Fiszman. "'*A biblyotek vos felt*' [A library that is lacking]: Planning and Creating the Book Collection *Musterverk fun der yidisher literatur* (Buenos Aires, 1957–1984)." *Journal of Jewish Identities* 10, no. 1 (2017): 135–53.

Clyne, Michael G. *Community Languages: The Australian Experience*. Cambridge and Melbourne: Cambridge University Press, 1991.

Cohen, Joseph. "Yiddish Film and the American Immigrant Experience." *Film and History* 28, nos. 1–2 (1998): 30–44.

Cohen, Nathan. "The Jews of Independent Poland: Linguistic and Cultural Changes." In *Starting the Twenty-First Century: Sociological Reflections and Challenges*, edited by Ernest Krausz and Gitta Tulea, 161–75. New Brunswick, NJ: Transaction Publishers, 2002.

– "The Yiddish Press and Yiddish Literature: A Fertile but Complex Relationship." *Modern Judaism* 28, no. 2 (2008): 149–72.

Cohen, Yolande. "The Migrations of Moroccan Jews to Montreal: Memory, (Oral) History and Historical Narrative." *Journal of Modern Jewish Studies* 10, no. 2 (2011): 245–62.

Comartin, Justin. "Opening Closed Doors: Revisiting the Canadian Immigration Record (1933–1945)." *Canadian Jewish Studies* 24 (2016): 79–102.

Conn, Stephanie. "Fitting between Present and Past: Memory and Social Interaction in Cape Breton Gaelic Singing." *Ethnomusicology Forum* 21, no. 3 (2012): 354–73.

Costa, James. "New Speakers, New Language: On Being a Legitimate Speaker of a Minority Language in Provence." *International Journal of the Sociology of Language* 2015, no. 231 (2015): 127–45.

Crasnow, S.J. "'I Want to Look Transgender': Anti-Assimilation, Gender Self-Determination, and Confronting White Supremacy in the Creation of a Just Judaism." *Journal of the American Academy of Religion* 88, no. 4 (2020): 1026–48.

Dabback, William. "A Community of Singing: Motivation, Identity, and *Communitas* in a Mennonite School Choir Programme." *Music Education Research* 20, no. 2 (2015): 242–51.

Davids, Leo. "Hebrew and Yiddish in Canada: A Linguistic Transition Completed." *Journal of Canadian Jewish Studies* 18–19 (2011): 39–76.

Dembling, Jonathan. "Instrumental Music and Gaelic Revitalization in Scotland and Nova Scotia." *International Journal of the Sociology of Language* 206 (2010): 245–54.

– "Joe Jimmy Alec Visits the Gaelic Mod and Escapes Unscathed: The Nova Scotia Gaelic Revivals." PhD diss., St Mary's University, 1997.

Desmoulins, Leisa, Melissa Oskineegish, and Kelsey Jaggard. "Imagining University/Community Collaborations as Third Spaces to Support Indigenous Language Revitalization." *Language & Literacy* 21, no. 4 (2019): 45–67.

Deutsch, Nathaniel. "The Forbidden Fork, the Cell Phone Holocaust, and Other Haredi Encounters with Technology." *Contemporary Jewry* 29, no. 3 (2009): 3–19.

Diner, Hasia. *We Remember with Reverence and Love: American Jews and the Myth of Silence after the Holocaust, 1945–1962.* New York: New York University Press, 2009.

Dinshaw, Carolyn, Lee Edelman, Roderick A. Ferguson, et.al. "Theorizing Queer Temporalities." *GLQ: A Journal of Lesbian and Gay Studies* 13, nos. 2–3 (2007): 177–95.

Draper, Paula. "Canadian Holocaust Survivors: From Liberation to Rebirth." *Canadian Jewish Studies* 4–5 (1996–97): 39–62.

Dudgeon, Pat, and Fielder, John. "Third Spaces within Tertiary Places: Indigenous Australian Studies." *Journal of Community & Applied Social Psychology* 16, no. 5 (2006): 396–409.

Dunbar, Robert. "The Gaelic Language (Scotland) Act 2005." *The Edinburgh Law Review* 9, no. 3 (2005): 466–79.

Dunmore, Stuart S. "Emic and Essentialist Perspectives on Gaelic Heritage:

New Speakers, Language Policy, and Cultural Identity in Nova Scotia and Scotland." *Language in Society* 50, no. 2 (2021): 259–81.

– "Language Policy and Prospects: Metalinguistic Discourses on Social Disruption and Language Maintenance in a Transatlantic, Minority Community." *Language & Communication* 76 (2021): 69–78.

– "Transatlantic Context for Gaelic Language Revitalisation." *Studia Celtica Posnaniensia* 5, no. 1 (2020): 1–20.

Dunsky, Shimshen. *Midrash Rabbah. Ester, Rus: Targum yidish*. Montreal: S. dunsky medresh fond komitet, 1962.

– *Midrash Rabbah. Eykhah: Mit yidisher iberzetsung, derklerungen un araynfir*. Montreal: S. dunsky medresh fond komitet, 1956.

– *Midrash Rabbah. Koheles: Targum yidish*. Montreal: S. dunsky medresh fond komitet, 1967.

– *Midrash Rabbah. Shir ha-shirim: Targum yidish*. Montreal: S. dunsky medresh fond komitet, 1973.

Edelman, Lee. *No Future: Queer Theory and the Death Drive*. Durham, NC: Duke University Press, 2004.

Elbaz, Mikhaël. "Les héritiers. Générations et identités chez les Juifs sépharades à Montréal." *Revue européenne des migrations internationales* 9, no. 3 (1993): 13–34.

Elberg, Yehuda. *Afn shpits fun a mast: Roman*. New York: Brider shulzinger, 1974.

– *L'empire de kalman l'infirme*. Translated by Pierre Anctil. Montreal: Leméac, 2001.

– *Kalmen kalikes imperye: Roman*. Tel Aviv: Farlag yisroel-bukh, 1983.

– *Ship of the Hunted*. Translated with Barbara E. Galli. Syracuse, NY: Syracuse University Press, 1997.

– *Unter kuperne himlen: Dertseylungen*. Buenos Aires, AR: Tsentral-arband fun poylishe yidn in argentine, 1951.

Eriksson, Svetlana. "Societal, Community, Family, and Individual Factors Affecting Russian Language Maintenance in Migrant Families in Ireland." *Russian Journal of Communication* 7, no. 2 (2015): 150–63.

Estraikh, Gennady. "On the Acculturation of Jews in Late Imperial Russia." *La Rassegna Mensile di Israel*, nos. 1–2 (1996): 217–28.

Fader, Ayala. *Mitzvah Girls: Bringing Up the Next Generation of Hasidic Jews in Brooklyn*. Princeton, NJ: Princeton University Press, 2009.

Farr, Joanna, Laura Blenkiron, Richard Harris, and Jonathan A. Smith. "'It's My Language, My Culture, and It's Personal!' Migrant Mothers' Experience of Language Use and Identity Change in Their Relationship with

Their Children: An Interpretative Phenomenological Analysis." *Journal of Family Issues* 39, no. 11 (2018): 3029–54.

Felsen, Vivian. "Preserving Yiddish Culture in Canada: The Remarkable Legacy of Chaim Leib Fuks." In *Kanade, di goldene medine? Perspectives on Canadian Jewish Literature and Culture*, edited by Krzysztof Majer, Justyna Fruzińska, Józef Kwaterko, and Norman Ravvin, 9–22. Toronto: University of Toronto Press, 2018.

Feuerverger, Grace. "Jewish-Canadian Identity and Hebrew Language Learning: Belonging (or Not Belonging) in Montreal and Toronto." In *Nation-Building, Identity and Citizenship Education*, edited by Joseph Zajda, Holger Daun, and Lawrence J. Saha, 117–30. Netherlands: Springer, 2008.

Fishman Gonshor, Anna and William Shaffir. "Commitment to a Language: Teaching Yiddish in a Hasidic and Secular School." In *Yiddish After the Holocaust*, edited by Joseph Sherman, 149–78. Oxford: Boulevard Books, Oxford Centre for Hebrew and Judaic Studies, 2004.

Fishman, Joshua A. *Language Loyalty in the United States: The Maintenance and Perpetuation of Non-English Mother Tongues by American Ethnic and Religious Groups*. The Hague, NL: Mouton, 1966.

– "Language: Planning and Standardization of Yiddish." YIVO *Encyclopedia of Jews in Eastern Europe*. 2011. https://yivoencyclopedia.org/article.aspx /Language/Planning_and_Standardization_of_Yiddish.

Fishman, Joshua A., ed. *Never Say Die! A Thousand Years of Yiddish in Jewish Life and Letters*. The Hague, Paris, and New York: Mouton, 1981.

– *Reversing Language Shift: Theoretical and Empirical Foundations of Assistance to Threatened Languages*. Clevedon, UK: Multilingual Matters, 1991.

– *Yiddish: Turning to Life*. Amsterdam: John Benjamins Publishing, 1991.

Fogel, Joshua, and Keith Weiser, eds. *Czernowitz at 100: The First Yiddish Language Conference in Historical Perspective*. Lanham, MD: Rowman and Littlefield, 2010.

Forman, Frieda, ed. *The Exile Book of Yiddish Women Writers: An Anthology of Stories That Looks to the Past So We Might See the Future*. Toronto: Exile Editions, 2013.

Forman, Frieda, Margie Wolfe, and Sarah Silberstein Swartz, eds. *Found Treasures: Stories by Yiddish Women Writers*. Toronto: Second Story Press, 1997.

Fox, Chaim Leib. *See* Fuks.

Fox, Sandra F. "Laboratories of Yiddishkayt: Postwar American Jewish Summer Camps and the Transformation of Yiddishism." *American Jewish History* 103, no. 3 (2019): 279–301.

– "'The Passionate Few': Youth and Yiddishism in American Jewish Culture, 1964 to Present." *Jewish Social Studies* 26, no. 3 (2021): 1–34.

Frankel-Zaltzman, Paula. *Haftling numer 94771: Iberlebenishn in daytshe lagern.* Montreal: Aroysgegebn fun a komitet, 1949.

Franzus-Garfinkle, Sheyndl. *Erev oktober: Roman.* Montreal: Aroysgegbn mit der hilf fun dem dr. hayim zshitlovski leyen krayz, 1947.

Frieden, Ken. *Classic Yiddish Fiction.* Albany: State University of New York Press, 1995.

Freidenreich, Fradle. *Passionate Pioneers: The Story of Yiddish Secular Education in North America, 1910–1960.* Teaneck, NJ: Holmes and Meier Publishers, 2010.

Friedgut, Theodore H. "Jewish Pioneers on Canada's Prairies: The Lipton Jewish Agricultural Colony." *Jewish History* 21, nos. 3–4 (2007): 385–411.

Friedman, Joshua B. "Serious Jews: Cultural Intimacy and the Politics of Yiddish." *Cultural Dynamics* 32, no. 3 (2020): 151–69.

– "Yiddish Returns: Language, Intergenerational Gifts, and Jewish Devotion." PhD diss., University of Michigan, 2015.

Friedman, Joshua B., and Moshe Kornfeld. "Identity Projects: Philanthropy, Neoliberalism, and Jewish Cultural Production." *American Jewish History* 102, no. 4 (2018): 537–61.

Frodon, Jean-Michel, ed. *Cinema and the Shoah: An Art Confronts the Tragedy of the Twentieth Century.* Translated by Anna Harrison and Tom Mes. Albany, NY: SUNY Press, 2010.

Fruchter, Temim. "Embracing the Multiple: A Conversation with Zohar Weiman-Kelman." *In geveb*, 1 June 2016. https://ingeveb.org/blog/embracing-the-multiple-talking-with-zohar-weiman-kelman.

Fuchs, Chaim Leib. *See* Fuks.

Fuerstenberg, Adam G. "Faithful to the Dream: The Proletarian Tradition in Canadian Yiddish Poetry." *Yiddish* 6, no. 1 (1985): 84–96.

– "From Yiddish to 'Yiddishkeit': A.M. Klein, J.I. Segal and Montreal's Yiddish Culture." *Journal of Canadian Studies* 19 (1984): 66–81.

Fuks, Chaim Leib. *Cent ans de littérature yiddish et hébraïque au Canada.* Translated by Pierre Anctil. Sillery, QC: Éditions du Septentrion, 2005.

– *Hundert yor yidishe un hebreyishe literatur in kanade.* Montreal: Kh. l. fuks bukh-fun, 1980.

Gambier, Yves, et al. *Subtitles and Language Learning: Principles, Strategies and Practical Experiences.* Bern, CH: Peter Lang, 2015.

Gauthier, Jennifer L. "Speaking Back with Similar Voices: The Dialogic Cinema of Zacharias Kunuk and Pierre Perrault." *Quarterly Review of Film and Video* 27, no. 2 (2010): 108–20.

Gerber, Jean. "Opening the Door: Immigration and Integration of Holocaust Survivors in Vancouver, 1947–1970." *Canadian Jewish Studies* 4–5 (1996–97): 63–86.

Giberovitch, Myra. "The Contributions of Holocaust Survivors to Montreal Jewish Communal Life." *Canadian Ethnic Studies* 26, no. 1 (1994): 74–84.

Gilbert, Shirli. "'We Long for a Home': Songs and Survival among Jewish Displaced Persons." In *"We Are Here": New Approaches to Jewish Displaced Persons in Postwar Germany*, edited by Michael Berkowitz and Avinoam Patt, 289–307. Detroit, MI: Wayne State University Press, 2010.

Gilman, Sandor L. *Jewish Self-Hatred: Anti-Semitism and the Hidden Language of the Jews*. Baltimore, MD: The John Hopkins University Press, 1986.

Glaser, Amelia. "From Polylingual to Postvernacular: Imagining Yiddish in the Twenty-First Century." *Jewish Social Studies* 14, no. 3 (2008): 150–64.

– "The Idea of Yiddish; Re-globalizing North American Jewish Culture." In *The Routledge Handbook of Contemporary Jewish Cultures*, edited by Laurence Roth and Nadia Valman, 259–71. New York: Routledge, 2017.

Glinert, Lewis. *The Story of Hebrew*. Princeton, NJ: Princeton University Press, 2017.

Gold, Elaine. "Yiddish Words in Canadian English: Spread and Change." In *Yiddish After the Holocaust*, edited by Joseph Sherman, 209–21, Oxford: Boulevard Books, Oxford Centre for Hebrew and Judaic Studies, 2004.

Gold, Muriel. "A Study of Three Montreal Children's Theatres." MA thesis, McGill University, 1972.

Goldberg, Adara. *Holocaust Survivors in Canada: Exclusion, Inclusion, Transformation, 1947–1955*. Studies in Immigration and Culture 14. Winnipeg: University of Manitoba Press, 2015.

Goldberg, Judith. *Laughter through Tears: The Yiddish Cinema*. East Brunswick, NJ: Associated University Presses, 1983.

Goldman, Eric A. *Visions, Images, and Dreams: Yiddish Film, Past and Present*. Teaneck, NJ: Holmes and Meier, 2011.

Goldman, Jess. *Schmutz*. Montreal: Museum of Jewish Montreal, 2020.

Gotlib, N.J. *Montreol*. Montreal: N.Y. Gotlib bukh-komitet, 1968.

Grainge, Paul, ed. *Memory and Popular Film*. Manchester, UK: Manchester University Press, 2003.

Green, Noam, and Tova Benjamin. "Seeking and Queering Utopia: A Chat About the Steiner Summer Yiddish Program." *In geveb*, 24 November 2017. https://ingeveb.org/blog/seeking-utopia-a-chat-about-the-steiner-summer-yiddish-program-1.

Greenstein, Michael, ed. *Contemporary Jewish Writing in Canada: An Anthology*. Lincoln, NB: University of Nebraska Press, 2004.

– *Third Solitudes: Tradition and Discontinuity in Jewish-Canadian Literature.* Kingston and Montreal: McGill-Queen's University Press, 1989.

Greenstein, Michael, Pierre Anctil, and Eugene Orenstein. "Canadian Literature." *Encyclopedia Judaica*, 2nd ed., vol. 4, edited by Michael Berenbaum and Fred Skolnick, 423–8. Detroit, MI: Macmillan Reference USA, 2007.

Grossman, Vladimir, ed. *Bibliotek bukh/Our Library 1914–1957.* Montreal: Jewish Public Library, 1957.

Grutman, Rainier. "Beckett and Beyond: Putting Self-Translation in Perspective." *Orbis litterarum* 68, no. 3 (2013): 188–206.

– "Refraction and Recognition: Literary Multilingualism in Translation." *Target* 18, no. 1 (2006): 17–47.

Gutkin, Harry, and Mildred Gutkin. *The Worst of Times, the Best of Times.* Markham, ON: Fitzhenry & Whiteside, 1987.

Hadda, Janet. "Imagining Yiddish: A Future for the Soul of Ashkenaz." *Pakn-Treger* 41 (2003): 10–19.

– "Transmitting Ashkenaz." *Shofar: An Interdisciplinary Journal of Jewish Studies* 25, no. 1 (2006): 114–26.

Halberstam, Jack. *In a Queer Time and Place: Transgender Bodies, Subcultural Lives.* New York: New York University Press, 2005.

– *The Queer Art of Failure.* Durham, NC: Duke University Press, 2011.

Halpern, Liora R. *Babel in Zion: Jews, Nationalism and Language Diversity in Palestine, 1920-1948.* New Haven, CT: Yale University Press, 2014.

Harshav, Benjamin. *The Meaning of Yiddish.* Stanford, CA: Stanford University Press, 1999.

Hedges, Inez. *World Cinema and Cultural Memory.* London: Palgrave Macmillan, 2015.

Heikkilä, Riina, "The Language Situation in Sweden: The Relationship between the Main Language and the National Minority Languages," *Sens Public: Revue Web*, 4 October 2010, http://www.sens-public.org /article763.html.

Hellerstein, Kathryn. *A Question of Tradition: Women Poets in Yiddish, 1586–1987.* Stanford, CA: Stanford University Press, 2014.

Hirschprung, Pinchas. *Fun natsishen yomertol: Zikhroynes fun a polit.* Montreal: Keneder adler, 1944.

– *The Vale of Tears: Memoirs of a Refugee.* Translated by Vivian Felsen. Toronto: Azrieli Foundation, 2017.

Hobart, Charles W. "Adjustment of Ukrainians in Alberta: Alienation and Integration." *Slavs in Canada* 1 (1966): 69–85.

Hoberman, Jay. *Bridge of Light: Yiddish Film between Two Worlds.* Lebanon, NH: University Press of New England, 2010.

Hoffman, Warren. *The Passing Game: Queering Jewish American Culture*. Syracuse, NY: Syracuse University Press, 2008.

Hollenberg, Donna Krolik. "At the Western Development Museum: Ethnic Identity and the Memory of the Holocaust in the Jewish Community of Saskatoon, Saskatchewan." *Oral History Review* 27, no. 2 (2000): 85–127.

Honeycutt, Courtenay. "Examining the Diffusion of CMC Technologies in Minority Languages: A Case Study of Welsh Language Blogging and Twittering." PhD diss., Indiana University, 2011.

Horn, Dara. "The Future of Yiddish – in English: Field Notes from the New Ashkenaz." *Jewish Quarterly Review* 96, no. 4 (2006): 471–80.

Hornsby, Michael. *Revitalizing Minority Languages: New Speakers of Breton, Yiddish and Lemko*. Basingstoke, UK: Palgrave Macmillan, 2015.

Houle, René. "Recent Evolution of Immigrant-Language Transmission in Canada." *Canadian Social Trends*, no. 92 (2011): 3–12.

Howe, Irving. *World of Our Fathers: The Journey of the East European Jews to America and the Life They Found and Made*. New York: Harcourt Brace Jovanovich, 1976.

Howe, Irving, and Greenberg, Eliezer. *A Treasury of Yiddish Poetry*. New York: Holt, Rinehart and Winston, 1969.

– *Voices from the Yiddish: Essays, Memoirs, Diaries*. Ann Arbor: University of Michigan Press, 1972.

Howe, Irving, and Ruth Wisse, eds. *The Best of Sholom Aleichem*. New York: New Republic Books, 1979.

Howe, Irving, Ruth R. Wisse, and Chone Shmeruk. *The Penguin Book of Modern Yiddish Verse*. New York: Viking, 1987.

Hua, Josephine, and Catherine Costigan. "The Familial Context of Adolescent Language Brokering within Immigrant Chinese Families in Canada." *Journal of Youth and Adolescence* 41, no. 7 (2012): 894–906.

Igartua, Iván. "Loss of Grammatical Gender and Language Contact." *Diachronica* 36, no. 2 (2019): 181–221.

Ingall, Marjorie. "How Sweden Became the Epicenter of Yiddish Children's Media." *Tablet Magazine*, 9 July 2019, https://www.tabletmag.com/sections/community/articles/sweden-yiddish-childrens-media.

Iqbal, Isabeau. "Mother Tongue and Motherhood: Implications for French Language Maintenance in Canada." *Canadian Modern Language Review* 61, no. 3 (2005): 305–23.

Isaacs, Miriam. "Haredi, *haymish* and *frim*: Yiddish Vitality and Language Choice in a Transnational Multilingual Community." *International Journal of the Sociology of Language* 138 (1999): 9–30.

– "Yiddish in the Aftermath: Speech Community and Cultural Continuity in Displaced Persons Camps." In *Jewishness: Expression, Identity, and Representation*, edited by Simon J. Bronner, 84–104. Oxford: Littman Library of Jewish Civilization, 2008.

Isenberg, Noah. "'Critical Post-Judaism'; or, Reinventing a Yiddish Sensibility in a Postmodern Age." *Diaspora* 6, no. 1 (1997): 85–96.

Jacobs, Neil G. *Yiddish: A Linguistic Introduction*. Cambridge: Cambridge University Press, 2005.

Jacobs, Paula. "Ladino and Yiddish Classes Boom Online." *Tablet Magazine*, 12 April 2021, https://www.tabletmag.com/sections/community/articles/ladino-and-yiddish-classes-boom-online.

Jacobson, Marion. "With Song to the Struggle: An Ethnographic and Historical Study of the Yiddish Folk Chorus." PhD diss., New York University, 2004.

Jedwab, Jack. "Canada's 'Other' Languages: The Role of Non-Official Languages in Ethnic Persistence." In *Rethinking Heritage Language Education*, edited by Peter Pericles Trifonas and Themistoklis Aravossitas, 237–53. Cambridge: Cambridge University Press, 2014.

– "The Politics of Dialogue: Rapprochement Efforts between Jews and French Canadians, 1939–1960." In *Renewing Our Days: Montreal Jews in the Twentieth Century*, edited by Ira Robinson and Mervin Butovsky, 42–74. Montreal: Véhicule Press, 1995.

Johnson, Matthew, and Corbin Allardice. "*Confessions of a Yiddish Writer and Other Essays*: An Interview with Goldie Morgentaler." *In geveb*, January 2020. https://ingeveb.org/blog/confessions-of-a-yiddish-writer-and-other-essays-an-interview-with-goldie-morgentaler.

Jones, Faith. "The Autobiography of Esther Shechter: Yiddish Print Culture in Winnipeg in Transnational Context." MA thesis, University of British Columbia, 2014.

– "A Chimney on the Canadian Prairies: Yiddish-Language Libraries in Western Canada, 1900 to the Present." *Judaica Librarianship* 12 (2006): 49–68.

– "The Vancouver Peretz Institute Yiddish Library: The Social History of a Jewish Community Library." MLIS thesis, University of British Columbia, 1999.

Jones, Faith, and Cynthia Ramsay. "Un mir zingen freylekhe lider: The Vancouver Jewish Folk Choir as Alternative Jewish Space." Paper presented at the annual conference of the Association for Canadian Jewish Studies, Vancouver, 2 June 2019.

Kachru, Braj, Yamuna Kachru, and Cecil Nelson. *The Handbook of World Englishes*. Oxford: Blackwell Publishing, 2006.

Kafrissen, Rokhl. "Queer Yiddishkeit, Rokhl's Golden City: Finding a Home in Yiddishland While Challenging the Status Quo." *Tablet Magazine*, 19 June 2019, https://www.tabletmag.com/sections/community/articles/golden-city-queer-yiddishkeit.

Kage, Joseph. *Tsvey hundert yor fun yidisher imigratsiye in kanade*. Montreal: Eagle Publishing, 1960.

– *With Faith and Thanksgiving: The Story of Two Hundred Years of Jewish Immigration and Immigrant Aid Effort in Canada, 1760–1960*. Montreal: Eagle Publishing, 1962.

Katz, Dovid. "Language: Yiddish." *YIVO Encyclopedia of Jews in Eastern Europe*. 2011. https://yivoencyclopedia.org/article.aspx/Language/Yiddish.

– *Words on Fire: The Unfinished Story of Yiddish*. New York: Basic Books, 2004.

– "The Yiddish Conundrum: A Cautionary Tale for Language Revivalism." In *The Palgrave Handbook of Minority Languages and Communities*, edited by Gabrielle Hogan-Brun and Bernadette O'Rourke, 553–87. London: Palgrave Macmillan, 2019.

Kats, Yosef, and John Campbell Lehr. *The Last Best West: Essays on the Historical Geography of the Canadian Prairies*. Jerusalem: Magnes Press, The Hebrew University, 1999.

Kelley, Ninette, and M.J. Trebilcock. *The Making of the Mosaic*. Toronto: University of Toronto Press, 1998.

Kelman, Ari Y. *Station Identification: A Cultural History of Yiddish Radio in the United States*. Berkeley: University of California Press, 2009.

Kerner, Aaron. *Film and the Holocaust: New Perspectives on Dramas, Documentaries, and Experimental Films*. New York: Continuum, 2011.

Kirshenblatt-Gimblett, Barbara. "Sounds of Sensibility." In *American Klezmer: Its Roots and Offshoots*, edited by Mark Slobin, 211–19. Berkeley: University of California Press, 2001.

– "Yiddish Studies: Toward a Twenty-First-Century Mandate." In *Choosing Yiddish: New Frontiers of Language and Culture*, edited by Lara Rabinovitch, Shiri Goren, and Hannah S. Pressman, xi–xiv. Detroit, MI: Wayne State University Press, 2012.

Kirzane, et al., eds. "Online Yiddish Language Instruction: A Conversation." *In geveb*, 12 December 2018. https://ingeveb.org/pedagogy/online-yiddish-language-instruction-a-conversation.

Kleine, Ane. "Standard Yiddish." *Journal of the International Phonetic Association* 33, no. 2 (2003): 261–5.

Koos, Leonard. "Films Without Borders: An Introduction." *Post Script – Essays in Film and the Humanities* 25, no. 2 (2006): 3–18.

Koprov, Ariel. *Jewish Life in Bessarabia*. Toronto, 1995.

– *Tsvishn tsvey velt milhomes*. Toronto, 1991.

Korn, Rachel. *Generations: Selected Poems*, edited by Seymour Mayne. Oakville, ON: Mosaic Press, 1983.

– *Heym un heymlozikayt*. Buenos Aires, AR: 1948.

– *Paper Roses*. Translated by Seymour Levitan. Toronto: Aya Press, 1985.

Kornhauser, Bronia. "Music and the Continuity of Yiddish Language and Culture in Melbourne." *Australian Journal of Jewish Studies* 27 (2013): 85–118.

Krauss, Michael. "Classification and Terminology for Degrees of Language Endangerment." In *Language Diversity Endangered*, edited by Matthias Brenzinger, 1–8. Berlin and Boston: de Gruyter, 2015.

Krishtalka, Aaron. *Gut morgn dir, velt!* Montreal, 1953.

Krogh, Steffen. "How Satmarish Is Haredi Satmar Yiddish?" in *Leket: Yiddish Studies Today*, edited by Marion Aptroot, Efrat Gal-Ed, Roland Gruschka, and Simon Neuberg, 483–506. Düsseldorf, DE: Düsseldorf University Press, 2012.

Krutikov, Mikhail. "Yiddish Literature: Yiddish Literature after 1800." *YIVO Encyclopedia of Jews in Eastern Europe*, 2016. https://yivoencyclopedia.org /article.aspx/Yiddish_Literature/Yiddish_Literature_after_1800.

Kuznitz, Cecile. "Yiddish Studies." In *The Oxford Handbook of Jewish Studies*, edited by Martin Goodman, 541–71. Oxford: Oxford University Press, 2002.

– *YIVO and the Making of Modern Jewish Culture: Scholarship for the Yiddish Nation*. Cambridge: Cambridge University Press, 2014.

Lacasse, Simon-Pierre. "À la croisée de la révolution tranquille et du judaïsme orthodoxe: L'implantation de la communauté hassidique des tasher au cœur du Québec francophone et catholique (1962–1967)." *Histoire sociale/Social History* 50, no. 102 (2017): 399–422.

– "'A Curse or a Blessing?': Montreal Jews and the Politics of 1960s Quebec." *The Canadian Historical Review* 102, no 1 (2021): 1–26.

Laing, Jennifer, and Judith Mair. "Music Festivals and Social Inclusion: The Festival Organizers' Perspective." *Leisure Sciences* 37 (2015): 1–17.

Lansky, Aaron. "The Maximalist's Daughter." *PaknTreger* 75 (2017), https://www.yiddishbookcenter.org/language-literature-culture/pakn-treger/maximalist-s-daughter.

– *Outwitting History: The Amazing Adventures of a Man Who Rescued a Million Yiddish Books*. Chapel Hill, NC: Algonquin Books, 2004.

Lapidus, Steven. "The Forgotten Hasidim: Rabbis and Rebbes in Prewar Canada." *Canadian Jewish Studies* 12 (2004): 1–30.

Lappin, Ben. "Rehabilitation or Renaissance." *Judaism* 19, no. 2 (Spring 1970): 174–82.

Larrue, Jean Marc. *Le théâtre yiddish à Montréal/Yiddish Theatre in Montreal.* Montreal: Éditions Jeu, 1996.

Lasry, Jean-Claude. "Essor et tradition: La communauté juive nord-africaine au Québec." In *Les juifs du Maghreb: Diasporas contemporaines*, edited by Jean-Claude Lasry and Claude Tapia, 15–54. Montreal: Les Presses de l'Université de Montreal, 1989.

Leach, Jim. *Film in Canada*, 2nd ed. Don Mills, ON: Oxford University Press, 2011.

Legutko, Agnieszka. "Yiddish in the 21st Century: New Media to the Rescue of Endangered Languages," *Handbook of Foreign Language Education in the Digital Age*, edited by Lisa Winstead and Penny Wang, 236–51. Hershey, PA: IGI Global, 2016.

Levendel, Lewis. *A Century of the Canadian Jewish Press: 1880s–1980s.* Ottawa, ON: Borealis Press, 1989.

Levin, Nora. *While Messiah Tarried: Jewish Socialist Movements, 1871–1917.* New York: Schocken Books, 1977.

Levine, Marc V. *The Reconquest of Montreal: Language Policy and Social Change in a Bilingual City.* Philadelphia, PA: Temple University Press, 1990.

Lewis, Justin Jaron. "A New Yiddish Renaissance: Der Veker's Creative Writing Contest." Paper presented at the annual conference of the Association of Jewish Studies, Boston, 17 December 2018.

Lim, Bliss. "Queer Aswang Transmedia: Folklore as Camp." *Kritika Kultura* 24 (2015): 178–225.

Little, Sabine. "Whose Heritage? What Inheritance? Conceptualising Family Language Identities." *International Journal of Bilingual Education and Bilingualism* (2017): 1–15.

London, Frank. "An Insider's View: How We Traveled from Obscurity to the Klezmer Establishment in Twenty Years." In *American Klezmer: Its Roots and Offshoots*, edited by Mark Slobin, 188–205. Berkeley: University of California Press, 2002.

Lotherington, Heather. "Creating Third Spaces in the Linguistically Heterogeneous Classroom for the Advancement of Plurilingualism." *TESOL Quarterly* 47, no. 3 (2013): 619–25.

Macintyre, Peter D, Susan C. Baker, and Heather Sparling. "Flow Experiences and Willingness to Communicate: Connecting Scottish Gaelic

Language and Traditional Music." *Journal of Language and Social Psychology* 38, no. 4 (2019): 536–45.

– "Heritage Passions, Heritage Convictions, and the Rooted L2 Self: Music and Gaelic Language Learning in Cape Breton, Nova Scotia." *The Modern Language Journal* 101, no. 3 (2017): 501–16.

Mandel, Michael. *The Jewish Hour: The Golden Age of a Toronto Yiddish Radio Show and Newspaper*. Toronto: Now and Then Books, 2016.

Margolis, Rebecca. "Across the Border: Canadian-Jewish Writing." In *The Cambridge History of Jewish American Literature*, edited by Hana Wirth-Nesher, 432–48. New York: Cambridge University Press, 2015.

– "*Ale brider*: Yiddish Culture in Montreal and New York City." *EJJS* (*European Journal of Jewish Studies*) 4, no. 1 (2010): 137–64.

– "*Les belles-sœurs* and *Di shvegerins*: Translating Québécois into Yiddish for the Montreal Stage in 1992." In *Translation Effects: The Making of Modern Culture in Canada*, edited by Luise von Flotow and Sherry Simon, 461–78. Ottawa, ON: University of Ottawa Press, 2013.

– "Chava Rosenfarb's Yiddish Montreal." *Canadian Jewish Studies/Études juives canadiennes* 18–19 (2010–11): 159–77.

– "Choosing Yiddish in the Classroom: Montreal's Secular Jewish Schools, 1910–50." In *Choosing Yiddish: New Frontiers of Language and Culture*, edited by Shiri T. Goren, Hannah Pressman, and Lara Rabinovitch, 103–22. Detroit, MI: Wayne State University Press, 2012.

– "Culture in Motion: Yiddish in Canadian Jewish Life." *Journal of Religion and Popular Culture* 21, no. 4 (2009), 1–16.

– "Forays into a Digital Yiddishland: Secular Yiddish in the Early Stages of the Coronavirus Pandemic." *Contemporary Jewry* 41 (July 2021): 1–28.

– "French Canada as a Site of Holocaust Representation." In *Translated Memories*, edited by Bettina Hofmann and Ursula Reuter, 69–98. Lanham, Boulder, New York, London: Lexington Books, 2020.

– "Holocaust and Post-Holocaust Yiddish Theatre in Montreal: A Canadian Response to Catastrophe." In *Leket. Jiddistik Heute/Yiddish Studies Today/yidishe shtudyes haynt*, edited by Marion Aptroot, 525–40. Düsseldorf, DE: Düsseldorf University Press, 2012.

– "*In der heym*: Yiddish in Canada Today." In *No Better Home? Jews, Canada, and the Sense of Belonging*, edited by David Koffman, 261–83. Toronto: University of Toronto Press, 2021.

– *Jewish Roots, Canadian Soil: Yiddish Culture in Montreal, 1905–45*. Kingston and Montreal: McGill-Queen's University Press, 2011.

– "*Ken men tantsn af tsvey khasenes?* A.M. Klein and Yiddish." In *Failure's Opposite: Listening to A.M. Klein*, edited by Norman Ravvin and Sherry

Simon, 79–97. Kingston and Montreal: McGill-Queen's University Press, 2011.

– "Melekh Ravitch as Yiddish Catalyst: Montreal, 1941–1954." *East European Jewish Affairs* (EEJA) 46 no. 2 (2016): 192–209.

– "Montreal Yiddish Theatre as Youth Cultural Imperative." In *Performing Canadian Frontiers: Theatre and (Im)migration*, edited by Yana Meerzon, 129–46. Toronto: Playwrights Canada Press, 2019.

– "Negotiating Jewish Canadian Identity: Montreal Yiddish Literary Journals in the Interwar Period." *Shofar* 27, no. 4 (2009): 24–48.

– "New Yiddish Film and the Transvernacular." *In geveb*, 18 December 2016. https://ingeveb.org/articles/new-yiddish-film-and-the-transvernacular.

– "Sholem Shtern: Bridging the Gaps." In *New Readings of Yiddish Montreal/Traduire le Montréal yiddish/Taytshn un ibertaytshn yidish in montreol*, edited by Pierre Anctil, Norman Ravvin, and Sherry Simon, 93–102. Ottawa, ON: University of Ottawa Press, 2007.

– "Translating Jewish Poland into Canadian Yiddish: Symcha Petrushka's *Mishnayes*." *Traduction Terminologie Rédaction* (TTR) 22, no. 2 (2009): 183–202.

– "Yiddish and Multiculturalism: A Marriage Made in Heaven?" In *Multiculturalism in Canada: Theories, Policies and Debates*, edited by Shibao Guo, 159–70. Rotterdam, NE: Sense Publishers, 2015.

– "Yiddish at a Crossroads: The Jewish Public Library in 1954." In *The Future of the Past: The Jewish Public Library of Montreal, 1914-2014*, edited by Ira Robinson, Rivka Augenfeld, and Karen Biskin, 26–42. Montreal: Hungry I Books/Concordia Institute for Jewish Studies, 2015.

– "Yiddish Translation in Canada: A Litmus Test for Continuity." *Traduction Terminologie Rédaction* (TTR) 19, no. 2 (2006): 149–89.

Mayne, Seymour, ed. *Essential Words: An Anthology of Jewish Canadian Poetry*. Ottawa, ON: Oberon Press, 1985.

– *In Your Words: Translations from the Yiddish and Hebrew*. Toronto: Ronald P. Frye and Company, 2017.

Maza, Ida. *Vaksn mayne kinderlekh: Muter un kinder lider*. Montreal: Aroysgegebn mit der mithilf fun kanader yidishn kongres, 1954.

McDonald, Chris, and Heather Sparling. "Interpretations of Tradition: From Gaelic Song to Celtic Pop." *Journal of Popular Music Studies* 22, no. 3 (2010): 309–28.

McLeod, Wilson. "Gaelic in Contemporary Scotland: Challenges, Strategies and Contradictions." *Europa Ethnica* 71, no. 1 (2014): 3–12.

Medres, Israel. *Between Two World Wars: Canadian Jews in Transition*. Translated by Vivian Felsen. Montreal: Véhicule Press, 2003.

- *Montreal foun Nekhtn/Le Montréal juif d'autrefois*. Translated by Pierre Anctil. Sillery, QC: Éditions du Septentrion, 1997.
- *Montreal fun nekhtn*. Montreal: Keneder adler, 1947.
- *Le Montréal juif entre les deux guerres/Tsvishn tsvey velt milkhomes*. Translated by Pierre Anctil. Sillery, QC: Éditions du Septentrion, 2001.
- *Montreal of Yesterday: Jewish Life in Montreal, 1900–1920*. Translated by Vivian Felsen. Montreal: Véhicule Press, 2000.
- *Tsvishn tsvey velt milkhomes*. Montreal: Keneder adler, 1964.
Mendelson, Alan. *Exiles from Nowhere: The Jews and the Canadian Elite*. Toronto: Robin Brass Studio, 2008.
Menkis, Richard. "Jewish Communal Identity at the Crossroads: Early Jewish Responses to Canadian Multiculturalism, 1963–1965." *Studies in Religion/Sciences religieuses* 40, no. 3 (2011): 283–92.
Miransky, Peretz. *Between Smile and Tear: Poems and Poetic Fables*. Vilnius, LT: Versus Aureus, 2005.
Miransky, Peretz, and Anna Miransky. *Selected Poems and Fables*. Oakville, ON: Mosaic Press, 2000.
Miron, Dan. *A Traveler Disguised: The Rise of Modern Yiddish Fiction in the Nineteenth Century*. Syracuse, NY: Syracuse University Press, 1996.
Morgentaler, Goldie. "'I Am Still There: The Recreation of Jewish Poland in the Canadian Novels of Chava Rosenfarb." *Studies in American Jewish Literature* 35 (2016): 187–99.
- "Land of the Postscript: Canada and the Post-Holocaust Fiction of Chava Rosenfarb." *Judaism* 49 no. 2 (2000): 168–81.
Muñoz, José Esteban. *Cruising Utopia: The Then and There of Queer Futurity*. New York: New York University Press, 2019 (2009).
Myers Feinstein, Margarete. "Re-imagining the Unimaginable: Theater, Memory, and Rehabilitation in the Displaced Persons Camps." In *After the Holocaust: Challenging the Myth of Silence*, edited by David Cesarani and Eric J. Sundquist, 39–54. New York: Routledge, 2011.
Naar, Devin E. "On Words Reclaimed and the Fate of Ladino." In *Stavans Unbound: The Critic Between Two Canons*, edited by Bridget Kevane, 131–45. Boston, MA: Academic Studies Press, 2019.
Nance, Claire, Wilson McLeod, Bernadette O'Rourke, and Stuart Dunmore. "Identity, Accent Aim, and Motivation in Second Language Users: New Scottish Gaelic Speakers' Use of Phonetic Variation." *Journal of Sociolinguistics* 20, no. 2 (2016): 164–91.
Netsky, Hankus. "Klez Goes to College." In *Performing Ethnomusicology: Teaching and Representation in World Music Ensembles*, edited by Ted Solis, 189–201. Los Angeles: University of California Press, 2004.

- "An Overview of Klezmer Music and its Development in the U.S." *Judaism* 47, no. 1 (1998): 5–13.

Neugroschel, Joachim, and S. An-Ski. *The Dybbuk and the Yiddish Imagination: A Haunted Reader*. Syracuse, NY: Syracuse Press, 2000.

Newman, Zelda Kahan. "The Jewish Sound of Speech: Talmudic Chant, Yiddish Intonation and the Origins of Early Ashkenaz." *The Jewish Quarterly Review* 90, nos. 3–4 (2000): 293–336.

Niger, Shmuel, Jacob Shatzky, Berl Kagan, et.al. *Leksikon fun der nayer yidisher literatur*. New York: Alveltlekhn yidishn kultur-kongres, 1956–81.

Nora, Pierre, and Lawrence D. Kritzman. *Realms of Memory: Rethinking the French Past*. New York: Columbia University Press, 1996.

Norich, Anita. *Discovering Exile: Yiddish and Jewish American Culture during the Holocaust*. Stanford, CA: Stanford University Press, 2007.

- "*Harbe sugyes*/Puzzling Questions: Yiddish and English Culture in America during the Holocaust." *Jewish Social Studies* 5, nos. 1–2 (1998–99): 91–110.

- "Yiddish Literary Studies." *Modern Judaism* 10, no. 3 (1990): 297–309.

Nove, Chaya R. "The Erasure of Hasidic Yiddish from Twentieth Century Yiddish Linguistics." *Journal of Jewish Languages* 6, no. 1 (2018): 109–41.

- "Social Predictors of Case Syncretism in New York Hasidic Yiddish." *University of Pennsylvania Working Papers in Linguistics*, 24, no. 11 (2018): 87–95.

Oberman, Sheldon, and Elaine Newton, eds. *Mirror of a People: Canadian Jewish Experience in Poetry and Prose*. Winnipeg, MB: Jewish Educational Publishers of Canada, 1985.

O'Bryan, K.G., Jeffrey G. Reitz, and O. Kuplowska. *Non-Official Languages: A Study in Canadian Multiculturalism*. Ottawa, ON: Supply and Services Canada, 1976.

Oldenburg, Ray. *The Great Good Place: Cafes, Coffee Shops, Community Centers, Beauty Parlors, General Stores, Bars, Hangouts, and How They Get You Through the Day*. New York: Paragon House, 1989.

Olko, Justyna, and Julia Sallabank, eds. *Revitalizing Endangered Languages: A Practical Guide*. Cambridge: Cambridge University Press, 2021.

Orenstein, Benjamin. *Der umkum un vidershtand fun a yidisher shtot, tshenstokhov*. Montreal, 1949.

Orenstein, Eugene. Review of *Canadian Jewish Anthology/Anthologie juive du Canada*, ed. Yaacov Zipper and Chaim Spilberg; *Identifications: Ethnicity and the Writer in Canada* ed. Jars Balan; and *Uncle Mike's Edenbridge: Memoirs of a Jewish Pioneer Farmer*, by Michael Usiskin. *University of Toronto Quarterly* 53, no. 4 (1984): 496–8.

– "Yiddish Culture in Canada Yesterday and Today." In *The Canadian Cultural Mosaic*, edited by Morton Weinfeld, William Shaffir, and Irwin Cotler, 293–314. Rexdale, ON: John Wiley and Sons, 1981.

Orenstein, Eugene, Beyle Schaechter Gottesman, and Moyshe Steingart, eds. *Vidervuks: A nayer dor yidishe shrayber*. New York: Yugntruf, League for Yiddish, Congress for Jewish Culture, 1989.

O'Sullivan, Carol. *Translating Popular Film*. New York: Palgrave Macmillan, 2011.

Panofsky, Ruth. "Chava Rosenfarb's Early Life Writing: 'Bergen-Belsen Diary, 1945.'" *Women in Judaism: A Multidisciplinary E-Journal* 12, no. 1 (2016). https://wjudaism.library.utoronto.ca/index.php/wjudaism /article/view/26333.

– ed. *The New Spice Box: Canadian Jewish Writing*. Toronto: New Jewish Press, 2017.

Parigi, Paolo, and Rachel Gong. "From Grassroots to Digital Ties: A Case Study of a Political Consumerism Movement." *Journal of Consumer Culture* 14 (2014): 236–53.

Paskin, Sylvia, ed. *When Joseph Met Molly: A Reader on Yiddish Film*. Nottingham, UK: Five Leaves, 1999.

Peltz, Rakhmiel. "A Researcher Writes for His People: Who Writes What Language for Whom and When?" *International Journal of the Sociology of Language* 243 (2017): 39–65.

Petrushka, Symche. *Mishnayes mit iberzetsungen un peyrush in yidish*. 6 vols. Montreal, 1945–49.

– *Yidishe folks-entsiklopedye: Far yidishe religiye, geshikhte, filozofiye, literatur, biographiye, lender-kibutsim and andere inyonim*. Montreal: Keneder adler, 1943.

Piller, Ingrid. "Private Language Planning: The Best of Both Worlds?" *Estudios de Sociolingüística* 2, no. 1 (2001): 61–80.

Piller, Ingrid, and Livia Gerber. "Family Language Policy between the Bilingual Advantage and the Monolingual Mindset." *International Journal of Bilingual Education and Bilingualism* 21 (2018): 1–14.

Posner, Michael. *The Last Honest Man: Mordecai Richler: An Oral Biography*. Toronto: McClelland and Stewart, 2005.

Pritz, Alexandra. "Ukrainian Cultural Traditions in Canada: Theatre, Choral Music and Dance." PhD diss., University of Ottawa, 1977.

Raby, Eva. "'If You Build It, They Will Come': The Norman Berman Children's Library, 1983–2013." *Canadian Jewish Studies* 22 (2014): 87–107.

Ragusa, Angela, and Olivia War. "'Caught in the Web': Male Goths using

Online ICTs to Transcend Rural Reality." *Communication, Politics & Culture* 49 (2016): 1–24.

Rauch, Stefanie. "Understanding the Holocaust through Film: Audience Reception between Preconceptions and Media Effects." *History and Memory* 30, no. 1 (2018): 151–88.

Ravitch, Melech. *67 lirishe, satirishe, natsyonale, sotsyale un filozofishe lider fun di letste finf-zeks yor*. Buenos Aires, AR: Dovid Lerman, 1946.

– *Dos amolike yidishe varshe, biz der shvel fun dritn khurbn 1414–1939 in lid, balade, poeme, drame, dertseylung, roman, humoreske, glaykhvort, folkslid, geshikhte, zikhroynes, esey, publitsistik, zshornalistik, rede, reportazsh, khronik, fun 13*. Montreal: Farband fun varshever yidl in kanade, 1966.

– *Eynems yidishe makhshoves in tsvontsikstn yorhundert: Eseyen*. Buenos Aires, AR: Dovid Lerman, 1949.

– *Iker shokhakhti: Lider un poemes fun di yorn 1954–1969*. Montreal: M. Ravitch Committee at the Jewish Public Library, 1969.

– "Kanadisher tsvayg fun shtam: velt-literatur in yidish." In *Pinkes fun der forshung fun der yidisher literatur un prese*, edited by Shlomo Bikl, 230–52. New York: Congress for Jewish Culture, 1965.

– *Di kroynung fun a yungn yidishn dikhter in amerike: Poeme*. New York: D. Ignatov Literatur Fund, 1953.

– *Di lider fun mayne lider*. Montreal: M. Ravitch bukh-komitet, 1954.

– *Mayn leksikon: Yidishe shraybers, kintslers, aktiorn, oykh klal-tuers in di amerikes un andere lender*. Tel Aviv: I.L. Peretz Publishing House, 1980.

– *Dos mayse-bukh fun mayn lebn*. Tel Aviv: I.L. Peretz Publishing House, 1975.

– *Night Prayer and Other Poems*. Translated by Seymour Mayne and Rivka Augenfeld. Oakville, ON: Mosaic Press, 1993.

– "Yiddish Culture in Canada." In *Canadian Jewish Reference Book and Directory*, edited by Eli Gottesman, 75–80. Montreal: Mortimer, 1963.

Ravvin, Norman. *A House of Words: Jewish Writing, Identity, and Memory*. Kingston and Montreal: McGill-Queen's University Press, 1997.

– ed. *Not Quite Mainstream: Canadian Jewish Short Stories*. Calgary, AB: Red Deer Press, 2002.

– *Sex, Skyscrapers, and Standard Yiddish*. Toronto: University of Toronto Press, 1997.

Ravvin, Norman, and Sherry Simon, eds. *Failure's Opposite: Listening to A.M. Klein*. Kingston and Montreal: McGill-Queen's University Press, 2011.

Read, Anne. "The Precarious History of Jewish Education in Quebec." *Religion & Education* 45, no. 1 (2018): 23–51.

Reiter, Ester. "The Canadian Jewish Left: Culture, Community, and the Soviet Union." In *A Vanished Ideology: Essays on the Jewish Communist Movement in the English-speaking World in the Twentieth Century*, edited by Matthew B. Hoffman and Henry F. Srebrnik, 78–90. Albany, NY: SUNY Press, 2016.

– *A Future without Hate or Need: The Promise of the Jewish Left in Canada*. Toronto: Between the Lines, 2016.

Ringuet, Chantal. *À la découverte du Montréal yiddish*. Montreal: Fides, 2011.

– "Voix yiddish de Montréal." *Moebius* 139 (2013): 5–175.

Robin, Régine. *La Québécoite*. Montreal: XYZ Editeur, 1983.

Robinson, Ira. "Canadian Jews Engage with Hasidism in Yiddish in the Mid-Twentieth Century." Paper presented at the annual conference of the Association for Canadian Jewish Studies, Vancouver, 3 June 2019.

– "'A Letter from the Sabbath Queen': Yudel Rosenberg Addresses Montreal Jewry." In *The Canadian Jewish Studies Reader*, edited by Richard Menkis and Norman Ravvin, 126–40. Calgary, AB: Red Deer Press, 2004.

Robinson, Ira, Pierre Anctil, and Mervin Butovsky, eds. *An Everyday Miracle: Yiddish Culture in Montreal*. Montreal: Véhicule Press, 1990.

Robinson, Ira, and Mervin Butovsky, eds. *Renewing Our Days: Montreal Jews in the Twentieth Century*. Montreal: Véhicule Press, 1995.

Rogel, Joseph. *Confessions of an Auschwitz Number (A-18260)*. Translated by Joseph Rogel. Montreal: Dawson College, 1972.

– *Oyshvits: Lider*. Montreal: Aroysgegebn durkh a komitet fun shrayber, 1951.

Rojanski, Rachel. "Ben-Gurion and Yiddish after the Holocaust." In *The Politics of Yiddish*, Amsterdam Yiddish Symposium 5, edited by Shlomo Berger, 31–50. Amsterdam: Menasseh ben Israel Instituut, 2011.

– *Yiddish in Israel: A History*. Bloomington: Indiana University Press, 2020.

Rosenberg, Louis. *Canada's Jews: A Social and Economic Study of Jews in Canada in the 1930s*. Edited by Morton Weinberg. Kingston and Montreal: McGill-Queen's University Press, 1993 (1939).

– "Population Characteristics of the Jewish Community of Montreal." *Canadian Jewish Population Studies* no. 6 (1956): 1–66.

– "A Study of the Changes in the Population Characteristics of the Jewish Community in Canada, 1931–1961." *Canadian Jewish Population Studies*, no. 2 (1965): 1–21.

Rosenberg, Yudel. *The Golem and the Wondrous Deeds of the Maharal of Prague*. Translated by Curt Leviant. New Haven, CT: Yale University Press, 2007.

Rosenfarb, Chava. *Bociany*. Syracuse, NY: Syracuse University Press, 2000.

– *Botshani*. 2 vols. Tel Aviv: I.L. Peretz Publishing House, 1983.

– *Der boym fun lebn*. 3 vols. Tel Aviv: Hamenora, 1972.

– *Briv tsu abrashen*. Tel Aviv: I.L. Peretz Publishing House, 1992.

– "Canadian Yiddish Writers." In *Traduire le Montreal Yiddish/New Readings of Yiddish Montreal*, edited by Pierre Anctil, Norman Ravvin, and Sherry Simon, 11–18. Ottawa, ON: University of Ottawa Press, 2007.

– *Confessions of a Yiddish Writer and Other Essays*, edited by Goldie Morgentaler. Kingston and Montreal: McGill-Queen's University Press, 2019.

– *Of Lodz and Love*. Translated by Chava Rosenfarb. Syracuse, NY: Syracuse University Press, 2000.

– *Survivors: Seven Short Stories*. Translated by Goldie Morgentaler. Toronto: Cormorant Books, 2004.

– *The Tree of Life*. Translated by Chava Rosenfarb, with Goldie Morgentaler. Melbourne, AU: Scribe, 1985.

– *The Tree of Life: A Trilogy of Life in the Lodz Ghetto*. 3 vols. Translated with Goldie Morgentaler. Madison: University of Wisconsin Press, 2004–06.

Rosenthal, Henry, and S. Cathy Berson, eds. *Canadian Jewish Outlook Anthology*. Vancouver, BC: New Star Books, 1988.

Roskies, David G. *Against the Apocalypse: Responses to Catastrophe in Modern Jewish Culture*. Syracuse, NY: Syracuse University Press, 1999.

– "A City, a School, and a Utopian Experiment." In *The Jewish Search for a Usable Past*, 146–57. Bloomington: Indiana University Press, 1999.

– *The Literature of Destruction: Jewish Responses to Catastrophe*. New York: The Jewish Publication Society, 1988.

– "Yiddish in Montreal: The Utopian Experiment." In *An Everyday Miracle: Yiddish Culture in Montreal*, edited by Ira Robinson, Pierre Anctil, and Mervin Butovsky, 22–38. Montreal: Véhicule Press, 1990.

– *Yiddish Lands: A Memoir*. Detroit, MI: Wayne State University Press, 2008.

Roskies, David G., and Naomi Diamant. *Holocaust Literature: A History and Guide*. Waltham, MA: Brandeis University Press, 2012.

Rosten, Leo. *The Joys of Yiddish: A Relaxed Lexicon of Yiddish, Hebrew and Yinglish Words often Encountered in English from the Days of the Bible to Those of the Beatnik*. New York: McGraw Hill, 1968.

– *The Joys of Yinglish*. New York: McGraw Hill, 1989.

Roth, Lorna. *Something New in the Air: The Story of First Peoples Television Broadcasting in Canada*. Kingston and Montreal: McGill-Queen's University Press, 2005.

Rotman, Diego. "The 'Tsadik from Plonsk' and 'Goldenyu': Political Satire in

Dzigan and Shumacher's Israeli Comic Repertoire." In *A Club of Their Own: Jewish Humorists and the Contemporary World*, edited by Eli Lederhendler and Gabriel N. Finder. Oxford: Oxford University Press, 2016.

Rozhanski, Shmuel, ed. *Kanadish: Antologiye–Musterverk fun der yidisher literatur 62*. Buenos Aires, AR: Literatur-gezelshaft bam yivo in argentine, 1974.

Sack, Benjamin Gutelius. *Geshikhte fun yidn in kanade: Fun di friste onheybn biz der letster tsayt*. Montreal: Aroysgegebn durkh a komitet fun fraynt, 1948.

– *History of the Jews in Canada*. Montreal: Canadian Jewish Congress, 1945.

Samuel, Maurice. *In Praise of Yiddish*. New York: Cowles, 1971.

Sarna, Lazar and Abraham Boyarsky, eds. *Canadian Yiddish Writings*. Montreal: Harvest House, 1976.

Schachter, Allison. *Diasporic Modernisms: Hebrew and Yiddish Literature in the Twentieth Century*. Oxford: Oxford University Press, 2014.

Schaechter, Mordkhe. *The Standardized Yiddish Orthography: Rules of Yiddish Spelling*. 6th ed., and *The History of the Standardized Yiddish Spelling*. New York: YIVO and Yiddish Language Resource Center of the League for Yiddish, 1999.

Schaechter-Viswanath, Gitl, Paul E. Glasser, and Chava Lapin, eds. *Comprehensive English-Yiddish Dictionary*. Bloomington: Indiana University Press, 2016.

Scherbenske, Amanda. "From 'Folksmentshn' to Creative Individuals: Klezmer Transmission in the Twenty-First Century." *MUSICultures* 39, no. 2 (2012): 103–40.

Schlosberg, Mira. *Kugel Western*. Melbourne: Glom Press, 2021.

Schwarz, Jan. "A Portable Library for Polish Jews: The *Dos poylishe yidntum* Series Aimed to Rebuild Yiddish Culture in the Diaspora." *PaknTreger* 74 (2016). https://www.yiddishbookcenter.org/language-literature-culture/pakn-treger/portable-library-polish-jews.

– *Survivors and Exiles: Yiddish Culture after the Holocaust*. Detroit, MI: Wayne State University Press, 2015.

Seelig, Rachel. "Like a Barren Sheet of Paper: Rokhl Korn from Galician Orchards to Postwar Montreal." *Prooftexts* 34, no. 3 (2014): 349–77.

Segal, J.I. *Lider far yidishe kinder*. New York: Bildungs komitet fun arbeter ring, 1961.

– *Seyfer yidish: lider un poemen*. Montreal: J.I. Segal komitet, 1950.

– *Yidishe lider/Poèmes yiddish*. Translated by Pierre Anctil. Montreal: Le Noroît, 1992.

Shaffir, M.M. *A stezshke*. Montreal, 1940.

Shaffir, William. "Safeguarding a Distinctive Identity: Hassidic Jews in Montreal." In *Renewing Our Days: Montreal Jews in the Twentieth Century*, edited by Ira Robinson and Mervin Butovsky, 75–94. Montreal: Véhicule Press, 1995.

– "Separation from the Mainstream in Canada: The Hassidic Community of Tash." In *The Jews in Canada*, edited by Robert J. Brym, William Shaffir, and Morton Weinfeld, 126–41. Don Mills, ON: Oxford University Press, 1993.

Shandler, Jeffrey. *Adventures in Yiddishland: Postvernacular Language and Culture*. Berkeley: University of California Press, 2006.

– "Anthologizing the Vernacular." In *The Anthology in Jewish Literature*, edited by David Stern, 304–23. Oxford: Oxford University Press, 2004.

– "The Cultural Politics of Yiddish in the United States after the Holocaust." *Politics of Yiddish, Amsterdam Yiddish Symposium 5* (2011): 51–65.

– "Imagining Yiddishland: Language, Place and Memory." *History and Memory* 15, no. 1 (2003): 123–49.

– "Postvernacular Yiddish: Language as a Performance Art." *TDR: The Drama Review* 48, no. 1 (2004): 19–43.

– "Queer Yiddishkeit: Practice and Theory." *Shofar* 25, no. 1 (2006): 90–113.

– "The Savior and the Survivor: Virtual Afterlives in New Media." *Jewish Film & New Media* 8, no. 1 (2020): 23–47.

– *Shtetl: A Vernacular History*. New Brunswick, NJ: Rutgers University Press, 2014.

– *Yiddish: Biography of a Language*. New York: Oxford University Press, 2020.

– "The Yiddish-'Svives': A New Yugntruf Project." *TDR: The Drama Review* 48 no. 1 (2004): 19–42.

Shatan, Mirl Erdberg. *Nit fun kayn freyd: Lider*. Montreal, 1950.

– *Regnboygn: Lider, eseyen, zikhroynes*. New York: C.F. Shatan, 1975.

Sheftel, Anna, and Stacey Zembrzycki. "'We Started Over Again, We Were Young': Postwar Social Worlds of Child Holocaust Survivors in Montreal." *Urban History Review* 39, no. 1 (2010): 20–30.

Sherman, Nancy. "Voices from the Vault: Yiddish Writers Speak Again," *PaknTreger* 64 (2011), https://www.yiddishbookcenter.org/language-literature-culture/pakn-treger/voices-vault-yiddish-writers-speak-again.

Shneer, David. "Who Owns the Means of Cultural Production? The Soviet Yiddish Publishing Industry of the 1920s." *Book History* 6 (2004): 197–226.

– *Yiddish and the Creation of Soviet-Jewish Culture: 1918–1930*. New York: Cambridge University Press, 2004.

Shneer, David, and Karen Aviv, eds. *New Jews: The End of the Jewish Diaspora.* New York: NYU Press, 2005.

Shohat, Ella, and Robert Stam. "The Cinema after Babel: Language, Difference, Power." *Screen* 26, nos. 3–4 (1985): 35–58.

Shtern, Abraham. *Kvutses kitve agode.* Montreal, 1947.

– *Sefer hutim ha-meshulashim.* Montreal, 1953.

Shtern (Krishtalka), Shifre. *Yidish a lebedike shprakh: A lern-program far lerer.* 3 vols. Montreal: Jewish People's and Peretz Schools, 1992–97.

Shtern, Sholem. *Au Canada: Un roman en vers.* Translated by Tatania Hais. Montreal, 1984.

– *La Famille au Canada: Un roman en vers.* Translated by Tatania Hais. Montreal, 1984.

– *The Family in Canada: A Novel in Verse.* Translated by Tatania Hais. Montreal, 1984.

– *Ha-bayit ha-lavan be-harim*, 1972. Translation by Shimshon Meltser. Tel Aviv: Hamenorah, 1972.

– *The Household of Professor Sydney Goldstein: A Novel in Verse/La Maisonnée du Professor Sydney Goldstein: Un roman en vers.* Translated from English by Guy Maheux. Montreal, 1984.

– *In Canada: A Novel in Verse.* Translated by Judith Rotstein. Montreal, 1984.

– *In kanade.* 2 vols. Montreal: Sholem Shtern bukh-komitet, 1960–63.

– *Di mishpokhe in kanade un dos hoyzgesind fun profesor sidni goldstin: Tsvey noveln.* Montreal, 1975.

– *Shrayber vos ikh hob gekent: Memuarn un esayn.* Montreal: Adler Printing, 1982.

– *Tristesse et nostalgie: Mémoires littéraires du Montréal yiddish.* Translated by Pierre Anctil. Montreal: Éditions du Noroît, 2007.

– *Dos vayse hoyz.* New York: YKUF, 1967.

– *Velvl: Un roman en vers.* Translated from English by Guy Maheux. Montreal: Société de belles-lettres Guy Maheux, 1977.

– *The White House.* Translated by Max Rosenfeld. New York: Warbrooke Publishers, 1974.

Sicular, Eve. "'A yingl mit a yingl hot epes a tam': The Celluloid Closet of Yiddish Film." *Jewish Folklore and Ethnology Review* 16, no. 1 (1994): 40–5.

Siebert, Monika. *Indians Playing Indian: Multiculturalism and Contemporary Indigenous Art in North America.* Tuscaloosa, AL: University of Alabama Press, 2015.

Sienna, Noam. *A Rainbow Thread: An Anthology of Queer Jewish Texts from the First Century to 1969.* Philadelphia, PA: Print-o-Craft Press, 2019.

Simchovitch, Simkhe. *A shtifkind bay der vaysl*. Toronto: Aroysgegebn durkh a komitet, 1992.

– *Stepchild on The Vistula*. Toronto: Lugus Publications, 1994.

Simon, Sherry. *Translating Montreal: Episodes in the Life of a Divided City*. Kingston and Montreal: McGill-Queen's University Press, 2006.

Sims, Margaret and Elizabeth M. Ellis. "Raising Children Bilingually Is Hard: Why Bother?" *Babel* 49, no. 2 (2015): 28–35.

Sinclair, Gerri, and Morris Wolfe, eds. *The Spice Box: An Anthology of Canadian Writing*. Toronto: Lester and Orpen Dennys, 1981.

Singer, Esther. "Yiddish Melbourne: A Community in Transition." MA thesis, Monash University, 2019.

Sinha, Amresh. "The Use and Abuse of Subtitles." In *Subtitles: On the Foreignness of Film*, edited by Atom Egoyan and Ian Balfour, 172–190. Cambridge, MA: Alphabet City Media, 2004.

Skinazi, Karen E.H. "Kol Isha: Malka Zipora's Lekhaim as the Voice of the Hasidic Woman in Quebec." *Shofar* 33, no. 2 (2015): 157–81.

Slobin, Mark. *Fiddler on the Move: Exploring the Klezmer World*. Oxford: Oxford University Press, 2003.

– "Klezmer Music: An American Ethnic Genre." *Yearbook for Traditional Music* 16 (1984): 34–41.

Slucki, David. *The International Jewish Labor Bund after 1945: Toward a Global History*. New Brunswick, NJ: Rutgers University Press, 2012.

Slutzky-Kohn, Grunya. *Kinder lider*. Montreal: Farlag yidisher shul bay di montreoler folks shuln un peretz shuln, 1990.

– *Survivor*. Montreal, 2015.

Smith, Glenn. *Something on My Own: Gertrude Berg and American Broadcasting, 1929–1956*. Syracuse, NY: Syracuse University Press, 2007.

Smith-Christmas, Cassie, Noel P. Ó Murchadha, Michael Hornsby, and Máiréad Moriarty, eds. *New Speakers of Minority Languages Linguistic Ideologies and Practices*. London: Palgrave Macmillan, 2018.

Smulyan, Shayn. "The SoCalled Past: Sampling Yiddish in Hip-Hop." In *Choosing Yiddish: New Frontiers of Language and Culture*, edited by Lara Rabinovitch, Shiri Goren, and Hannah Pressman, 357–75. Detroit, MI: Wayne State University Press, 2012.

Soldat-Jaffe, Tatjana. "Yiddish without Yiddishism: Tacit Language Planning among Haredi Jews." *Journal of Jewish Identities* 3, no. 2 (2010): 1–24.

Sparling, Heather. "Music Is Language and Language Is Music." *Ethnologies* 25, no. 2 (2003): 145–71.

Speisman, Stephen A. *The Jews of Toronto: A History to 1937*. Toronto: McClelland and Stewart, 1979.

Spilberg, Chaim, and Yaakov Zipper, eds. *Kanader yidisher zamlbukh/ Canadian Jewish Anthology/Anthologie juive du Canada*. Montreal: National Committee on Yiddish, Canadian Jewish Congress, 1982.

Srebrnik, Henry. "Chasing an Illusion: The Jewish Communist Movement in Canada." In *A Vanished Ideology: Essays on the Jewish Communist Movement in the English-Speaking World in the Twentieth Century*, edited by Matthew B. Hoffman and Henry F. Srebrnik, 60–77. Albany, NY: SUNY Press, 2016.

Stavans, Ilan. *On Self-Translation: Meditations on Language*. New York: State University of New York Press, 2018.

Stein, Sarah Abrevaya. "Asymmetric Fates: Secular Yiddish and Ladino Culture in Comparison." *The Jewish Quarterly Review* 96, no. 4 (2006): 498–509.

Steir-Livny, Liat. "Shattered Encounters: From My Father's House (1947) to My Father's House (2008)." *Pivot: A Journal of Interdisciplinary Studies and Thought* 6, no. 1 (2017): 29–51.

Sternberg, Meir Sternberg. "Polylingualism as Reality and Translation as Mimesis." *Poetics Today* 2, no. 4 (1981): 221–39.

Stratton, Jon. "Seinfeld is a Jewish Sitcom, Isn't It? Ethnicity and Assimilation in 1990s American Television." In *Seinfeld, Master of Its Domain: Revisiting Television's Greatest Sitcom*, edited by David Lavery and Sara Lewis Dunne, 117–38. New York: Bloomsbury Academic, 2006.

Suchoff, David. *Kafka's Jewish Languages: The Hidden Openness of Tradition*. Philadelphia: University of Pennsylvania Press, 2012.

Sutzkever, Avrom. *Burnt Pearls: Ghetto Poems of Abraham Sutzkever*. Translated from the Yiddish by Seymour Mayne. Oakville, ON: Mosaic Press/Valley Editions, 1981.

Svigals, Alicia. "Whither Queer Yiddishkayt?" *In geveb*, 21 October 2021. https://ingeveb.org/blog/whither-queer-yiddishkayt.

– "Why We Do This Anyway: Klezmer as a Jewish Youth Subculture." In *American Klezmer: Its Roots and Offshoots*, edited by Mark Slobin, 211–20. Berkeley: University of California Press, 2002.

Szmigin, Isabelle, Andrew Bengry-Howell, Yvette Morey, et. al. "Socio-Spatial Authenticity at Co-Created Music Festivals." *Annals of Tourism Research* 63 (2017): 1–11.

Taft, Margaret, and Andrew Markus. *A Second Chance: The Making of Yiddish Melbourne*. Clayton, AU: Monash University Publishing, 2018.

Thiessen, Jack. *Yiddish in Canada: The Death of a Language*. Leer, DE: Verlag Schuster, 1973.

Tregebov, Rhea, ed. *Arguing with the Storm: Stories by Yiddish Women Writers*. New York: Feminist Press, 2008.

Trepman, Paul. *Among Men and Beasts*. South Brunswick, NJ: A.S. Barnes, 1978.

– *A gesl in varshe*. Montreal: Aroysgegebn fun a komitet in montreol, 1950.

Trifonas, Peter Pericles, and Themistoklis Aravossitas. "Introduction." In *Rethinking Heritage Language Education*, edited by Peter Pericles Trifonas and Themistoklis Aravossitas, xiii–xxi. Cambridge: Cambridge University Press, 2014.

Troper, Harold. *The Defining Decade: Identity, Politics, and the Canadian Jewish Community in the 1960s*. Toronto: University of Toronto Press, 2010.

Tulchinsky, Gerald. *Canada's Jews: A People's Journey*. Toronto: University of Toronto Press, 2008.

– "The Third Solitude: A.M. Klein's Jewish Montreal, 1910–1950." *Journal of Canadian Studies* 19, no. 2 (1984): 96–112.

Usiskin, Michael. *Oksn un motorn: Zikhroynes fun a yidishn farmer-pioner (di geshikhte fun idnbridzsh)*. Toronto: Farlag Vokhnblat, 1945.

– *Uncle Mike's Edenbridge: Memoires of a Jewish Pioneer Farmer*. Translated by Marcia Usiskin Basman. Winnipeg, MB: Peguis Publishers, 1983.

Vaisman, Ester-Basya. "Being Heard: The Singing Voices of Contemporary Hasidic Women." PhD diss., Harvard University, 2009.

Valencia, Heather. "'Yidishe Dikhterins': The Emergence of Modern Women's Poetry in Yiddish and Rokhl Korn's Poetic Debut." *European Judaism* 42, no. 2 (2009): 80–93.

Venables, Elizabeth, Susana A. Eisenchlas, and Andrea C. Schalley. "One-parent-one-language (OPOL) Families: Is the Majority Language-Speaking Parent Instrumental in the Minority Language Development?" *International Journal of Bilingual Education and Bilingualism* 17, no. 4 (2013): 429–48.

Waddington, Miriam. *Apartment Seven: Essays Selected and New*. Toronto, New York, Oxford: Oxford University Press, 1989.

– ed. *Canadian Jewish Short Stories*. Toronto: Oxford University Press, 1990.

Waddington, Miriam, and Ruth Panofsky. *The Collected Poems of Miriam Waddington*. Ottawa, ON: University of Ottawa Press, 2014.

Waldman, Rose. "New York's Yiddish Press Is Thriving." *Tablet Magazine*, 4 December 2018, https://www.tabletmag.com/sections/arts-letters/articles/new-yorks-yiddish-press-is-thriving.

– "Seizing the Means of Cultural Production: Hasidic Representation in Contemporary Yiddish Media." *In geveb*, 27 April 2018. https://ingeveb.org/blog/seizing-the-means-of-cultural-production-hasidic-representation-in-contemporary-yiddish-media.

Weiman-Kelman, Zohar. *Queer Expectations: A Genealogy of Jewish Women's Poetry*. Albany, NY: SUNY Press, 2018.

Weinfeld, Morton. *Like Everyone Else ... but Different: The Paradoxical Success of Canadian Jews*. Kingston and Montreal: McGill-Queen's University Press, 2018 (2001).

– "Myth and Reality: 'Affective Ethnicity.'" *Canadian Ethnic Studies* 13, no. 3 (1981): 80–100.

Weinreich, Max, *History of the Yiddish Language*. Translated by Shlomo Noble and Joshua A. Fishman. New Haven, CT: Yale University Press, 2008 (1980).

Weinreich, Uriel. "Notes on the Yiddish Rise-Fall Intonation." In *For Roman Jakobson: Essays on the Occasion of his Sixtieth Birthday*, edited by Morris Halle, 633–43. The Hague: Mouton, 1956.

Weintraub, Aviva. "Bordering on 'Lehavdl': Michael Wex, Performing Yiddish, and a Discourse of Discomfort." *Shofar* 26, no. 2 (2008): 1–12.

Weisbord, Merrily. *Strangest Dream: Canadian Communists, the Spy Trials, and the Cold War*. Toronto: Lester & Orpen Dennys, 1983.

Weissenberg-Akselrod, Perl. *Y.M. vaysenberg: Zayn lebn un shafn, 1878–1938*. Montreal: Y.M. Weissenberg bukh-fond, 1986.

Wex, Michael. *Born to Kvetch: Yiddish Language and Culture in All Its Moods*. New York: St Martin's Press, 2005.

– *Just Say Nu: Yiddish for Every Occasion (When English Just Won't Do)*. New York: Harper Collins, 2008.

Wisse, Ruth. *Free as a Jew: A Personal Memoir of National Self-Liberation*. New York: Wicked Son, 2021.

– *I.L. Peretz and the Making of Modern Jewish Culture*. Seattle and London: University of Washington Press, 1991.

– *A Little Love in Big Manhattan*. Cambridge and London: Harvard University Press, 1988.

– *The Modern Jewish Canon: A Journey through Language and Culture*. Chicago, IL: University of Chicago Press, 2003.

– "The Politics of Yiddish." *Commentary* 80, no. 1 (1985): 29–35.

– *The Schlemiel as Modern Hero*. Chicago, IL: University of Chicago Press, 1971.

– *Shtetl and Other Yiddish Novellas*. Detroit, MI: Wayne State University Press, 1986.

– "Shul Daze: Is Yiddish Back from the Dead?" *The New Republic*, 27 May 1996: 16–19.

Wolfe, Morris, and Gerri Sinclair, eds. *The Spice Box: An Anthology of Jewish Canadian Writing*. Toronto: Lester and Orpen Dennys, 1981.

Wolofsky, Hirsh. *Journey of My Life: A Book of Memoirs*. Translated by A.M. Klein. Montreal: Eagle Publishing, 1945.

– *Mayn lebens-rayze*. Montreal: Keneder adler, 1946.
– *Mayn lebens-rayze. Un demi-siècle de vie Yiddish à Montréal et ailleurs dans le monde*. Translated by Pierre Anctil. Sillery, QC: Éditions du Septentrion, 2000.

Wolters-Fredlund, Benita. "'We Shall Be Better Canadians by Being Conscious Jews': Multiculturalism and the Construction of Canadian Identity in the Toronto Jewish Folk Choir." *Intersections* 25, nos. 1–2 (2005): 187–201.

– "'We Shall Go Forward with Our Songs into the Fight for Better Life': Identity and Musical Meaning in the History of the Toronto Jewish Folk Choir, 1925–1959." PhD diss., University of Toronto, 2005.

Wood, Abigail. *And We're All Brothers: Singing in Yiddish in Contemporary North America*. London, UK: Routledge, 2016.

– "(De)constructing Yiddishland: Solomon and SoCalled's HipHop-Khasene." *Ethnomusicology Forum* 16, no. 2 (2007): 253–70.

– "The Multiple Voices of American Klezmer." *Journal of the Society of American Music* 1, no. 2 (2007): 367–92.

– "Pop, Piety and Modernity: The Changing Spaces of Orthodox Culture." In *Routledge Handbook of Contemporary Jewish Studies*, edited by Laurence Roth and Nadia Valman, 286–96. New York: Routledge, 2017.

– "Yiddish Song in Twenty-First Century America: Paths to Creativity," in *Mazal Tov, Amigos! Jews and Popular Music in the Americas*, edited by Amalia Ran and Moshe Morad, 142–52. Leiden, Boston: Brill, 2016.

Yam, Joseph. "Selected Data on the Canadian Population Whose Mother Tongue is Yiddish." *Canadian Jewish Population Studies*, Canadian Jewish Congress, 1973. https://www.bjpa.org/search-results/publication/20116.

Yampolskaya, Sonya. "The Concept of 'Dead Language' as Exemplified by Hebrew." *Vestnik of Saint Petersburg University*, series 13 (2016): 16–30.

Yanofsky, Joel. "What's the Yiddish Word for Comeback?" *The Walrus*, 31 July 2017. https://thewalrus.ca/yiddish-is-on-the-verge-of-a-comeback. Republished as "Is Yiddish Making a Comeback?" *The Reader's Digest*, 1 December 2018.

Young, Judy. "No Longer 'Apart'? Multiculturalism Policy and Canadian Literature." *Canadian Ethnic Studies* 33, no. 2 (2001): 88–116.

Yudika. *Tsar un freyd: Lider un dramatishe poemen*. Toronto, 1949.

Zaretsky, Natasha. "Singing for Social Change: Nostalgic Memory and the Struggle for Belonging in a Buenos Aires Yiddish Chorus." In *Rethinking Jewish-Latin Americans*, edited by Jeffrey Lesser and Raanan Rein, 231–65. Albuquerque: University of New Mexico Press, 2008.

Zaritt, Saul Noam, and the editors. "Yiddish Lives! *Loshn* of the Living

Dead." *In geveb*, 9 March 2017. https://ingeveb.org/blog/loshn-of-the-living-dead.

Zarrow, Sarah Ellen. "The Digital Yiddish Classroom: Reflections on Teaching Yiddish in the Digital Age." *In geveb*, 27 March 2017. https://ingeveb.org/pedagogy/the-digital-yiddish-classroom-reflections-on-teaching-yiddish-in-the-digital-age.

Zierler, Wendy. *Movies and Midrash: Popular Film and Jewish Religious Conversation*. New York: Routledge, 2017.

Zimmerman, David. "'Narrow-Minded People': Canadian Universities and the Academic Refugee Crises, 1933–1941." *Canadian Historical Review* 88, no. 2 (2007): 291–315.

Zipper, Yaakov. *Araynblikn in yidishn literarishn shafn, in guter demonung fun khaverim un tuer*. Montreal: Adler Printing, 1983.

– *The Far Side of the River: Selected Short Stories*. Translated by Ode Garfinkle and Mervin Butovsky. Oakville, ON: Mosaic Press, 1985.

– *The Journals of Yaakov Zipper, 1950–1982*. Translated by Ode Garfinkle and Mervin Butovsky. Kingston and Montreal: McGill-Queen's University Press, 2004.

– *Meever le-nahar bug: Roman*. Tel Aviv: M. Neuman, 1957.

– *Oyf yener zayt bug*. Montreal, 1946.

Zolf, Falek. *Di letste fun a dor: Heymishe geshtaltn*. Winnipeg, MB: Israelite Press, 1952.

– *Oyf fremder erd/On Foreign Soil*. Translated by Martin Green. Winnipeg: Benchmark, 2000.

– *Undzer kultur hemshekh: Eseyen*. Winnipeg: Universal Printers, 1956.

Zuckermann, Ghil'ad. *Revivalistics: From the Genesis of Israeli to Language Reclamation in Australia and Beyond*. Oxford: Oxford University Press, 2020.

Index